W0079175

Communications in Computer and Information Science 963

Commenced Publication in 2007
Founding and Former Series Editors:
Phoebe Chen, Alfredo Cuzzocrea, Xiaoyong Du, Orhun Kara, Ting Liu,
Dominik Ślęzak, and Xiaokang Yang

More information about this series at http://www.springer.com/series/7899

Salah Kabanda · Hussein Suleman
Stefan Gruner (Eds.)

ICT Education

47th Annual Conference of the Southern African
Computer Lecturers' Association, SACLA 2018
Gordon's Bay, South Africa, June 18–20, 2018
Revised Selected Papers

 Springer

Editors
Salah Kabanda
Department of Information Systems
University of Cape Town
Cape Town, South Africa

Stefan Gruner
University of Pretoria
Pretoria, South Africa

Hussein Suleman
Computer Science
University of Cape Town
Rondebosch, Cape Town, South Africa

ISSN 1865-0929   ISSN 1865-0937 (electronic)
Communications in Computer and Information Science
ISBN 978-3-030-05812-8   ISBN 978-3-030-05813-5 (eBook)
https://doi.org/10.1007/978-3-030-05813-5

Library of Congress Control Number: 2018964125

This Springer imprint is published by the registered company Springer Nature Switzerland AG
The registered company address is: Gewerbestrasse 11, 6330 Cham, Switzerland

This book is dedicated to the memory of **Helene Gelderblom**,
Professor of Informatics at the University of Pretoria.

* 27th Nov. 1963
† 7th April 2018

She supervised and promoted 4 doctoral candidates,
and published a large number of often-cited papers.[1]
She was an inspiration for colleagues and students,
and will be remembered for kindness and creativity.

---

[1] https://scholar.google.co.za/citations?user=Z_mhjgMAAAAJ&hl=en
The photography printed on this page is in the Public Domain (Internet).

Preface

This volume of CCIS contains the revised selected papers of SACLA 2018, the 47th Annual Conference of the Southern African Computing Lecturers' Association, held in Gordon's Bay (South Africa),[1] during June 18–20, 2018.

SACLA 2018 provided a forum for the discussion of original research and practical experiences in tertiary teaching and learning of information systems, computer science, information technology, and related disciplines, as well as the use of software tools in support of education more broadly.

The program of SACLA 2018 had a mixture of keynote addresses, contributed papers, panel sessions, and workshops, to meet the needs of a diverse range of attendees from across many different facets of computing education.

The keynote speakers were: Richard Baskerville, Professor of Information Systems at Georgia State University and Professor in the School of Information Systems at Curtin University, Perth, Australia, who spoke about cybersecurity in a digital world, and Mark Horner, CEO of Siyavula, who spoke about adaptive and individualized learning. The invited paper to Baskerville's keynote lecture is included in this volume.

Contributed papers were selected through rigorous double-blind peer-review with our international Program Committee. Every paper was peer-reviewed by at least three members of the Program Committee. In all, 79 papers were initially submitted.

Though most of those came from within the Republic of South Africa, we also received several international submissions with co-authors from (in alphabetical order) Canada, UK, Germany, Kenya, Mauritius, Namibia, The Netherlands, the USA, Zambia, and Zimbabwe. Whereas most of those papers were submitted by authors from the above-mentioned disciplines, one submission came from a department of computer engineering.[2]

Out of these initial submissions, the best 23 papers ($\approx$ 29%) were accepted for publication in this volume. A further 24 papers (not included in this volume) were accepted for presentation at the conference. All papers in this volume were revised and finalized after incorporating feedback from both the anonymous reviewers and the discussions at the conference.

The Best Paper Award was presented to Douglas Parry and Daniel le Roux for their paper titled "Off-task Media Use in Lectures: Towards a Theory of Determinants."

The conference's program included two affiliated workshops, which are summarized briefly in the Appendix of this volume —one on the dividing line between schools and universities in the teaching of IT, and another one about accreditation of IT diploma programmes— as well as a tutorial to assist young authors to prepare publications (with LaTeX) for Springer's CCIS format.

---

[1] https://sacla.uct.ac.za/.

[2] Indeed the participation of computer engineers ought to be encouraged more strongly in future editions of our conference: see Baskerville's keynote paper on this topic.

We wish to thank all members of the Program Committee and the additional reviewers for diligently reviewing the submitted papers, as well as helping to solicit submissions and publicize the conference in general. This year there were 42 members on the Program Committee. Approximately half of them were from outside South Africa, and 15 were from outside Southern Africa, the region of focus for the conference.

We also thank conference session chairs, presenters of papers, invited speakers, and staff who assisted with producing a high-quality program.

Last but not least, many thanks also to our sponsors, iitpsa, oracle, and sap, as well as to the many staff members of our publisher, Springer, without the help of whom this volume would not have appeared. Our publisher also donated several valuable computer science and informatics textbooks for inspection; after the conference, these books were handed over to academic libraries in South Africa for the benefit of the local students and their lecturers.

July 2018

Salah Kabanda
Hussein Suleman
Stefan Gruner

The supporters and sponsors of SACLA 2018 are herewith gratefully acknowledged

Organization

General Chair

Lisa Seymour	University of Cape Town, South Africa

Program Committee Co-chairs

Salah Kabanda	University of Cape Town, South Africa
Hussein Suleman	University of Cape Town, South Africa

Local Arrangements and Technical Support

Stephan Jamieson	University of Cape Town, South Africa
Aslam Safla	University of Cape Town, South Africa
Pitso Tsibolane	University of Cape Town, South Africa

Publications Chair and CCIS Proceedings Co-editor

Stefan Gruner	University of Pretoria, South Africa

Program Committee

Millicent Agangiba	University of Mines and Technology, Ghana
Tibebe Beshah	Addis Ababa University, Ethiopia
Madhulika Bhatia	Maharshi Dayanand University, India
Torsten Brinda[*]	Universität Duisburg-Essen, Germany
Emma Coleman	University of the Witwatersrand, South Africa
Donald Flywell	University of Cape Town, South Africa
Peter Forbrig[*]	Universität Rostock, Germany
Malcolm Garbutt	University of Cape Town, South Africa
Kurt Geihs[*]	Universität Kassel, Germany
Roelin Goede[*]	North-West University, South Africa
Leila Goosen[*]	University of South Africa, South Africa
Irene Govender[*]	University of Kwa Zulu Natal, South Africa
Stefan Gruner[*]	University of Pretoria, South Africa

Mmaki Jantjies	University of the Western Cape, South Africa
Norbert Jere	Walter Sisulu University, South Africa
Salah Kabanda	University of Cape Town, South Africa
Eduan Kotzé[*]	University of the Free State, South Africa
Herbert Kuchen[*]	Westfälische Wilhelms-Universität Münster, Germany
Horst Lichter	RWTH Aachen, Germany
Janet Liebenberg[*]	North-West University, South Africa
Linda Marshall[*]	University of Pretoria, South Africa
Matthew Mullarkey[*]	University of South Florida, USA
Lakshmi Narasimhan[*]	University of Botswana, Botswana
Liezel Nel[+]	University of the Free State, South Africa
Gabriel Nhinda[*]	University of Namibia, Namibia
Brian Nicholson	University of Manchester, UK
James Njenga[*]	University of the Western Cape, South Africa
Benny Nyambo[*]	University of Zimbabwe, Zimbabwe
Kwete Nyandongo[*]	University of Johannesburg, South Africa
Vreda Pieterse[*]	University of Pretoria, South Africa
Karen Renaud[*]	Abertay University, UK
Markus Roggenbach[*]	Swansea University, UK
Ian Sanders[*]	University of South Africa, South Africa
Andreas Schwill	Universität Potsdam, Germany
Lisa Seymour[*]	University of Cape Town, South Africa
Hussein Suleman	University of Cape Town, South Africa
Estelle Taylor[*]	North-West University, South Africa
Mark van den Brand	Technische Universiteit Eindhoven, The Netherlands
Marko van Eekelen[*]	Radboud Universiteit Nijmegen, The Netherlands
Corné van Staden[*]	University of South Africa, South Africa
Albert Zündorf	Universität Kassel, Germany
Olaf Zukunft[*]	Hochschule für angewandte Wissenschaften Hamburg, Germany

PC members marked with [*] are continuing PC members from the previous year's conference, SACLA 2017 [Springer-Verlag: **CCIS 730**], and PC members marked with [+] had acted as additional reviewers for SACLA 2017.

Additional Reviewers

Alagappan, Annamalai
Alexander, Peter
Barosan, Ion
Breytenbach, Johan
Cilliers, Liezel
Cleophas, Loek
Eickhoff, Christoph
Fredivianus, Nugroho
Fuchs, Andreas
Gabriels, Joost
Hacks, Simon
Hamunyela, Suama
Harun, Firdaus
Hooda, Madhurima
Huizing, Cornelis
Jakob, Stefan

Jokonya, Osden
Kumar, Nand
Lindel, Stefan
Maoneke, Pardon-Blessings
Ntinda, Maria-Ndapewa
Opfer, Stephan
Ossenkopf, Marie
Plewnia, Christian
Raesch, Simon-Lennert
Reischmann, Tobias
Rieger, Christoph
Schneegans, Lena
Venkata, Yugendra
von Hof, Vincent
Wrede, Fabian

"Prove all things; hold fast that which is good"
[Paul of Tarsus ($\approx 5 - \approx 64...67$ AD)].

Contents

Teaching Programming

Adaptation and Learning

Teamwork and Projects

Learning Systems

Topic Teaching

APPENDIX: Summaries of Affiliated Workshops

Invited Lecture

Information Security: Going Digital (Invited Lecture)

Richard Baskerville[1,2]([envelope]) [iD]

[1] Department of Computer Information Systems, Georgia State University,
Atlanta, USA
baskerville@acm.org
[2] School of Management, Curtin University, Perth, Australia

Abstract. Because 'going digital' regards using digital technologies to fundamentally change the way things get done, information security is necessarily engaged in going digital. Society and science are going digital. For the sciences, this digitalization process invokes an emerging model of the science of design that incorporates the assembly of information systems from a wide variety of platform ecosystems. According to principles of bounded rationality and bounded creativity, this mode of design requires more creativity to develop needed functionality from a finite set of available platforms. Going digital requires more creativity in designers of all types of information systems. Furthermore, the designers' goals are changing. The traditional model of information systems is representational: the data in the system represents (reflects) reality. Newer information systems, equipped with 3D printing and robotics actually create reality. Reality represents (reflects) the data in the system. This invited paper explores the example of information security. Designers of security for information systems not only must be more creative, they must design for more goals. The security task is no longer just protecting the digital system, the security task is protecting the products of the digital system. These innovations have particular implications for information systems curricula at university, too.

Keywords: Digitalization · Digital artifacts · Information systems
Information security · Information privacy · Education at university
Invited keynote lecture

1 Introduction

Going digital is an expression with differing meanings. For some, it is simply a synonym for computerization: adopting a digital technology to communicate or process data. But in the business world, the expression has a deeper meaning. Going digital regards fundamentally changing the way things get done. Going digital creates new frontiers, new experiences, and new capabilities [3]. So inevitably, information security is going digital. This change in its nature does

© Springer Nature Switzerland AG 2019
S. Kabanda et al. (Eds.): SACLA 2018, CCIS 963, pp. 3–14, 2019.
https://doi.org/10.1007/978-3-030-05813-5_1

not imply that information security has not always been at least partly digital. It is meant to imply that the information being protected is going digital in a societal way [13]. It is also meant to imply that many things in the world are going digital, among them societal information, and information security is now charged with protecting them all.

Society is itself going digital. This unfolding event envelopes and engages myriad aspects of information systems research such as digital natives, digital immigrants, ubiquitous information systems, pervasive computing, interorganizational information systems, IT diffusion and adoption, user acceptance of IT, mobile computing, enterprise systems, IT and new organizational forms, and the like [11].

As society goes digital, it is changing, and in keeping with this societal change, the reasoning about security also has to change. Such changes demand a fundamental rethink of the theoretical basis of information security [1]. A form of security reasoning has been common which could be regarded as security reasoning *around* the technology. As a result of the societal change, this reasoning must shift to security reasoning *through* the technology. In order to understand the shift in security reasoning, we will need to discuss what it means to be going digital with information systems.

2   The Digitalization of Society and Science

Information systems [7] (Sect. 1.1) are going through a thrilling period. The current period is thrilling because the rest of the world is discovering the marvels of digital technology. Society began going digital as mobile telephone technology began to operate in a digital mode. It quickly became obvious that information systems were being used as much for communications as they were for information processing. Many started using 'ICT' (information and communications technology) as a term instead of 'IT' (information technology). Soon after the availability of digital services on mobile telephones, together with the availability of personal computing, sparked the rise of myriad new kinds of applications: online shopping, online banking, social media, the Internet of Things, big data, FinTech, etc. As part of this emerging digitalization, science is going digital.

Gradually evolving scientific disciplines have become more and more prominent. Examples of these new natural-science-related disciplines included computational biology, computational physics, computational chemistry, computational neuroscience, and *in silico* medicine. Essentially every field of commerce, social engagement, science, knowledge, etc. has either digitalized or developed a digital counterpart.

The field of information systems has recognized that much of these digital developments have been focused on the notion of a digital device *broadly defined*. Such a digital device includes not just information processing, but networking, and software applications or 'apps'. It is an integrated, often personal, information system within a single device. In the field of information systems, this recognition has led us to become interested in developing Herbert Simon's original notions of the sciences of the artificial [9]. This interest has developed in information systems as *Design Science Research.* Information systems research recognizes that, as society goes digital, more and more human activities are organized with the aim of designing and creating digital artifacts. Thus the list of societal arenas and scientific disciplines that are now engaged in digital operations has expanded. These have quietly become, perhaps unrecognized by themselves, sciences of the artificial. Simon's original notions were based on an assumption that the natural sciences were different from the sciences of the artificial. The digitalization of the natural sciences is increasing making this assumption obsolete. For example with the development of biological science *in silico*, computational biology and laboratory biology are fast growing indistinguishable; merging into one discipline. Many logical experiments can take place within a computer. In this way digital biology is as much a science of the artificial as it is a natural science.

3   Digitalization and the Science of Design

Unrecognized here is that all of these scientific fields, natural or otherwise, are engaging in the science of design. That is, they are scientifically designing artifacts and studying the processes of design decisions. This form of design science constitutes the branch of design science research within information systems. This increasing engagement places information systems design science research in a leadership position. This position could well serve as a model for the progression toward digital systems design in other disciplines.

These processes of design decisions have been consistently part of Herbert Simon's work across his career. Simons work in decision-making is best known for what he called classical decision theory. Simon distinguished between classical decision theory and design decisions:

> *"Classical decision theory has been concerned with choice among given alternatives"*
> [10](p.172).

The decision process involved choosing from among alternatives that could be found. But design decisions are quite different. Design decisions have a degree of creativity. Design decisions are not only concerned with searching for alternatives but also through the elaboration of these alternatives. These alternatives were not just found, they were made:

> *"Design is concerned with the discovery and elaboration of alternatives"*
> [10](p.172).

These design decisions actually guide subsequent search to a certain degree. Taking a design decision has the impact of confining future design decisions. It is a form of bounded rationality in which the boundaries are created piecemeal as a design progresses. Each design decision defines constraints on subsequent design decisions. If the constraints prove overwhelming, it is always possible to return to a previous design decision and rethink it:

"The evaluations and comparisons that take place during this design process are not, in general comparisons among complete designs. Evaluations take place, first of all, to guide the search[, to] provide the basis for decisions that the designs should be elaborated in one direction rather than another"
[10](p.172).

This means that designers create their own future design prisons. All designs are bounded by rationality. Bounded rationality means that individuals and organizations are limited by their collective knowledge, cognitive abilities, and the constraints of finite resources. But because our design decisions guide the search for future designs, and design decisions must be elaborated, design decisions are also bounded by creativity. Because one design decision constrains future design decisions, such constraints create a frame of reference, a confining box within which new design decisions must be taken. Whenever you have such a frame of reference, such as rational constraints, you actually have a more creative situation: all the constraints put new demands on human creativity in order to create solutions to achieve goals in a highly constrained environment [6, 12]. Individuals are known to be more creative when given operating limits [4].

The growth of digitalization means that there are growing creative demands being placed on people who are now engaged in digital design in all walks of society. These creative demands are actually stronger than those that were placed on the pioneers of information systems. This increasing demand strength is because the pioneers of information systems had such a broad range of design decisions that they could take; and they had so few constraints on these design decisions. But today designers and disciplines of wide variety are constrained by the existing consumer devices and platforms from which they must work. Their creative problem is, how to create a functional system that provides the means to their goals [7], out of the existing panoply of digital devices and platforms.

This problem is well-known. It is similar to the design of junk art. Junk yards offer domains of miscellaneous objects that have been thrown away, discarded, or sold for scrap. The junk artist assembles works of beauty from these *found objects*. They design and create junk art from the junk. While it is totally unfair to suggest that the marvels of the digital devices we have available today can be construed to be junk, the idea nevertheless is similar. The digital world is the domain of miscellaneous digital found objects that are available to consumers at very low cost. Across all walks of society and science, we are now assembling marvelous information systems out of these found objects. It involves a higher degree of rationality, and a higher degree of creativity, because of the boundaries being placed on the ultimate designs by these pre-determined, and pre-defined objects.

The notion that today's computer information systems are junk art is not new. Such agile mash-ups are a return to notions of bricolage. Information systems bricolage is the pulling together of just the right kinds of digital technologies to solve the information problems [2]. In today's rapid digitalization of society and science, these found objects include digital platforms, ecosystems, apps,

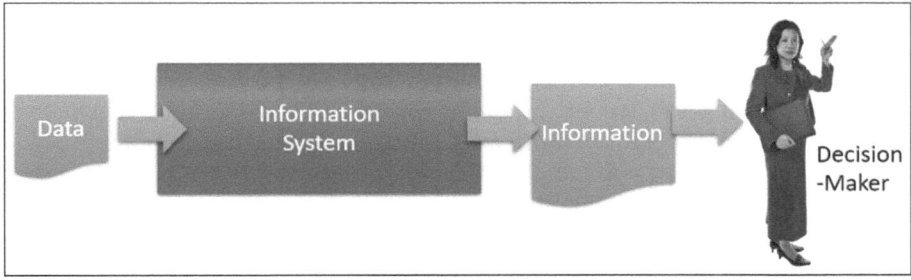

Fig. 1. Early 4-element information system

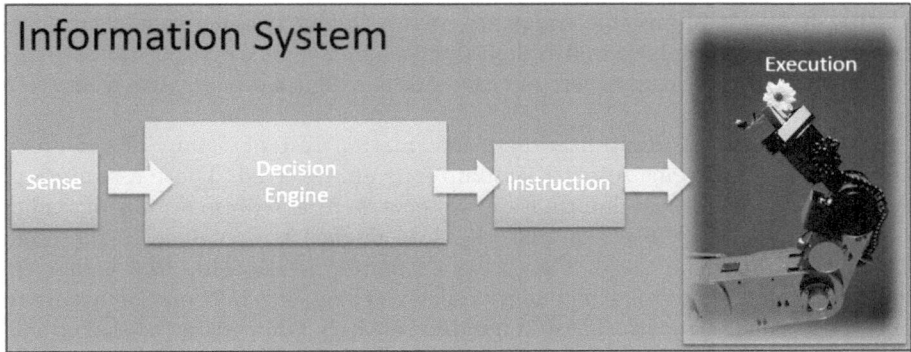

Fig. 2. Emerging 'Digital' information systems

devices, etc. Our design task in information systems is to assemble useful information systems out of this constellation of digital platforms, ecosystems, apps, devices, etc.

4   Descriptive Versus Prescriptive Information Systems in a Digital Society

This progression of digitalization has not only changed the way we design systems, it has also changed the underlying systems themselves. Information systems have evolved. Yesterday's information system essentially processed the data into information which was then used by a human decision-maker. It was a simple four element system with input data, the information system, the output information, and the decision-maker: see Fig. 1.

Tomorrow's information system may be quite different. It is still a simple four-part system, but now it includes a decision engine that makes many of our decisions *in silico*. So the four parts are quite different in some cases, namely sense, decide, instruct, and execute: see Fig. 2.

This revised system comes about because we have the Internet of Things to enable us to sense data as it is created (an event), we have artificial intelligence to make the decisions within the digital system, and we have robotics to actually execute, producing the system products without necessarily involving human actors. In this way the information system must be designed to go from events to products. The designs use found objects, and involve as little human interference as possible. Such information systems are not that far in the future. These newer kinds of information systems already decide what music we will hear and what movies we will watch. They do this by sensing our listening and viewing patterns, using artificial intelligence to decide what other music and videos we might wish to watch, and then executing these by offering us those digitally determined pre-selections for our enjoyment. With the increasing use of robotics and digital printing it is not impossible today to create similar systems that themselves create physical products as well as digital products. For such systems the stepwise process is sense, decide, instruct, and execute. The digital process runs from event to product.

As a result of this digitalization of information systems, many of our previous information systems research assumptions are inverted. Those assumptions included the notion that information systems were a *representation* of reality [7] (pp. 3–4, Fig. 1.1). For example, the data models are assumed to represent information about the world. They have a semantic relationship that is descriptive. Our notion of information quality relied on things like information accuracy, objectivity, timeliness, etc. These venerated research assumptions no longer hold in the digital world. Our new assumption ground holds that information systems now *create* and *shape* reality. The real world is often a reflection of the system, not the other way around. This inversion arises because information systems create reality. They have a semantic relationship that is prescriptive. There is even an ethical dimension: is it morally proper to create the reality that is digitally determined? The implications for information security are profound. Information security is no longer obligated to protect a representation of an existing reality. It is becoming an obligation to protect a representation of a future reality. The security task becomes one of protecting our next world. Information security is thus moving from protecting the digital assets and is now becoming involved in the digital consequences. In other words, today's information security is protecting not only the information system, but also protecting the products that it is producing. For security this is a means-end inversion. When information systems represented reality, that reality was the end, and the information system was the means. When information systems create reality, the information systems is the end, and reality is the means.

5   Security Around the System Versus Security Through the System

The previous mode of information systems, that of reflecting reality, defines the traditional information security goals of protecting the information and the

Fig. 3. Case IH Magnum autonomous tractor in field with a planter implement

system that produces it. But the newer mode for information systems, that of producing reality, forces us to ask: what exactly are we securing? Are we still protecting the computer system itself? If so it means the security concept is one of *providing a protection perimeter around the information system*. Alternatively we can ask, are we protecting the digital consequences of this information system? If the security concept is one of protecting not only the system but its digital consequences, its digital and physical products, then now we must think of providing a protection perimeter that encompasses not only the information system but also the products of that system. Security protects the products *through the system* rather than just *around the system*.

As a simple example, let us consider the Case IH Magnum autonomous tractor of Fig. 3.[1] It is a driverless robotic tractor designed to be released into a field with whatever implements and attachments that are required for agriculture. The tractor does its work under computer control that is guided by electronic signals (such as GPS locations) and other Internet of Things devices. In previous times, the security mission would be that of protecting the computer system, and the security mission would seek to provide *security around* the computer system. The protection perimeter would extend around the computer, the communications network, and the various data input devices. It is security around the system.

But with newer modes of digital systems, the whole ag-robotic tractor becomes part of the system. The tractor is conceptually the robotic endpoint of the information system. This incorporation of robotic output extends the protection boundary to include the robotic tractor as well as the other information elements. We would still provide *security around* computer system, the network elements and now the ag-robotic tractor: see Fig. 4. But such security designs

---

[1] http://www.cnbc.com/2016/09/16/future-of-farming-driverless-tractors-ag-robots.html.

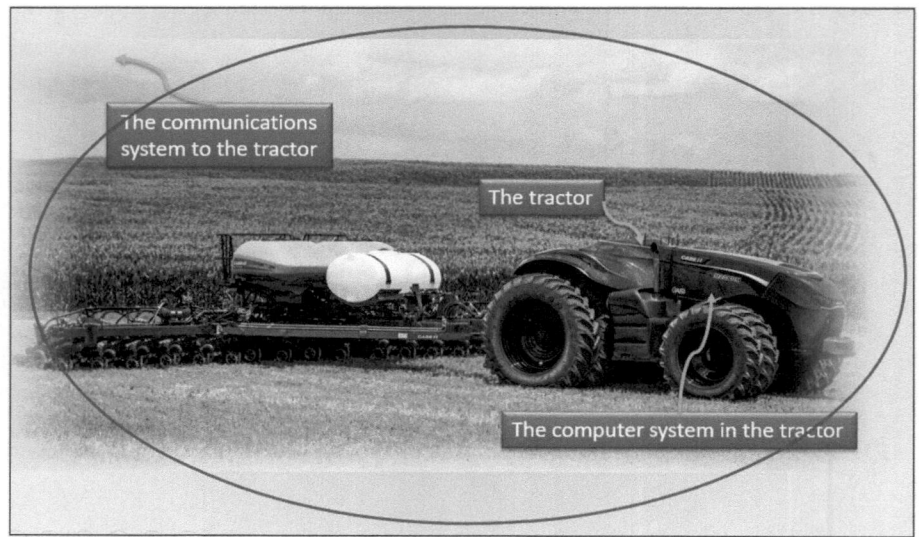

Fig. 4. Security around the system, protecting the tractor system

are made problematic because of the increasing use of platforms in the design. Security perimeters must account for the platforms and platform ecosystems that become involved in 'going digital'.

However, this system is not a traditional information system in which the human decision-maker is receiving information. This artifact is an information system that is producing agricultural products. In this case, this information system (because of its links to sensors artificial intelligence and its robotics) is producing a crop. The information in the system is creating a crop. In this way the mission of information security is no longer just protecting the tractor, its computer, and its communications. Now, the mission of information security includes protecting the crop. It requires a reset in the goals of information security. Information security now has the mission to protect the crop *through* information security: see Fig. 5. This shift is a dramatic extension of the mission of information security and extends the information security perimeter in order to protect the system products.

For information security, going digital means a new set of design principles to guide the convergence of information security and the security of its product. The first of these principles is that when data integrity falls, so can the integrity of our reality. When data is irrationally changed in an information system, it can change reality in irrational ways. This consequence arises because reality is the product that is an output of this information system. Because this product may be either digital or physical, changing the data will change the real world. The result arises from the inversion of the system-reality relationship in that data is no longer representing reality, reality is representing the data.

Fig. 5. Security through the system, protecting the crop

For example, suppose we gain access to change the viewing history data for an online, on-demand entertainment system. If we can configure this history to indicate that a happy and peaceful community prefers angry and violent films, then the intelligence routine of the entertainment system may shift to one that suggests only angry and violent films to the community. As a consequence, angry and violent films may become ever so slightly more popular, and it may even be possible that the community itself becomes ever so slightly more angry and violent. Changing the viewing system can create a different reality.

6   Discussion

Going digital in information security also highlights how security is itself evolving into a digital construction. Information security is no different than other aspects of reality. This evolution means that security exists first in the digital world, and this digital existence creates security in the physical world. Such an evolution would mean that it is no longer possible to have physical security where there is digital insecurity. As a result of such logic, digital security is now security of the first kind. It is the antecedent of security in the other aspects of our world. Physical security such as locks, fences, gates, and burly guards may become ineffective if digital security is absent. They cannot operate correctly without operating digital security correctly first.

Unfortunately, it appears to be the current case that our digital security is growing less and less effective. We have tended to underinvestment in security, at least partly because simply measuring security is difficult [8]. While our dependence on digital security grows deeper and deeper, digital security is encountering more and more issues. Currently, these problems surface as the inability of our information systems to prevent privacy losses that are a consequence of security failures [1]. Digital perimeters are highly permeable and difficult to protect [5]. They are easily violated. There is also an asymmetry between the attacker and the defender that makes attacks on digital systems easy. We currently have few effective ways to adjust this asymmetry such that attacks become more difficult, more dangerous, more costly, and more work.

These problems have fundamental implications for *how we teach* information security at the university level. Our present curriculum is focused on security systems such as the model in Fig. 1. Such courses only consider risks to a digital system that has data inputs and information outputs. When digital systems are modeling the physical world as it is about to become, *the scope of the curriculum must broaden to encompass the physical reality* that will be generated by the digital system.

Information security curricula must evaluate risks that the system generates with its outputs. The subject of risk analysis is the outputs of the system as well as the system. This means the risks to the physical realities affected by the digital system should be inventoried and estimated. Information security curricula must also ensure that the security control set encompasses the physical realities created by the digital system. Designing information security controls must consider their utility for protecting the physical realities generated by the system. For example, if the system generates a classroom meeting for learning security, the system must be designed not only to provide security for the system (as traditional) but also for the classroom meeting. When dealing with incident response and disaster recovery, information security curricula must now consider detection and recovery not only of the digital system, but how that digital system can regenerate an operational physical reality when this reality is interrupted. For example, if the system generates a classroom meeting, and a fire disrupts this meeting, security controls within the information system must be available to detect the disruption and provide recovery mechanisms to restore classroom operations.

Of course these examples assume that the information system is generating a physical reality. In 'going digital', many previously physical realities themselves grow more digital. For example, the physical classroom meeting used in the examples above may indeed become online, existing only as a digital reality. The extension of scope remains just as important. In previous curricula, we have taught students how to recover the computing system. 'Going digital', we must also teach students how to recover the digital realities generated by these systems.

Because 'going digital' implies that information systems generating physical and digital realities will encompass myriad digital devices (large and small), the task of information systems professionals will increasingly incorporate the Internet of Things. Data capture devices, 3D digital printers, robotics, and process control embedded in machinery grow increasingly under the purview of information systems designers. As we have discovered with data scientists, it is difficult to find single individuals with all of the skills necessary to perform such designs. Design teams must grow diverse to incorporate experts in the platforms and devices being integrated into the information system. The *socio-technical* world of the information systems security designer is gradually becoming the *techno-social* world. 'Going digital' can *shift the center of the information systems security designer's world from the social to the technical.* Of course it will be impossible to create a 'super-curriculum' that will cover the traditional social and economic focus of information systems security, *plus* the computer science, *plus* the computer engineering that the new designers will encounter. But the curriculum can extend to *better prepare the information systems professionals to work in teams made up not only of users, but also of more technical professionals with computing and engineering expertise.* For example, student projects with wider scope 'gone digital' topics could include a 'mixture' of team members from students of information systems, computer science, and computer engineering.

7   Conclusion

Future research is needed into ways to overcome such fundamental problems. The issues are in motion: both the issues of *what* information security is charged to protect; and *how* information security must go about protecting it. In terms of *what* information security is charged to protect, the security perimeter is moving outward. First, to incorporate the (multiple) platforms and platform ecosystems that are inevitably drawn into the digital system design. Second, to include the digital consequences of information systems. These consequences include an increasingly broad range of digital and physical products. In terms of *how* information security goes about achieving such protection, our security mode is shifting from one of security *around* the system to one of security *through* the system. More creativity is required on the part of the security designer because the platforms create more rational and creative boundaries, and because the goals of information security have grown.

Currently, the provision of security on the basis of reasoning around the system is growing less and less effective in proportion to the broadening demands society is placing on its information systems. Such a system only provides security for a representation of the world without providing security for the world that the representation creates. Reasoning information security through the system is growing more essential as we progressively increase our use of systems that create reality. Reasoning about the protection of the world that is being created by digital technology has potential to provide a more thorough approach.

This unfolding world of digitally generated realities *broadens the scope of information and computer security curricula.* Students must be prepared for this wider scope and the wider range of expertise that this scope will require. This curricula not only must deliver concepts for protecting and recovering information systems, but also deliver the additional concepts needed to enable the information systems to protect, regenerate and recover any digital realities that these systems have generated. Digital security designers will increasingly work with more technical professions. Our curricula should also prepared students for this new, more diverse work environment.

References

1. Anderson, C., Baskerville, R., Kaul, M.: Information security control theory: achieving a sustainable reconciliation between sharing and protecting the privacy of information. J. Manag. Inf. Syst. **34**, 1082–1112 (2017)
2. Ciborra, C.U.: From thinking to tinkering: the grassroots of strategic information systems. Inf. Soc. **8**, 297–309 (1992)
3. Dörner, K., Edelman, D.: What 'digital' really means. McKinsey (2015)
4. Finke, R.A., Ward, T.B., Smith, S.M.: Creative Cognition: Theory, Research, and Applications. MIT Press, Cambridge (1992)
5. Griffy-Brown, C., Lazarikos, D., Chun, M.: How do you secure an environment without a perimeter? Using emerging technology processes to support information security efforts in an agile data center. J. Appl. Bus. Econ. **18**, 90–102 (2016)
6. Hoegl, M., Gibbert, M., Mazursky, D.: Financial constraints in innovation projects: when is less more? Res. Policy **37**, 1382–1391 (2008)
7. Olivé, A.: Conceptual Modeling of Information Systems. Springer, Heidelberg (2007). https://doi.org/10.1007/978-3-540-39390-0
8. Pfleeger, S.L., Cunningham, R.K.: Why measuring security is hard. Secur. Priv. **8**, 46–54 (2010)
9. Simon, H.A.: The Sciences of the Artificial. MIT Press, Cambridge (1996)
10. Simon, H.A.: Theories of bounded rationality. In: Decision and Organization: A Volume in Honor of Jacob Marschak, pp. 161–176. North-Holland (1972)
11. Vodanovich, S., Sundaram, D., Myers, M.D.: Digital natives and ubiquitous information systems. Inf. Syst. Res. **21**, 711–723 (2010)
12. Ward, T.B.: Cognition, creativity, and entrepreneurship. J. Bus. Ventur. **19**, 173–188 (2004)
13. Yoo, Y.: Computing in everyday life: a call for research on experiential computing. MIS Q. **34**, 213–231 (2010)

Playfulness

Continuance Use Intention of a Gamified Programming Learning System

Marisa Venter[✉] and Arthur James Swart

Department of Information Technology, Central University of Technology,
Bloemfontein, South Africa
marisa@cut.ac.za

Abstract. The gamification of education offers various advantages including increased engagement of students. Limited research is currently available that can shed light on the influence of various gamification elements in on-line learning environments on the engagement and continuance use intention of students. The objective of the study was therefore to investigate the influence of gamification elements in on-line learning environments on the engagement of students and consequently on the continuance use intention of students. The population of the study consisted of 192 second-year Information Technology students enrolled at the Central University of Technology (Free State). An on-line questionnaire was used to collect data from students. The results indicated that the rewards that students received, as well as their self-expression and status in a gamified programming learning environment are very important to enhance their engagement in these environments. Furthermore, the study revealed that meaningful experiences in on-line learning environments is the leading predictor of continuance use intention of students in gamified programming learning environments. The results of this study could assist instructors in information technology departments of higher education institutions to incorporate gamified programming learning environments into their learning offerings.

Keywords: Gamification · Online learning environments
Khan Academy

1 Introduction

Gamification of education is an emerging approach for increasing student engagement and motivation in educational settings [9]. The excitement surrounding gamification results from the belief in its potential to make monotonous tasks more enjoyable [24]. The term 'gamification' has been defined in several ways, such as 'the phenomenon of creating gameful experiences' [16], or 'the use of game design elements in non-game contexts' [8]. Gamification in education refers to the introduction of gameful experiences and game design elements in the design of learning processes [9].

© Springer Nature Switzerland AG 2019
S. Kabanda et al. (Eds.): SACLA 2018, CCIS 963, pp. 17–31, 2019.
https://doi.org/10.1007/978-3-030-05813-5_2

Regardless of the widespread belief in the benefits of gamification, various studies have stressed the difficulty of sustaining user engagement due to the fact that effects of game elements are often short-lived [18,30]. A substantial percentage of gamified information system users seemingly discontinue their engagement with the system within a short period after initial system adoption [15,31]. Therefore, it is essential to understand the mechanisms that explain why users would continue to use gamified information systems in higher education settings [9]. Without an understanding of how a gamified electronic learning system engages students and encourages them toward continued system use, higher education institutions will forfeit the opportunity to make productive use of these emerging technologies [40].

The purpose of this paper is to investigate the influence of gamification elements in on-line learning environments on the engagement of students and consequently on the continuance use intention (CUI) of students. The paper is structured to provide an overview of prior research conducted on CUI with regard to e-learning contexts in Sect. 2, followed by an explanation of the gamified on-line learning environment that was used in this study (called Khan Academy) in Sect. 3. In Sect. 4, the development of the theoretical model for the study is discussed. Section 5 presents the research method, followed by the results in Sect. 6. Discussions are given in Sect. 7 and the conclusions in Sect. 8.

2   CUI in the E-learning Context

While previous research in e-learning has focused on the initial adoption [43] the ultimate success of an information system (IS) is really determined by the continued usage thereof. Until the continuous usage of an IS can be confirmed, it is premature to classify it as a success [44]. CUI can be defined as an individual user's intention to continue using a particular IS or the long term usage intention of a technology [2]. A review of prior research that was conducted in the wider e-learning domain in terms of CUI is summarized in Table 1, sorted according to the year of study.

After analysing the tabulated CUI research from the broader e-learning domain, the following trends were observed. Only two studies focused on game-based learning environments [23,42], with other e-learning environments not featuring any game based elements. Furthermore, studies focusing on the CUI of e-learning systems have only been conducted in countries like Brazil, Canada, Taiwan, USA and Turkey. It can be concluded that research on CUI in the e-learning context has not yet reached maturity, since approximately only one study per year was conducted over the last ten years. This study will therefore contribute to the limited existing body of knowledge of CUI in the broader e-learning context and specifically in a gamified electronic learning context in an area that has not featured prominently in the literature.

Table 1. Prior research conducted on CUI in the e-learning context

Reference	Year	Country of study	Type of e-learning
[35]	2005	Canada	On-line learning system
[33]	2006	International	E-learning course
[42]	2009	Taiwan	Business simulation games
[21]	2010	Taiwan	Web-based learning system
[23]	2011	Taiwan	Business simulation games
[5]	2012	USA	Information-oriented mobile applications
[32]	2015	Brazil	Learner management system (Moodle)
[7]	2016	Turkey	On-line learning portal

3   Khan Academy

3.1   Learning Environment

Khan Academy originated as a set of YouTube tutorials which MIT graduate Sal Khan made for his cousin who was struggling with mathematics. Today it is a multi-million-dollar non-profit organization with the stated mission of 'not-for-profit with the goal of changing education for the better by providing free world-class education for anyone anywhere' [27]. It provides a comprehensive set of resources, with over 5000 courses delivered in 65 languages. The Khan Academy website has delivered more than 600 million lessons worldwide, with four million exercises completed per day [27].

In addition to mathematics, Khan Academy covers many areas of science, arts, humanities, computing and economics. The computer programming section of Khan Academy offers the following subjects: Introduction to JavaScript and Animation; Introduction to HTML/CSS: Making web pages; Introduction to SQL: Querying and managing data; Advanced JavaScript: Games and Visualizations; Advanced JavaScript: Natural simulations [19].

The Khan Academy learning environment mainly comprises watching a video explanation of the topic followed by self-assessments in the form of questions (multiple choice or short answer). In contrast, the computer programming learning environment involves a code editor and execution window as shown in Fig. 1 [27]. The programming subject, from Khan Academy, that was investigated in this paper was 'Introduction to SQL: Querying and managing data'. The code editor and execution window of one of the SQL lessons are shown in Fig. 1.

The left-hand frame comprises an editor with the SQL code that produces the output in the right-hand frame. The video is a demonstration of how to code the solution for a given topic. In this example, it is restricting group results with HAVING in SQL [19]. The video contains a developer discussing the development of the code. While the code is being generated, the output on the right changes instantaneously to reflect the code that is added in the editor window [19]. At any

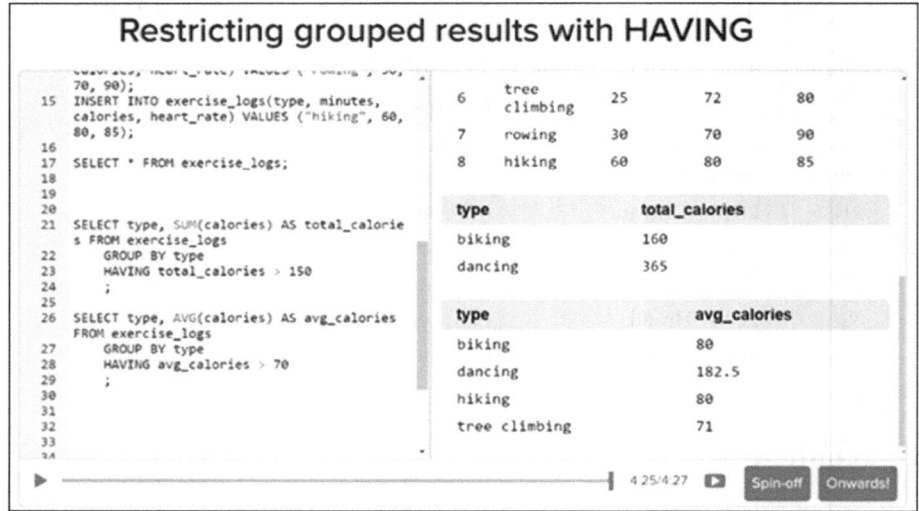

Fig. 1. SQL programming environment

given time, the user can pause the video and start to change the code, and the alterations are instantly reflected in the right-hand frame [19]. The SQL lessons demonstrate various SQL topics and directly after the video demonstration on a particular concept, the user is provided with the opportunity to complete a challenge by typing SQL code into the editor window. Instead of compilation errors, a character appears in the output frame with the explanation of the error, along with a prompt to show the user where the error occurs in the code as shown in Fig. 2 (on the left). Once the error has been corrected, and the challenge is successfully completed, the user is rewarded with points and a character that appears on the screen telling the user that all steps have been completed; see Fig. 2 on the right.

3.2 Gamification

Khan Academy has implemented several specific gaming elements within its on-line environment including badges, points, specific goals, leader boards and progress indicators which will be discussed next. Khan Academy has five different types of badges which can be earned while interacting with the learning material: see Fig. 3 [19]. The most common badge is the Meteorite (viewed as entry-level) with the Black Hole being the rarest (viewed as advanced-level). In addition, completing activities will allow the students to earn energy points, which are then displayed on their personalised dashboard, along with the number of videos they have completed. Moreover, Khan Academy gives a student the opportunity to enroll in a class with an instructor. The instructor can assign various goals to

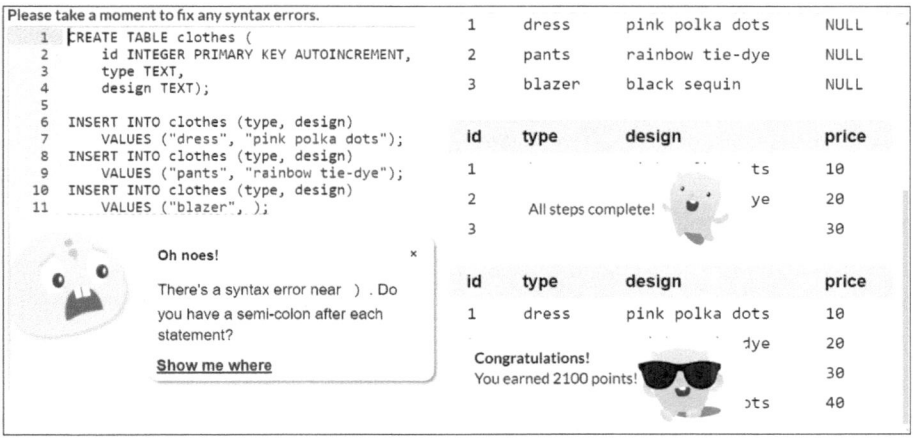

Fig. 2. Error condition (left), success condition (right)

students with due dates when these goals should be achieved. Goals can also be suggested by the system, based on past performance, or may be defined by the user.

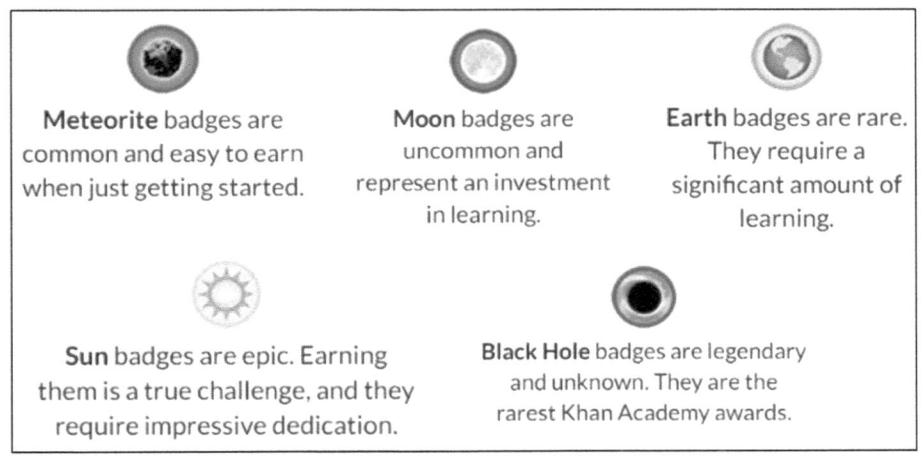

Fig. 3. Badge types in Khan Academy

In order for users to see their status on a leader board in Khan Academy, they must be enrolled in a subject with an instructor. The instructor has access to the leader board consisting of a list of students and the number of energy points they have gained and minutes they have spent on specified activities. In order for users to see their rankings, the instructor should post the leader board for all users to see. Furthermore, Khan Academy provides several different indicators for showing progress to the user. It will display information for achieving goals (Fig. 4: on the left) as well as activity indicators (Fig. 4: on the right).

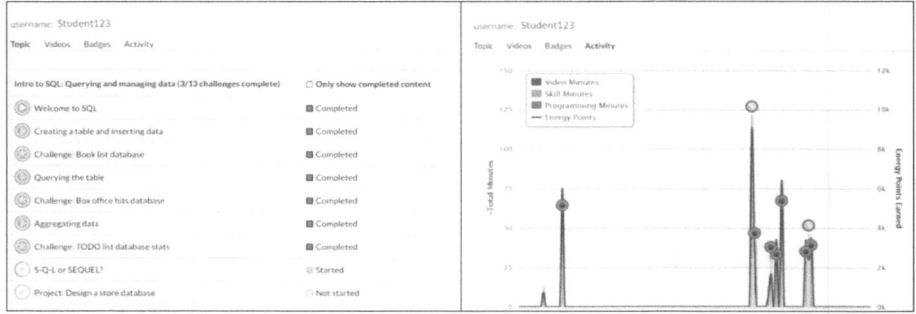

Fig. 4. Progress indicators in Khan Academy

Activity information is displayed through a bar graph indicating the amount of activity within Khan Academy each day and how many energy points were earned within a specific time period. Khan Academy also sends each registered user an email once a week detailing the progress that was made during that particular week.

4   Theoretical Model

A theoretical model was developed in order to predict the influence of gamification elements in the Khan Academy on-line learning environment on the engagement of students and consequently on the CUI of students. Gamification research over the past decade provided many constructs that might predict a user's CUI, including social influence [13], attitude toward a gamified IS [14], self-efficacy and satisfaction [40]. Flow experience (FE) is one of the predominant constructs that has been used to explain the CUI of users in various gamification and game-based learning environments [17,23]. Flow is a concept that was recognised and named by [6] to describe the psychological state of operation in which a person performing an activity is completely immersed in an emotion of full immersion, energised focus and enjoyment [6]. This emotional state is considered to be so rewarding that a person is inherently motivated to repeat the activity for its own sake [12]. When studying the CUI of users, researchers find this characteristic of flow particularly useful to predict the CUI of users. According to [6], the characteristics of flow include a loss of self-consciousness, a distortion of time, intense concentration, and a sense of being in control [37]. FE is therefore the first construct that was included in the theoretical model in order to predict the CUI of students towards a gamified learning environment. FE in the current study was measured by a combination of four constructs namely enjoyment, immersion, time distortion and control [1].

FE has been used extensively in IS research as a construct that represents the depth of engagement from a hedonic viewpoint. However, researchers presently stress that a gamified IS should not rely solely on hedonic user experience that is based on deep engagement, but it should also focus on the creation of pathways that will assist users to discover meaningful relations between their own interests and system use [30, 39]. Meaningful engagement (ME) refers to a state of mind in which a person experiences a sense of meaning and deeply comprehends the essence of the experienced events [40]. ME derives its theoretical basis from the Self-Determination Theory which is focused on what motivates an individual to make choices without external influence [29]. In a ME state, people are constantly aware of the contextual situation in which given tasks are performed, and people actively discover new paths to achieve their goals and feel that they are utilising power to meet environmental challenges [30]. Consequently, a users' ME in the interaction with the gamified IS has been proposed as a key determinant for the continued use of the system [4]. ME was therefore selected as the second construct that was included in the theoretical model in order to predict CUI. Drawing on existing literature, ME was measured in the current study by a combination of three constructs, namely self-expansion, meaning, and active discovery [40].

One of the key objectives of gamification is to make an activity more engaging [9]. To identify the antecedents of FE and ME, a literature search was conducted in order to identify frequently used gamification elements that influence user engagement. Four gamification elements were identified from gamification literature, namely rewards, status, competition, and self-expression, that may increase user engagement in the context of gamification [3, 16, 36, 38]. The rewards construct in this study refer to the perception of students that it is possible for them to earn and accumulate points, and that they will have the possibility to earn more points if they try harder [18]. In addition, the status construct refers to the perception of students that it is possible for them to have a higher status than others, and to be regarded highly by others, and that it is possible for them to increase their status [47]. Moreover, the self-expression construct in the study refers to the perception of users that it is possible for them to express their identity through game elements in a way that is distinct from others [25]. Finally, the competition construct refers to the perception of students that it is possible for them to compete with others and that it is possible for them to compare their performance to other students and to threaten the status of other students through their active participation [20]. These four constructs were therefore entered into the model created for the study as antecedents of FE and ME. The theoretical model that was developed for the study is shown in Fig. 5.

5   Method

The research instrument that was used to test the theoretical model of the study is a survey. Multiple-item summated rating scales were used to measure each construct that consisted of a 7-point Likert scale with two anchor points namely (1) 'Strongly Disagree' and (7) 'Strongly Agree'. The items in these scales were

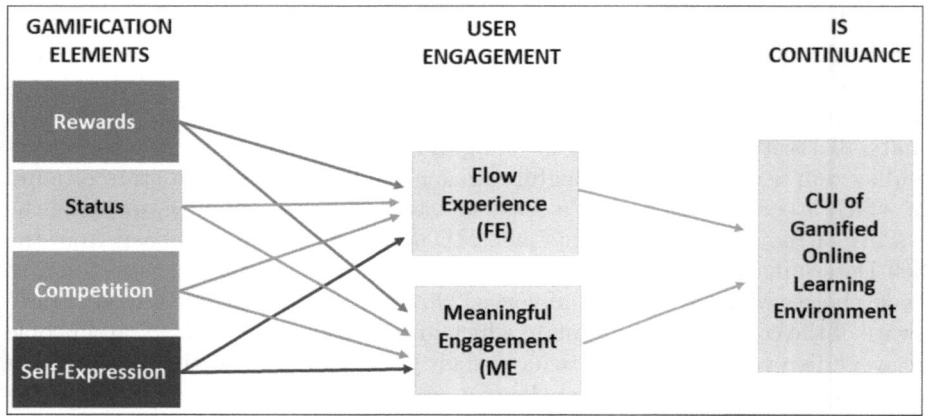

Fig. 5. Theoretical model for CUI of gamified on-line learning environments

adapted from existing literature in order to ensure content validity of the survey instrument. The items were adapted by replacing the specific type of IS used in the original wording of the item to 'Khan Academy'. For example if the original item was 'I enjoy using the Web' [1], the adapted item would be 'I enjoy using Khan Academy'.

Scales for CUI contained 3 items that were adapted from [22]. Scales for FE contained 14 items and 4 sub scales, namely immersion (3 items), time distortion (3 items), control (3 items) and enjoyment (3 items) that were adapted from [1]. Scales for ME contained 9 items and 3 sub scales, namely self-expansion (3 items), meaning (3 items) and active discovery (3 items) that were adapted from [40]. Scales for rewards contained 3 items and were adapted from [18]. In addition, scales for status contained 3 items and were adapted from [47]. Scales for self-expression contained 3 items and were adapted from [25]. Finally, the scales for competition contained 3 items and were adapted from [20]. The reliability of each scale of the survey instrument was evaluated by calculating Cronbach's alpha [11]. Acceptable values of alpha range from 0.70 to 0.95 [11]. Cronbach's alpha for the constructs were as follows: CUI (0.77); FE (0.85); immersion (0.70); time distortion (0.78); control (0.70); enjoyment (0.75); ME (0.91); self-expansion (0.75); meaning (0.75); active discovery (0.71); rewards (0.74); status (0.70); self-expression (0.70) and competition (0.70). All scales fell into the acceptable range and the data collection tool for the study was deemed to be a reliable measuring instrument. Regression analysis using SPSS version 19 was used to analyse the collected data.

The population for the study was limited to students enrolled for the subjects Databases II (DBS216C) and Information Systems II (NIL20DB) at the Central University of Technology in the Free State province. The content of these subjects offered in the first semester are the same. The theory component of the subjects focus on database design while the practical component focuses on SQL database programming. In the practical periods of these subjects, students were exposed to the 'Introduction to SQL subject on Khan Academy. The lecturer of these subjects created a subject on Khan Academy (called Databases II) and then enrolled all the students for this subject. The instructor assigned various tasks to students in Khan Academy, which they had to perform in the Khan Academy environment. All these assignments were part of the 'Introduction to SQL' subject on Khan Academy.

Students were exposed to the Khan Academy on-line platform for the first academic term. After this period, a survey was administered on-line by making use of QuestionPro. The link to the questionnaire was placed in the learning management system used by the students, and students were asked to voluntary complete the questionnaire. Ethical procedures as stipulated by the Central University of Technology were adhered to.

6   Results

From Table 2 it can be seen that 72% of the students were male, and 28% female. Furthermore, Table 3 shows that the majority of students (64.7%) accessed Khan Academy two or three times a week, and that 15.7% of students accessed Khan Academy more than three times a week.

Table 2. Gender

Gender	n	Percent
Male	139	72%
Female	53	28%
Total	192	100%

Table 3. Khan Academy Access per Week

Access per week	n	Percent
Not at all	3	1.5%
About once a week	31	15.2%
Two or three times a week	132	64.7%
More than three times a week	32	15.7%
Total	204	100.0%

Three regression models were constructed in order to test the theoretical model of the study. These results are discussed next. The first stepwise multiple regression model was constructed in order to determine what predictive power the four gamification elements (rewards, status, competition and self-expression) had towards FE. Three gamification elements, namely rewards ($\beta = 0.333$, $p <$ 0.001), self-expression ($\beta = 0.317$, $p < 0.001$) and status ($\beta = 0.233$, $p <$ 0.001) made a statistical significant contribution to the prediction of FE and were entered into the model. This resulted in a significant model $R^2 = 0.559$, F(3,192) = 84.53, $p < 0.001$, adjusted $R^2 = 0.552$. The adjusted R^2 value indicates that approximately 55% of the FE construct could be accounted for by the rewards, self-expression and status constructs. Competition ($\beta = 0.018$, $p = 0.789$) was the only construct that did not make a statistically significant contribution toward the prediction of FE. The following guidelines, presented by [10], were used to interpret R^2: very weak (0–4%); moderate (16–36%); strong (36–64%) and very strong (64–100%). From these guidelines, it can be seen that the model that was constructed had strong predictive power towards the FE construct.

The second stepwise multiple regression model was constructed in order to determine what predictive power the four gamification elements had towards ME. The following three gamification elements, namely rewards ($\beta = 0.492$, $p < 0.001$), self-expression ($\beta = 0.266$, $p < 0.001$) and status ($\beta = 0.148$, $p = 0.017$) made a statistical significant contribution to the prediction of ME and were entered into the model. This resulted in a significant model $R^2 =$ 0.606, F(3,192) = 102.41, $p < 0.001$, adjusted $R^2 = 0.600$. The adjusted R^2 value indicates that approximately 60% of the ME construct could be predicted by the rewards, self-expression and status constructs. As with FE, competition ($\beta = 035.018$, $p = 0.567$) did not make a statistically significant contribution toward the prediction of ME. From the guidelines presented by [10], it can be seen that the model that was constructed had a strong predictive power towards the ME construct.

The last stepwise regression model was constructed in order to determine what predictive power the FE and ME constructs had towards CUI. Both ME ($\beta = 0.464$, $p < 0.001$) and FE ($\beta = 0.276$, $p = 0.002$) made a statistical significant contribution to the prediction of CUI and were entered into the last regression model. This resulted in a significant model $R^2 = 0.503$, F(3,192) = 101.90, $p < 0.001$, adjusted $R^2 = 0.499$. The adjusted R^2 value indicates that approximately 50% of the CUI construct could be predicted by the FE and ME constructs. The resulting model had strong predictive power towards CUI, according to [10]. The results of the stepwise multiple regression models are shown in Fig. 6.

7   Discussion

When the results are investigated, it can be seen that the rewards gamification element had the strongest predictive power towards FE and ME. This result is consistent with research that found that rewards in mobile educational games was one of the most important reasons learners wanted to continue playing these

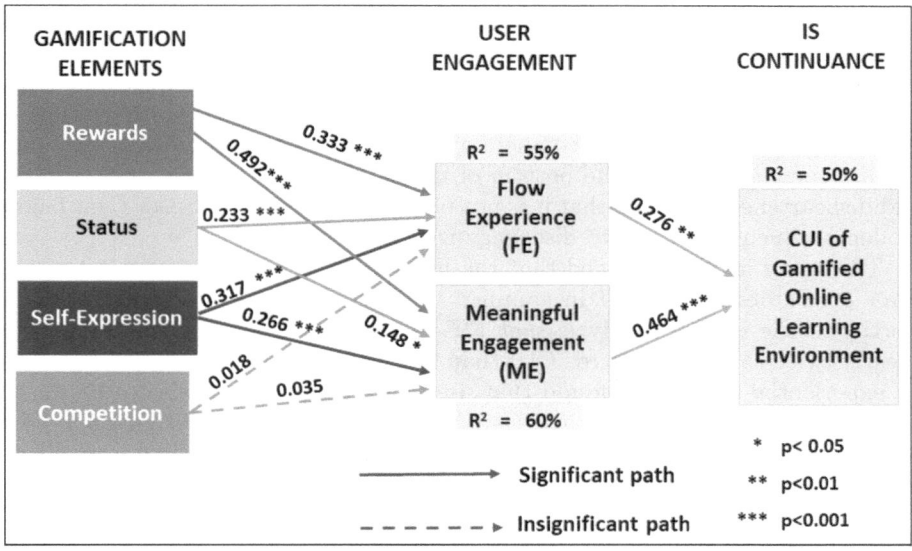

Fig. 6. Results of multiple stepwise regression

games [46]. Moreover, the strong motivational appeal of rewards found in this study can be compared with research that found that learners enjoyed an educational game with in-game rewards twice as much as an educational game without rewards [28]. The implication of this finding is that the rewards that students earn in a gamified on-line learning environment could sustain engagement in these environments which could lead to higher levels of CUI.

The self-expression construct had the second strongest predictive power towards FE and ME. This finding is consistent with prior research that found that providing users with opportunities to express their self-identity through choosing the types and names of their avatars, increased their intrinsic motivation and learning of the subject matter [34]. In Khan Academy, users can customise their profiles by selecting their own avatar which develops and grows as the user makes progress. The implication of this finding is that in a gamified learning environment it is important to provide users the opportunity to express their unique identity in order for them to distinguish themselves from others.

The status gaming element also made a statistical significant contribution towards the prediction of FE and ME. Users will be able to observe a higher status in a gamified environment if they notice that they can efficiently track their performance and level-up when they achieve certain mileposts [41]. These results can be compared to research conducted by [40] that indicated that the status construct made a statistical significant contribution towards the prediction of FE ($\beta = 0.388$, $p < 0.001$) and ME ($\beta = 0.326$, $p < 0.01$) in their study. This implies that when users are able to effectively track their performance in a gamified learning environment, it could improve the engagement of users.

The only gamification element that did not make any statistical significant contribution towards the prediction of FE or ME was the competition construct. These results are similar to various findings in digital game-based learning environments that showed that learners strongly preferred to collaborate with other learners and did not want to compete with them [45, 46]. Another reason could be that some students at the bottom of the leader board become downtrodden and disheartened, thinking that it is not possible for them to surpass their fellow students, which lead them to disengage with the system [46].

The study lastly confirmed that the FE and ME are both statistical significant predictors of the CUI in gamified learning environments. What is noteworthy in the current study is that ME had a much higher predictive power (nearly twice as much) towards CUI than FE. This finding is in accordance with an experiential study that found that users of a gamified IS consider FE to be less important than ME for their CUI [26]. This study showed that users who perceive their interaction with an IS as personally meaningful were more likely to continue to use the IS [26]. This implies that it is more important for students to perceive that they are meaningfully engaged by the system, as opposed to experiencing a state of flow. Moreover, higher perceptions of ME will lead to higher levels of CUI.

8   Conclusions

The contribution of this study is that it sheds lights on the influence that several gamification elements have on sustaining a user's engagement in a gamified programming learning environment. Moreover, the theoretical model of the study made a novel contribution to the literature on CUI by incorporating gamification elements as predictors of FE and ME in a CUI model for an e-learning context. The model developed for the study indicated that the rewards that students receive, as well as their self-expression and status in a gamified learning programming environment are very important to enhance their engagement in these environments. Furthermore, the study revealed that ME in on-line learning programming environments is the leading predictor of CUI of students in these environments.

A shortcoming of the current study is that the population was limited to two student groups in one province in South Africa with only one gamified learning environment being investigated. Therefore, the results obtained from the study cannot be generalised to the broader population of South Africa or to other gamified learning systems. Suggestions for future research would therefore be an invitation to researchers at institutions from other provinces to test the model developed for the study in similar or other gamified learning environments in order to validate the findings of the current study.

References

1. Agarwal, R., Karahanna, E.: Time flies when you're having fun: cognitive absorption and beliefs about information technology usage. MIS Q. **24**(4), 665–694 (2000)
2. Bhattacherjee, A.: Understanding information systems continuance: an expectation-confirmation model. MIS Q. **25**(3), 351–370 (2001)
3. Bunchball: Gamification 101: An Introduction to the Use of Game Dynamics to Influence Behavior (2010)
4. Chen, Y., Burton, T., Mihaela, V., Whittinghill, D.M.: Cogent: a case study of meaningful gamification in education with virtual currency. Int. J. Educ. Technol. **10**(1), 39–45 (2015)
5. Chen, L., Meservy, T.O., Gillenson, M.: Understanding information systems continuance for information-oriented mobile applications. Commun. Assoc. Inf. Syst. **30**, 127–146 (2012)
6. Csíkszentmihályi, M.: Finding Flow: The Psychology of Engagement with Everyday Life. Harper Perennial, New York City (1990)
7. Dagan, G., Akkoyunlu, B.: Modeling the continuance usage intention of online learning environments. Comput. Hum. Behav. **60**, 198–211 (2016)
8. Deterding, S., Dixon, D., Khaled, R., Nacke, L.: From game design elements to gamefulness: defining gamification. In: Proceedings of 15th International Academic MindTrek Conference: Envisioning Future Media Environments, pp. 9–15 (2011)
9. Dichev, C., Dicheva, D.: Gamifying education: what is known, what is believed and what remains uncertain: a critical review. Int. J. Educ. Technol. High. Educ. **14**(1), 1–36 (2017)
10. Evans, J.: Straightforward Statistics for the Behavioral Sciences. Brooks/Cole, Boston (1996)
11. Field, A.: Discovering Statistics Using SPSS. SAGE, Newcastle upon Tyne (2009)
12. Finneran, C.M., Zhang, P.: A person-artefact-task (PAT) model of flow antecedents in computer-mediated environments. Int. J. Hum. Comput. Stud. **59**(4), 475–496 (2003)
13. Hamari, J.: Transforming homo economicus into homo ludens: a field experiment on gamification in a utilitarian peer-to-peer trading service. Electron. Commer. Res. Appl. **12**(4), 236–245 (2013)
14. Hamari, J., Koivisto, J.: Social motivations to use gamification: an empirical study of gamifying exercise. In: ECIS 2013 Proceedings of the European Conference on Information Systems, pp. 1–12 (2013)
15. Hamari, J., Koivisto, J.: Working out for likes: an empirical study on social influence in exercise gamification. Comput. Hum. Behav. **50**, 333–347 (2015)
16. Hamari, J., Koivisto, J., Sarsa, H.: Does gamification work? A literature review of empirical studies on gamification. In: Proceedings of the Annual Hawaii International Conference on System Sciences, pp. 3025–3034 (2014)
17. Hamari, J., Shernoff, D.J., Rowe, E., Coller, B., Asbell-Clarke, J., Edwards, T.: Challenging games help students learn: an empirical study on engagement, flow and immersion in game-based learning. Comput. Hum. Behav. **54**, 170–179 (2016)
18. Kankanhalli, A., Taher, M., Cavusoglu, H., Kim, S.: Gamification: a new paradigm for online user engagement. In: Proc. 33rd International Conference on Information Systems, pp. 1–10 (2012)
19. Khan Academy Environment (2018). https://www.khanacademy.org/
20. Lee, C.L., Yang, H.J.: Organization structure, competition and performance measurement systems and their joint effects on performance. Manag. Account. Res. **22**(2), 84–104 (2011)

21. Lee, M.C.: Explaining and predicting users' continuance intention toward e-learning: an extension of the expectation-confirmation model. Comput. Educ. **54**(2), 506–516 (2010)
22. Lee, M.C., Tsai, T.R.: What drives people to continue to play online games? An extension of technology model and theory of planned behavior. Int. J. Hum.-Comput. Interact. **26**(6), 601–620 (2010)
23. Liao, Y.W., Wang, Y.S.: Investigating the factors affecting students' continuance intention to use business simulation games in the context of digital learning. In: Proc. International Conference on Innovation, Management and Service, pp. 119–124 (2011)
24. Liu, D., Santhanam, R., Webster, J.: Toward Meaningful Engagement: a framework for design and research of gamified information systems. MIS Q. **41**(4), 1011–1034 (2017)
25. Ma, M., Agarwal, R.: Through a glass darkly: information technology design, identity verification, and knowledge contribution in online communities. Inf. Syst. Res. **18**(1), 42–67 (2007)
26. Mekler, E.D., Brühlmann, F., Opwis, K., Tuch, A.N.: Disassembling gamification: the effects of points and meaning on user motivation and performance. In: Proceedings of CHI 2013 Extended Abstracts on Human Factors in Computer Syststem, p. 1137 (2013)
27. Morrison, B.B., di Salvo, B.: Khan academy gamifies computer science. In: SIGCSE 2014 Proceedings of 45th ACM Technical Symposium on Computer Science Education, pp. 39–44 (2014)
28. Nagle, A., Wolf, P., Riener, R., Novak, D.: The use of player-centered positive reinforcement to schedule in-game rewards increases enjoyment and performance in a serious game. Int. J. Serious Games **1**(4), 2384–8766 (2014)
29. Nicholson, S.: A user-centered theoretical framework for meaningful gamification. In: Games + Learning + Society 8.0 (2012)
30. Nicholson, S.: Two paths to motivation through game design elements: reward-based gamification and meaningful gamification. In: Proceedings of iConference, pp. 671–672 (2013)
31. Patel, M.S., Asch, D.A., Volpp, K.G.: Wearable devices as facilitators, not drivers, of health behavior change. J. Am. Med. Assoc. **313**(5), 459–460 (2015)
32. Pereira, F.A.D.M., Ramos, A.S.M., Andrade, A.P.V.D., Oliveira, B.M.K.D.: Use of virtual learning environments: a theoretical model using the decomposed expectancy disconfirmation theory. J. Inf. Syst. Technol. Manag. **12**(2), 333–350 (2015)
33. Roca, J.C., Chiu, C.M., Martínez, F.J.: Understanding e-learning continuance intention: an extension of the technology acceptance model. Int. J. Hum. Comput. Stud. **64**(8), 683–696 (2006)
34. Ryan, R.M., Rigby, C.S., Przybylski, A.: The motivational pull of video games: a self-determination theory approach. Motiv. Emot. **30**(4), 347–363 (2006)
35. Saadé, R., Bahli, B.: The impact of cognitive absorption on perceived usefulness and perceived ease of use in on-line learning: an extension of the technology acceptance model. Inf. Manag. **42**(2), 317–327 (2005)
36. Santhanam, R., Liu, D., Shen, W.C.M.: Research note: gamification of technology-mediated training: not all competitions are the same. Inf. Syst. Res. **27**(2), 453–465 (2016)
37. Sherry, J.: Flow and media enjoyment. Commun. Theory **14**(4), 328–347 (2004)

38. Stanculescu, L., Bozzon, A., Sips, R., Houben, G.: Work and play: an experiment in enterprise gamification. In: CSCW 2016 Proceedings of 19th ACM Conference on Computer Supported Cooperative Work and Social Computing, pp. 346–358 (2016)
39. Suh, A.: Applying game design elements in the workplace. In: ICIS 2015 Proceedings of 36th International Conference on Information Systems, pp. 1–11 (2015)
40. Suh, A., Cheung, C.M.K., Ahuja, M., Wagner, C.: Gamification in the workplace: the central role of the aesthetic experience. J. Manag. Inf. Syst. **34**(1), 268–305 (2017)
41. Suh, A., Wagner, C., Liu, L.: The effects of game dynamics on user engagement in gamified systems. In: Proceedings of Annual Hawaii International Conference on System Sciences, pp. 672–681 (2015)
42. Tao, Y.H., Cheng, C.J., Sun, S.Y.: What influences college students to continue using business simulation games? The Taiwan experience. Comput. Educ. **53**(3), 929–939 (2009)
43. Tarhini, A., Masa'deh, R., Al-Busaidi, K.A., Mohammed, A.B., Maqableh, M.: Factors influencing students' adoption of e-learning: a structural equation modeling approach. J. Int. Educ. Bus. **10**(2), 164–182 (2017)
44. Thong, J.Y.L., Hong, S.J., Tam, K.Y.: The effects of post-adoption beliefs on the expectation-confirmation model for information technology continuance. Int. J. Hum. Comput. Stud. **64**(9), 799–810 (2011)
45. Tüzün, H., Yilmaz-Soylu, M., Karaku, T., Inal, Y., Kizilkaya, G.: The effects of computer games on primary school students' achievement and motivation in geography learning. Comput. Educ. **52**(1), 68–77 (2009)
46. Venter, M.: Continuance use intention of primary school learners towards mobile mathematical learning games. Dissertation: Computer Science Department, University of the Free State (2017)
47. Wang, Y., Fresenmaier, D.: Assessing motivation of contribution in online communities: an empirical investigation of an online travel community. Electron. Markets **13**(1), 33–45 (2003)

Robotics: From Zero to Hero in Six Weeks

Romeo Botes$^{(\boxtimes)}$ ⓘ and Imelda Smit ⓘ

School of Computer Science and Information Systems, North-West University,
Vanderbijlpark, South Africa
{romeo.botes,imelda.smit}@nwu.ac.za

Abstract. In the Information Technology course offered at the North-West University, students do two subject modules during their second year on Information Systems Development. During their third year the course scaffolds on this knowledge base by extending exposure to novel technologies including robotics, cyber security, etc. The focus of this paper is on the design and evaluation of the robotics project offered over a six-week period. After the project a focus group interview with several students provided feedback regarding their experience.

Keywords: Robotics · Project based learning · Learning tools
Arduino · JellyBeanBot

1 Introduction

During the exit year of study in the Information Technology (IT) degree offered at the North-West University, students complete a project based subject module. This module challenges students to explore new and unfamiliar technologies with the purpose to prepare them for industry. Some projects are industry projects provided by industry partners that are at times set up as a competition, with scholarships or internships offered to the winning students. Other projects are more focused on the introduction of new concepts such as mobile applications. During 2017 the robotics interest group at the North-West University had the opportunity to offer a six-week project course on robotics with the purpose to expose students to the basic concepts of robotics. In this paper we describe and discuss our experiences with this project.

2 Related Work

In education, *robotics* is applied in a variety of ways and for a multitude of purposes [15]. Robotics may relate to education in one of two ways [15]: first, robotics *in* education and, second, robotics *for* education. The latter refers to robotics being used as an educational tool, whereas the first is goal orientated using robotics to have fun while teaching something useful.

© Springer Nature Switzerland AG 2019
S. Kabanda et al. (Eds.): SACLA 2018, CCIS 963, pp. 32–46, 2019.
https://doi.org/10.1007/978-3-030-05813-5_3

Table 1. Core robotic concepts adapted from [2]

Core concept	Sub-categories
Robotics and society	History, application, manufacturing, ethics
Hardware	Components, embodiment, mechanical design
Sensors/perception	Distance/proximity, tactile
Types of error	Sensors, thinking, acting
Planning/thinking/control schemes	Remote control, autonomous control, feedback control, behavior-based control, navigation, localization, mapping
Acting	Actuators, motors, manipulators, wheels, gears, kinematics, forward, inverse
Algorithms	Conditionals, loops, interrupts

Inexperienced lecturers would sometimes shy away from teaching with technology, because they are not aware of its uses and abilities [10]. Unfortunately, such inexperience not only limits the use of technology in education and robotics for education, but also poses a problem for robotics in education; since the inability to use technological tools forms gaps in the knowledge acquired by students. Consequently they do not have the necessary opportunities to utilize new technology in their learning and therefore do not become aware of advances prevalent beyond textbook theory.

With the intention to provide students with some background knowledge regarding key robotics concepts, the facilitators of the robotics course have drawn on the research of [2] who proposed a list of core robotic concepts: see Table 1.

In the robotics course of [16] at university, LEGO kits were used which culminated in a contest in the context of a predetermined theme. Students collaborated with a peer with the intention to ease frustrations and challenges accompanying working with hardware [16]. In a similar course for a high school [20], students designed and produced a feature-rich programmable robot that would be robust for hundreds of hours of use.

Arduino[1] includes software and hardware on a prototyping platform that is electronics-based. The software is open-source and written in Java [23]; the hardware is user friendly and usable in more than one context, making it attractive to people working in interactive environments. The Arduino UNO includes the following components: a microcontroller (ATmega328 microprocessor), a USB to serial chip, and a DC power connector. An Integrated Development Environment (IDE) installed on a user's computer allows such a user to program the Arduino UNO. The IDE includes a number of features such as LEDs, sound, etc. In Table 2, reasons are given for using Arduino as a learning tool according to [8, 11].[2]

---

[1] http://www.arduino.cc/.
[2] https://massimobanzi.com/.

Table 2. Reasons for using Arduino as a learning tool

Reason	Description
An active community of users exist	A group of people who uses the Arduino microprocessor makes up its user community. They act as support when problems are encountered by the newcomers in this community. The expert users also guide the development of the open source code and hardware[a]
Developed in an educational environment	The Arduino micro-processor was developed in the context of education, keeping students in mind in its design
The hardware is affordable	The Arduino hardware is relatively inexpensive, while designs are free to obtain. Damaged components may be replaced at a nominal fee. This allows users to focus on tinkering
Hardware and software are both open-source	Given the free license for Arduino hardware and software designs, users may make changes and build circuits without paying Arduino [13, 14]
Based on the processing IDE	The development environment [19] in the processing software was designed to be easy-to-learn
Programmable via USB cable	With the absence of serial ports from computers and the introduction of USB cables, the Arduino board becomes accessible outside the formal laboratory environment [9]
It is a multi-platform environment	The Arduino IDE being written in Java, it can run on various platforms, including Windows, Linux and mac OS X

[a]http://www.fastcolabs.com/3025320/howarduino-is-becoming-the-worlds-social-network-for-hackers-and-makers

In the work environment of computer science or information systems professionals one expects that problems need to be solved, and that in many cases these problems would be complex problems requiring a group of people with a variety of skills to solve the problem jointly. When imitating such scenarios at university, *project-based* and *problem-based* learning (PBL) is well-suited. To distinguish between the two approaches it is sufficient to say that problem-based learning would center around individual study units, while project-based learning would integrate a number of study units (possibly all the study units) of a subject module [22]. The constructionist approach to PBL, where students work in teams to solve open-ended projects large enough to challenge a group [7], enables such students to acquire knowledge, learn skills, and build confidence in their abilities. Cappelleri and Vitoroulis, for example, replaced a semester-long robotics competition with project-based learning tasks stretching over one week periods [4]. They found that this changed approach made the course easier to manage and more enjoyable for their students [4].

The course offering reported on in this paper was building on the strengths and knowledge of the studies mentioned above; with the guidance of one robotics expert three facilitators offered the robotics course. The course culminated in a competition to stimulate students' interest; the course utilized a robot that was built in-house to save costs. The students worked in groups to draw on the benefits of project-based learning within a constricted budget.

A *focus group interview* (FGI) uses interaction to generate data [17]. Carey elaborates by classifying FGIs as a group interview guided by a moderator [5]; questions are semi-structured, the setting is informal, and data are collected on a focused theme. Various authors are not in agreement regarding the nature of the data collected. For example [3] claims that data gathered may be qualitative and quantitative, while [1] classifies data to be qualitative. This study aims to hear the students and understand their experiences, relating to qualitative data and an interpretive stance towards the topic under discussion.

The number of groups to be used in research is also a point of contention among various authors. As many as 12 are suggested by [12], while [18] deems 10 to be mostly redundant. As a minimum, [21] suggests that four FGI are sufficient, whereas [24] claim that there are no rules when it comes to the optimum number of FGIs; one FGI may already be enough. The notion of 'saturation' [17] may be of much value here, since it may guide each study accurately. In the study under discussion the fairly small group of students and the invitation to students to willingly participate resulted in one FGI.

The size of the focus group influences the actual discussion [6]. Fern found that a larger group of eight tends to generate more concepts than a smaller group of four [6], but he also poses that it is easier to manage smaller focus groups. Therefore focus groups should be large enough to provide a sufficient number of concepts [17], but also small enough to allow all participants to participate freely. In this study a group of three students participated with one facilitator-researcher and one researcher.

3   Setting

The aim of the study is to establish a formalized robotics subject module to be offered as part of the IT course. Towards this purpose a subject sub-module covering introductory robotics concepts along with a project, are suggested in this paper. The offering was conducted during the first part of the second semester of 2017. After the finalization of the offering students were invited to participate in a focus group interview (FGI). The purpose of the interview was to learn from

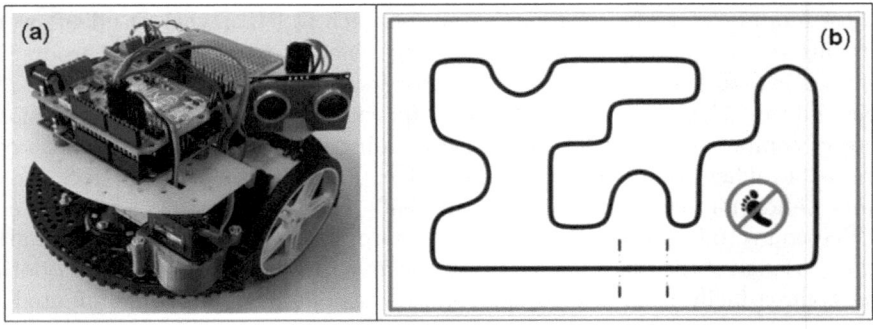

Fig. 1. (a) Robot used during the course. The playing field (b)

the student-experience and to gather data that may guide subsequent offerings of the robotics project.

At the start of the FGI, participants were informed regarding the purpose of the study, their privacy were assured, and they were allowed to ask questions. The moderators participated in the FGI along with the students, testing their observations and opinions as well as guiding the conversation. Data were gathered using an audio-recorder. The recordings were transcribed and analyzed.

A number of factors had an influence on the form the robotics project took on. Within the confinements of the subject module, six weeks were allocated to the robotics project. A strict budget was made available to attain the components necessary to construct the robots to be used in the projects. The budget was not sufficient to supply each of the 64 students enrolled for the module with his or her own prebuild, ready to program, robot and students needed to form groups of four members. Groups were formed by the facilitators based on students' second year Java marks to ensure groups include both stronger and weaker students. As an example, the best Java student would form a group with the person in the 16th position, the 31st, and the 46th. A large percentage of students from the Vaal Campus, where this intervention took place, come from disadvantaged families. For this reason, students were not expected to buy robots; the robots were returned to be used in subsequent years. The intention is to extend the number of robots to allow for future growth in the course, and accommodate groups of at most three members and possibly only two in future offerings.

The set of robots that was constructed to be used in this course made use of the Arduino platform which uses the Arduino Uno 3 as a microcontroller. The microcontroller board were supported by a custom designed shield known as JellyBeanBot. Two sensors were utilized as input for navigation purposes, a 3-line sensor and an ultra-sonic sensor, finally all this were fitted to a Romi-Chassis which provided for a base for the robot, driving motors and wheels. Figure 1(a) shows the complete robot used during the course.

Students were not allowed to remove the robots from the laboratory, and all work needed to be completed in the 3 h per week over the six weeks allocated to the offering. Initially classes were started with an offering of the supporting theoretical concepts before students worked on their robots. During the last few weeks only practical work were done during class time. With this being a first offering, some teething problems were experienced. Initially the groups of students were not allocated a particular robot and picked the next one upon entering class, but slight differences between the robots posed a problem with this strategy and from week 3 it was decided that a robot will be marked for the use of a particular group.

The final objective of this project was for the groups to complete a playing field. Successful completion awarded a project pass. The playing field included the aspects of line following, object detection and object avoidance. Figure 1(b) shows the playing field designed to be completed by each robot.

Although three facilitators were tasked with the responsibility of this offering, only one had the expertise to acquire and build components, and to construct the robots. This route was taken because of the substantial saving that realized from constructing robots from self-bought and 3D-built components, instead of buying prepared kits. Unfortunately, a difference in opinion among the facilitators resulted in 16 groups of four students being formed, instead of 10 groups of six students. This was suggested by the facilitator responsible for building the robots, based on the available funding which allowed for acquiring the components for only 10 complete robots. The extra six robots were to be assembled by using old equipment from other robotics projects and courses stripped for parts to be re-used in creating six robots similar to the 10 already acquired.

4   The Robotics Course

The aim of the robotics project was to introduce students to the novel technology of robotics. The associated concepts that was covered, include micro-processor programming, movement, object detection and object avoidance. Providing the groups of students with a constructed robotic, moved the focus of the intervention from being inter-disciplinary (including both engineering and computer science disciplines) to centering on programmatically preparing the robot for the tasks set out. The practical preparation and testing of a preconstructed robot to follow a simple line with some obstacles along the way was the end goal of the project. The six-week project subject sub-module is discussed subsequently.

The components included in the construction of the robot allow students to use programming code to prepare the robot for its tasks on the playing field. These components are listed, described, and shown in Table 3. The completely assembled robot is shown in Fig. 1(a). The discussion of the design and assembly of the robot is beyond the scope of this paper. The cost incurred in acquiring the components are listed as well. It may be noted that the cost incurred for a similar project is in the region of R1400.00; this compares favorably to off-the shelf kits ranging between R2256.00 (AfrikaBot) and R5800.00 (LEGO Mindstorms EV3).

As a tool to guide student groups through the project, continuous assessment was utilized since its initiation. Every week groups were required to submit the

Table 3. Planned six-week robotics group project

Item and Cost	Description	Use	Visual
Arduino UNO Estimated Cost: R179.40	The Arduino UNO is a micro controller based on the ATMEGA 328 Chip. The Arduino UNO R3 was used	This is the brain of the robot and needs to be programmed to execute the programmers commands	
Romi-Chassis Estimated Cost: R447.35	The Romi-chassis is a basic embodiment kit	It includes basic mechanical components such as motors and wheels, making it an easy setup to be used for the course	
JellyBeanBot Shield Estimated Cost: R600.00	This shield is custom designed and developed by the robotics expert as facilitator to facilitate easy interaction	The board is use to connect the Romi-chassis motors and the various sensors to the board for interaction with the Arduino UNO	
Sensor Ultrasonic - HC-SR04 Estimated Cost: R67.85	The HC-SR04 is an economical ultrasonic sensor. It provides a range for detection from 2cm to 400cm of non-contact measurement functionality	The sonar sensor provides a way of detecting the opponent	
Line Follower Module Estimated Cost: R28.75 (each, 3 needed)	This Infrared (IR) reflective sensor utilizes a TCRT5000 reflective optical sensor to detect color and distance	Infrared rays are emitted and returned to detect if it reflects or not. These sensors are mostly used in line following robots, because this module can sense if a surface is white or black	

code they generated, as well as a video clip of the accomplishments of their robot. The facilitators used the code and videos to determine obstacles and bottlenecks in the learning that took place that week. This action allowed the facilitators to address these problems at the start of a subsequent class with the purpose to enhance the learning. In the subsequent sub-sections reference are made to these components as they are introduced throughout the robotics offering.

4.1 Week 1: Introduction to Robotics

The objective of week 1 is to provide an overview of robotics, its place in society and to introduce students to the Arduino UNO micro-processor board. An overview on the functionality of Arduino UNO, focusing on the possibilities it opens up for users are covered. Student are requested to reflect on possibilities that are not available without using the Arduino micro-processor. Then they are guided towards using the Arduino platform and the software associated with the boards. The basic electronic concepts are discussed, along with what to do and not to do in robotics, as well as tips and tricks. The basic concept of input and output are discussed. An important focus during this session is on the communication and coding of the Arduino UNO by using a USB-Type-B cable and the software downloadable which students had to download from the Arduino website. In addition to introducing concepts from a theoretical point of view, the project groups are formed and a shield, the Arduino experimentation shield, are introduced to students to facilitate the interaction with hardware. The shield (see Fig. 2) is a simple interaction interface that was developed and used in the first year IT extended undergraduate course. This shield features three buttons, 10 LEDs, a variable resistor, two servo motor output pins-sets, and a buzzer. Project groups are prompted to interact with the hardware by being tasked to illuminate a light-emitting diode (LED) by means of the push of a button. Also, for each subsequent button push, another LED should light up.

4.2 Week 2: Motor Functions

The objective of week 2 is to provide an overview on movement functions associated with robotics. Therefore, the focus is on motors responsible for enacting movement. Three types of motors are introduced, namely stepper motors, direct current (DC) motors and servo motors, covering the requirements, functionality, advantages and disadvantages of each. Students were also introduced to the JellyBeanBot shield, its functionality and how to utilize it correctly. From an implementation point of view, project groups are challenged to do the coding necessary to direct the motors to move around the outer skirts of a playing field. The same playing field to be introduced in week 4 is used, but students use the outer border of the field to practice on. This red outer border can be seen in Fig. 1(b). The objective of this challenge is to show students that without the use of sensors, navigating a straight line or making a 90-degree turn is not simple. Furthermore, students should understand that not all hardware components such as motors are created equal and therefore differences may arise between the same models of a motor.

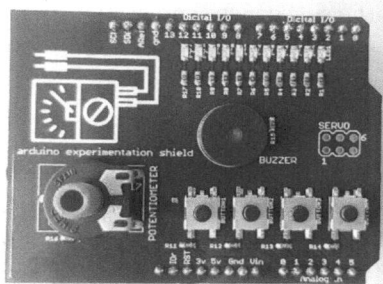

Fig. 2. Arduino experimentation shield

4.3   Week 3: Sensors

The objective of week 3 is to introduce two sensors, the line sensor and the ultra-sonic sensor to project groups. Line sensors enable a robot to navigate around a field, while a sonar-sensor detects obstacles with the purpose to avoid them. After week 2 students should appreciate the value of using sensors as a means to orientate and navigate a robot successfully. The project group challenge for this week is similar to that of last week, but this week the groups are to make use of line sensors to follow the black line all around the playing field. In a separate task students have to use the ultrasonic sensors to avoid the wall by remaining 30 cm from it, while moving perpendicular to it.

4.4   Week 4: The Playing Field

The objective of week 4 is to introduce the complete playing field (Fig. 1(b)) to the students. Time is also spent on the expectations regarding the successful completion of the line-following on the playing field, as well as obstacles to be identified. The playing field requires the robot to follow the black line diligently, and at indicated instances (Fig. 1(b)), stop to perform an action, specifically to avoid an obstacle, this allows interaction with the ultrasonic sensor introduced during week 3. From an implementation perspective, at this point, groups are familiar with all components and are allowed time to refine their program through practice during this session.

4.5   Week 5: A Working Robot

No new concepts are introduced at this point and project groups are using the time to test and refine their robotic system. Since robots are not allowed out-side the robotics laboratory, groups requested additional time in the laboratory. This additional time was provided by utilizing a smaller laboratory. Students could sign out their robot and returned it after the session. The following rules and penalties were communicated to the students in preparation for the final evaluation of the project:

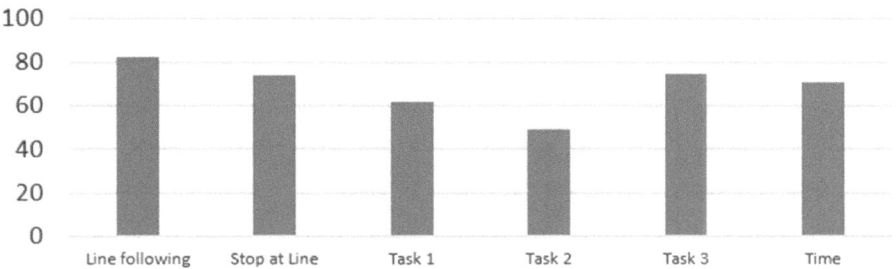

Fig. 3. Average results per assessment task

– Robot starts with a 5 s delay.
– Robot must follow the line to the end of the course (except at the wall and at task 1).
– Robot must stop dead at the end of the course with no movement afterwards.
– The course may be restarted only once.
– Any robot available to the class may be used, but each group's code needs to be implemented.
– Any group found using another group's code will be deemed as plagiarism.
– Code uploaded to the robot should be done with at least one assessor present.
– Time limit per group to complete assessment is 10 min.
– Every robot touch is a penalty.
– Removing the wall is a penalty.

4.6   Week 6: Game Time

The last class is allocated to the final assessment of the programming code. This is done on the playing field, performing the explicit tasks (such as following the line and avoiding obstacles) and implicit tasks (induced by the playing field, the rules and penalties introduced). Marks allocated are indicated in brackets. The assessment schedule is shown in Table 4.

The graph in Fig. 3 shows the average percentage of each task completed. It shows that the line following task as the main outcome of the project had the highest success rate. However, task two, object avoidance, were the least successful. From the assessment of all groups only one of the 16 groups failed the project (pass rate 93.5%) and the average mark obtained was 72.25%.

5   Discussion

At the end of the second semester the students were contacted and invited to a FGI. Six students indicated that they would participate in the FGI, but only three attended. The session was moderated by us. With the first cycle of analysis a coding table was compiled. Table 5 shows the suggested codes and its corresponding descriptions.

Table 4. Assessment schedule

	Achieved	Partly achieved	Not achieved
Complete circuit			
Explicit task 1: Line following	Lost the line at one turn only **(8)**	Lost the line several occasions **(5)**	Could not complete the circuit at all **(2)**
Explicit task 2/Implicit task 2: Stop at two indicated black blocks	Both targets reached **(2)**	One target reached **(1)**	No action **(0)**
Isolated implicit tasks			
Implicit task 1: Wall avoidance	Avoid the wall successfully **(2)**	Avoid wall but fails to find line **(1)**	No action **(0)**
Implicit task 3: Stop at and/or avoid object	Stop and move around object **(2)**	Stop or move around object **(1)**	No action **(0)**
Implicit task 2: Stop at line for 5 s	Successfully stops at black block for 5 seconds **(2)**	Stops at black block **(1)**	No action **(0)**
Time limit			
Complete the circuit within time limit	Complete within 3 min **(2)**	Complete within 4 min **(1)**	>4 min **(0)**
Team spirit & documentation			
Documentation	Complete **(2)**	Limited **(1)**	No action **(0)**
Team spirit	Enthusiastic, everyone did their part **(2)**	Not everyone is enthusiastic **(1)**	No action **(0)**

It should be noted that since one FGI was conducted, only one discussion is analyzed. This fact realizes the manifestation of short discussions on issues that are not brought up more than once. In some cases, a challenge (as an example) is mentioned, all participants agree, and the discussion moves on to a next topic of discussion. Also, every participant is cognizant of what all other participants says. In some limited instances, an issue will be discussed more than once, in different contexts. These multiple conversation threads are all listed.

The small group did facilitate all participants to actively take part in the discussion. In addition, from the discussion it was clear that discourses took place during the robotics project offering, since participants mentioned challenges and issues that was not necessarily their own experience. For each of the eleven codes identified in Table 5, a representative response is also listed with the responsible participant (P_i) mentioned. The participants are numbered, where P1 is the researcher-moderator who was not part of the facilitation team, P2 is

Table 5. Encoding and description of FGI responses

Code	Description and responses
Group formation < STU:GF>	How groups were formed and the experience of participants regarding group formation: *P3 = We would also prefer it if we could choose our own groups. I think it would have been a better experience if he had ten complete fully functional robots and six members in a group. It would have been a better experience, because there is not a lot of us third years here. I've heard enough of everybody complaining about the robots. Some of them are not working as they should, etc.*
Team work < STU:TW>	How well groups of students worked together in their teams: *P5 = If you tell group members they should help you with this and they never come up with a solution: I feel like they were not committed to the project*
Reflection < STU:R>	Students reflecting on the success of their implementations: *P5 = We tested our code before we presented. Obstacle avoidance, read with numbers, sensors. After the facilitator placed the instrument to measure the speed, our robot ended up seeing those as objects and tried to avoid them: that's why it couldn't go through the line. So I think the manner in which we coded the application was where the problem lies. I feel if we did know those objects were going to be placed there, we could have found a solution to avoid those and not recognize the speed measuring instrument as an object*
Laboratory access < STU:LA>	Students were not allowed to take robots out of the robotics laboratory, their feedback regarding this limitation: *P5 = Because of this, we only got to work with them while we were on campus*
Hardware malfunction < STU:HM>	Identification of hardware malfunctions: *P5 = Our sensors were not working, or we could not find the right pins or where they are connecting*
Time constraints < STU:TC>	The time-constraints experienced with the project: *P5 = If there were enough robots and they would let us work not only on Mondays, I think we could have accomplished a lot more with our project. We only found out late that there was extra time to use*
Variety of robots < STU:VOR>	Project groups were receiving any robot at each subsequent class, while robots differed which implied that the work done during a previous week needed to be revised: *P3 = I did not like the fact that some robots had more on it than the others. Some of them had extra boards on it, which I'm not exactly sure what for. On the top left side there was that little board that restricted your view of the sensors or your sonar*
Higher-orderthinking < STU:HOT>	Challenging concepts encountered in completing the project: *P3 = I would have liked if we created the groups and build your own little robot. The group knew the wiring and exactly how to do it, because if you know how the circuitry works the coding is easy. In our group, one time we used a mobile battery pack on it to get it to work*
Job opportunity < STU:JO>	A robotics job opportunity presented itself: *P4 = I think robotics should continue, because as I can say right now yesterday I went for an interview and it was for a robotics company, so I think it has an advantage for us*
Coding < STU:C>	The experience regarding the coding, the main focus of the intervention: *P3 = I did learn that there are about ten different ways to just code line-following*
Learning < STU:L>	According to the participants, did they learn, and how well? *P3 = I learned sort for the first time, that was kind of fun*

the researcher-moderator who was the facilitator who acted as robotics expert, whereas P3, P4 and P5 represent the student participants.

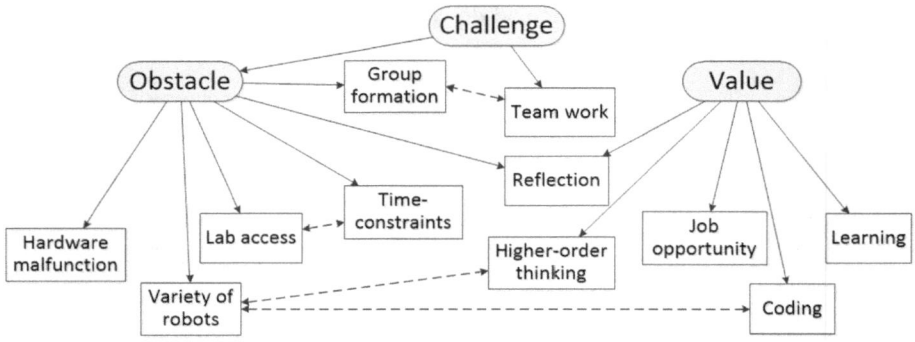

Fig. 4. FGI response categories: network diagram

After extracting the responses per code, they were analyzed once more with the purpose to categorize codes; resulting in three categories, namely challenges experienced by students, obstacles that may be addressed in future to improve the course, and the value of the robotics project. These three categories are not isolated from one another, since some challenges may be perceived as an opportunity to improve the next robotics project offering, a challenge may also be perceived as an opportunity to learn about robotics, which may improve its value. The three categories and their relation to the codes, as well as inter-code relationships are shown in Fig. 4 which lists the network diagram for this study. The three categories are used to guide the subsequent discussion of participant responses.

Critically analyzing the responses of participants, it is clear that the differences in the construction of the robots posed the biggest challenge to students <STU:VOR>. The experience during the first few weeks where each group weekly received a different robot, provided much confusion due to minor differences between the robots such as the wiring of components <STU:VOR>. Although this was addressed later by labelling each robot and making sure each group selects the robot they used before, it is important to note this for future course offerings. To some extent this experience did prove valuable value since groups were challenged to work with what they had <STU:HOT> and forced to overcome these differences with their coding <STU:C>.

The second biggest challenge to students were the formation of groups and the subsequent team work <STU:GF, STU:TW>. From their responses it is clear that students would have preferred to select their own group members <STU:GF> or even work alone <STU:TW>. This is mainly due to group members not working together or not doing their assigned tasks. Unfortunately all students do not share the same passion for learning and robotics. Juxtaposed to this notion, having access to a complete and fully working robot was high on the agenda of students and they would have elected to work in larger (than four members) groups rather than having to work with malfunctioning robots <STU:GF, STU:HM>. In future offerings this issue need to be addressed, even with funding being limited: the standard components acquired from funding provided to build the initial 10 robots should be expanded, since the six additional robots were the ones causing much confusion.

Thirdly, students mentioned that working beyond the allocated sessions would have enabled them to accomplish a lot more <STU:LA,STU:TC>. This an important point for consideration in future offerings since the credits and the accompanying notional hours worked by students need to be coordinated in this 16 credit project module.

It is encouraging that reflection occurred among participants <STU:R>. In this particular case the participants' group did not manage to complete all tasks, but through reflection realized their mistakes. Students were grateful for the exposure to robotics and found the course to be fun and enjoyable <STU:L>. It even presented one of the students with a job opportunity <STU:JO>.

6   Conclusion

The six-week robotics project offering suggested and presented in a third year project module at the North-West University provided a valuable learning opportunity. The 93% pass rate for the project groups makes the success of the offering evident. Feed-back received during a FGI provided valuable feedback regarding the offering. Students were exposed to new, unknown and novel concepts. The course presented students with the opportunity to code actual programs to communicate with hardware while interacting with peers in a fun environment. The course stretched over six weeks in which students had to prepare a robot to do line following, stop at an obstacle, and pick up an object on the playing field. In addition to these explicit tasks, implicit tasks also realized, such as starting and stopping the robot, wall (of the playing field) avoidance, and completion within a specified time. To gain insight into the students' experiences during the project offering, the evaluation of the course were done by a FGI. Feedback received included both valuable and challenging aspects, indicating what students gained from doing the project offering, as well as aspects for improvement to be considered for the next iteration. Some of the challenges faced by students were group dynamics and associated team work, but also the differences in the construction of the robots due to challenges in funding this offering. It is clear that more funding is required to purchase more robots. Lastly, students indicated that they did learn much about robotics and that the project was an enjoyable way to learn new concepts.

References

1. Basch, C.E.: Focus group interview: an underutilized research technique for improving theory and practice in health education. Health Educ. Q. **14**(4), 411–448 (1987)
2. Berry, C.A., Remy, S.L., Rogers, T.E.: Robotics for all ages: a standard robotics curriculum for K-16. IEEE Robot. Autom. Mag. **23**(2), 40–46 (2016)
3. Calder, B.J.: Focus groups and the nature of qualitative marketing research. J. Mark. Res. **14**(3), 353–364 (1977)

4. Cappelleri, D.J., Vitoroulis, N.: The robotic decathlon: project-based learning labs and curriculum design for an introductory robotics course. IEEE Trans. Educ. **56**(1), 73–81 (2013)
5. Carey, M.A.: The group effect in focus groups: planning, implementing, and interpreting focus group research. In: Critical Issues in Qualitative Research Methods, vol. 225, pp. 225–240 (1994)
6. Fern, E.F.: The use of focus groups for idea generation: the effects of group size, acquaintanceship, and moderator on response quantity and quality. J. Mark. Res. **19**(1), 1–13 (1982)
7. Fernandes, S.R.G.: Preparing graduates for professional practice: findings from a case study of Project-based Learning (PBL). Procedia Soc. Behav. Sci. **139**, 219–226 (2014)
8. Galadima, A.A.: Arduino as a learning tool. In: Proceedings of 11th IEEE International Conference on Electronics, Computer and Computation, ICECCO 2014 , pp. 1–4 (2014)
9. Gibb, A.M.: New media art, design, and the Arduino microcontroller: a malleable tool. M. thesis, Pratt Institute (2010)
10. Hacker, L.: Robotics in education: ROBOLAB and robotic technology as tools for learning science and engineering. Project report, Department of Child Development, Tufts University (2003)
11. Jamieson, P., Herdtner, J.: More missing the Boat: Arduino, Raspberry Pi, and small prototyping boards and engineering education needs them. In: Proceedings of IEEE Frontiers in Education Conference, FIE 2015, pp. 1–6 (2015)
12. Krueger, R.A., Casey, M.A.: Focus Groups: A Practical Guide for Applied Research, 5th edn. SAGE, Thousand Oaks (2015)
13. Lakhani, K.R., von Hippel, E.: How open source software works: free user-to-user assistance. Res. Policy **32**(6), 923–943 (2003)
14. Laurent, A.M.S.: Understanding Open Source and Free Software Licensing: Guide to Navigating Licensing Issues in Existing and New Software. O'Reilly, Springfield (2004)
15. Malec, J.: Some thoughts on robotics for education. In: Proceedings of AAAI Spring Symposium on Robotics and Education (2001)
16. Mataric, M.J.: Robotics education for all ages. In: Proceedings of AAAI Spring Symposium on Accessible, Hands-on AI and Robotics Education (2004)
17. McLafferty, I.: Focus group interviews as a data collecting strategy. J. Adv. Nurs. **48**(2), 187–194 (2004)
18. Millward, L.J.: Focus groups. Res. Method Psychol. **2**, 274–292 (1995)
19. Noble, J.: Programming Interactivity: A Designer's Guide to Processing, Arduino, and OpenFrameworks. O'Reilly, Springfield (2009)
20. Nourbakhsh, I.R., et al.: The robotic autonomy mobile robotics course: robot design, curriculum design and educational assessment. Auton. Robots **18**(1), 103–127 (2005)
21. Nyamathi, A., Shuler, P.: Focus group interview: a research technique for informed nursing practice. Journ. Adv. Nurs. **15**(11), 1281–1288 (1990)
22. Perrenet, J.C., Bouhuijs, P.A.J., Smits, J.G.M.M.: The suitability of problem-based learning for engineering education: theory and practice. Teach. High. Educ. **5**(3), 345–358 (2000)
23. Reas, C., Fry, B.: Processing: A Programming Handbook for Visual Designers and Artists. MIT Press, Cambridge (2007)
24. Stewart, D.W., Shamdasani, P.N., Rook, D.W.: Focus Groups: Theory and Practice. SAGE, Thousand Oaks (1990)

Media and Classrooms

Off-Task Media Use in Lectures: Towards a Theory of Determinants

Douglas A. Parry[✉] and Daniel B. le Roux

Department of Information Science, Stellenbosch University,
Stellenbosch, South Africa
dougaparry@sun.ac.za

Abstract. A growing body of evidence indicates that university students frequently engage in off-task media use (OTMU) during lectures. While the bulk of research in this area has considered the frequency and impact of such behaviour, little work concerning the subjective and contextual factors that determine OTMU in academic settings has been conducted. In this study we adopt a qualitative approach to consider the determinants of this behaviour. Seven key factors that determine students' OTMU in lectures are identified: OTMU policy, OTMU norms, Fear of missing out, Grit, Control over technology, Quality of lecture, and Visibility of peers' OTMU. We propose a model which specifies the relationships between these factors and discuss how institutions and lecturers can navigate the challenges posed by OTMU in lectures.

Keywords: Off-task media use · Cyber-slacking · Media multitasking

1 Introduction

Extensive use of digital media has become a distinguishing feature of today's university students [20]. A growing collection of studies investigate the influence of this behaviour on students' academic activities [15, 19, 22, 34]. From these studies a body of evidence has emerged indicating, firstly, that students frequently interact with a variety of digital media while engaging in academic activities, secondly, that these interactions are mostly *off-task* (unrelated to their academic work), and finally, that they have come to change how students approach learning. Fried, for example, reports that during a 75-min lecture students used their laptops for off-task activities for an average of 17 min [15]. Junco reports that 69% of students engage in texting during lectures [19], while Roberts and Rees found that 66% of students engage with email, instant messaging and social networking during lectures [31]. In a subset of these studies researchers have investigated the implications of media use for academic performance [19, 20, 22, 35]. Van der Schuur et al., through a review of studies examining the effect of media use on academic performance, found evidence of a negative correlation between media use in academic settings and academic performance [38]. While these findings underscore the importance of understanding the dynamics of students' behaviour

© Springer Nature Switzerland AG 2019
S. Kabanda et al. (Eds.): SACLA 2018, CCIS 963, pp. 49–64, 2019.
https://doi.org/10.1007/978-3-030-05813-5_4

with media in learning settings, there remains uncertainty about how learning processes are influenced by media use.

While many studies consider the frequency of media use in academic settings [15,19,20], or the relationships between this use and academic performance [19,20,22,35], little work concerning the subjective and situational factors that determine *off-task media use* (OTMU) or *cyber-slacking* [40] in academic settings has been conducted. This is particularly the case in developing countries. Additionally, with few exceptions, researchers in this domain have opted for quantitative methodologies, utilising data collected through surveys or quasi-experiments. Against this backdrop this paper reports the findings of a qualitative investigation of media use during university lectures. The aim of this study was to develop a rich descriptive account of the OTMU patterns students adopt in lectures. To this end we conducted five focus groups involving a total of 30 undergraduate students at a large, residential South African university.[1] We analysed the resulting data in accordance with grounded theory principles and identified seven factors that underlie OTMU in lectures.

2   Related Work

We briefly review literature concerning the ubiquity of media in students' lives, followed by research into the motivations for media use in academic settings.[2]

Studies of student media use suggest that, on average, students spend between one and two hours of their days online [20]. In a survey study Jacobsen and Forste found that two-thirds of students use media while in class or studying [18]. Rosen et al. similarly, found that students averaged less than six minutes on a task before switching to another task [32]. Specifically, a number of studies [7,15,19,22] indicate that OTMU has become increasingly common during university lectures.

While data is limited, South African students seem to be little different from their peers in developed countries. North et al. found that, in their sample of 362 South African students, only 1% did not own a mobile phone, or had not owned one recently [25]. In another study of South African students, Leysens et al. found that over 95% of students use instant messaging at least once during a lecture [22]. This was followed by social networking with over 20% of students using it at least every ten minutes during a 50-min lecture. As is the case in other studies, they found that few students engaged in task-related media use.

Guo et al. identified seven dimensions of motivation for media use in academic settings [17]: (i) information seeking; (ii) convenience; (iii) connectivity; (iv) problem solving; (v) content management; (vi) social presence; and (vii) social context cues. In a subsequent study Zhang found that different needs predicted different types of media use [43]. They clustered these needs into three

---

[1] The university is currently ranked among the top 400 on the 2017/2018 Times Higher Education World University Rankings.

[2] Our use of the term 'academic setting' is inclusive of formal lecture environments, practical or tutorial classes, group work settings or personal study sessions.

categories. The first, and most common category—'convenient/easy/instant'—includes gratifications which are only possible given media's technical capabilities (e.g., instant messages), as well as those possible without media (e.g., maintaining social connections). The second category—'control/habitual'—suggests media gratifies both habitual needs, and that it allows personal control over the pace of information intake. The third category—'social/affective/relaxation'—emphasises the emotional needs associated with media use. Interestingly we found that, while differences in intentions exist, they do not moderate any relationships with academic performance [27].

Following a series of semi-structured interviews Blackburn et al. report that, for students, use of technology is an active process voluntarily engaged in [7]. Interviewees described using their laptops in class for multiple tasks, switching between on or off-task activities. Congruent with [26], participants acknowledged that in-lecture media use is often an attempt to be entertained in response to experiences of boredom. Likewise, Annan-Coultas found that, in addition to academically-related tasks, students reported the usage of laptops for off-task purposes whilst in lectures, particularly when becoming bored or disengaged with lecture content [3]. Williams and Cox found that students defend their in-lecture media use by arguing that content covered during the lecture could be attained from other sources at a later time [42]. This awareness devalued the lecture and created a justification for students to engage in OTMU.

Through a series of semi-structured interviews Aagaard found that OTMU in a lecture is seen to be normal [1]. Upon considering the rationale for this behaviour the author notes that, in contrast to theories of reasoned action, for instance the *Theory of Planned Behaviour* (TPB) [2], and Blackburn et al.'s findings [7], students reported that they engage in OTMU automatically, without conscious choice. Two lecture-related factors were reported to increase the likelihood of this behaviour. First, students reported that, when they considered material to be 'too hard', they distracted themselves. Second, boredom was reported to precede instances of OTMU. Aagaard offers two interpretations of his findings [1]. First he suggests that OTMU is a *habitual distraction* for students. He argues, accordingly, that allocation of attention to OTMU is neither endogenous nor exogenous—it occurs as a *"deeply sedimented relational strategy"* [1] (p. 5). Second, he suggests that instances of boredom 'triggering' OTMU occur as a result of a *mediated impatience*. A lecture is perceived to be boring not because of the content of the lecture itself, but rather, it is viewed as boring because students can readily access more entertaining mediated stimulation.

This constant presence of potentially rewarding mediated experiences has prompted consideration of a specific form of anxiety, the *fear of missing out* (FoMo), or the *"pervasive apprehension that others might be having rewarding experiences from which one is absent"* [28] (p. 1841). This form of anxiety is characterised by a desire to stay continually updated with the activities of ones' social connections. Consequently, people feel that they 'miss out' on potentially rewarding experiences when they are off-line. Rosen et al. investigated relationships between media use and a number of psychiatric symptoms, finding the highest prevalence of anxiety related to an inability to check text-messages and social media feeds [33]. Moreover, symptoms of obsessive compulsive disorder were predicted by media-anxiety, media use, and task-switching frequency. Commenting on this outcome, they postulate that the need to stay connected, and the anxiety related to missing out foster an 'obsession' to check media for updates.

Taneja et al. considered students' attitudes and intentions to engage in OTMU during a lecture [40]. Adopting the TPB as a theoretical framework, they proposed a model describing students' intentions to *cyber-slack*, or engage in OTMU. The model includes attitudes, subjective norms, descriptive norms and perceptions of behavioural control as predictors of the intention to cyber-slack. Evaluation of the model through a survey study involving 267 students revealed that it could explain ≈52% of the variation in intention to cyber-slack, while ≈40% of this variation could be explained only by students' attitudes towards this behaviour. Specifically, they found that consumerism, escapism, and lack of attention positively predicted such attitudes. In contrast, OTMU related anxiety and peer-related distractions negatively predicted attitudes towards OTMU. Taneja et al. found that a lack of attention to a lecture was positively predicted by apathy towards the class material [40]. In contrast, both intrinsic and extrinsic motivation, as well as class engagement negatively predicted a lack of attention.

3   Research Design

Grounded theory presents an inductive approach to the study of social life [16]; theory is derived through the analysis of patterns and themes present in qualitative data [4]. A study using grounded theory may commence with the specification of a research question, or with the collection of qualitative data. As researchers review the data collected, repeated ideas or concepts become apparent, and are tagged with codes, which have been extracted from the data. To guide our investigation we formulated a single, primary RESEARCH QUESTION:

What are the determinants of students' off-task media use during lectures?

Our study extends the body of qualitative research concerning students' OTMU in lectures by investigating the determinants of such behaviour through a series of focus groups. This approach allowed us to interpret the meanings, explanations and personal narratives students attach to their behaviour. Mason explains that a qualitative approach is interpretative [23], considering both the individuals in question, and the social context in which the data is produced. As such, an interpretivist ontology is adopted in this study: meaning is seen to be socially constructed and subjective.

During focus groups data are produced through a process of interaction between the participants and researchers. While not providing the data necessary for statistically determining the strength of the emergent relationships, such an approach is, nonetheless, capable of producing valid causal descriptions of behaviour. Participants' accounts of the relationship between actions and subsequent events provide an understanding of cause-effect processes, as they perceive and interpret them. In the broader context of an increasing number of studies reporting negative correlation between media use and academic performance, obtaining a textured understanding of the range of factors that influence OTMU is a desired outcome. In particular, it is our view that understanding the subjective, normative and environmental factors that interact to produce OTMU in lectures, will serve to enlighten the manner in which personal media use impacts the learning process. Kitzinger explains that one of the key tenets of a focus group methodology is the ability of group processes to aid the participants in exploring and explaining their perceptions and experiences [21]. The group dynamics at play in a focus group allow for the emergence of unexpected narratives and interpretations. As a consequence of the social and normative nature of this behavioural phenomenon, the subjective, interpretative procedures characterising focus groups were deemed appropriate to address the specified aim of the study.

3.1 Participants

To obtain participants for the study several advertising techniques were used. These included: Posters placed in each academic building of the main campus of the university; announcements in four undergraduate modules;[3] and a radio interview on the campus radio station. While some of these procedures were indiscriminate in their targeting, with any eligible student standing a chance of becoming aware of the opportunity, others, *unintentionally* restricted this possibility. Participation was incentivised through an amount of $50 \cdot$ ZAR ($\approx 5 \cdot$ USD). These procedures may have affected the representativity of the sample, with some students missing one or more of these techniques. Nonetheless, it is believed that sufficient measures were put in place to ensure adequate diversity in the sample and, therefore, representativity of the population on the campus.

Following these calls 30 students ($n = 15$ female; eight 1st year, 17 2nd year, and five 3rd year) responded, all meeting the inclusion criteria of being enrolled in an undergraduate program at the institution. As the number of respondents matched the intended sample size, a convenience approach was adopted. Each participant selected one of five available sessions. With the exception of session one (six participants) and session four (nine participants), the remaining three sessions included five participants each. These sizes are in line with the prescriptions of Morgan, who explains that focus groups must be small enough to provide each participant with an opportunity to provide input, while still being large enough to enable a diversity of views [24]. The participants represented four of the eight faculties at the main campus of the university: Education, Law, Arts and Social Sciences, and Economic and Management Sciences. Therefore, in terms of representativity, only 50% of the faculties were accounted for in the sample. However, these four faculties represent over 60% of all students on campus. While this may provide a limitation for this study, it is believed that, given a focus group methodology, and the homogeneity of the population in this regard, the sample achieved is representative enough to capture the nature of the phenomenon under study.

---

[3] Reaching over 3000 students, from first to third year in three faculties.

3.2   Procedures

A topic guide to direct the discussion in each session was developed. This guide included prompts to initiate discussion relating to attitudes towards, beliefs about and motivations for media use in lectures, perceptions of social and sub-jective norms associated with media use, beliefs about the factors which trigger, facilitate or hinder media use, as well as beliefs about the potential consequences thereof.[4] The topic guide was developed based on, firstly, the relevant literature reviewed, and, secondly, the objective of the study. The suitability of the topic guide was assessed through a pilot study involving a single focus group conducted with five students several weeks prior to the primary focus groups. Following this procedure several prompts in the topic guide were rephrased to avoid ambiguity.

Each focus group was moderated by the primary researcher of this study and lasted between 60 and 70 min. The five focus groups took place over a two week period, with two in the first week and three in the second week. This number of sessions is in line with the suggestions of Richie et al., who state that such a number should achieve a saturation point in terms of new findings [30]. All focus groups were recorded using a 360° digital recorder. The focus groups took place in a large classroom-style venue at a round table in the centre of the room. All participants sat around the table, with a recording device in the centre, and the researcher amongst them. No-one else was present in the room. The primary researcher, who moderated the focus groups, is a 'white' male in his mid-twenties who conducted his undergraduate and postgraduate studies at the same institution where the study was performed. The participants were unknown to him prior to the sessions.

3.3   Data Analysis

The data were analysed using an inductive thematic analysis method [8]. Adopt-ing the constant comparative method proposed by Glaser and Strauss [16] as part of the grounded theory methodology, analysis occurred in an iterative manner through data collection, open coding, and code integration, to a point of theoreti-cal saturation. In the first phase of analysis the audio recordings were transcribed into a textual format using *Atlas.ti*, with each participants' quotes associated with an anonymous identifier. Next, guided by recurring elements in the data, preliminary codes were produced. Subsequently, these codes were then applied to the data. Where necessary, these preliminary codes were either modified, or augmented with additional codes as the analysis proceeded. Finally, through considering patterns in emergent codes, initial themes were identified. Through considering these initial themes in relation to the relevant coded extracts final themes were produced. This process of constant comparison with the data was

---

[4] Ethical clearance for the study was granted by the institution's research ethics board. Prior to the commencement of the focus groups each participant provided informed consent, in full knowledge of the study procedures, the voluntary nature of their participation, data protection measures, and reporting confidentiality.

conducted in four rounds of inductive analysis: open coding, a priori coding, theme development, and theme refinement through data checking.

In addition to the provision of rich, thick descriptions of participants' accounts presented in the findings section, the credibility and trustworthiness of the findings presented in this study were supported through three strategies. First, credibility was strengthened through data triangulation which, as argued by Twining et al. [41], involves comparing data from different participants, in different groups, conducted at different times. Second, as Elliott et al. explain [11], in involving two researchers in the coding process a degree of investigator triangulation is achieved. To further support inter-rater reliability cross checking of codes and peer debriefing procedures were conducted. Third, as Babbie suggests [4], the processes of data collection, coding, and thematic analysis were documented to provide an audit-trail of decisions made.

4   Findings

We present our findings in three subsections. First we consider a theme relating to norms surrounding OTMU in lectures. Second we consider three themes concerning the role of stable, personal traits. Finally we consider two themes concerning subjective situational factors. Within each of these subsections descriptions of the themes are provided, accompanied by a sample of associated supporting quotes using a coding system to identify contributions made by participants. Each participant was coded as $Px - y$, where x is the number of the focus group and y is the individual within that group. In this way a data-grounded interpretative narrative is provided.

4.1   OTMU Norms

Models of human behaviour broadly acknowledge the role of social norms in determining behavioural intentions [12]. Norms reflect what *"people approve and disapprove within the culture"* and serve to *"motivate action by promising social sanctions for normative or counter normative conduct"* [29] (p. 104). Our data revealed that the prevailing norm at the institution was that OTMU is an acceptable, though not endorsed, form of behaviour during lectures. This norm functioned as a justification (even a motivation) among students to initiate instances of OTMU. Based on our data few lecturers at the institution explicitly forbid OTMU during their lectures. In the absence of such top-down mechanisms, OTMU norms were established through group behaviour.

P2-3: *In a lecture room you can hide behind other people, not physically, but mentally. It's a group behaviour so you feel like it's okay to do it. It's not disrespect aimed at the lecturer, it's a group mentality. If everyone else is doing something then obviously more people are going to pick up on that behaviour.*

P4-9: *It's scary when you look back and you see how many people are actually listening to the lecturer: everyone's like* [indicates looking down at phone under desk]*; you see someone in front of you on Instagram.*

P4-6: *Sometimes I feel really bad actually, that I'm on my phone in class, and I'll stop and then I look around me, everyone else is on their phone.*

P4-4: *In all my classes there are at least like 20 laptops out at any given point. I can count, there is at least like 90% of those people are not on the page of the slides.*

4.2   Personal Traits

Our data suggest that three traits of individual subjects determined their OTMU intentions. The first is the experienced need to stay connected or up to date with online activities to avoid missing out on potentially rewarding experiences. In accordance with previous studies [9, 28, 33] we refer to this factor as 'FoMo' and argue that it is a key determinant of students' OTMU intentions. An interesting aspect of this factor is subjects' awareness of the accessibility of their devices. Awareness of the ease with which the device can be accessed (i.e., the *nearness* of the online experience) seemed to influence experiences of FoMo. This effect is highlighted by Sapacz et al. who found that subjects' anxiety increased when their devices were present as opposed to out of sight [37].

P2-1: *Most of the time, I open it. I mean, it's like sitting right there, looking at me, I need to see what's happening.*

P1-4: *If you're not part of that conversation, you come in, like after the lecture. Even just an hour later. You're like I could say something now, but it doesn't matter, the conversation has passed.*

P2-4: *I think if you see someone using their phone, it's just an automatic thing. I wonder what's going on, on my phone; let me just check quickly.*

P1-2: *Although they're teaching you, I'm not paying any attention. I may be writing down what you're saying. But I'm actually thinking: "I wonder what's happening on Facebook" and "oh I saw this was trending on Twitter and I'm missing it because I'm doing this".*

The second trait which emerged from our data related to students' attempts to suppress their FoMo and remain focused on their academic goals (i.e., paying attention to lecture material). The success of these attempts typically depends on their ability to resist the various triggers (intrinsic and extrinsic) directing their attention to OTM. Duckworth et al. use the notion of *grit* to express an individual's *"perseverance and passion for long-term goals"* [10] (p. 1087). Individuals high in grit *"do not swerve from their goals, even in the absence of positive feedback"*. In the context of our data we believe grit can be used as an indicator of a student's ability to remain focused on his/her academic goals despite the lure of OTM. *"The gritty individual approaches achievement as a marathon, his or her advantage is stamina. Whereas disappointment or boredom signals to others that it is time to change trajectory and cut losses, the gritty individual stays the course"* [10] (p. 1088). Our data suggest that students are aware of the negative impact OTMU during lectures will have on attempts to attain their academic goals. Consequently, instances of OTMU typically followed conscious deliberation of the costs, mostly expressed in terms of future study time, that may result from not paying attention in a lecture. This trend corroborates earlier findings by Flanigan and Babchuk [13].

P1-4: *It's not like we don't know that we are doing the wrong thing. We're aware of the costs, but, at that point in time, that immediate satisfaction factor is just too high.*

P2-4: *When I'm listening to the lecturer if I don't really find it useful, or they're just losing me. Then I'll go on my phone.*

P1-1: *I know that if I need to stay up to four in the morning to finish this work, I will do it, because this is what I get for playing on my phone and not working.*

P2-1: *I think social media, it effects in the fact that we don't listen in class and all these things, but I know that I'm gonna do the work at the end of the day.*

P1-4: *We're all pretty conscious of the fact that when we decide to postpone, we are postponing the work. Meaning, we're going to have to do it, we're going to regret it later that we didn't do at at that point in time.*

P3-2: *I keep wanting to go on Instagram and Facebook. If it's still in front of me and on, then the resistance is very low.*

The third trait we identified relates to students' exertion of some form of control over their devices in an attempt to protect themselves from OTM distractions. We refer to this factor as *control over technology* (CoT) and argue that it plays a significant role in determining OTMU behaviour. Among our subjects CoT often involved limiting the visibility or proximity of media for particular time segments when academic goals received priority. It also involved manipulation of the features or settings of devices and applications to limit the triggers that may lead to instances of OTMU. The emerging behavioural pattern, also reported by Aagaard [1], is characterised by planned segments of on-task (work) time punctuated by OTMU sessions. OTMU, in this pattern, is framed as a *reward* that is earned by completing a certain amount of on-task time.

P4-2: *Do not disturb mode is the only thing getting me through exams.*

P3-2: *I put my phone completely away, out of sight, because it's distracting.*

P4-4: *I have to put it away, otherwise I'll check it every two seconds; I have to put it somewhere else.*

P3-1: *I typically have a piece of paper, a pen, a highlighter and my laptop and then everything switched off, like no WiFi, I switch my phone off otherwise I will get distracted.*

An interesting dimension of this theme is students' inability to control the *amount* of content that is presented to them. The manner in which many content providers design interfaces to present a *never-ending stream* or *feed* of content kept students engaged in OTMU longer than they initially intended.

P2-3: *It's like a snowball effect; it's a conversation and next thing you know you've spent an hour talking to one person.*

P4-9: *It's also because it's unlimited. I think, say, for instance you have a news-paper, one article and you're done. But with Instagram, you look at one photo and then it's like there's still a million more, I can just continue scrolling.*

4.3   Subjective Situational Factors

Our data revealed that instances of OTMU were often initiated in response to experiences such as boredom or disengagement. It is important to frame these experiences as the products of both subjective factors (e.g., a lack of interest in the subject area) and situational factors (e.g., the enthusiasm, preparedness and presentation style of the lecturer). Now we turn our attention to the role of these factors in determining OTMU.

As found by Flanigan and Babchuk as well as Taneja et al. [13, 40], there was a clear relation between the degree to which a lecture is perceived as *engaging* and the tendency to initiate OTMU. We use the term *engaging* here to refer to a combination of the lecturer's presentation skills (which includes aspects like enthusiasm and authoritativeness) and the nature of the content taught. It is acknowledged, however, that this is a subjective factor—students' preferences play an important role in determining perceptions of a lecture or lecturer.

P4-5: *It depends on the lecturer's enthusiasm. Because if the lecture is going to be boring, I'm not going to want to listen, and then I'll be Whatsapping.*

P4-8: *Well I started out in the beginning of the year taking notes on my laptop, but then by the second semester I was so bored with all my classes, so I just record all my classes and then I just spend all my time on social media.*

P1-3: *Most of the lectures are quite boring to say the least. It's stuff that you can read when you're at home. It's basically someone reading slides that you have. So, it's not engaging. So then I'm like: well, I'm not going to do anything, so I'm gonna play on my phone.*

P4-2: *If it's a theoretical subject, I tend to take notes while the lecturer speaks on my laptop. But, as soon as it gets boring or I lose focus, I tend to go onto other sites that I've opened, so like Instagram or Pinterest on my phone or social communication like Whatsapp.*

P4-3: *During lectures or tutorials I would prefer to, if I do get bored, use social media. But if a lecturer is compelling, I'll be like yes! That is wonderful, please don't ever stop talking.*

An important finding which emerged from the data is the effect that peers' OTMU had on subjects. Our data suggest that awareness of peers' OTMU has three effects. The first is that it strengthens norms around OTMU during lectures. Subjects' awareness that their peers engaged in OTMU often provided the justification they needed to initiate OTMU themselves; (see Sect. 4.1). The second is that students often follow their peers' screens (as opposed to the lecturer), taking interest in whatever is displayed there. The third is that it acts as a trigger for the initiation of OTMU. When students see their peers engaging in OTMU they frequently follow suit, often in response to experiences of FOMO. This confirms previous findings in this regard [15, 36].

P1-2: *You see someone else on Youtube and then I'm like: you know what, actually, that's a better idea. The people around you influence you and stuff. Also, in class if you see other people on their laptop or phones, and then you're like: "ooh that video!"*

P2-1: *If I have somebody sitting right next to me and they're on 9Gag, I want to see what meme that is. I don't want to listen to the lecture right now. I get distracted very easily.*

P2-3: *I have a friend who is always on his phone in class, always. I think sometimes it does disrupt me to a certain extent. He doesn't even have to say look, I just start looking at what he's doing. I think that disrupts me.*

P1-6: *If someone's like scrolling through their pictures. I don't think I could stop watching. If someone is on their laptop in front of me and they're doing other things, that's where my eyes are.*

5   Discussion

We discuss our findings in two sections. The first proposes a model for OTMU in lectures. In the second section, on the basis of this model, we discuss a number of recommendations for higher educational institutions and lecturers to navigate the challenges posed by students' OTMU use in lectures.

5.1   A Proposed Model for OTMU in Lectures

We propose that the factors elicited from our data can be expressed in the form of a model describing the determinants of OTMU in lectures. Our proposed model is presented in Fig. 1 and discussed below.

Our data suggest that lecturers at the institution where the study was performed tended not to formulate explicit OTMU policies in their classes. This aligns with findings by Berger who reports that the majority of university lecturers adopt a passive stance towards OTMU in their classes despite being aware of its occurrence [6]. Consequently, we have little empirical evidence to support the argument that establishing and enforcing a specific OTMU policy would influence student behaviour. However, Beland and Murphy investigated the effects of policies *banning smartphone use at high schools*,[5] and found that students performed significantly better when these are enforced [5]. It is conceivable that higher education institutions may adopt similar policies in future (some already have [39]) and we therefore include the construct in our model. We envision that such policies will influence OTMU norms.

Our data provides evidence of the role social norms for OTMU play in determining the OTMU behaviour of individuals. An awareness that peers are engaging in OTMU during a lecture encourages the initiation of OTMU sessions and provides a basis for the retrospective justification of the decision to do so. In accordance with the TPB [2] we envision norms to influence intentions to engage in OTMU.

---

[5] Note, for instance, the newest legislation on this matter in France, 2018.

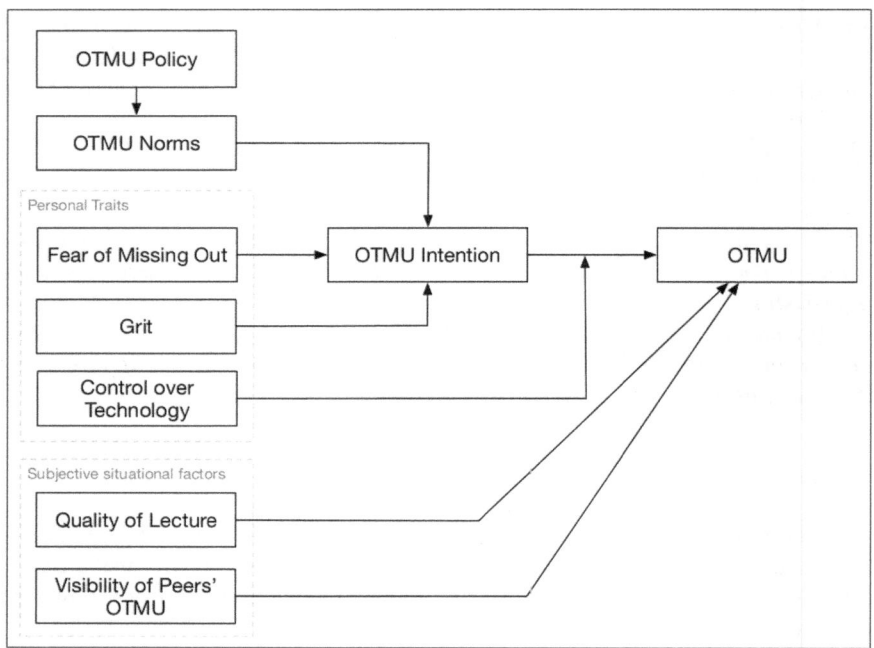

Fig. 1. Proposed model of OTMU determinants in academic environments

Our model includes the three personal traits emerging from our data. We argue that FoMo, together with Grit, influence OTMU intentions. The interaction between these two constructs produce, what may be termed, the individual's *attentional strategy* in the academic environment. This strategy is jointly shaped by the individual's academic performance goals and the desire to engage in rewarding online experiences. Consequently, we propose that individuals with high FoMo and low Grit are likely to engage in OTMU more frequently than their peers, and *vice versa*. The model also includes control over technology as a moderator of the relationship between OTMU intention and OTMU. This construct has not received explicit attention from researchers in prior studies. We argue that the exertion of control over devices and applications moderates OTMU by manipulating the triggers which typically precede instances of OTMU. Importantly, this exertion of control is a combination of both the preference and ability to take control over device and application settings. There is also an emerging trend to use smartphone applications which enable tracking and control of usage volume (e.g., Moment and QualityTime).

Two subjective situational factors which we deem to be determinants of OTMU are included. Both factors are applicable at the level of a particular academic setting (e.g., a lecture or tutorial). Quality of lecture describes the degree to which the lecture is perceived as stimulating and engaging. This construct includes aspects of the lecturer, the content and the style of presentation.

Our data provided evidence that feelings of disengagement or boredom trigger OTMU. The second factor is the visibility of peers' OTMU which, we argue, is largely determined by the physical attributes of the lecture theatre. In theatres where rows increase in height towards the back, students are likely to have a clear view of the screens of devices of peers' sitting in the rows in front of them. In traditional class rooms where seats are at an equal height the visibility of peers' screens would be lower.

5.2 Recommendations for Institutions and Lecturers

On the basis of our findings we briefly discuss how institutions and lecturers can navigate the challenges posed by OTMU in lectures. While there is evidence of increased academic performance at institutions enforcing a ban on smartphones, we acknowledge that this is neither an attractive nor practical policy for many institutions. Not only does it nullify the potentially valuable role these devices can play in the learning process, but it also creates an artificial environment. Flanigan and Kiewra suggest rather than enforcing a ban and *"verbally reprimanding students when they violate it, instructors should explain how the policy benefits student learning"* [14] (p. 5). This can be done by highlighting the detrimental effects of frequent task switching on primary task performance (in academic and other settings).

We also support the views of Flanigan and Kiewra who state that *"although enforced course policies might alleviate the temptation to cyber-slack in the classroom, such policies have no direct influence on students' out-of-class behavior"* [14] (p. 8). Lecturers should strive to *"train students to be self-regulated learners"* and monitor how they spend their attention. In accordance with our model, one way to encourage self-regulation among students is through increasing their ability to exert control over their devices. This, we suggest, can be done by providing guidelines to control device and application settings to minimise distracting notifications.

Although lecturers typically have minimal control over the physical structure of their theatres (classrooms), we propose a strategy to decrease the distracting effects of the visibility of peers' screens. By dividing the class into halves and declaring one half to be a *device-free zone*, students that feel they are easily distracted by devices can be supported in their self-regulation efforts. If the class does not allow easy left-right division, the front half of the class can be used for this purpose. At our institution this policy was recently employed with success [publication forthcoming].

6 Conclusion

Our study utilised qualitative data collected through focus groups involving 30 undergraduate students to investigate the determinants of OTMU in lectures. Based on the results of thematic data analysis we propose a model describing these determinants and their interrelationships. Unlike the theory-derived model proposed by Taneja et al. [40], we derived our model from the results of our qualitative data analysis. Based on the model we discuss various recommendations for institutions and lecturers to encourage self-regulation of OTMU among students.

While qualitative data enabled us to gain rich descriptions of students' experiences in lectures, the limitations of this form of research should be acknowledged. In particular, students' interpretations of their own experiences and, in turn, our interpretations of their expressions thereof, imply that our findings (like those of all qualitative studies) are necessarily infused with the frames of reference of the researchers. This includes, of course, our personal experiences as lecturers. Additionally, limitations resulting from the representativity of our sample should be acknowledged. In particular, the convenience sampling technique and self-selection of participants may imply biases in the data produced. Additionally, as the focus group moderator was a lecturer at the institution, this may have introduced a degree of moderator bias into the sessions, with participants potentially being reticent to share their experiences. Notwithstanding these limitations, the findings provide valuable insights into students' OTMU patterns and their perceptions of this behaviour. Future research building on the findings should endeavour to test the validity of the model we propose. In some cases (e.g., OTMU Policy) some work is required to identify or establish appropriate instruments for measurement at the individual level.

References

1. Aagaard, J.: Drawn to distraction: a qualitative study of off-task use of educational technology. Comput. Educ. **87**, 90–97 (2015)
2. Ajzen, I.: From intentions to actions: a theory of planned behavior. In: Kuhl, J., Beckmann, J. (eds.) Action Control. SSSSP, pp. 11–39. Springer, Heidelberg (1985). https://doi.org/10.1007/978-3-642-69746-3_2
3. Annan-Coultas, B.D.L.: Laptops as instructional tools: student perceptions. TechTrends **56**(5), 34–42 (2012)
4. Babbie, E.: The Practice of Social Research, 13th edn. Cengage, Boston (2012)
5. Beland, L.P., Murphy, R.: Ill communication: technology, distraction & student performance. Labour Econ. **41**, 61–76 (2016)
6. Berger, P.: Beyond plain acceptance or sheer resistance: a typology of university instructors' attitudes to students' media use in class. Teach. Teach. Educ. **67**, 410–417 (2017)
7. Blackburn, K., Lefebvre, L., Richardson, E.: Technological task interruptions in the classroom. Fla. Commun. J. Technol. Interruptions **XLI** (2013)
8. Braun, V., Clarke, V.: Thematic analysis revised. Qual. Res. Psychol. **3**(2), 77–101 (2006)
9. Cheever, N.A., Rosen, L.D., Carrier, L.M., Chavez, A.: Out of sight is not out of mind: the impact of restricting wireless mobile device use on anxiety levels among low, moderate and high users. Comput. Hum. Behav. **37**, 290–297 (2014)
10. Duckworth, A.L., Peterson, C., Matthews, M.D., Kelly, D.R.: Grit: perseverance and passion for long-term goals. J. Pers. Soc. Psychol. **92**(6), 1087–1101 (2007)
11. Elliott, R., Fischer, C.T., Rennie, D.L.: Evolving guidelines for publication of qualitative research studies in psychology and related fields. Br. J. Clin. Psychol. **38**, 215–229 (1999)

12. Fishbein, M., Ajzen, I.: Predicting and Changing Behavior: The Reasoned Action Approach. Taylor & Francis, Milton Park (2010)
13. Flanigan, A.E., Babchuk, W.A.: Social media as academic quicksand: a phenomenological study of student experiences in and out of the classroom. Learn. Individ. Differ. **44**, 40–45 (2015)
14. Flanigan, A.E., Kiewra, K.A.: What college instructors can do about student cyberslacking. Educ. Psychol. Rev. **30**(2), 585–597 (2017)
15. Fried, C.B.: In-class laptop use and its effects on student learning. Comput. Educ. **50**(3), 906–914 (2008)
16. Glaser, B.G., Strauss, A.L.: The Discovery of Grounded Theory: Strategies for Qualitative Research. Aldine, Chicago (1967)
17. Guo, Z., Tan, F.B., Cheung, K.: Students' uses and gratifications for using computer-mediated communication media in learning contexts. Commun. Assoc. Inf. Syst. **27**(1), 339–378 (2010)
18. Jacobsen, W.C., Forste, R.: The wired generation: academic and social outcomes of electronic media use among university students. Cyberpsychol. Behav. Soc. Netw. **14**(5), 275–280 (2011)
19. Junco, R.: In-class multitasking and academic performance. Comput. Hum. Behav. **28**(6), 2236–2243 (2012)
20. Junco, R., Cotten, S.: A decade of distraction? How multitasking affects student outcomes. In: Proceedings of Symposium on the Dynamics of the Internet and Society, pp. 1–38. Oxford Internet Institute (2011)
21. Kitzinger, J.: Qualitative research: introducing focus groups. B. M. J. **311**(7000), 299–302 (1995)
22. Leysens, J.L., le Roux, D.B., Parry, D.A.: Can I have your attention, please? An empirical investigation of media multitasking during university lectures. In: SAICSIT 2016 Proceedings of the Annual Conference of the South African Institute of Computer Scientists and Information Technologists, Paper #21 (2016)
23. Mason, J.: Qualitative Researching. SAGE, Newcastle upon Tyne (2002)
24. Morgan, D.: Focus groups as qualitative research. Qual. Res. Methods Ser. **16**(2), 6–17 (1997)
25. North, D., Johnston, K., Ophoff, J.: The use of mobile phones by South African university students. Issues Informing Sci. Inf. Technol. **11**, 115–138 (2014)
26. Parry, D.A.: The digitally-mediated study experiences of undergraduate students in South Africa. M.-Thesis, Stellenbosch University (2017)
27. Parry, D.A., le Roux, D.B.: In-lecture media use and academic performance: investigating demographic and intentional moderators. S. Afr. Comput. J. **30**(1), 85–107 (2018)
28. Przybylski, A.K., Murayama, K., Dehaan, C.R., Gladwell, V.: Motivational, emotional, and behavioral correlates of fear of missing out. Comput. Hum. Behav. **29**(4), 1841–1848 (2013)
29. Reno, R.R., Cialdini, R.B., Kallgren, C.A.: The transsituational influence of social norms. J. Pers. Soc. Psychol. **64**(1), 104–112 (1993)
30. Ritchie, J., Lewis, J., McMaughton-Nichols, C., Ormston, R.: Qualitative Research Practice: A Guide for Social Science Students and Researchers. SAGE, Newcastle upon Tyne (2013)
31. Roberts, N., Rees, M.: Student use of mobile devices in university lectures. Australas. J. Educ. Technol. **30**(4), 415–426 (2014)
32. Rosen, L.D., Carrier, M., Cheever, N.A.: Facebook and texting made me do it: media-induced task-switching while studying. Comput. Hum. Behav. **29**(3), 948–958 (2013)

33. Rosen, L.D., Whaling, K., Rab, S., Carrier, L.M., Cheever, N.A.: Is Facebook creating 'iDisorders'? The link between clinical symptoms of psychiatric disorders and technology use, attitudes and anxiety. Comput. Hum. Behav. **29**(3), 1243–1254 (2013)
34. le Roux, D.B., Parry, D.A.: A new generation of students: digital media in academic contexts. CCIS **730**, 19–36 (2017)
35. le Roux, D.B., Parry, D.A.: In-lecture media use and academic performance: does subject area matter? Comput. Hum. Behav. **77**, 86–94 (2017)
36. Sana, F., Weston, T., Cepeda, N.J.: Laptop multitasking hinders classroom learning for both users and nearby peers. Comput. Educ. **62**, 24–31 (2013)
37. Sapacz, M., Rockman, G., Clark, J.: Are we addicted to our cell phones? Comput. Hum. Behav. **57**, 153–159 (2016)
38. van der Schuur, W., Baumgartner, S.E., Sumter, S.R., Valkenburg, P.M.: The consequences of media multitasking for youth: a review. Comput. Hum. Behav. **53**, 204–215 (2015)
39. Strauss, V.: Why a leading professor of new media just banned technology use in class. Technical report (2014). https://goo.gl/hzejkd
40. Taneja, A., Fiore, V., Fischer, B.: Cyber-slacking in the classroom: potential for digital distraction in the new age. Comput. Educ. **82**, 141–151 (2015)
41. Twining, P., Heller, R., Nussbaum, M., Tsai, C.: Some guidance on conducting and reporting qualitative studies. Comput. Educ. **106**, 1–9 (2017)
42. Williams, J.A., Cox, D.: I got distracted by their being distracted. East. Educ. J. **40**(1), 48–56 (2011)
43. Zhang, W., Zhang, L.: Explicating multitasking with computers: gratifications and situations. Comput. Hum. Behav. **28**(5), 1883–1891 (2012)

An Evaluation of Social Media Use in the Classroom at a Traditional University

Obrain Murire[1], Liezel Cilliers[1(✉)], and Kim Viljoen[2]

[1] Department of Information Systems, University of Fort Hare,
East London, South Africa
lcilliers@ufh.ac.za
[2] Department of Business Management, University of Fort Hare,
East London, South Africa

Abstract. Emerging technologies, such as social media, have become essential tools to increase student-lecturer interaction, collaboration and communication in academia. Despite the popularity of social media, few lecturers use these tools for learning purposes. The purpose of the study was to evaluate social media usage in teaching and learning at a traditional university in the Eastern Cape, South Africa. The substitution, augmentation, modification and redefinition (SAMR) model was used as the theoretical foundation for this study. The data was collected using a quantitative survey method. A questionnaire was distributed to the academics at the traditional university, with a response rate of 39% achieved. From these, descriptive statistics were used to analyse the data. The study found that the use of social media at the traditional university can be placed at level two of the model (augmentation) while technology use in the class is further along at the modification level. Barriers that prevent lecturers from using social media for teaching purposes included lack of management support, inadequate resources, lack of training of traditional university lecturers and resistance to change. The study, therefore, recommends that management at traditional universities should reinforce the use of emerging technologies by lecturers to improve student-lecturer interaction, communication and promoting collaborative learning amongst students.

Keywords: Social media · Teaching and learning
Traditional universities

1 Introduction

The throughput rate at traditional universities has been impacted by the massification of teaching and learning [18]. More students have enrolled at traditional universities annually, despite a lack of resources to support academic activities

This work is based on the research supported in part by the National Research Foundation (NRF) of South Africa: Unique Grant No. TTK150713125504.

S. Kabanda et al. (Eds.): SACLA 2018, CCIS 963, pp. 65–77, 2019.
https://doi.org/10.1007/978-3-030-05813-5_5

[11]. Fifty-five percent of first-year students will not graduate while only 5% of the enrolled black and colored students will finish their undergraduate degrees in the prescribed time [9, 28]. Traditional universities must identify new solutions, such as emerging technologies, to solve the challenges of massification [11].

Mobile technology has become a preferred mode of communication for young adults [25]. A recent study suggested that university students are the most active mobile phone users with the functions most often used including text messaging, gaming and the Internet [10]. Given the popularity of mobile communication amongst the university students, the potential to use social media to improve the learning environment at universities is immense to improve the throughput rate as it assists in increasing student-lecturer interaction, collaboration and communication in academia [8]. However, the incorporation of social media tools such as social networks at traditional universities in South Africa is low due to limited knowledge and proficiency required to use social media effectively as a pedagogical tool amongst lecturers [20].

The study was conducted at a traditional university and focused on the lecturer perspective on using social media in teaching and learning. The purpose of the study was to evaluate social media use in teaching and learning at a traditional university in the Eastern Cape, South Africa. The study will also provide an overview of the barriers that prevent lecturers from adopting these tools in academia. The paper is outlined as follows: Sect. 2 discusses social media tools in higher education which is followed by an introduction to the SAMR model. Section 4 then provides an overview of the methodology employed in the study. A discussion of the results is given thereafter, which includes an analysis of the barriers of social media. The conclusions and recommendations of the study are provided in Sect. 7.

2   Social Media Tools in Higher Education

Social media adoption in the teaching and learning environment has increased in the past few years [19]. Tarantino, McDonough and Hua describe social media as a range of web-based tools and services that are designed to encourage community development through collaboration and information sharing [27]. Figure 1 illustrates the various social media tools that may be used in teaching and learning.

Some studies have revealed that lecturers are turning to social media in the academic environment with the aim to create an innovative learning environment [4, 6]. However, in the South African higher education system, this trend has not been investigated. Madhav, Joseph, and Twala found that most students are aware of social media tools [16], e.g. Facebook, Twitter and Whatsapp. They are also willing to integrate these tools in academia as they provide convenience, e.g. no need to visit the university computer laboratory to check for announcements as it is posted online. This is supported by Mbodila, Ndebele and Muhandji whose study conducted at the University of Venda in South Africa indicated that students, tutors and lecturers are using social media to communicate with each other [17].

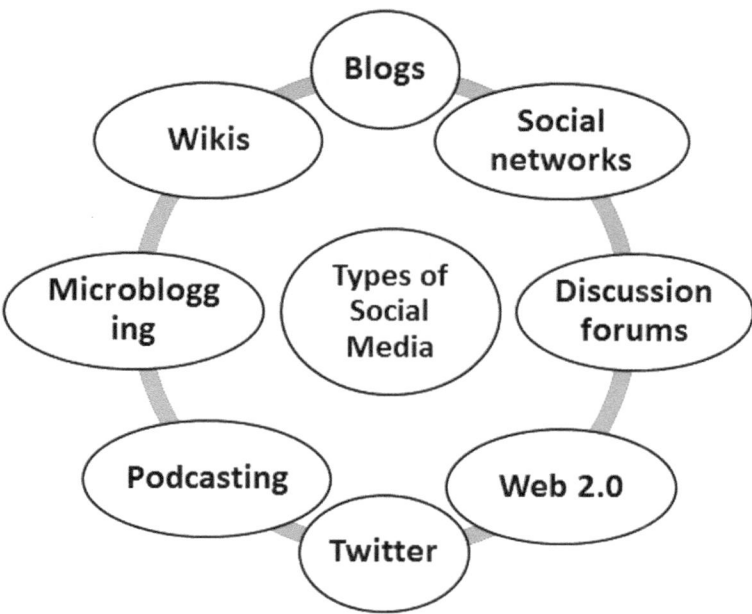

Fig. 1. Types of emerging technologies according to [13]

There are several advantages when social media is adopted in the academic environment. Nurulrabihah, Hajar, Norlidah, Saedah and Ridhuan state that emerging technologies such Wikis, Twitter and Facebook have a positive effect in the academic setting [21]. The use of emerging technologies in the academic setting will allow lecturers and students to communicate in real time and therefore offers virtual office hours. Furthermore, other types of technologies, such as blogs and wikis allow students to engage in online discussions. These tools provide features that help to manage students and promote student-lecturer interaction [12,13].

Even though the benefits of incorporating emerging technologies at the traditional university include communication as well as collaboration, some students report that they are distracted by the numerous kinds of entertainment that are offered by the various devices, for instance, playing games and 'surfing the net'. Some students perceive social networking sites as their personal space and do not want their studies to intrude in this space. Furthermore, some students tend to communicate or text their peers during lectures which will distract them from learning [14,20]. As a result, students' concentration levels in class are reduced. To counter this, mechanisms must be in place to discourage the use of social media and mobile devices while students are attending lectures. This conclusion is supported by Kopcha who postulates that some students will find it challenging to balance their online activities and their academic work [14].

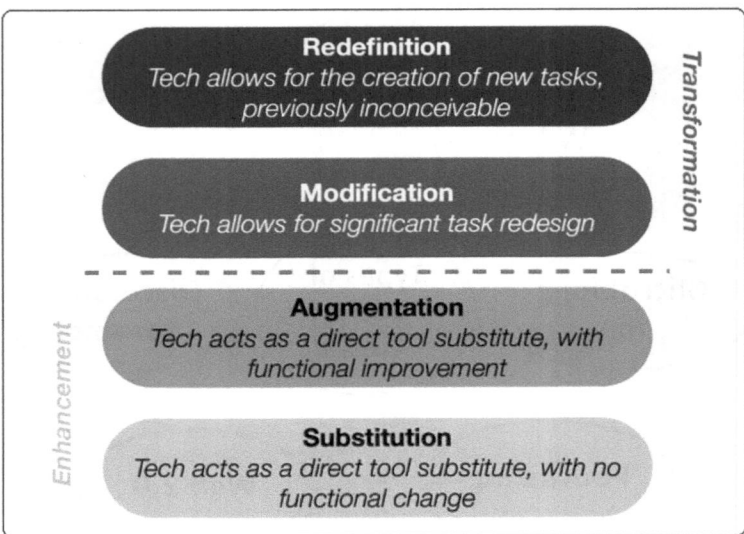

Fig. 2. The SAMR model according to [24]

The following section discusses the SAMR model, which is the underpinning model adopted for this study.

3   Substitution, Augmentation, Modification, Redefinition Model (SAMR)

The substitution, augmentation, modification and redefinition model (SAMR) was used as a theoretical foundation for this study. Puentedura developed the SAMR model which assists lecturers to incorporate technology in the classroom [24]. The SAMR model depicts four levels which consist of the enhancement and transformation sections. The substitution and augmentation levels fall under enhancement while modification and redesign are under transformation, which is where most learning takes place [24]. The model portrays levels of incremental technology integration in the teaching and learning environments. Figure 2 depicts the SAMR model which is explained in more detail below.

Substitution is the first level where technology is used as a substitute by both lecturers and students. Technology is employed to accomplish the tasks that were done before the arrival of computers and Web 2.0 technologies. For instance, lecturers used to post announcements on notice boards which would now be substituted when lecturers use social media such as Facebook and Twitter to deliver announcements to students [5]. The task is the same, and there is no functional change.

With the *augmentation level*, social media is used to complete tasks more efficiently [22]. Social media offers an effective tool to perform everyday tasks. A case study conducted by Lubega, Mugisha and Muyinda states that social media can be useful to replace ordinary ways of accomplishing academic activities [15], however with little functional change. For example, when a lecturer uses subject communities such as wikis, blogs and chat rooms to look for relevant research content instead of making use of textbooks borrowed from the library.

The *modification level* allows for the creation of new tasks [22]. Cilliers describes how educators can create new tasks with social media [8]. For instance, lecturers may use group discussion facilities on a wiki to facilitate academic activities as well as collaborations amongst students.

The *redefinition level* allows social media to be used for significant task redesign [22]. Lubega et al. describe how lecturers redesign teaching and learning using social media [15]. For example, lecturers may ask students to create their notes from the discussions they make on social networking sites, or when educators use social media to express, share thoughts and ideas with students as well as peers with a common interest.

The model can be used to identify the level of social media integration in the classroom. Therefore, the model can also be employed to *evaluate the adoption of social media in teaching and learning* at a traditional university [22]—see the following section for the details of the method.

4   Method

A quantitative survey tool was used to collect the data at one traditional university in the Eastern Cape. The questionnaire was adapted from Puentedura [24] (chosen after extensive literature reviews) to test social media acceptance among lecturers in a higher education institution. The question was adapted to reflect the social media context of the study.

The study population was limited to full-time lecturers at one traditional university where data was collected, and a convenience sampling method was used as the study made use of the readily available study population. A link to the web-based questionnaire was emailed to the participants with detailed instructions for completion of the questions. An aggregate of 116 responses was received, resulting in a response rate of 39%. Before this, the questionnaire was piloted to 10 lecturers for suitability, user-friendliness and un-ambiguousness.[1]

All responses to the questionnaire were analysed as quantitative variables. Statistical Package for the Social Science (SPSS 24) was used to analyse primary data. Data were analysed using descriptive statistics. Also, relationships between variables were tested using the Pearson chi-square test.

5   Results

The majority of our participants were between 30–50 years of age. Interestingly, more than half of the academics did indicate that they do not make use of social media: see Table 1.

---

[1] 'Ethical clearance' was received from our university's research ethics committee.

Table 1. Details of participants

Item	Category	Frequency	%
Gender	Male	53	45.8
	Female	63	54.2
Age	<30	9	10.8
	30–40	29	34.9
	41–50	33	39.8
	>50	12	14.5
Faculty	Science and agriculture	27	32.5
	Management and commerce	24	28.9
	Social sciences and humanities	10	12.0
	Others	9	10.8
	Education	7	8.4
	No indiaction	4	4.8
	Law	2	2.4
Years in academia	<3	13	15.7
	3–6	27	32.5
	7–10	13	15.7
	11–14	14	16.9
	15+	15	18.0
	No indication	1	1.2
Social media use	Daily	15	18.1
	Once a week	6	7.2
	Once a month	15	18.1
	Rarely (when inevitable)	28	33.7
	Never	19	22.9

Substitution ICTs is when technology, in this context social media, is used as a replacement for standard practices with no functional change. With respect to Table 2, the majority (47.0%) of the lecturers indicated that they have never used social media for assignments, while 39.0% of the lecturers point out that they do not use social media to deliver announcements to their students. By contrast, only 7.2% and 23.0% of the lecturers always use social media for assignments and to deliver announcements respectively. By contrast, the majority of lecturers (47.3%) always make use of projectors and smart boards in the lecture venues. The use of emerging technologies in academic setting fosters effective communication between lecturers and students [8, 20]. The findings indicated that majority of the lecturers (57.8%) sometimes use social media to communicate with students. These findings entail that personal communication is more acceptable than a group discussion. A possible reason for using Facebook, Twitter and

Table 2. Substitution of ICTs

Substitution of ICTs	Never	Sometimes	Always	Total
I use **Social Media** for assignments in teaching and learning	47.0%	45.8%	7.2%	100%
I use **Social Media** to deliver announcements to students	39.0%	38.0%	23.0%	100%
Technology: I use projectors and smart boards in the lecture venues	35.5%	17.3%	47.3%	100%

Table 3. Augmentation ICTs

Augmentation ICTs	Never	Sometimes	Always	Total
Social Media: I use subject communities such as wikis, blogs and chat rooms to look for research content	37.5%	41.3%	21.2%	100%
Technology: I use word processor applications to correct grammatical errors in assignments and research projects	33.6%	15.5%	50.9%	100%
Technology: I use track changes on a word processor to review students' work	34.2%	14.9%	50.9%	100%

WhatsApp for communication with students could be that it is fun using it for academic purposes and students already have access to and are using these technologies. Table 2 provides descriptive statistics for substitution of ICTs.

In the augmentation dimension, social media are used to complete tasks more efficiently but with little functional change. The results, as per Table 3, indicated that the majority of lecturers (41.3%) sometimes use subject communities when looking for research material, while 21.2% of the lecturers always use subject communities to search for relevant research content in their disciplines. Thus, lecturers have adopted augmentation ICTs to support their scholarly research work. These results are congruent to the results obtained by Lubega et al. who found that lecturers are more likely to make use of technology for augmentation than social media to change practices in the classroom [15]. These results, similarly to the previous section, illustrate that lecturers are aware of technologies, e.g. PowerPoint and projectors, and utilise them more frequently than social media. Thus, technology is more acceptable than social media at this level. Table 3 provides descriptive statistics for augmentation.

The majority of lecturers (50.9%) stated that they always use word processor applications to correct grammar on student's assignment or research project. The same results were found as the majority of lecturers (50.9%) indicated that they always use track changes in a word processor to review students' work. The majority of the lecturers (67.5%) reported that they have never allowed students to use group discussion facilities such as wikis. Thus, group discussion

Table 4. Modification ICTs

Modification ICTs	Never	Sometimes	Always	Total
Social Media: I use group discussion facilities on wikis	67.5%	25.3%	7.2%	100%
Social Media: I use Facebook and WhatsApp to communicate with the students	25.3%	57.8%	16.9%	100%
Technology: I use the Internet to give students topics for assignment purposes	12.0%	55.5%	32.5%	100%

Table 5. Redefinition ICTs

Redefinition ICTs	Never	Sometimes	Always	Total
Students use social media to make their notes	54.2%	38.6%	7.2%	100%
Blogs provide useful information for my lecturers	56.6%	39.8%	3.6%	100%
I use social media to express and share thoughts and ideas with students	50.6%	42.2%	7.2%	100%

facilities found on wikis are less used in teaching and learning. These results are consistent with the results by Cilliers who found that the majority of students lack knowledge about the role of wikis in teaching and learning [8]. Students ought to be taught on the potential benefits of a wiki as it improves collaboration. Table 4 provides the details for modification.

The most common modification ICT is the Internet. The findings indicated that majority of the lecturers (57.8%) sometimes use Facebook and WhatsApp to communicate with students. Furthermore, more than half of lecturers (55.5%) sometimes use the Internet to find student topics for assignment or research, while 32.5% of the participants stated that they only assign work to students from the Internet. The reason for these results could be that lecturers found the Internet a helpful resource to provide current assignments to the students while the students could easily access and find supporting material on the Internet. This indicates that the lecturers are comfortable in making use of the Internet to modify their teaching and learning.

Under the redefinition stage, technology allows for the creation of new tasks previously impossible to develop. As can be seen in Table 5, the majority of lecturers (54.2%) are hesitant to ask students to make their notes from discussion threads on social networking sites, whereas 7.2% allow students to write notes from discussion groups. Similarly, 56.6% of the lecturers indicated that they have never used blogs as a source of information for teaching and learning, while only 3.6% made use of blogs to facilitate the teaching and learning process. The majority of the lecturers (50.6%) responded that they have never used social media to express and share thoughts and ideas, whereas 7.2% exchange ideas and share thoughts on social networks with peers. Low percentages (7.2%, 3.6% and 7.2%) were recorded for the always column. These results indicate that the lecturers are not comfortable to make use of social media to redefine their teaching and learning. Table 5 provides the details for redefinition.

The study results that the traditional university academics can be placed at level two of the SAMR model (Augmentation). Academics indicated that they always use word processor applications to correct grammar on students' assignment or research project as well as track changes in a word processor to review students' work. To improve to level three and four, there is a need for management support in sponsoring workshops of how social media can be adopted in teaching in the academic setting. The next section discusses some of the factors that can be considered as barriers to social media adoption in the academic setting.

The results are consistent with the findings from a previous study by Lubega et al., according to which lecturers are more likely to make use of technology than social media to replace standard practices in the classroom [15]. The reason for this finding is that most lecturers are familiar with technologies such as projectors or microphones in the class. One of the reasons that lecturers are not comfortable with employing emerging technologies to substitute activities in the academic environment is the lack of a social media policy at the traditional university. Additionally, the little substitution which is taking place is based on the lecturers' efforts.

6   Barriers to Social Media in Teaching and Learning

The incorporation of social media in the academic environment is limited. Barriers include poor administrative-, leadership- and technical support, resistance to change, and lack of sufficient equipment [3,14]. In this study, the lecturers were provided with a predefined list that was developed from the literature study and asked to indicate whether they thought the listed barriers would impede social media use in teaching and learning. The list consists of students' attitude, internet connectivity, lack of resource, students' IT literacy level, lack of management support for innovation, resistance to new technology, lecturer attitude and beliefs and inadequate time to adopt new technology. The discussion below is based on these results displayed in Fig. 3.

Some of the lecturers indicated that allowing social media in the academic setting will prevent students from concentrating in lecture venues or classrooms. Classrooms at a traditional university do not have computers; where students make use of their devices, they are discouraged to use it as lecturers fear it will distract them. Chetty described similar results indicating that students will spend more time on their devices while doing non-academic activities [7], for instance, downloading music and videos. Additionally, some students will develop a habit texting in lecture venues when they are not allowed, e.g. during a test.

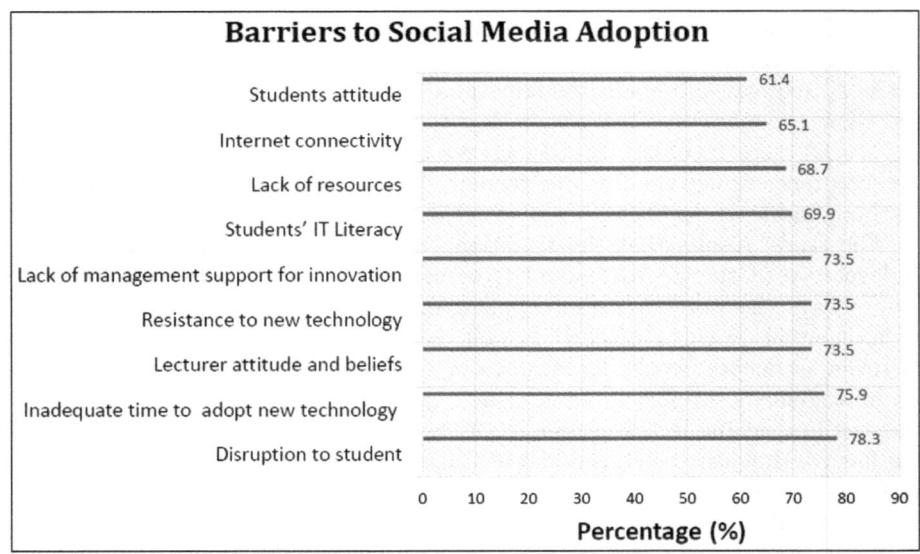

Fig. 3. Barriers to social media adoption in the classroom

Lecturers also indicated that they do not have adequate resources to adopt new technologies. Almeshal states that some lecturers find it challenging to integrate social media because some of the venues do not have computers and Internet access [1]. Further to this, most of the students at a traditional university come from the poor social, economic background; they cannot afford to buy data and do not have the necessary hardware resources to access social media. Additionally, most of the students at had access social media in university computer labs and libraries with poor Internet connectivity.

A further barrier identified by lecturers is lack of management support. Lecturers indicated that management does not support social media adoption and the little integration that is taking place is based on lecturers' efforts. In addition to this, there is no Technology-Enhanced Learning (TEL) or social media policy in place at this specific traditional university. No budget has been allocated for technology in teaching and learning only technology support, for instance, laptops and projectors. Management plays a crucial role in teaching and learning as it provides the needed financial resources, develops a vision and plan for social media integration, and provides incentives and encouragement [26]. Thus, there is a need for management support for social media to be adopted in teaching and learning.

Lecturers indicated that they lack time to integrate emerging technologies which is another barrier to incorporate emerging technologies in the academic environment at a traditional university. This is due to the fact that lectures at traditional universities lack training in this regard. It can however be noted that technology in the classroom is a small component of the Post Graduate

Diploma in Higher Education. Comparable results were found in a research study conducted by Oye, Iahad and Rahim which highlighted that time and technical support were the most significant barriers affecting ICT adoption at Adamawa State University in Ghana [23].

Lecturers' attitude and beliefs were found to be further reasons affecting the adoption of social media in academia. Similar results were found in a study by Bexheti, Ismaili and Cico who found that lecturers' attitude plays a critical role in facilitating the use of social media at traditional university [2]. Thus, effective and successful incorporation of social media in the academic environment is subject to a lecturer's positive attitude toward the new technology. Conversely, results from the literature indicated this, but it is not the similar case at the traditional university, as the majority of lecturers (73.5%) were positive that they would adopt social media in their teaching and learning activities shortly. Similarly, 71.1% of the lecturers expect to employ emerging tools in the next 12 months. Furthermore, the majority of the lecturers (75.9%) plan to use social media in academia in the next 12 months. This is due to lecturers identified that social media is a useful tool, and most of the academics are knowledgeable about social media tools. These results indicate that lecturers will adopt social media in the teaching and learning environment as they are influenced by four main factors (substitution, augmentation, modification and redefinition).

7 Conclusion

Various factors such as management support and prior knowledge of social media were found to be important for the acceptance of social media among lecturers. The study therefore recommends that the management of traditional universities should prioritise social media to improve student-lecturer interaction, communication and promoting collaborative learning among students.

Emerging technologies at traditional universities has a substantial impact in teaching and learning, however it is affected by barriers such as management support, inadequate resources, lack of training of traditional university lecturers and resistance to change. This analysis shows that lecturers at the specified traditional university can be placed at level two of the model (augmentation) due to the under-utilisation of social media tools in academic environment. The little enhancement that is taking place is entirely reliant on the lecturers' individual efforts. Therefore, social media are essential tools in teaching and learning and could be used by lecturers to increase the interaction reduced by massification which is taking place at a traditional university.

One of the constraints to the research study is that data was collected from one traditional university, assuming that all universities in South Africa have the same teaching and learning context as this university. The sample size was small. Additionally, a survey method was employed in the research study, therefore results are only based on quantitative data, and thus there was no follow up with qualitative interviews. Future research on adoption of social media in the teaching and learning environment in South Africa must draw a comprehensive sample including at least one traditional university from each province in South Africa. The analysis of the results can also investigate the relationship between gender and age and the use of social media.

References

1. Almeshal, T.: Social media adoption in learning and teaching by higher education faculty. In: Proceedings of the 9th International Technology, Education and Development Conference, pp. 1–10 (2015)
2. Bexheti, L.A., Ismaili, B.E., Cico, B.H.: An analysis of social media usage in teaching and learning: the case of SEEU. In: Proceedings of International Conference on Circuits, Systems, Signal Processing, Communications and Computers, pp. 90–94 (2014)
3. Bingimlas, K.A.: Barriers to the successful integration of ICT in teaching and learning environments: a review of the literature. Eurasia J. Math. Sci. Technol. Educ. **5**(3), 235–245 (2009)
4. Birch, A., Irvine, V.: Preservice teachers' acceptance of ICT integration in the classroom: applying the UTAUT model. Educ. Media Int. **46**(4), 295–315 (2009)
5. Bulbulia, Z., Wassermann, J.: Rethinking the usefulness of Twitter in higher education. Educ. Sci. **11**(1), 31–40 (2015)
6. Chen, B., Bryer, T.: Investigating instructional strategies for using social media in formal and informal learning. Int. Rev. Res. Open Distrib. Learn. **13**(1), 87–104 (2012)
7. Chetty, P.: The top 5 intellectual property risks on social media. Technical report. http://smetoolkit.businesspartners.co.za/en/content/top-5-intellectual-property-risks-social-media
8. Cilliers, L.: Wiki acceptance by university students to improve collaboration in higher education. Innov. Educ. Teach. Int. **54**(5), 485–493 (2017)
9. Higher Education South Africa: Strategic framework for HESA 2015–2019. Technical report (2014). http://www.hesa.org.za/
10. Cilliers, L., Viljoen, K.L.A., Chinyamurindi, W.T.: A study on students' acceptance of using mobile phones to seek health information in South Africa. Health Inf. Manag. J. **47**(2), 59–69 (2018)
11. Council on Higher Education: A proposal for undergraduate curriculum reform in South Africa: the case for a flexible curriculum structure. Report of the Task Team on Undergraduate Curriculum Structure, Discussion Document (2013)
12. Kagohara, D.M., van der Meer, L., Ramdoss, S., O'Reilly, M.F., Lancioni, G.E., Davis, T.N.: Using iPods and iPads in teaching programs for individuals with developmental disabilities: a systematic review. Res. Dev. Disabil. **34**(1), 147–156 (2013)
13. Kaplan, A.M., Haenlein, M.: Users of the world, unite! The challenges and opportunities of Social Media. Bus. Horiz. **53**(1), 59–68 (2010)
14. Kopcha, T.J.: Teachers' perceptions of the barriers to technology integration and practices with technology under situated professional development. Comput. Educ. **33**, 1100–1121 (2012)
15. Lubega, J.T., Mugisha, A.K., Muyinda, P.B.: Adoption of the SAMR model to asses ICT pedagogical adoption: a case of Makerere University. Int. J. e-Educ., e-Bus., e-Manag. e-Learn. **4**(2), 106–115 (2014)

16. Madhav, N., Joseph, M.K., Twala, B.: Creating social learning spaces to enhance the learning experience. Technical report, University of Johannesburg (2015)
17. Mbodila, M., Ndebele, C., Muhandji, K.: The effect of social media on students' engagement and collaboration in higher education: a case study of the use of Facebook at a South African University. J. Commun. **5**(2), 115–125 (2014)
18. Mohamedbhai, G.: The Effects of massification of Higher Education in Africa. Report from the Working Group on Higher Education of the Association for the Development of Education in Africa (2008, 2012)
19. Motamedi, V.: Integration of technology in our classrooms: a divisive issue. Technical report, Teheran (2012)
20. Murire, O., Cilliers, L.: Social media adoption among lecturers at a traditional university in Eastern Cape Province of South Africa. S. Afr. J. Manag. **19**(1), 1–6 (2016)
21. Nurulrabihah, M.N., Siti-Hajar, A.R., Norlidah, A., Saedah, S., Mohd-Ridhuan, M.J., Zaharah, H.: Usage of Facebook: the future impact of curriculum implementation on students in Malaysia. In: Proceedings of 13th International Educational Technology Conference, pp. 1261–1270 (2013)
22. Oxnevad, S.: Using the SAMR model to teach above the line. Technical report, 13 July 2013. http://gettingsmart.com/2013/07/
23. Oye, N.D., Iahad, N.A., Rahim, N.A.: The history of UTAUT model and its impact on ICT acceptance and usage by academicians. Educ. Inf. Technol. **19**, 251–270 (2014)
24. Puentedura, R.: Transformation, technology, and education. Technical report (2006). http://www.hippasus.com/resources/tte/
25. Robinson, G.: Why tablets are a key learning tool in special education. TabTimes Technical report (2014). http://tabtimes.com/
26. Schlenkrich, L., Sewry, D.A.: Factors for successful use of social networking sites in higher education. S. Afr. Comput. J. **49**, 12–24 (2012)
27. Tarantino, K., McDonough, J., Hua, M.: Effects of student engagement with social media on student learning: a review of literature. J. Technol. Stud. Aff. **1**(8), 1–8 (2013)
28. Zulu, C.: Empowering first year (post-matric) students in basic research skills: a strategy for education for social justice. S. Afr. J. Educ. **31**(3), 447–457 (2011)

It Seems to Have a Hold on Us: Social Media Self-regulation of Students

Lushan Chokalingam, Machdel Matthee$^{(\boxtimes)}$, and Marié J. Hattingh

Department of Informatics, University of Pretoria, Pretoria, South Africa
{machdel.matthee,marie.hattingh}@up.ac.za

Abstract. Social media play a positive role in the lives of students by providing social networking, communication and information functionalities. However, social media also act as a distraction, resulting in multitasking between social media and studying which leaves fragmented time intervals for focused concentration. Self-regulation is emphasized as an essential skill necessary to manage the use of social media when planning or performing learning activities. In this paper we determine whether students are aware of the need for social media self-regulation behavior during their studies and, if so, which measures they take. Some of these include the physical removal of the phone, using technological functions to limit access (e.g. removing the battery, uninstalling apps), or sheer will-power. Nevertheless there remains a strong 'pulling' power of social media which makes the implementation of those plans difficult. Reasons for this phenomenon include fear-of-missing-out (FOMO) and the habit-forming nature of social media and mobile devices. Another factor is the two 'worlds' of social media as perceived by students: they can be used both academically and socially. How to ignore the one and focus on the other? We emphasise the importance of awareness amongst students and lecturers regarding the need for self-regulation of social media use as well as strategies to manage them.

Keywords: Social media self-regulation · Zimmerman
Cyclical self-regulation · Social media habits · Distraction · Learning

1 Introduction

The term 'social media' (SM) refers to online tools available on mobile or desktop devices, which allow people to interact through texting, phone calls, sharing or posting photos, videos and audio clips. Well-known social media platforms include Facebook, Instagram, LinkedIn, Twitter, WhatsApp, YouTube, Snapchat, etc. The affordances of social media result in their widespread adoption in both developed and developing countries. In South Africa, for example, Facebook is used by half of people older than 13 [7]. Young people in particular seem to embrace social media. Lau reports that social media usage of young adults in the USA has climbed from 12% in 2005 to 90% in 2015 [8]. In South

S. Kabanda et al. (Eds.): SACLA 2018, CCIS 963, pp. 78–92, 2019.
https://doi.org/10.1007/978-3-030-05813-5_6

Africa, the age groups 18–24 and 25–34 were the largest user groups of Facebook during 2016–2017 [14].

Educators and students alike use the opportunities provided by social media to their benefits in learning environments. Although mostly incidental and informal, some of the positive uses include the sharing of resources, access to course material, unofficial substitutes for a learning management system, increased collaboration between students, and improved communication with lecturers [8,9]. However, social media can be distracting [18], 'luring' students away from academic engagement and deep concentration [1].

To advise students to simply focus on their studies does not seem to have the desired effect, as recent studies point towards the addictive and habit-forming properties of social media [5,11].

Self-regulation is mentioned as a necessary skill for students to combat the distractions presented by social media [16]. Self-regulation is defined as the capacity of human beings to alter their own behavior [2]. The habitual, embodied nature of social media use makes self-regulation difficult so that teachers and lecturers should support students in this process [1]. One example is where teachers implement an 'open/close' policy where students get permission to use devices only during certain parts of a lecture. According to [1], students welcome these measures (even if some of them carry on with mobile phones under the desks). The study indicated that students use similar measures to self-manage their technology-use in class [1]. Methods vary from closing a tab, quitting a browser, to closing the lid of the laptop. As a result of [1], Aagaard contemplated students' self-management of technological distractions outside the classroom, e.g. while in a café with friends or around a dinner table. Similar to [1] we are interested in how students manage their social media use both in and out of the classroom. To date there is not yet much research with this specific focus.

The purpose of this paper is thus to investigate the self-regulative behaviour of students towards social media use during learning activities (i.e. study, attend lectures, complete academic work) in formal and informal settings. We conducted interviews with 50 students at a South African university and analysed their answers w.r.t. self-regulation as understood by Zimmerman [21].

In the next section we recapitulate the distracting properties of social media with applicability to university students. Section 3 gives an overview of Zimmerman's cyclical self-regulation model. Section 4 describes our research method. In Sects. 5, 6 and 7 we present and discuss our findings and conclusions.

2   Social Media as Habit and Distraction

Researchers ascribe the irresistible nature of social media to varying factors. On the one hand, social media provides highly effective ways for communication, information-seeking and forming social connections: Wang, Lee and Hua consider these uses as normal and harmless [20]. However, these activities become habits which can eventually lead to irrational behaviour or excessive use. With the intensification of habit, users focus on the emotional rewards gained, at the cost of other longer term goals [18]. Nadkami and Hofmann listed some of the emotional rewards provided by SM (Facebook) as a sense of 'belonging' and as an opportunity for self-presentation [10]. Another concept closely related to excessive use of social media is the 'fear of missing out' (FOMO). Przybylski describes this as *"the pervasive apprehension that others might be having rewarding experiences from which one is absent—FOMO is characterized by the desire to stay continually connected with what others are doing"* [13] (p. 1841). The craving for this emotional gratification, and the need to know what the 'group' is up to, can lead to social media dependence.

Another factor contributing to social media dependence is the habit-forming nature of IT devices [1,11]. Oulasvirta (et al.) describe the checking habit formed with mobile devices: the almost constant inspection of the content of the device [11], including social media, e-mail, news apps, etc. Aagaard argued that habitual use of IT (including social media) is 'deeply sedimented' and embodied to such an extent that the user is no longer aware of doing it [1]: *"the process of logging onto Facebook has become embodied in ones fingers and happens almost automatically"* (p. 91). As such, users have a 'pre-reflective attraction' towards certain websites (e.g. Facebook) which implies that it does not involve rational choices nor reactions to stimuli [1] (p. 94).

Whatever the reasons for social media's pervasive use, the fact is that it can distract students from focusing on their academic work with possible adverse effects on their studies. Several papers focus on this topic by linking social media to concepts like 'cognitive distraction' [19], 'multitasking' [8,18], 'off-task use' [1], and 'media-induced task-switching' [15]. Their authors agree that human cognitive resources are limited and that placing competing demands on cognition can lead to decreased task performance [4]. Moreover, Lau found that social media multitasking has a negative effect on students' academic performance [8].

Considering the effect of students' self-regulation, personality traits and trust on the use of Facebook, the authors of [16] stated that students who are generally more self-regulated also control their use of social media more effectively. In [4] we find a positive correlation between deficient self-regulation and excessive mobile phone use at the expense of focusing on more important tasks.

Thus it is clear that being a student in the 21st century demands strong self-regulation ability. But what exactly is meant with 'self-regulation'—particularly w.r.t. learning? The next section recapitulates some literature on the concept of self-regulation and learning.

3   Self-regulation and Learning

Panadero and Alonso-Tapia consider self-regulation related to learning as *"the control that students have over their cognition, behaviour, emotions and motivation through the use of personal strategies to achieve the goals they have established"* [12] (p. 450). Zimmerman explained that self-regulation of learning involves not only the application of knowledge but the self-motivation, self-awareness and skill to know when to apply the knowledge [21]. Baumeister and

Vohs highlighted the role played by motivation in self-regulation [2]: they argued that there are conflicting motivations at play during self-regulation and that "*self-regulation is often employed to restrain motivations, but the motivation to self-regulate is often crucial to the success of engaging in self-regulation*" (p. 116). According to [21], good self-regulation skills are largely dependent of students' perceptions of their efficacy regarding a subject as well as their interest in the subject. Zimmerman considers self-regulatory processes as taking place in a cycle of three phases: the *forethought* phase, the *performance* phase, and the *self-reflection* phase (Fig. 1). The cyclical nature of the model shows the importance of including feedback from previous efforts in changing strategies for new tasks. Panadero and Alonso-Tapia provided an overview of the cyclical phase model of Zimmerman in appreciation of its important role in the scientific literature. The three phases of the model according to [12, 21, 22] are recapitulated below.

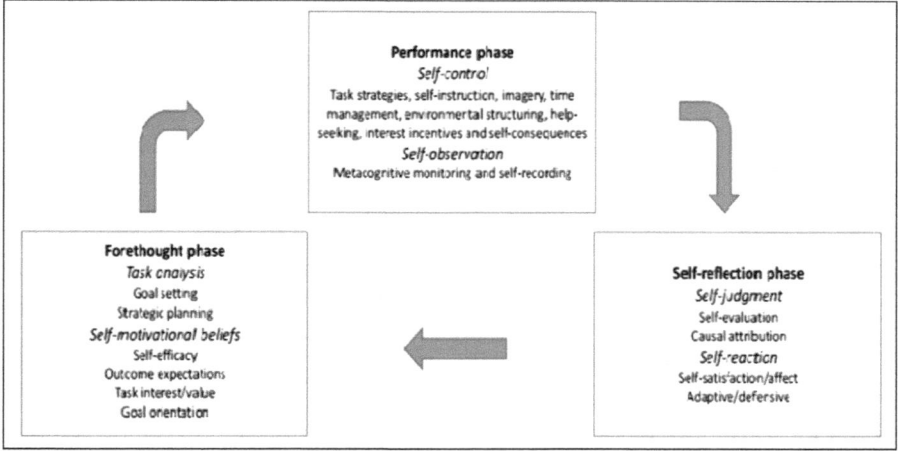

Fig. 1. Zimmerman's cyclical phase self-regulation model [22]

3.1   The Forethought Phase

This phase is divided into two processes: task analysis and self-motivation. Task analysis comprises two activities: goal setting and strategic planning. Studies show that students with effective self-regulation behaviour start by setting goals for themselves and devising strategies to attain such goals. Students take into account the assessment criteria against which the performance will be judged. The desired level of performance also plays a role [12]. However, these strategies will be to no avail if students do not believe in themselves. Self-efficacy forms part of self-motivation. Self-efficacy refers to a person's beliefs about his/her capability to perform a task. The outcome expectations of students also play a role in motivation: what do they expect the success of a study-task to be? Other ingredients of self-motivation are intrinsic interest and goal orientation. Both these concepts refer to a student's perceived intrinsic value of the specific study-task as well as the general goal of the process of learning (i.e. focus on developing competence rather than focusing on short-term performance rewards) [21].

3.2   The Performance Phase

This phase refers to the self-regulative processes during the learning process itself. These processes are divided into two classes: self-control and self-observation. Typical self-control processes include imagery, self-instruction, time management, structuring the learning environmental, help-seeking, incentives to maintain their interests and self-consequences. Visualization of a problem or concepts and drawing sketches are examples of imagery, whereas describing to yourself (can be 'aloud') how to approach the task can be seen as self-instruction. A learning environment structuring activity can be to make sure that the room where you study is quiet and away from distracting noises, or not sitting next to a class mate who talks during class [12]. Help-seeking is a learning strategy only if students are not trying to avoid the activity but are willing to learn from the answer. Incentives to maintain interest and self-consequences refer to self-directing messages about the importance of an activity, self-praise, and self-rewards. Two important self-observation processes are self-recording and self-monitoring. As an illustration of self-recording, consider a student comparing the time he/she takes to study a topic early in the morning to the time it takes to study a similar topic late at night. In this way a student learns when the ideal time is for him/her to study that type of topic. Self-monitoring refers to the self-assessment of the quality of the process followed [12].

3.3   The Self-reflection Phase

The two major processes in this phase are self-judgment and self-reaction. Self-judgment includes self-evaluation that involves the comparisons made by the learner of his/her own performance against some standard. Another important component of self-judgment is the looking for causes of one's errors or misunderstandings. Students who believe that the cause of the errors is an inherent inability to comprehend the subject matter will become despondent, whereas students who believe that the cause of the errors can be attributed to wrong strategies will be motivated to try different approaches. Zimmerman refers to this process as 'causal attribution'. Self-reaction in the self-reflection phase involves feelings of self-satisfaction. An increase in self-satisfaction leads to positive affect enhancing motivation regarding the learning experience. On the other hand a decrease in self-satisfaction may hinder the learning process. Students may show defensive responses in this phase by avoiding learning-challenges. Students in this phase can also adapt their strategies to increase the effectiveness of their learning process.

3.4 The Cyclical Nature of Self-regulation

The 'cyclical nature' of the self-regulation process refers to the influence of the different phases on each other. For example, self-dissatisfaction in the self-reflection phase leads to lower self-efficacy in the forethought phase. In [21] significant correlations were shown between students' processes in the forethought-, performance-, and self-reflection phases.

4 Research Method

We followed the qualitative research approach of [6] with the aim of understanding and interpreting the social phenomena, students' use of social media, and the influence on their learning activities, through their own frames of reference.

Answers were collected from 50 students at a large South African university. We approached randomly selected students (as they entered the IT building) on campus during several consecutive days. Approachable students were interviewed with a semi-structured questionnaire, and all interview answers were transcribed. The semi-structured questionnaire focused on four main areas: (1) type, frequency of and reasons for social media used, (2) whether social media are distracting, (3) the perceived impact of social media on learning activities, and (4) how their usage is managed.

We used *thematic content analysis* (TCA) as the data analysis technique for this paper, because TCA is suitable for analysing written, verbal or visual messages [3]. Accordingly, sub-themes were identified relating to the first three focus areas of the questionnaire, whereas the self-regulation model of Zimmerman was used to deductively analyse the data regarding the fourth focus (management of social media usage).

5 Data Analysis and Findings

We present our findings in two sub-sections: the first one on demographics of the respondents and their social media usage, the second one on the results of the data analysis according to Zimmerman's Self-Regulation Model.

5.1 Demographics and Social Media Usage

Demographics. The only demographics recorded were *gender* and *age* of the respondents. Out of the 50 respondents the majority (58%) were male, the others female. 26% of all respondents were between 16–19 years of age, 54% between 20–23 years, and the rest between 24–27 years.

Social Media Used. The answers indicated that the most common social media platform among the respondents was 'WhatsApp', used by 49 of the 50 (98%) of the respondents. The second most frequently used platform was 'Facebook' that was used by 37 (74%) of the respondents. 32 (64%) of the respondents stated that they used 'Instagram', 20 (40%) used 'Twitter', 19 (38%) used 'YouTube', 9 (18%) used 'SnapChat', 5 (10%) used 'LinkedIn', 3 (6%) used 'Tinder' and 2 (4%) used 'Google+'. Many respondents used more than one of those media.

Frequency of Social Media Usage. A word count of all the words expressed by respondents w.r.t. a specific media usage time period indicated that the word 'daily' occurred 25 times. The word 'hourly' was expressed 24 times, 'every minute' 14 times, 'all the time' 7 times, 'weekly' three times, and 'every second' once in all responses. From these numbers we can see that majority of the respondents access their social media platforms daily and even hourly.

Purpose of Social Media Usage. The answers indicated *six types of purposes* of social media usage by the respondents.

1. *Communication:* Respondents stated that they used social media for communication purposes. This theme was supported by statements like: *"Mostly to talk to my friends"*; *"Basically, communicating with other people, making sure my voice is heard, and so that I can help you or send a message, just communication basically"*; *"It's for communicating, I mainly use WhatsApp that is generally the way that everyone communicates these days"*.
2. *Entertainment:* This theme was supported by statements like: *"I guess it's for entertainment mostly and you can alleviate boredom"*; *"Just look at people and laugh at them and for entertainment I guess"*.
3. *Education:* Some respondents stated that they used social media for educational purposes. For example: *"Nowadays it's mainly for academic purposes because we have class groups to discuss what's happening"*.
4. *Keeping up-to-date:* This theme was supported by statements like *"... to keep up to date as to what is happening around the world"*.
5. *Business:* Some indicated that this was their main purpose for using social media. One said: *"Well, for example with LinkedIn I look for potential clients and look at which areas I can expand in to the market"*.
6. *Alleviate boredom:* For an example see the 'entertainment' statement quoted above.

The answers indicated that the respondents used social media for more than one purpose. For example the following quote speaks of the business, entertainment, communication and education themes: *"Well, for example with LinkedIn I look for potential clients and look at which areas I can expand into the market. For Facebook: I use it for entertainment and for keeping in touch with long distance family. YouTube I use for watching educational videos and football highlights"*.

Inclination to Check Social Media. The majority of respondents indicated that they feel inclined to constantly 'check' their social media services. For example: *"Yes, I ... check it at least once an hour or once every two hours. I do feel inclined to check my social media so I can stay updated"*, as well as: *"Yes, sometimes I feel like I have to check what people are up to"*. Table 1 illustrates the reasons with supporting statements of why students feel inclined to constantly check their social media accounts. The table includes 'boredom' and the need to 'keep up to date'.

Eight of the respondents indicated that they do *not* feel an inclination towards checking their social media services constantly. For example: *"No, I just check it whenever I want or whenever I can"*. One student out of the 50 responses stated that he only 'sometimes' feels the inclination to check social media services.

Table 1. Reasons for checking social media accounts

Motivation	Quotes
Boredom	*"... when you are bored or when I'm following something or when I've been busy and I want to take a break or take a walk, then I'll log onto social media"*
	"... when I am bored. I feel like I get bored a lot, and social media keeps me busy"
Keep up to date	*"I do feel inclined to check my social media so I can stay updated"*
	"Yes, because I need to be updated with what's happening around me"
	"I think it's a norm these days to frequently check what's going on in the world"

5.2   Self-regulation Behavior

As discussed above, Zimmerman's cyclical Self-Regulation Model consist of three phases: forethought, performance and self-reflection. We start the discussion with the self-reflection phase since we argue students will not employ any self-management techniques if they are not aware of the distracting nature of social media while preparing for and participating in learning activities. This awareness will typically transpire in the self-reflection phase. In this phase we therefore asked the students whether they experience social media as a distraction, and, if so, what the perceived impact is on their academic performance. The forethought process gives the strategies they have whereas the performance phase discusses the deployment of the plans. The data (answers) associated with each of these phases are discussed next.

The Self-reflection Phase. The self-reflection phase is concerned with self-judgment (including self-evaluation) and self-reaction (including adapting). During the self-evaluation phase students become aware of the distraction of social media as well as the impact of social media on their studies.

Are Social Media Distracting? The majority of students indicated that they found social media distracting, whereas a few indicated they do not, and one person indicated 'sometimes'. Figure 2 shows the themes that were identified from the analysis of those respondents that indicated that they found social media distracting.

From those respondents that classified social media as 'distracting' the following was found: some stated that having a break in concentration when completing their learning activities caused them to pick up their devices and access social media. An example of this is: *"Social media is a way of just grabbing your attention and you never know when to stop. It can be problem at times"*. Respondents reported that they feel the urge to respond rapidly when receiving a message: *"If your phone is near and a WhatsApp message comes in I find myself not focusing on my work and I want to respond to the message"*. The appealing content shared on social media lead the respondent astray, as illustrated here: *"... when you are checking, it can lead to an hour — when you find something interesting which leads to the following up stories and what is trending. Some trends can take forever"*. Another theme that emerged is when the respondents take a break from learning activities by browsing social media but then get distracted: *"... when you're studying sometimes you take a break that is supposed to be ten minutes but it ends up being one hour or something like that"*. Group chats are also distracting, as indicated by this quote: *"It's distracting when your friends talk to you on WhatsApp, when there is a group chat and it goes on and on. YouTube can also take my whole day"*. Another theme that has emerged was the fear of missing out (FOMO) illustrated by the following quote: *"It is distracting in terms of when you are in class trying to listen but there's a message coming in on WhatsApp and you just have to attend to it because of FOMO"*.

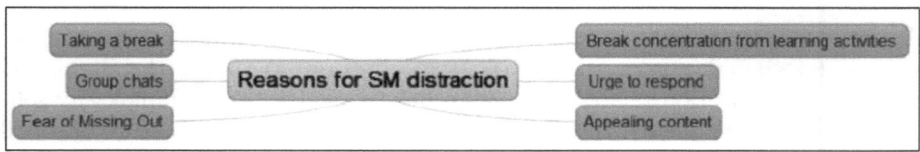

Fig. 2. Reasons for social media distraction

Those respondents who indicated that social media did not distract them mainly reasoned that they were disciplined and that they did not allow social media to become a distraction. One student out of the 50 stated that social media distracted him 'sometimes'.

What is the Impact of Social Media on Your Academic Performance? The thematic analysis conducted on the answer-data revealed that social media have not only had negative effects on students' academic performance but also some positive impact. 44% reported a negative impact and 36% reported that social media also had a positive effect on their learning activities. 22% of the respondents said that social media have had both a positive and a negative effect on their academic performance, whilst 8% reported no effect. Table 2 summarises the responses.

Students who stated that social media affected their academics positively used social media as a tool to communicate with fellow students with the aim of gathering information for academic purposes. Some students stated that social media could cause distractions but also be used as a good research tool to find information and do research. The majority of students who found social media distracting also found their studies being affected negatively. One student went so far to see this as the reason for his academic failure: *"Always chatting caused me to fail; I learnt my lesson and started reducing social media"*.

The Forethought and Performance Phases. In the forethought phase, during task analysis, students do strategic planning to prepare for the performance phase. These plans are implemented in the performance phase through the self-control process. The performance phase also includes structuring the environment to maximize concentration and focus during the learning activity.

The answers indicated that the respondents employ a number of social media management strategies to prepare themselves for learning activities. Only two respondents indicated that they have no social media management technique. The social media regulation techniques employed by the respondents were divided into three different categories: limiting access through technological functions, limiting access through physical removal strategies, and limiting access through willpower. Will-power has a role to play in each category, but some students believe that will-power (or self-discipline) alone is sufficient. Table 3 presents these categories together with quotes that describe how the strategies are implemented in the performance phase.

All in all our interviews seem to have *created awareness* about the problem, as two respondents indicated that they had never thought of managing their social media use before, but that they will definitely consider it for the future, given its distractive nature.

6   Discussion

Although students have a number of strategies to manage their social media use, some of them find it challenging to keep to their social media management plans during the performance phase: *"I thought that turning off the notifications would help, but I keep going back on the app just to check if I have any messages"*. Students also seemed perplexed by the hold social media has on them: *"You're not sure why you do it, but it seems to have a hold on us"*. They described a

Table 2. Reported effects of social media usage on learning activities

Effect	Quotes
Positive	"I think it has, because you have academic WhatsApp groups where they post papers and advice so it really helps"
	"WhatsApp I use it a lot for academic purposes to communicate with students about work, so that would have more of a positive effect"
	"YouTube has assisted as well as Google Drive to back up information. My academic studies have improved because of social media"
Negative	"It's just that sometimes you can procrastinate and end up on your phone a bit longer than you should"
	"Procrastination is already a problem for me and social media is just a thing that makes it worse"
	"I would find myself googling people and pictures"
	"I end up focusing on watching YouTube videos and watching series instead of studying, and you find yourself on Facebook, and then one hour later you say: oh shucks, I was supposed to be done with something else"
Positive and Negative	"… it has helped me with getting notes from different students, and has also affected me negatively when I get caught up logged into Instagram or looking at memes"
	"… it is a bit of both, positively and negatively. Sometimes I use social media to get notes from friends, and sometimes it distracts me when I study and people want to talk to me"
	"There is a negative and there is a positive: Negatively because I get super-distracted and I don't cover as much work as I should have; positively because I get news feeds on Twitter and they usually tell me what's going on around South Arica and provide me with news"
None	"No, it has not affected my academic studies"
	"No it has not; I can manage my social time"

certain helplessness using words like being 'caught up' or being 'trapped': "It limits me from doing things that I should be doing in reality; I get so caught up in the virtual world"— "I usually find myself back in the trap".

Students tried to explain the enticing nature of social media in different ways. In accordance with existing literature they noticed FOMO—see [13]—as well as the habit-forming nature of social media and mobile devices—see [1,11]. Some students were explicitly aware of the concept of FOMO and mentioned this term in their answers, whereas others circumscribed it as the need to keep up to date with what is going in others' lives.

Table 3. Categories, forethought strategies, and implementation

Theme	Forethought phase strategies: quotes	Performance phase implementation: quotes
Technological functions	"Switch off the WIFI", "switch off data", "do not buy data", "impose a data limit", "shutdown device", "mute conversations", "turn off notifications", "delete applications", "delete accounts", "activate flight-mode", "set profile on do-not-disturb", "switch off device", "put phone on silent", "disassemble device", "remove battery"	"Sometimes I switch off my data or put my phone on 'silent'. Also, when I get notifications I check them but I decide whether or not it's important enough to attend to"
		"I try to save my time by disabling my mobile data or switch off my phone. Sometimes I delete, if it's exam time"
		"For me it's hiding my phone and disassembling my phone. Taking out the battery, hiding one part in one room and another part in another room. That way I'm too lazy to get up and find all those pieces and I just don't remember where they are. I'll remember when I'm disassembling my room"
Physical measure	"Remove device from room", "put device far away", "leave device at home"	"I try to leave my phone at home before coming to campus if I know that I have a busy day or a test to write"
Willpower	"Will-power", "mind over matter", "manage my social time", "prioritise", "ground myself", "manage", "setting a time limit"	"I set an alarm to study then another alarm for the amount of time I should be using social media"
		"... you firstly just need to arrange your time schedule and also be aware of the fact that it's time-consuming and distractive"

Students refer to their social media as part of their habits, whereas one student observed that his/her social media use is triggered by certain events or environments: *"For me it is environmental; you've created habits of when you check it, and in what situations you check social media more than others"*. Similarly, Aagaard mentioned the embodied nature of social media habits by saying that logging onto Facebook is *"in ones' fingers"* [1](p. 91). The embodiment of the habit is facilitated by the physical device, as illustrated by one respondent: *"I found that one of the useful things is not to download social media applications on your phone, because your phone is quite invasive. So your phone tends to be very easily accessible. You usually always have it with you, so it would be the least form of resistance to access social media"*. Similarly, Oulasvirta (et al.) mentioned the strong checking habit associated with mobile devices [11]. They determined that checking behavior (brief times spent on the device) becomes a habit. In [11], users checked devices briefly, focusing on one application only, whereas some only viewed ('touched') the home screen for one second. Motivators for this habit are listed as entertainment, killing time, and awareness. In our study students reported similar checking behavior with social media with very similar reasons for doing it.

Finally, we argue that another factor making self-regulation of social media challenging during learning activities is the fact that mobile phones and social media merge traditionally separate worlds in one device or one platform. Students mentioned diverse uses of social media such as maintaining and building business connections, educational purposes, entertainment and communication. They knew that social media can be distracting, but they still wanted access to some of the communication functionalities—e.g., only switching off 'data' when studying because of still wanting to be able receive calls on the phone at the same time—or they wanted to have the device nearby to do research on the internet without being 'pulled' into other content: *"I need to do work on the internet; social media is there on the internet and is just a click away. It is distractive because most of the work done nowadays requires the internet, so, if you wander off, you can easily find yourself on social media"*. This implies that students should invest more effort in the self-reflection phase (to evaluate their own actions around social media) and the forethought phase (to do a thorough task analysis to decide which parts of the task require social media access or not) in order to prepare themselves for their learning activities.

This paper can be seen as an initial exploration of the topic. A more diverse sample (e.g. respondents from different academic faculties, different ethnic groups, different home languages, etc.) might have provided more insightful results. Future research avenues might include focusing on those students already managing their social media usage well: which specific self-regulation skills do they possess? Other research possibilities include quantitative studies to determine the influence of various parameters and student 'characteristics' on social media management (e.g. intrinsic motivation, FOMO), etc.

7 Conclusion

Our data analysis shows that our respondents are aware of the distracting nature of social media and the impact on their academic performance. Most of them have a number of strategies to manage their social media use. The strategies all relate to limiting or stopping access to social media. These strategies were categorized as limiting access through physical measures (e.g. leave phone at home), technological functions (e.g. uninstall app, switch off data), and will-power. Will-power has a role to play in each category, but some students believed will-power or self-discipline alone to be sufficient. A smaller number of students did not find social media to be a distraction and welcome its entertainment value to 'kill time' as well as its information sharing value to stay informed and connected. We found that the social media self-regulation is particularly challenging because of the emotional rewards gained from social media usage, the habit-forming nature of social media and mobile device usage, and the merging of academic and social worlds in these platforms. In line with [1] we think that it is wise for lecturers and institutions to provide guidelines to students to manage their social media usage. Indeed students should be informed of specific tools to help them to manage their social media use: at home students can use internet distraction management tools like 'OffTime', the 'News Feed Eradicator', 'Forest' or the more recent 'Hold' app. By using 'Hold', for example, students can earn points for every 20 min without social media, to be exchanged for goods and services from partners like 'Amazon' or their app marketplace. 'Hold' is already used by just under half of all students in Norway, Denmark, and Sweden [17]. In our study most students were not even aware of the existence of such apps. Since social media are currently 'the norm' as indicated by one student—*"WhatsApp is always there; that's a norm; if you text me now I will reply now"*—students should be made aware of the need for self-regulation of social media use during learning activities as well as possible strategies for doing it.

References

1. Aagaard, J.: Drawn to distraction: a qualitative study of off-task use of educational technology. Comput. Educ. **87**, 90–97 (2015)
2. Baumeister, R.F., Vohs, K.D.: Self-regulation, ego depletion, and motivation. Soc. Pers. Psychol. Compass **1**(1), 115–128 (2007)
3. Braun, V., Clarke, V.: Using thematic analysis in psychology. Qual. Res. Psychol. **3**(2), 77–101 (2006)
4. David, P., Kim, J.H., Brickman, J.S., Ran, W., Curtis, C.M.: Mobile phone distraction while studying. New Media Soc. **17**(10), 1661–1679 (2015)
5. van den Eijnden, R.J.J.M., Lemmens, J.S., Valkenburg, P.M.: The social media disorder scale. Comput. Hum. Behav. **61**, 478–487 (2016)
6. Fitzgerald, B., Howcroft, D.: Competing dichotomies in IS research and possible strategies for resolution. In: Proceedings of the international conference on Information systems. ICIS 1998, pp. 155–164 (1998)
7. Goldstuck, A., du Plessis, T.: SA social media landscape 2017. http://www.worldwideworx.com/wp-content/uploads/2016/09/Social-Media-2017-Executive-Summary.pdf
8. Lau, W.W.F.: Effects of social media usage and social media multitasking on the academic performance of university students. Comput. Hum. Behav. **68**, 286–291 (2017)

9. Mao, J.: Social media for learning: a mixed methods study on high school students' technology affordances and perspectives. Comput. Hum. Behav. **33**, 213–223 (2014)
10. Nadkarni, A., Hofmann, S.G.: Why do people use Facebook? Personality Individ. Differ. **52**(3), 243–249 (2012)
11. Oulasvirta, A., Rattenbury, T., Ma, L., Raita, E.: Habits make smartphone use more pervasive. Pers. Ubiquit. Comput. **16**(1), 105–114 (2012)
12. Panadero, E., Alonso-Tapia, J.: How do students self-regulate? Review of Zimmerman's cyclical model of self-regulated learning. An. Psicol. **30**(2), 450–462 (2014)
13. Przybylski, A.K., Murayama, K., de Haan, C.R., Gladwell, V.: Motivational, emotional, and behavioral correlates of fear of missing out. Comput. Hum. Behav. **29**(4), 1841–1848 (2013)
14. Qwerty Digital: The digital landscape in South Africa 2017. https://qwertydigital. co.za/wp-content/uploads/2017/08/Digital-Statistics-in-South-Africa-2017-Repo rt.pdf
15. Rosen, L.D., Carrier, L.M., Cheever, N.A.: Facebook and texting made me do it: media-induced task-switching while studying. Comput. Hum. Behav. **29**(3), 948–958 (2013)
16. Rouis, S., Limayem, M., Salehi-Sangari, E.: Impact of Facebook Usage on Students' academic achievement: role of self-regulation and trust. Electron. J. Res. Educ. Psychol. **9**(3), 961–994 (2011)
17. Tamblyn, T.: Hold app cures smartphone addiction by rewarding users with freebies. https://www.huffingtonpost.co.uk/entry/hold-app-cures-smartphone-addict ion-by-rewarding-users-with-freebies_uk_5a97bed7e4b09c872bb14a44 (2018)
18. Terry, C.A., Mishra, P., Roseth, C.J.: Preference for multitasking, technological dependency, student metacognition, and pervasive technology use: an experimental intervention. Comput. Hum. Behav. **65**, 241–251 (2016)
19. Tess, P.A.: The role of social media in higher education classes (real and virtual): a literature review. Comput. Hum. Behav. **29**(5), a60–a68 (2013)
20. Wang, C., Lee, M.K.O., Hua, Z.: A theory of social media dependence: evidence from microblog users. Decis. Support Syst. **69**, 40–49 (2015)
21. Zimmerman, B.J.: Becoming a self-regulated learner: an overview. Theory Into Pract. **41**(2), 64–70 (2002)
22. Zimmerman, B.J., Moylan, A.R.: Self-regulation: where metacognition and motivation intersect. In: Handbook of Metacognition in Education, pp. 299–316. Routledge (2009)

Academia and Careers

Research Barriers Experienced by South African Academics in Information Systems and Computer Science

Dhriven Hamlall and Jean-Paul Van Belle[(✉)] [iD]

Centre for IT and National Development, University of Cape Town,
Cape Town, South Africa
jean-paul.vanbelle@uct.ac.za

Abstract. Information Systems (IS) and Computer Science (CS) research can provide a much-needed knowledge foundation for social development, innovation and economic growth. The purpose of this paper is to determine the main research productivity barriers that affect South African academics in IS and CS; to gain an insight into what motivates or incentivizes IS and CS researchers to conduct research and publish their work; and to identify what changes are necessary in order to increase IS and CS researchers' productivity. There were 38 respondents in this study. The main research barriers identified were: lack of adequate time for research due to too many simultaneous tasks, too many other official duties and teaching. Poor institutional support and lack of funding, reward, compensation or recognition also emerged as significant research barriers. The results from this paper aim to positively influence government policies with regards to research productivity in SA HEIs. The details of this study are available to all researchers, possibly to lobby their institutions.

Keywords: Research productivity · Research barriers
Research incentives · Research policy

1 Introduction

There are several highly productive researchers in African 'flagship' universities. Despite this, research productivity of universities in Africa is still quite behind in comparison to other universities in the world [2,9]. Academic research can contribute hugely to African societies. Research into topics such as health care, education and science and technology in Sub-Saharan African universities can provide a much-needed knowledge foundation for social development, innovation and economic growth [11]. Universities need their academics to increase their research productivity to enhance competitiveness, visibility and institutional prestige [18]. Sadly, South African (SA) university research funding has declined steadily over time in real terms [11]. Consequently, researchers spend

© Springer Nature Switzerland AG 2019
S. Kabanda et al. (Eds.): SACLA 2018, CCIS 963, pp. 95–107, 2019.
https://doi.org/10.1007/978-3-030-05813-5_7

more time looking for and applying for research funding due to increased competition and an overall reduced envelope of resources [5].

This paper focusses specifically on the Information Systems (IS) and Computer Science (CS) community of researchers. Our study has the following objectives:

- To determine the main research productivity barriers that affect South African academics in IS and CS. The 'Research Productivity Factors Framework' [2] was chosen to guide the research because it combines the different research productivity factors relating to the general factors affecting the research productivity of university academics.
- To gain an insight into what motivates or incentivizes researchers to conduct research and publish their work in the IS and CS fields.
- To identify what measures can be taken to increase IS and CS researchers' productivity.

2 Related Work

2.1 Research Productivity in South Africa

South African universities face many challenges with respect to research productivity. In SA Higher Education Institutions (HEIs) only a third of the permanent staff have doctoral degrees [3]. South Africa faces the challenge of retaining their researchers and scientists. There is approximately one researcher in South Africa for every thousand members in the South African workforce [13]. Researchers play a crucial role in knowledge production and sharing and should be recognised beyond the confining walls of their institutions [12].

Some of the challenges faced in conducting research in Africa are the costs of gathering data, the small number of PhD graduates and the non-existence of incentives for international publications [7]. The most disquieting issue is that most of the university lecturers do not have PhD degrees. Other areas of concern are that there is a failure among academics to distinguish between high-quality international journal publications and lower-quality locally accredited journals, which affects their incentive to publish [12].

2.2 Research Productivity in Computer Science

The collaboration level, number of research outputs and number of active authors in the Computer Science field is not as high as other scientific fields [6]. However, the number of scientific publications in Computer Science has increased greatly over the past few years. This stems from the pressure on academic researchers to publish in order to acquire promotions and qualify for applications for grants or projects [4]. Conference publications have dominated journal publications in CS research [17] although not all researchers are comfortable with conference papers being a primary means of publication in CS research [15].

Some CS researchers believe that different sub-areas should follow different publishing practices. CS sub-areas favour and value conferences and journal publications differently; for example, bioinformatics seems more journal-oriented, whereas computer architecture seems more conference-oriented [15]. It is also plausible that CS sub-areas dealing mainly with data (such as IPCV) are more likely to have greater productivity than areas in which evaluation procedures require users (such as HCI), programmers (such as SE), and organisations (such as MIS) [15]. Researcher productivity in these human- and organisation-based areas are bound by the difficulty of carrying out the empirical evaluations the fields require [15].

2.3   Research Productivity in Information Systems

Information Systems (IS) is an important field to conduct research in, as digital innovations are emerging at a rapid pace. These digital innovations include, but are not limited to, digital infrastructures, advanced middle-ware layers, and mobile and ubiquitous technologies [14]. With the rapid advancement of a new and complex array of information systems and technologies, organisations continually face complexities with regards to the understanding of IS and IT capabilities [16]. Social media and the availability of a wide range of IT-enabled devices have now made IT an integral part of organisations and individuals. Organisations face challenges in understanding the practices, usages, and the impact of IS and IT [16].

Departments and research groups can reduce barriers to research productivity by improving their organisation's research culture [5], whereby *"researchers affiliated with high-status institutions published, on average, more articles in the top five IS journals than researchers affiliated with middle-status institutions and low-status institutions"* [8]. Their study also found a positive relationship between academic affiliation and research productivity in terms of quantity and quality in IS. They suggest that HEIs should grow and maintain a faculty of productive researchers, by creating an organisational culture that encourages, promotes, and remunerates research productivity. Organisational factors such as incentives and support for research, linked with greater research expectations appear to be efficacious motivators to produce research [8].

2.4   Research Productivity Factors

Collaboration between researchers allows the sharing and exchange of knowledge and techniques, which help to improve research productivity [1]. Research outputs involving collaborations between different countries, institutions, or disciplines generally have a higher visibility and attract more citations than papers with single authors [6]. In South Africa, scientific collaboration is an accepted practice among scientists: research institutes appear to favour domestic collaboration, whereas universities favour international collaboration, despite the lack of encouragement from the government [13]. However, collaborative research does not seem to be encouraged in South Africa under the contemporary scientific system [12]. The South African New Funding Framework (NFF) does not encourage collaboration with researchers who are not affiliated with a South African HEI [19]. Also, if a paper is co-authored, the subsidy is split between all the authors; thus researchers may opt for the choice of single-authored research and publications [12].

Age and gender have also been found to affect average research productivity. Research experience and self-efficacy positively impact the research outputs of academics [3]. Studies conducted in the American context found that for almost every age group in their respective data sets, men publish more than women [10]. According to [10], research productivity tends to increase with age, reaching a peak before gradually lessening off towards retirement. However, in [12] we can find the opposite claim, namely that the productivity of academics and researchers declines with age.

ICT adoption also has an impact on research productivity. ICT (Inf. and Communic. Techn.) with training increases researcher performance in terms of research productivity [2].

The use of *incentives* such as monetary rewards in academia can help to improve the advancement of core academic activities such as teaching, supervision of postgraduate students and academic research [18]. Publications are important as they help researchers to achieve a permanent academic appointment and promotions [5]. The current system being used to encourage research productivity at SA HEIs is largely intended to be a financial reward-based system [19]. Government subsidies to HEIs depend on the subsidy granted by the DHET for publications in officially recognised journals. At most of the HEIs in SA, authors receive a fraction of the total subsidy [19]. Following the 'publish or perish' culture and having strong publication incentives could create a focus on quantity and productivity rather than on the quality and relevance to a research topic [5].

These and a number of other factors have been summarized in the 'Research Productivity Factors Framework' in the study done by [2] as shown in Fig. 1.

3   Method

We adopted a positivist paradigm and used a survey approach. A questionnaire was used as a predetermined and highly structured data collection technique. The research time frame was cross-sectional. Our purpose was to determine the main research productivity barriers that affect South African academics in IS and CS. The main *research questions* are the following:

- What are the main research barriers that affect researchers from conducting quality research and publishing their work in IS and CS?
- What motivates or incentivizes researchers to conduct research and publish their work in IS and CS?
- What would IS and CS researchers change in their environment, if they could, to increase their research productivity?

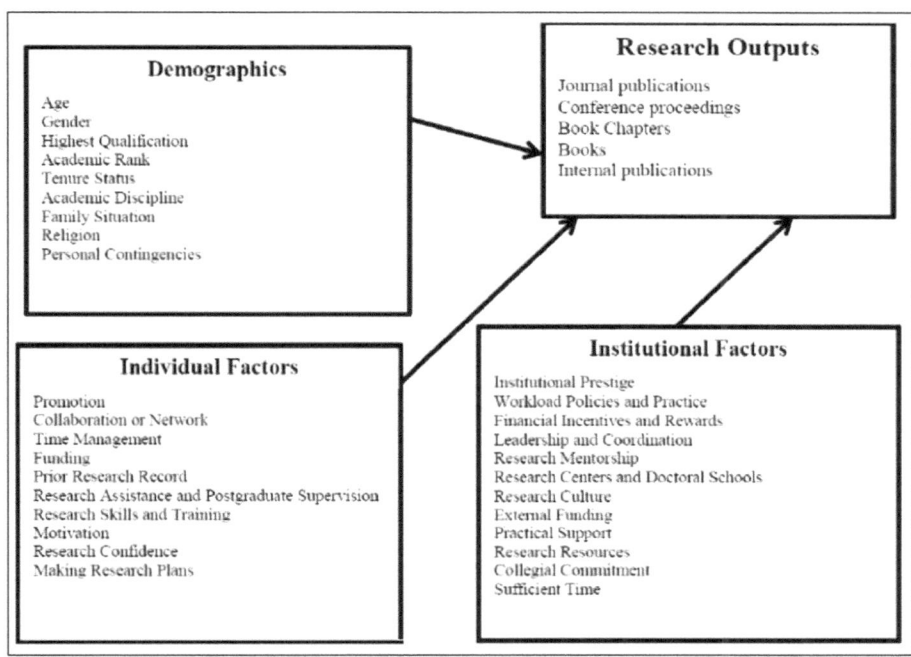

Fig. 1. Factors potentially influencing research productivity [2]

The questionnaire was designed based on the 'Research Productivity Factors Framework' adapted from [2]. Additional open-ended questions were added and the instrument was also aligned with that used in a collaborative study being conducted in India. Thematic analysis was used to identify the main themes in the open-ended questions. The sample included researchers and academics at Southern African Higher Education Institutes. Potential participants were approached using the Southern African Computer Lecturers' Association (SACLA) and South African Institute of Computer Scientists and Information Technologists (SAICSIT) mailing lists. Additional researchers and academics email addresses were taken from various university websites.

4   Data Analysis

4.1   Descriptive Statistics

The sample consisted of 38 respondents with 25 respondents being male and 11 respondents being female. Two respondents indicated 'prefer not to answer'. Respondents were separated according to their departments: Information Systems (IS), Computer Science (CS) and Information Technology (IT). The number of respondents per department was 19, 11 and 8 respectively. Information Technology (IT) was one of the disciplines that emerged from the data set.

Respondents were asked to indicate their percentage of time spent on teaching, research and administrative tasks: researchers spend most of their time on teaching (42% of their time) followed by research (35%) and then administrative tasks (26%).

4.2   Research Barriers

Various factors potentially preventing researchers from conducting quality research were listed and respondents answered using a Likert scale. The 16 highest rated barriers are shown in Fig. 2, sorted by average rating. Lack of adequate time for research due to too many simultaneous tasks; lack of adequate time for research due to too many other official duties; and lack of adequate time for research due to teaching appear to be the top 3 factors that prevent researchers from conducting quality research. All other barriers were, in fact, *not* rated by more than half the respondents as barriers. The complete list of possible factors presented to the respondents is provided in Appendix A: Table 5.

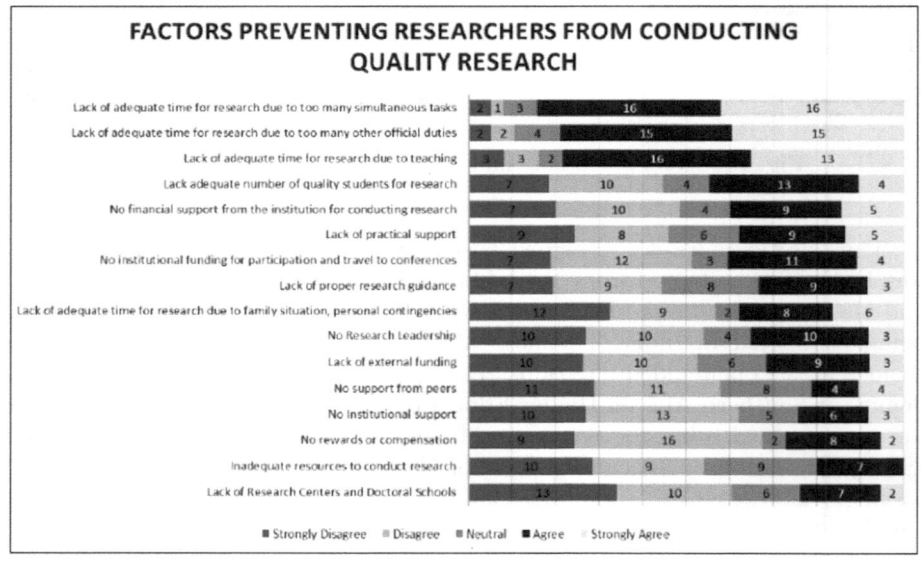

Fig. 2. 16 factors preventing researchers from conducting quality research (high-low)

The respondents were also asked in an open question based on what they considered to be their main research barrier, apart from work load. The main research barriers that emerged from this question could be classified under the themes of lack of time, lack of support and guidance, lack of funding, lack of collaboration, a lack of postgraduate students and university politics: Table 1.

Some specific responses under the theme, Lack of support and guidance were *"poor practical support in HR and Finance"*, *"lack of a personal assistant"*,

Table 1. Main research barriers (open-ended question)

Main barrier	IS	CS	IT	Total
Lack of time	7	2	2	11
Lack of support and guidance	3	1	3	7
Lack of funding	1	2	1	4
Lack of postgraduate students	1	2	-	3
University politics	1	2	-	3
Lack of collaboration	2	-		2

and *"lack of research champions"* (i.e. professors in our department and campus to help and guide us). University politics (which was an unexpected barrier in this research) did emerge as the main (number one) research barrier for two CS researchers and one IS researcher. Other unique responses as main research barriers were *"the research structure"*, *"limited research experience"*, *"bureaucratic ethical clearance processes"* and *"professional service"* (i.e. review papers, examine theses, journal editor, conference organisation, and the like).

4.3   Motivators or Incentives to Conduct and Publish Research

There were 35 valid responses when asked about their main motivator or incentive to publish. Five researchers gave more than one explanation as to what motivates or incentivizes them to conduct research and publish their work. 'Intrinsic motivation' was the most frequent response by researchers as to *what motivates or incentivizes them to conduct research and publish their work.* One IS researcher stated: *"I enjoy research, I consider myself a researcher by nature"*. Other frequent responses were grouped into 'making a difference (contribution) to knowledge', 'personal recognition (promotion)', and 'collaboration'. An IT researcher stated that she is motivated or incentivized *"to improve organisational work processes and for personal satisfaction to know that I have made a difference to make the world a little bit better"*. An IS researcher indicated that he is motivated or incentivized by *"growing African scholars to increase African standing globally"*. Table 2 indicates the frequency of responses by the researchers (per department) under the following themes. Interestingly, CS respondents seem less motivated by 'knowledge contribution' or 'interest' in their field, whereas IT researchers are more focussed on personal recognition or promotion. Of course, a larger sample would be needed to generalise these statements.

4.4   Desired Environmental Change to Increase Research Productivity

Researchers were asked, in an open question, about the key change to be effected in their environment to increase their research productivity. Table 3 indicates the responses which we grouped under the following themes: *reduce administrative*

Table 2. Main research motivator (open-ended question)

Main motivator	IS	CS	IT	Total
Intrinsic motivation	5	4	1	10
Personal/recognition/promotion	3	2	4	9
Growth of others	2	1	3	6
Knowledge contribution	5	-	1	6
Collaboration	2	2	-	4
Extrinsic motivation	1	2	-	3
Interest	1	-	1	2

duties, reduce teaching, more collaboration, increase time for research, proper guidelines, more funding for research and quicker processes. Interestingly, CS respondents did not rate increased time as important as the IS/IT researchers.

Table 3. Key change in environment which would increase research productivity

Proposed change	IS	CS	IT	Total
Reduce administrative duties	4	4	1	9
Increase time for research	5	1	2	8
More collaboration	4	2	-	6
Proper guidelines	1	1	2	4
Quicker processes	2	-	1	3
Reduce teaching load	1	-	1	2
More research funding	1	1	-	2

Some specific responses under the theme *reduce administrative duties* were: *"less admin—and the only way we would accomplish that would be by finding good admin staff who actually want to and do the things they are paid to do. At our institution most of the admin staff seem to be paid on the basis of how much of their work they can pass on to the academics"*, and *"change current research admin staff or train them in how to administer research-related efforts"*. Specific responses under the theme *more collaboration* were: *"stronger collaborations with other peers from other universities"* and *"increase number of events to share research internally to build internal cross-disciplinary links"*. There was one unique response as to what a researcher would change in the environment, if possible, to increase their research productivity: *"less bureaucracy"*.

4.5   Desired Policy Change to Increase Research Productivity

Only 25 respondents answered what policy changes they wanted to see in order to increase their research outputs, with some giving more than one answer: Table 4. Surprisingly, only IS/IT researchers punted for more funding (incentives) and none of the CS researchers. IS researchers, on the other hand, did not indicate anything related to research culture.

Table 4. Key policy change which would increase research productivity

Change policies w.r.t.	IS	CS	IT	Total
Funding/incentives	5	-	3	8
Defining/understanding what counts as 'research output'	3	2	-	5
Research culture?	-	3	1	4
Consistent/relevant/quality research?	2	-	1	3
Division of duties?	2	1	-	3
No comment/all is fine?	1	2	-	3
Quicker processes?	1	1	-	2
Appropriate staff-student-ratios?	2	-	-	2

Two noteworthy unique responses from IS researchers with regards to policy changes were: *"policies must recognise that research is a primary component of the overall chain of value-generating activity that leads to effective education; research must be seen in that context"*, and *"the university uses an IPMS app-roach that is not in line with research. The IPMS treats each employee as a unit of production"*.[1]

5   Discussion

The main research barriers identified in this paper that prevent researchers from conducting quality research and publishing their work are lack of adequate time for research due to too many simultaneous tasks; lack of adequate time for research due to too many other official duties; and lack of adequate time for research due to teaching. Poor organisational or institutional support and lack of funding/reward/compensation/recognition also emerged as significant research barriers. Researchers (but only males) indicated that there is a lack of institu-tional funding for participation and travel to conferences and that there is a lack of financial support from the institution for conducting research. These results are further backed up by [5] which states that researchers spend a great deal of

---

[1] IPMS = 'integrated performance management system'.

time looking for and applying for financial funding due to increased competition and a lack of resources. According to the literature, lack of collaboration appears to be one of the significant research barriers that researchers face; however, lack of peer support/collaboration is ranked last. South African researchers do not see lack of collaboration as one of their main research barriers.

We found that intrinsic motivation is the main reason why researchers conduct research and aim to publish their work. This was an expected finding. However, there is always pressure for academic researchers to publish their work which is necessary for promotions [4]. In South Africa, career advancement and promotions for academic researchers are attached to publications [12]. The second finding (motivated by recognition or promotion) is in alignment with the literature as it indicates that researchers conduct research for personal reasons, i.e. for recognition and promotion. Moreover, organisational factors such as incentives and support for research appear to be efficacious motivators to produce research [8]. The goal of research and publishing is to combine knowledge and to advance the truth in an area of study [5]. There were a number of responses under 'making a difference/contribution to knowledge'. This reinforces the point that researchers do not only conduct research for monetary gain.

We found that researchers would prefer (in order of priority) reduced administrative burdens, increased time for research, more collaboration, proper guidelines, quicker processes, lower teaching loads and more funding for research, to increase their research productivity. It would make sense that researchers would want to collaborate more as through collaboration researchers share and exchange knowledge and techniques which help to improve research productivity [1]. More funding for research would improve research productivity [11], lack of funding has major impacts on the nature and sustainability of research capacity and productivity. Increasing time for research by removing administrative burdens and excessive teaching loads are possible solutions that have been highlighted in this study frequently as a way to improve research productivity.

6   Conclusion

The importance of academic research cannot be over-emphasised. Academic research can contribute significantly to African societies. Research into topics such as education and science and technology can provide a much-needed knowledge foundation for social development, innovation and economic growth. The main purpose of this paper was to determine the major research productivity barriers that affect South African academics in IS and CS. The main research barriers identified were: lack of adequate time for research due to too many simultaneous tasks; lack of adequate time for research due to too many other official duties; and lack of adequate time for research due to teaching. Lack of funding/reward/compensation/recognition and poor organisational or institutional support also emerged as significant research barriers. We also found that intrinsic motivation is the main reason why researchers conduct research and aim to publish their work. Researchers are also motivated because they want to make a difference and contribute to the knowledge in their field. Financial reasons and collaboration did emerge as motivators, but these were not the most frequent motivators.

Finally, our study indicated that researchers would prefer (in order of priority) reduced administration burdens, more time for research, more collaboration, proper guidelines, quicker processes, lower teaching loads and more funding for research, to increase their research productivity. Researchers also indicated that they would like policy changes in how research is funded and incentivized in South Africa.

The validity and generalisability of the research is limited by the relatively small number of responses: only 38 researchers responded. However, the population of IS and CS in South Africa is relatively small and the sample probably represents more than 10% of the research-'population' in our field. Interviews would have provided more insight and uncovered more complex issues. Future research might want to do a mixed method approach incorporating interviews or focus groups. Hopefully future research, perhaps institutionalized by means of one of the regular local conferences (e.g. SACLA or SAICSIT) can provide a longitudinal perspective and also increase the sample size to provide further validity and confirm generalisability of our findings.

Some institutional recommendations emanating from this research would relate to freeing up more time for researchers, e.g. by hiring research assistants and statisticians to help IS and CS researchers in their teaching and research or reducing administrative burdens. Also, the HEIs need to create an organisational culture that encourages, promotes, and rewards research productivity in IS, CS and IT. A national policy recommendation is the need to look at the funding, especially in IS and IT where lack of time combines with lack of funding as significant barriers; forcing researchers to spend more of their scarce time on chasing research funding instead of actually doing research seems to be counter-productive.

A   All Research Barriers Scores by Respondants

For the following data Table 5, these five Likert scale values are defined: L1 = 'strongly disagree', L2 = 'disagree', L3 = 'neutral', L4 = 'agree', L5 = 'strongly agree'. Moreover, 'average' is abbreviated as 'avg'.

Table 5. Key change in environment to increase research productivity

Factor possibly impeding research	Avg	L1	L2	L3	L4	L5
Lack of time due to too many simultaneous tasks	4.13	2	1	3	16	16
Lack of time due to too many other official duties	4.03	2	2	4	15	15
Lack of time due to teaching	3.89	3	3	2	16	13
Lack adequate nr. of quality students for research	2.92	7	10	4	13	4
No financial support from the institution	2.86	7	10	4	9	5
No institutional funding for conference travel	2.81	7	12	3	11	4
Lack of practical support	2.81	9	8	6	9	5
Lack of proper research guidance	2.78	7	9	8	9	3
Lack of time due to family/personal situation	2.65	12	9	2	8	6
No Research Leadership	2.62	10	10	4	10	3
Lack of external funding	2.61	10	10	6	9	3
No support from peers	2.45	11	11	8	4	4
No Institutional support	2.43	10	13	5	6	3
No rewards or compensation	2.41	9	16	2	8	2
Inadequate resources to conduct research	2.37	10	9	9	7	–
Lack of Research Centers/Doctoral Schools	2.34	13	10	6	7	2
Lack of collaboration and networking	2.3	14	8	6	8	1
Difficult to develop research plans	2.27	12	12	5	7	1
Not updated about latest research techniques	2.11	13	15	4	5	1
Lack adequate software tools	2.05	15	13	4	5	1
Limited research experience	2.03	16	13	2	6	1
Lack of inner drive to conduct research	1.97	18	10	5	3	2
Poor research rules and regulations	1.97	21	6	2	6	2
Lack adequate research laboratory facilities	1.81	19	12	1	4	1
Research is not part of annual promotions	1.78	23	5	4	4	1
No research emphasis in the institution	1.78	18	13	1	3	1
Lack interest in research	1.78	19	11	3	1	2
Lack research skills	1.74	19	13	3	3	–
Lack adequate library information resources	1.68	18	16	1	1	1
Not part of my job description	1.5	26	9	1	–	2
We are not a research institution	1.33	23	5	1	1	–

References

1. Balasubramani, R., Parameswaran, R.: Mapping the research productivity of Banaras Hindu University: a scientometric study. J. Theor. Appl. Inf. Technol. **59**(2), 367–371 (2014)
2. Basak, S.K.: A model using ICT adoption and training to improve the research productivity of academics. Doctoral Dissertations: Department of Information Technology, Faculty of Accounting and Informatics, Durban University of Technology (2014)

3. Callaghan, C.W., Coldwell, D.: Research versus teaching satisfaction and research productivity. Int. J. Sci. Educ. **7**(1), 203–218 (2014)
4. Cavero, J.M., Vela, B., Caceres, P.: Computer science research: more production, less productivity. Scientometrics **98**(3), 2103–2111 (2014)
5. Eikebrokk, T., Busch, P.A.: Progress and stewardship in information systems research: addressing barriers to cumulation through active process ownership. In: AMCIS 2016 Proceedings of 22nd Americas Conference on Information Systems, paper #7, San Diego (2016). https://aisel.aisnet.org/amcis2016/Phil/Presentations/7/
6. Franceschet, M.: Collaboration in computer science: a network science approach. J. Assoc. Inf. Sc. Technol. **62**(10), 1992–2012 (2011)
7. Lages, C.R., Pfajfar, G., Shoham, A.: Challenges in conducting and publishing research on the middle east and Africa in leading journals. Int. Mark. Rev. **32**(1), 52–77 (2015)
8. Long, R., Crawford, A., White, M., Davis, K.: Determinants of faculty research productivity in information systems: an empirical analysis of the impact of academic origin and academic affiliation. Scientometrics **78**(2), 231–260 (2008)
9. Maassen, P.: Research productivity at flagship African universities. World University News, no. 357 (2015). https://www.chet.org.za/
10. Murray, M.: Predicting scientific research output at the University of KwaZulu-natal: research letter. S. Afr. J. Sci. **110**(3/4), 1–4 (2014)
11. Musiige, G., Maassen, P.: Faculty perceptions of the factors that influence research productivity at Makerere University. In: Knowledge Production and Contradictory Functions in African Higher Education, Ch. 6, pp. 109–127. African Minds (2015)
12. Sooryamoorthy, R.: Publication productivity and collaboration of researchers in South Africa: new empirical evidence. Scientometrics **98**(1), 531–545 (2014)
13. Sooryamoorthy, R.: Scientific collaboration in South Africa. S. Afr. J. Sci. **109**(5/6), 1–5 (2013)
14. Sørensen, C., Landau, J.S.: Academic agility in digital innovation research: the case of mobile ICT publications within information systems 2000–2014. J. Strateg. Inf. Syst. **24**(3), 158–170 (2015)
15. Vardi, M.Y.: Conferences vs. journals in computing research. Commun. ACM **52**(5), 5–5 (2009)
16. Venkatesh, V., Brown, S.A., Bala, H.: Bridging the qualitative-quantitative divide: guidelines for conducting mixed methods research in information systems. MIS Q. **37**(1), 21–54 (2013)
17. Wainer, J., Eckmann, M., Goldenstein, S., Rocha, A.: How productivity and impact differ across computer science subareas. Commun. ACM **56**(8), 67–73 (2013)
18. Wangenge-Ouma, G., Lutomiah, A., Langa, P.: Academic incentives for knowledge production in Africa: case studies of Mozambique and Kenya. In: Knowledge Production and Contradictory Functions in African Higher Education, Ch. 7, pp. 128–147. African Minds (2015)
19. Woodiwiss, A.J.: Publication subsidies: challenges and dilemmas facing South African researchers: editorial. Cardiovasc. J. Afr. **23**(8), 421–427 (2012)

Top IT Issues for Employers of South African Graduates

Jean-Paul Van Belle[1]([✉])(iD), Brenda Scholtz[2](iD), Kennedy Njenga[3],
Alexander Serenko[4], and Prashant Palvia[5]

[1] Centre for IT and National Development, University of Cape Town,
Cape Town, South Africa
jean-paul.vanbelle@uct.ac.za
[2] Department of Computing Sciences, Nelson Mandela University,
Port Elizabeth, South Africa
brenda.scholtz@mandela.ac.za
[3] Department of Applied Information Systems, University of Johannesburg,
Johannesburg, South Africa
knjenga@uj.ac.za
[4] Faculty of Business Administration, Lakehead University, Thunder Bay, Canada
aserenko@lakeheadu.ca
[5] Information Systems and Supply Chain Management, University of North Carolina,
Greensboro, USA
pcpalvia@uncg.edu

Abstract. Technology trends and challenges in industry today are pressurising higher education institutions to rethink their curricula design, particularly for IT programmes. The World IT Project was designed to examine important issues confronting IT employers in many parts of the world. The purpose of this paper is to critically analyse the findings of a survey of South African IT employees, particularly related to the top technical and organisational IT issues faced by IT management and other IT staff. The results obtained were compared to those previously reported in earlier years, and to those of other countries that participated in the World IT Project. We found that the top technical and organisational issues in South Africa are not necessarily those receiving the most hype; rather, bread-and-butter issues such as reliable, efficient IT infrastructure or enterprise application integration are key concerns: issues often receiving insufficient attention in our academic curricula. Another important finding with educational policy implications is that the IT skills shortage is of much higher priority in South Africa than in the developed world; this highlights the need for additional resources in IT education.

Keywords: IT issues · SA employers · IT curricula · IT skills shortage

1 Introduction and Research Questions

Recent technology trends in industry continue to affect the competitiveness of organisations globally. Graduates with the necessary skills and competencies

© Springer Nature Switzerland AG 2019
S. Kabanda et al. (Eds.): SACLA 2018, CCIS 963, pp. 108–123, 2019.
https://doi.org/10.1007/978-3-030-05813-5_8

capable of addressing these challenges will be highly sought-after [39]. Technological innovation continues to improve productivity in organisations; however, this could also lead to displacement of unskilled workers and graduates without the required competencies. Indeed, technology changes raise the concerns about the likely increase in technological unemployment and segmentation of the labour market. Studies have long shown that education plays an important role in technology developments and that educated and skilled graduates have a relative advantage in the use and implementation of new technology [3].

When considering the relationship between technology, skills and employment [39], the design of Information Technology (IT) programmes at universities becomes more critical. In India for instance, the IT industry employs close to 10 million workers, contributing to 67% of the market (US\$ 124–130 · 10^9), with an expected growth of 12–14% over 2017 and beyond [13]. In this regard Indian universities continue to explore ways to revise technology and engineering curricula in order to meet the changing needs of industry and society [32]. India is part of the 'BRICS' group of emerging nations which also includes South Africa. The majority of studies relating to technology and employment issues were conducted in more technology advanced countries and may thus be biased in their views. South Africa, as a developing country, may not face the same challenges as those regions, and research relating to contexts such as the ones found in Africa is thus needed.

This paper describes some aspects of a larger research project, the 'World IT Project'. It curbs the bias in Information Systems (IS) research towards American or Western views by means of a global study and a survey of the perceptions of IT staff in organisations [31]. The information captured pertained to organisational, technological and individual IT issues, and related these to cultural and organisational factors. This paper investigates a subsection of these issues and analyses the top technology and organisational IT issues faced by South African organisations. The research questions answered by this paper are:

– *What are the top technological and organisational IT issues reported by small, medium and large South African organisations?*
– *How do these issues differ from those reported in the international literature?*

2   Related Work

2.1   IT Graduate Employment: Supply and Demand Perspectives

Supply. There is consensus in South Africa that the lack of needed IT skills is one of the main issues many IT graduate employers face. Studies are now suggesting an increased imbalance between the supply side (effective graduates) and the demand side (IT graduate employers) for South African IT employment needs, with supply not adequately meeting demands [29]. The demand for skilled IT graduates in South Africa is continually mounting [7]. Though the number of IT graduates appears to be growing, IT employers are still constantly faced with the task of recruiting skilled graduates into their organisations [23]. Lotriet (et al.) have proposed a 'rethink' of how both universities and IT employers could cooperate towards solving the IT skills shortage that South Africa faces. The imbalance between supply and demand for IT graduates has motivated academics and educators to suggest new *curricula* [12], new *teaching styles* and techniques [35], as well as new *topics* [38] to close the gap between commercial needs and graduates' capabilities.

From a supply perspective, the Centre for Higher Education Transformation's findings on South Africa's education landscape suggest that the country has been experiencing high skill attrition rates coupled with insufficient capacity for adequate skill production [8]. Popescu highlighted the role of the South African government in the dynamics of structuring, regulating and financing the supply-side of higher education institutions [34].

Higher education continues to experience phenomenal changes that can be considered 'revolutionary' [2], wherein technology continues to play a big role. In the context of the 'information age', information has become a significant foundation for globalisation; its production is growing daily. Technology in education has been regarded as playing an important role in the information age [6]. Technological advances have paved the way for the restructuring of education and business models. Universities are under pressure to constantly revise approaches to education and curricula design for educating IT graduates with proper capabilities for the information age.[1] Modern education systems are therefore being redesigned with technology in mind. It is generally agreed that educating IT graduates is a challenge for higher education institutions. The notorious 'expectation gap' between industry needs and academic preparation has made the institutions the targets of severe criticism [1,33]. An important issue emerging in higher education is how to restructure programmes for 'continuous education' [33]. Due to the ever-changing skills needed in IT [9], part-time programmes should be designed that focus on continuous 'upskilling' of IT professionals.

Because of the role IT plays in education, studies have shown that higher education in South Africa (and other African countries) is technologically more marginalised than outside of the continent [40]. In this regard, African universities face problems of generating, accessing and disseminating information. This makes it even more difficult for them to respond to business challenges [34].

Demand. As a result of the changing educational landscape, many businesses now seek IT graduates who are conversant with emergent technological changes that can assist businesses' readiness in the '4th industrial age'. From a demand side and from the IT graduate employers' perspective, having an understanding of the critical IT issues is considered crucial in enabling these businesses to function more effectively [31]. This understanding can assist with effective IT graduate recruitment and the development of competitive IT policies and strategies. IT employers are prioritising to become pro-active w.r.t. attracting,

---

[1] Several papers on this topic can be found in the SACLA'2018 post-proceedings: see *this volume* of CCIS.

developing and retaining valuable talent, since this has a large impact on an organisation's success [16].

Employers now require qualified IT specialists with high expertise in networking, computing, and programming, and who are able to design, develop, and deploy pervasive computing systems and communication architectures for business sustainability [21]. These business requirements have motivated changes in the IT curriculum [22]. For example, *accounting* firms recommend that 'Big Data', information technology, and IS be integrated into accounting coursework to enable graduates to work in data-centric environments [36].

2.2   Issues Faced by IT Staff and Management (1994–2004)

Since 1980, surveys have been conducted annually with the aim of identifying the key IT issues faced by management. The Society for Information Management (SIM) spear-headed this research by outlining American issues with the hope of aiding IT executives globally. The first SIM study surveyed American organisations and identified key areas of technological investment reported by those organisations [4]. A comparative analysis of the top 10 issues faced by IT staff and management during 1994 and 2002 can be found in [15].

2.3   Issues Faced by IT Staff and Management (2005–2017)

Next we review the literature on issues faced by IT staff and management from 2005 to 2017. Our review includes organisational IT issues as well as specific technological and application issues in various countries.

Organisational IT Issues. A survey of 31 CIOs in South African organisations in 2006 revealed that the top five organisational IT issues were security and control, building a responsive IT infrastructure, IT value management, service delivery, and improving IS strategic planning [15]. In 2009, the SIM project extended the survey to include not only U.S.-American organisations but also several European and Chinese ones [24]. The issues are summarised in Table 1.

The top 10 IT management issues have remained relatively constant over time as management considerations evolve slowly under normal circumstances [24]. The 2016 SIM study [18] reported that the top 10 organisational IT issues were IT-business alignment, security and privacy, innovation, agility and flexibility (of IT), agility and flexibility (of business), cost reduction controls (business), cost reduction controls (IT), speed of IT delivery and time to market, strategic planning, as well as productivity and efficiency. Two issues that were in the top four for importance to organisations and to IT leaders in the two most recent SIM studies of 2015 [17] and 2016 [18] were IT and business alignment as well as security and privacy. These are briefly discussed below.

Table 1. Top 10 Org.-issues (top-down) for IT staff and management (2004–2016)

2004: USA [26]	2006: SA [15]	2009: USA, China, EU [24]	2014: USA, China, EU [17]	2016: USA, China, EU [18]
IT and business alignment	Security and control	Business productivity, cost reduction	IT and business alignment	IT and business alignment
Attracting, developing, retaining IT professionals	Building a responsive IT infrastructure	IT and business alignment	Security and privacy	Security and privacy
Security and privacy	IT value management	Business agility, speed to market	Business agility and flexibility	Innovation
IT strategic planning	Service delivery	Business process re-engineering	Business productivity	Agility and flexibility (IT)
Speed and agility	Improving IT strategic planning	IT cost reduction	IT time-to-market, speed of delivery	Agility and flexibility (business)
Government regulations	Disaster recovery	IT reliability and efficiency	IT value proposition in the business	Cost reduction controls (business)
Complexity reduction	Aligning IS organisation within the enterprise	IT strategic planning	Velocity of change in the business	Cost reduction controls (IT)
Measuring performance of IT organisation	Using IS for competitive advantage	Revenue-generating IT innovations	Innovation	Speed of IT delivery, time-to-market
Creating an information architecture	Effective use of data resources	Security and privacy	Business cost reduction, controls	Strategic planning (business)
IT governance	Developing and implementing an information architecture	CIO leadership role	Revenue-generating IT projects	Productivity, efficiency

Alignment of IT and Business. Alignment of IT and business is a persistent issue and elusive goal for IT management. Its importance is confirmed by its constant presence in the top 10 management issues since it first appeared in 1984 [10,17]. According to [11,37], while IT business alignment has improved globally, there is a strong correlation between the maturity of the alignment and an organisation's performance. One reason as to why it remains a consistent issue is due to ever-changing organisations, markets, economics, and technologies, which require alignment to be a continuous activity [17].

Security and Privacy. Organisations are prioritising on security and privacy issues due to the increase in high profile cybersecurity breaches [17]. Security and privacy have been a constant concern for management, remaining in the top 10 list since 2003 [25]. In 2015 there was a global shift in the importance of security and privacy, moving to 2nd position from previous years when it placed around 6th–9th [17]. This increase in importance was due to the large number of security breaches reported at Adobe, Community Health Systems, Experian, Facebook, Home Depot, Neiman Marcus, PF Chang, Target, Twitter, the U.S. Department of Homeland Security, the U.S. Federal Reserve Bank, etc.

Other Issues for the Organisation, IT Management and IT Employees reported as important are business agility and productivity. For an organisation to be relevant in today's competitive economy, business agility is essential for business growth [10]. Since 2009, business agility has ranked in the top three positions of management issues, moving to the 3rd place in 2015. This ongoing high rank suggests that the greater uncertainty and increasing pace of change that characterise the current times correspondingly increase the need for organisations to be more flexible and responsive to market, economic, regulatory, legal, and other changes [17]. IT Time-to-Market is an enabler of agility, productivity and the IT value proposition [20].

Since its introduction into the SIM IT Trends in 2007, business productivity has remained in the top 10 list of issues, which shows that organisations are still trying to 'do more with less'. The importance of business productivity varies, moving from the 7th place in 2008 to the 1st in 2009 on the list of management issues globally [10,25].

IT reliability and efficiency is an issue that has grown in importance due to the growing complexities of IT systems and ever-increasing reliance of business operations on IT [28]. This issue refers to the accuracy, timeliness and accessibility of the data and information delivered by IT [24]. In 2008, when it was introduced into the SIM survey, it ranked 8th. Its importance increased from 2009 to 2010 where it ranked 6th and 4th respectively. However, 2010 was its final year as a combined organisational concern; thereafter it was separated into two categories: IT reliability and IT efficiency.

Technological Issues. The SIM survey also reports on the top IT (i.e. technology) issues as perceived by the staff. These are listed in Table 2. The SIM survey of 2004 [26] identified the top six application and technology development issues as: security technologies, business intelligence (BI), business process management (BPM), Web Services, customer portals, and data synchronisation. Half of these technologies were new to the list of top developments.

The top five important technology investments reported by the most recent SIM study of 2016 [18] are analytics/BI/Big Data, application software development, (cyber)security, cloud computing, and customer relationship management (CRM). BI has remained as one of the top three major IT investments since 2003 [10]. BI refers to a diverse set of technologies and applications for gathering, storing, analysing and providing access to data to identify valuable trends [5]. Credit card companies, for example, use BI systems to compare each new charge with previous transactions to identify possible fraud. As BI has remained a high ranking IT investment across various countries, it seems that IT leaders know that their organisations are 'rich in data but poor in insight' [25].

Cloud computing and mobile applications first appeared in the SIM surveys in 2009 and were identified as priority technologies [10]. Cloud computing was ranked as the 17th most important technology whilst mobile and wireless applications came 24th. The following year cloud computing jumped to the 5th most important technology and has remained within the top five ever since. Mobile personal devices and tablets are increasingly supported by IT as a replacement for office desktop or laptop computers [25]. Subsequent years have shown the increasing importance of mobile/wireless applications: in 2010 they ranked 9th, and in 2011 4th. However, from 2012 their position has fallen to 13th in 2014.

CRM systems aim to facilitate interactions between customers and clients by automating, organising and synchronising business processes related to sales, marketing and customer service [25]. By using CRM systems, companies can enhance quality and efficiency, decrease overall costs and promote enterprise agility. In 2009, CRM systems first appeared in the SIM surveys at rank 13, moving up to the 9th place in 2010 and to the 5th place in 2011. During times of economic recession, European and Asian companies invested more into CRM systems in order to focus on improving customer trust and intimacy [28].

Enterprise resource planning (ERP) systems have remained in the top five largest technology investments from 2009 until 2014 [10]. However, in the most recent SIM survey they dropped to the 6th place [17]. Using ERP systems is an effective method to enable IT to help businesses to reduce costs and improve productivity [30]. ERP systems can provide the foundation for a wide range of e-commerce-based processes including web-based ordering and order tracing, inventory management, and built-to-order goods.

Business process management (BPM) has been a persistent issue in the SIM surveys since 2004 [28]. Since its introduction it varied between 3rd and 18th place [27,28]. BPM is a discipline that can significantly contribute to meeting an organisation's objectives by means of improvement, ongoing performance management, and governance of the core business processes [14]. BPM focuses on the technology of process management. It was introduced as a key technology in 2010 [28]. Since its introduction on this list it varied between 9th and 16th positions [10,19]. In the most recent SIM survey, however, BPM no longer listed in the top 10 in either the most important management issues nor in the list of the largest IT investments in organisations. It appears 16th in the technology (IT) investment ranking of [18].

Table 2. Top 10 Tech.-issues (top-down) for IT staff and management (2004–2016)

2004: USA [26]	2009: USA, China, EU [24]	2014: USA, China, EU [17]	2016: USA, China, EU [18]
Security technologies	Business Intelligence (BI)	Analytics, Business Intelligence (BI)	Analytics, BI, data mining, forecasting, big data
Business Intelligence (BI)	Server virtualisation	Data center infrastructure	Application software development, maintenance
Business Process Management (BPM)	Enterprise Resource Planning (ERP) systems	Enterprise Resource Planning (ERP)	Security, cybersecurity
Web services	Customer and corporate portals	Application and software development	Cloud computing (SaaS, PaaS, IaaS)
Customer portals	Enterprise Application Integration Management (EAI, EAM)	Cloud Computing (SaaS, PaaS, IaaS)	Customer Relationship Management (CRM)
Data synchro-nisation	Continuity planning, disaster recovery	Customer Relationship Management (CRM)	Enterprise Resource Planning (ERP)
Mobile and wireless applications	Collaborative and workflow tools	Security, cybersecurity	Data center, infrastructure
Enterprise application integration management	ITIL, IT process management practices	Integration, application integration	Network, telecommuni-cations
Enterprise resource planning	Service-Oriented Architecture (SOA)	Network, telecommuni-cations	Integration: application-, data-
Customer Relationship Management (CRM)	Storage virtualisation	Big data	Legacy software: maintenance, update, consolidation

3 Research Method

This paper is part of the 'World IT Project' (arguably the largest global IS academic empirical research project ever undertaken) and followed its research method, the details of which are described in [31]. We collected quantitative data from IT employees by means of a survey in a cross-sectional time-frame. The sampling technique was a mixture between stratified, convenience, and purposive sampling. The World IT Project focusses on larger organisations. The three South African-based ('local') researchers concentrated on the regions closest to their home universities. The instrument was a standardised questionnaire designed by the World IT Project 'core team' to allow for international comparison. The IT issues were based on [25,28]. The instrument was presented as an online survey (205 responses) as well as a paper-based format (105 responses). Only 9 responses had to be excluded because of insufficient quality, leaving 301 usable responses that could be analysed. Generally, the quality of responses was very high, as evidenced in a number of validity tests as well as the high reliability of sub-construct test items where some items were phrased negatively. The data were cleaned in two steps: first by the 'local' researchers, then by the World IT Project core team. 'Statistica' was used for statistical analysis and 'MS-Excel' for some of the descriptive analysis.[2]

4 Data Analysis and Discussion

Of the 301 usable responses, 70% of the respondents were below 40 years old: 38% aged 30–39, and 32% aged 21–29. 72% were male. They were also reasonably well-educated (48% with Bachelor degree, 16% with Master or Ph.D., 11% with merely high-school education). This corresponds well with the IT industry's overall demographic profile. Thus our sample can be regarded as representative of the IT industry (albeit perhaps with a slight bias towards better educated employees). Our respondents appear to be fairly experienced, with one-third of them having 10–19 years of work- and IT experience. Most of them work for large organisations, i.e. those with more than 1000 employees, rather than with medium-sized IT departments (51–100 IT staff). Hence we have a bias towards the larger organisations in line with the intended focus of the World IT Survey. Nevertheless our sample still contains a significant number of employees working in small and medium-sized organisations.

4.1 Top Organisational Issues of South African IT Employers

Respondents were asked to rate 18 organisational issues arising from their organisation's IT engagement according to their perceived relative importance on a 5-point Likert-type scale. Figure 1 presents the results, sorted by the mean. IT reliability and efficiency were clearly of top priority, followed by the IS/business

---

[2] Ethics-committee approval was obtained from our home universities as well as from the corporates who agreed to participate officially (i.e. by name) in this survey.

alignment and by security/privacy concerns; those were the top three issues. Interestingly, related to the notorious shortage of IT skills in the country, attracting and retaining IT staff is an important issue, but it ranks only 6th. At the opposite end of the spectrum, globalisation and outsourcing are not seen as major issues here in South Africa, and the often hyped 'BYOD' (Bring Your Own Device) issue was not even mentioned.

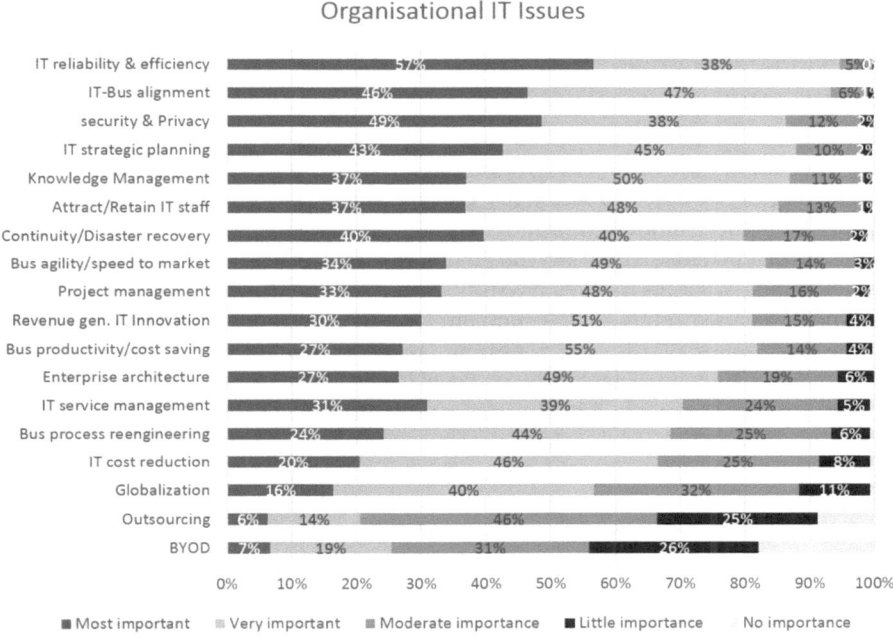

Fig. 1. Organisational issues ranked by South African IT employers ($n = 301$)

Comparing the South African issues with those in the previous SIM surveys we can see that the issues of alignment, security and privacy were also rated as very important: they usually feature among the top three issues both in the USA as well as in Europe and China. Similarly, most of the issues rated as less important in South Africa were also not ranked highly overseas.

However, IT reliability and efficiency, the most important issue in South Africa, did not even rank amongst the top five issues in any of the international surveys. By contrast, [15]—with a different list of issues—found in an admittedly small sample that building a responsive IT infrastructure, IT value management, and service delivery were three of the top four issues; these can arguably be said to align with what we called 'IT reliability and efficiency' in our survey. Also important to note is that attracting, developing and retaining IT skills only came into the top 10 in the 2004 SIM U.S.-American survey alone, and has not featured again in the later surveys. So there is strong support for the argument that the IT skills shortage is much more acute in South Africa than in the developed world. This underlines the importance of IT education in South Africa.

We also looked at which of the organisational issues that were in the top 10 of the SIM studies were also ranked by at least two-thirds of South African IT professionals as very or most important (i.e., found as part of our 15 most important issues). Remarkably, all of the top 10 issues in the SIM surveys of 2016 and 2014, and 9 of the top 10 issues of the SIM 2009 survey were also considered 'very' or 'most' important by two-thirds of the South African respondents. By contrast, only five issues from the top 10 of the 2004 survey are in our top 15 list (even after mapping 'closely related' issues).

As an additional exercise, we did an exploratory principal component analysis of the issues to see if some issues could be grouped in higher-order clusters using the empirical data. Four larger factors emerged. The factor accounting for the biggest variance in the data groups consists of four items: IT/business alignment, agility, innovation, and IT skills attraction/retention. We can thus perhaps conceptualise these as the issues relating to the organisation reacting to or engaging with its market environment. The factor with the second-largest explained variance refers to distinct internal management abilities or concerns loading the issues of disaster planning, project management, and knowledge management. The third factor loads security/privacy with reliability/efficiency and service management, which appear to group the operational business concerns (two of which feature in the top-three concerns). A fourth factor loads IT cost reduction, productivity as well as IT strategy planning (with business process re-design and enterprise architecture loading more than 40%). These seem like more specific IT-internal concerns, although a more natural descriptor is not so evident. A fifth factor, low in importance, combines globalisation with outsourcing and can thus be seen as one of the international concerns.

The implications for the South African academic IS curriculum appear to be rather small. The issues of aboce are generally all covered quite well by senior or 'capstone' IS management courses at most universities. Of note is that the BYOD, globalisation and outsourcing issues appear to be less important in industry. The relatively high ranking of continuity/disaster recovery planning (7th) belies its sometimes low visibility in many university curricula. The largest surprise is that the rather mundane issue of ensuring a reliable and efficient IT infrastructure is still the foremost concern of IT practitioners, ranked quite distinctly above all other, sometimes much 'sexier' IT concerns.

4.2   Top Technology Issues of South African IT Employers

Under a separate heading the respondents were also asked to rate each of 16 contemporary technology issues w.r.t. their importance on a 5-point Likert scale (from 'most' to 'no' importance).

Like with the business issues, the most important issue stood out quite clearly from the others. In the case of technologies, business intelligence/analytics is seen as the most important technological issue, rated by 84% as 'very' or 'most'

Technology Issues

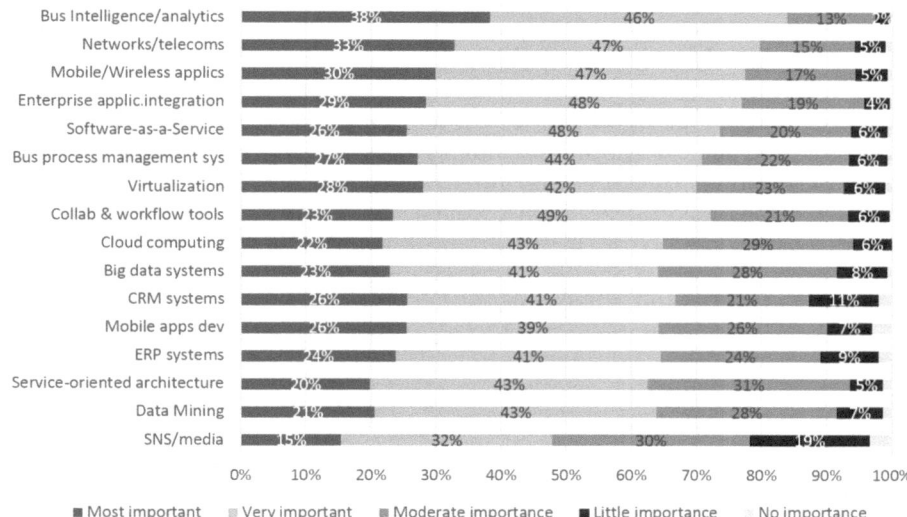

Fig. 2. Technological issues ranked by South African IT employers ($n = 301$)

important; hardly anyone (2%) sees it having 'little' or 'no' importance (Fig. 2). The often undervalued network/telecoms infrastructure is seen as the second most important technical issue.[3] Mobile/wireless applications, partly related to the telecoms issue, came third, and Enterprise Application Integration (EAI)—often hardly visible in academic curricula—were also regarded as 'very' or 'most' important by three-quarters of the respondents. Interestingly, software-as-a-service is ranked 5th, even though cloud computing in general is ranked only 9th. Service oriented architecture (SOA) and data mining were seen by less than two-thirds of respondents as very important technology issues, while social networking systems/media ranked lowest.

This makes for an interesting comparison with the international SIM studies. In all four SIM studies, business intelligence (BI) was also ranked as the top concern. However, our 'second-most important' networking/telecoms issue was ranked only 8th and 9th in the last two surveys respectively, and not evident at all in the prior SIM surveys. Only one of our top six concerns appears in the top six concerns in any of the other SIM surveys, namely EAI (4th in South Africa); it was the number-5 issue in the 2009 international SIM survey. That year, virtualisation (our number 6), was the second-most important issue in the same SIM survey. Perhaps this marks South Africa as 'lagging' in some respects or issues, although the issues of mobile applications, SaaS and cloud computing are definitely recent global developments.

---

[3] This is perhaps not surprising in a developing country.

We also conducted an exploratory principal component analysis to see which of these issues could be bundled based on their variability. Interestingly, the factor accounting for most of the explained variance in the empirical data loads Business Process Management (BPM), Enterprise Resource Planning (ERP), customer relationship management (CRM) with Enterprise Application Integration (EAI) and workflow/collaboration—these are indeed logically and conceptually linked technologies, which are often grouped together in a single academic course. Perhaps our colleagues lecturing this course can appeal to this fact as support for the importance of their course in our undergraduate major curriculum. The second-largest (w.r.t. variance) factor groups mobile/wireless, app development, networking and social networking/media. The third factor groups not only BI, Big Data and data mining (which are often taught together), but somehow also SOA; (this might just be an accidental 'data artifact'). Finally, virtualisation and SaaS load on the same factor although cloud computing loaded separately on its own factor.

Our findings strongly support the recent importance accorded to BI and analytics given by most universities—not only by the IS or computer science departments but also the management and accounting disciplines. However, the importance of Big Data and data mining seems secondary in this context, indicating that South African organisations still need to master the basic BI tools and apply analytics productively before venturing into more advanced Big Data and data mining applications. Another important finding was that, similar to what we found in the organisational issues context, the most pressing issues are not always the 'sexiest' ones: the rather staid networking and telecommunications issue is rated second-highest, but not necessarily perceived as such by the academic community (except of course for those working in that field). Even more surprising is that EAI is also seen as a crucial issue, even though it is largely absent in most university curricula. The exploratory factor analysis confirmed some of the naturally occurring topic groupings in the typical academic curricula, especially concerning ERP, workflow and BPM, but also BI, data mining and Big Data.

5   Conclusion

This paper identified the most urgent and pressing organisational and IT issues perceived by IT professionals and managers working for South African organisations, i.e., the employers of our graduates. We were fortunate in securing a large sample (301 respondents) representative of South African companies in both geographic diversity and different organisational sizes. Validity analysis confirms that our dataset contains data of high quality.

The *major finding* is that the issues rated as important by our IT students' employers do not always match what the vendors or academics perceive as popular, urgent or current. For instance, a reliable and efficient IT infrastructure was by far the most highly ranked organisational issue, something which is hardly ever foregrounded in our MIS or ISM courses. In the pure technical issues, the networking/telecommunication infrastructure (often perceived as rather mundane) and EAI (often absent from academic curricula) were ranked as 2nd and 4th most important issues respectively. By contrast, 'sexy' topics such as globalisation, outsourcing, BYOD (organisational) or SNS/Social Media and data mining (technical) were not seen as major issues. Hopefully these findings will lead to some interesting discussions regarding 'capita selecta' topic choices in curriculum design.[4]

Another crucial finding is that attracting and retaining quality IT staff ranked 6th in our survey and is seen as a major organisational issue—unlike in similar surveys conducted in Europe, the USA and China, where this has not been a top 10 issue for the past decade. This vindicates the need for providing more prominence and for plowing additional resources into IT education to address our ongoing IT skills shortage.

Future research could map the key issues more systematically onto the 'official' 2015 ACM curriculum. Given that this survey was conducted in 37 other countries around the world, we intend comparing our findings to those in other developing countries; (sadly, only one other African country has a quality data set so far). We also intend mining our dataset further for differences in rankings according to size of company or role of respondent; space limitations prevented us from including this analysis here. Finally, a longitudinal analysis using standardised methods and instruments may provide further validity and insights into the dynamics of the IT industry and its demands on the educational sector.

References

1. Akcam, B., Hekim, H., Guler, A.: Exploring business student perception of information and technology. Procedia Soc. Behav. Sci. **195**, 182–191 (2015)
2. Altbach, P., Reisberg, L., Rumbley, L.: Trends in global higher education: tracking an academic revolution. UNESCO/Sense (2010)
3. Bartel, A.P., Lichtenberg, F.R.: The comparative advantage of educated workers in implementing new technology. Rev. Econ. Stat. **69**, 1–11 (1987)
4. Brancheau, J.C., Wetherbe, J.C.: Key issues in information systems management. MIS Quart. **11**(1), 23–45 (1987)
5. Brijs, B.: Business Analysis for Business Intelligence. CRC Press, Boca Raton (2012)
6. Büyükbaykal, C.I.: Communication technologies and education in the information age. Procedia Soc. Behav. Sci. **174**, 636–640 (2015)
7. Cardinali, R.: Business school graduates: do they meet the needs of MIS professional? Words **16**(3), 33–35 (1988)
8. Cloete, N.: Differentiation: reasons, and purposes, systems and methodologies. Technical report, HESA Center For Higher Education Tranformation (2011) http://www.chet.org.za/files/uploads/reports/HesaFinalAugust11_for~website.pdf
9. Davis, P.: What computer skills do employees expect from recent college graduates? J. Tech. Horizons Educ. **25**(2), 74 (1997)

---

[4] For comparison see the 'Invited Lecture' of SACLA'2018 in *this volume* of CCIS.

10. Derksen, B., Luftman, J.: European key IT and management issues & trends for 2014: results of an international study. Technical report, CIONET (2015). http://www.fm-house.com/wp-content/uploads/2015/01/ITTrends_2014print.pdf
11. Dorociak, J.: The alignment between business and information system strategies in small banks: an analysis of performance impact. Capella University, Doctoral dissertation (2007)
12. Dougherty, J.P., Kock, N.F., Sandas, C., Aiken, R.M.: Teaching the use of complex IT in specific domains: developing, assessing and refining a curriculum development framework. Educ. Inf. Tech. **7**(2), 137–154 (2002)
13. India Brand Equity Forum: Infographics on IT Industry & ITeS in India (2016). https://www.ibef.org/industry/informationtechnologyindia/info-graphic
14. Jeston, J., Nelis, J.: Business Process Management. Routledge, Abingdon (2014)
15. Johnston, K., Muganda, N., Theys, K.: Key issues for CIOs in South Africa. Electr. J. Inf. Syst. Dev. Countries **30**(1), 1–11 (2007)
16. Joo, B., Park, S.: Career satisfaction, organizational commitment, and turnover intention. Leadersh Organ. Dev. J. **31**(6), 482–500 (2010)
17. Kappelman, L., Mclean, E., Gerhart, N., Johnson, V.: The 2015 SIM IT trends study: issues, investments, concerns, and practices of organizations and their IT executives. MIS Quart. Exec. **15**(1), 55–83 (2014)
18. Kappelman, L., et al.: The 2016 SIM IT key issues and trends study. MIS Quart. Exec. **16**(1), 47–80 (2017)
19. Kappelman, L., McLean, E., Luftman, J., Johnson, V.: Key issues of IT organizations and their leadership: the 2013 SIM IT trends study. MIS Quart. Exec. **12**(4), 227–240 (2013)
20. Kappelman, L., Mclean, E.R., Vess, J., Gerhart, N.: The 2014 SIM IT key issues and trends study. MIS Quart. Exec. **13**(4), 237–263 (2014)
21. Klimova, A., Rondeau, E.: Education for cleaner production in information and communication technologies curriculum. In: Proceedings of 20th IFAC World Congress 50(1), 12931–12937 (2017)
22. Klimova, A., Rondeau, E., Andersson, K., Porras, J., Rybin, A.V., Zaslavsky, A.: An international Master's program in Green ICT as a contribution to sustainable development. J. Cleaner Prod. **135**, 223–239 (2016)
23. Lotriet, H.H., Matthee, M.C., Alexander, P.M.: Challenges in ascertaining ICT skills requirements in South Africa. S. Afr. Comput. J. **46**, 38–48 (2010)
24. Luftman, J., Ben-Zvi, T.: Key issues for IT executives 2009: difficult economy's impact on IT. MIS Q. Executive **9**(1), 17–28 (2009)
25. Luftman, J., Ben-Zvi, T.: Key issues for IT executives 2011: cautious optimism in uncertain economic times. MIS Q. Executive **10**(4), 202–212 (2011)
26. Luftman, J.: Key issues for IT executives 2004. MIS Q. Executive **4**(2), 269–285 (2005)
27. Luftman, J., McLean, E.: Key issues for IT executives. MIS Q. Executive **3**(2), 89–104 (2004)
28. Luftman, J., Zadeh, H.S., Derksen, B., Santana, M., Rigoni, E.H., Huang, Z.: Key information technology and management issues 2011–2012: an international study. J. Inf. Tech. **27**(3), 198–212 (2012)
29. Maneschijn, M.M., Botha, A., van Biljon, J.A.: A critical review of ICT skills for higher education learners. In: ICAST 2013 Proceedings of International Conference on Adaptive Science and Technology, pp. 1–13. IEEE (2013)
30. O'Leary, D.E.: Enterprise resource planning (ERP) systems: an empirical analysis of benefits. J. Emerg. Technol. Account. **1**(1), 63–72 (2004)

31. Palvia, P., et al.: The World IT project: history, trials, tribulations, lessons, and recommendations. Commun. AIS **41**(1), 389–413 (2017)
32. Parashar, A.K., Parashar, R.: Innovations and curriculum development for engineering education and research in India. Procedia Soc. Behav. Sci. **56**, 685–690 (2012)
33. Pillay, P.: Barriers to information and communication technology (ICT) adoption and use amongst SMEs: a study of the South African manufacturing sector. Master thesis, University of the Witwatersrand (2016)
34. Popescu, F.: South African globalization strategies and higher education. Procedia Soc. Behav. Sci. **209**, 411–418 (2015)
35. Prat, N.: Teaching information systems with cases: an exploratory study. J. Comput. Inf. Syst. **52**(3), 71–81 (2012)
36. PricewaterhouseCoopers: Data driven – what students need to succeed in a rapidly changing business world (2015). https://www.pwc.com/us/en/faculty-resource/assets/pwc-data-driven-paper-feb2015.pdf
37. Ryan, T.K.: Business-IT alignment maturity: the correlation of performance indicators and alignment maturity within the commercial airline industry. Capella University, Doctoral dissertation (2010)
38. Seethamraju, R.: Enterprise systems software in business school curriculum: evaluation of design and delivery. J. Inf. Syst. Educ. **18**(1), 69–83 (2007)
39. Silva, H.C., Lima, F.: Technology, employment and skills: a look into job duration. Res. Policy **46**, 1519–1530 (2017)
40. Teferra, D., Greijn, H.: Higher Education and Globalisation: Challenges. Threats and Opportunities for Africa, MUNDO (2010)

Towards a Knowledge Conversion Model Enabling Programme Design in Higher Education for Shaping Industry-Ready Graduates

Hanlie Smuts[✉] and Marie J. Hattingh

Department of Informatics, University of Pretoriam, Pretoria, South Africa
{hanlie.smuts,marie.hattingh}@up.ac.za

Abstract. The increase in the requirement for competent and skilled Information Systems graduates has prompted higher education institutions to adapt learning strategies. One way of achieving this is through the application of knowledge conversion processes, transforming data to capability. Knowledge conversion processes can be utilised to optimise learning in higher education institutions. The purpose of this paper is to propose a knowledge conversion model grounded in educational theory and organisational theory within a real-world context. The model was applied to an Information Systems undergraduate programme at a major higher education institution in South Africa. It was established that the Information Systems programme conformed well with the principles of knowledge conversion as it enabled industry-ready Information Systems graduates. Furthermore, the knowledge conversion model can be utilised as a blueprint for programme design as well as identifying potential gaps in existing programmes.

Keywords: Higher education · Information Systems
Industry-ready graduates · Knowledge conversion · Programme design

1 Introduction

Upon graduating, alumni need to make a positive contribution to the commercial environment packed with dynamic problems and opportunities [42]. The dynamic problems and opportunities are partly created by ubiquitous computing where most systems are computerised. The design, development and implementation of these computerised systems increased the demand for aptly trained Information Systems graduates or informaticians. This demand has placed increased pressure on higher education institutions (HEIs) and educators to improve their educational practices in order to deliver students that are 'ready' to operate in the real world [39].

Rapid changes in the commercial environment, changing industry demands, new market trends and changes in technology have a direct impact on how

© Springer Nature Switzerland AG 2019
S. Kabanda et al. (Eds.): SACLA 2018, CCIS 963, pp. 124–139, 2019.
https://doi.org/10.1007/978-3-030-05813-5_9

effective students can learn and how effective they will be in the workplace [19]. Many educational teaching methods have been adopted and tested to respond to the educational challenges associated with preparing towards 'real-world-ready' [10,47]. Some of them are teacher-centred, while others are student-centred. However, all of them share the same goal, which is to provide students with the best education and knowledge as possible. However, this knowledge is not static and when considering informaticians in particular, the field of system analysis and design (SAD) is dynamic and continually adjusting to the needs of organisational information systems [47]. Flexibility is needed in the field to ensure that students are learning new methodologies and the techniques necessary to deliver a product that meets the needs of industry, the client [47]. Therefore, the purpose of this paper is to ensure that industry-ready graduates are shaped by applying a model for knowledge conversion facilitating programme design in HEIs.

The remainder of this paper is structured as follows: In Sect. 2 we provide background information from the literature. Our own approach is discussed in Sect. 3, whereafter we propose our new education knowledge conversion model in Sect. 4. In Sect. 5 we complete a mapping of an Information Systems curriculum to the knowledge conversion model for education in order to illustrate the proposed model's suitability for academic programme design. We summarise our findings and conclude the paper in Sect. 6.

2   Related Work

Higher education institutions deal with multiple challenges and resource burdens such as rising costs, funding problems and remaining at the leading edge of all subject areas [4,48]. These challenges entice universities to seek relationships with industry in order to relieve societal pressure to show contribution to economic growth through education and knowledge generation [8]. The collaboration between HEIs and industry refers to the interaction between any parts of the higher educational system and industry aiming to encourage innovation through knowledge and technology exchange [4].

The main aim of HEIs is to create new knowledge and to educate, while organisations in industry focus on capturing knowledge that can be leveraged for competitive advantage [8]. These pressures on both parties have led to an increasing incentive for identifying and developing collaboration opportunities that aim to enhance innovation and economic competitiveness at institutional levels via knowledge conversion between academic and commercial domains [7].

In the following sub-sections we consider the nature of knowledge, as well as higher education institution-industry collaboration and in particular the relevance of knowledge conversion as an organisational prerogative in the education domain.

2.1   The Nature of Knowledge

The definition of knowledge has drawn a substantial amount of speculation in the literature [14]. Polanyi, a chemist and philosopher, was the first to articulate the concept of two different, mutually exclusive, dimensions of knowledge, namely 'tacit' knowledge, whereby *"there are things that we know but cannot tell"* [38], and 'explicit' knowledge. Cognitive psychologists divided knowledge into 'declarative' and 'procedural' knowledge. Declarative knowledge refers to the descriptions of facts, methods and procedures that can be articulated. Procedural knowledge refers to motor (manual) skills and cognitive (mental) skills observable in actioning something [1,35]. What these definitions make clear however, is that knowledge is a combination of various elements [21,35].

Knowledge that has been articulated and formally recorded in document databases, knowledge bases, manuals, handbooks and program code is explicit knowledge [20]. Implicit knowledge, which is far less tangible than explicit knowledge, is knowledge in a person's internal state and refers to knowledge deeply embedded into an organisation's operating practices [13]. Implicit knowledge that is difficult to articulate is referred to as tacit knowledge and includes relationships, norms and values. In this instance the knowing is in the doing and tacit knowledge is therefore much harder to detail, reproduce or share [12].

Comparable to tacit and explicit knowledge, distinction is made between 'action-centred' skills and 'intellective' skills. Action-centred skills are developed through learning by doing. Intellective skills combine abstraction, explicit reference and procedural reasoning, making it easily representable and therefore easily exchangeable [32]. In educational theory, Bruning suggested that knowledge can be procedural (action-centred) or declarative (non-action-centred) [9]. Procedural knowledge is implicit in this instance and declarative knowledge is explicit. However, learning of procedural skills may access explicit descriptions, while knowledge on how procedures are applied in a specific environment may only be learnt as implicit knowledge via 'doing' or socialising [9].

Irrespective whether education or organisations are considered, both must be able to accomplish the explicit-to-implicit knowledge and the implicit-to-explicit knowledge transition [6,30].

2.2 The Learning Process Hierarchy

Kolb defines the learning process as the method whereby *"knowledge is created through the transformation of experience"* [28] (p. 38). Driscoll highlights that learning *"must come about as a result of the student's experience and interaction with the world"* [15] (p. 11), while Siemens defines the learning process as *"the act of internalizing knowledge"* [44] (p. 3). These definitions point to the fact that learning essentially considers the combination of two different processes: an internal psychological process of acquisition and elaboration, and, secondly, an external interaction process between the student and the student's social, cultural or material environment [24]. As both of these processes must actively be effected for any learning to take place, the stages are reflected in the learning process hierarchy consisting of four layers (Fig. 1): data, information, knowledge and capability [7].

Data consists of structured recordings of transactions and events and is presented without context [12]. Information is data with relevance and purpose

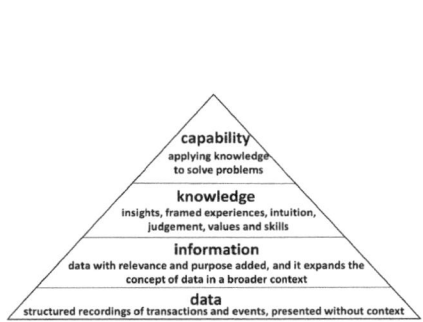

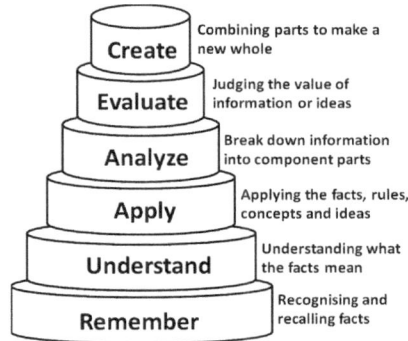

Fig. 1. Learning process hierarchy [7]   **Fig. 2.** Bloom's taxonomy [29]

added, and it expands the concept of data in a broader context [33]. Information becomes individual knowledge when it is accepted and retained as appropriate representations of the relevant knowledge. Knowledge comes with insights, framed experiences, intuition, judgement and values and encompasses the scope of understanding and skills that are mentally created by people [12]. The process of applying knowledge to solve problems leads to capability [7]. Capability is an *"integration of knowledge, skills, personal qualities and understanding used appropriately and effectively"* [45] (p. 2). Capability enables people to not only apply their knowledge and skills within different and ever-changing environments, but to also continuously develop their knowledge and skills long after they have left formal higher education, enabling them to take appropriate action within unfamiliar and changing circumstances [45].

The learning process in higher education is usually a bottom-up process and starts from the data layer, moving up slowly to the capability layer [7]. The purpose of the learning process is to engage the student to develop their personal capability. The nature of the process, the content and context of the learning, the products for assessment each require some degree of growth in personal autonomy from the student [45]. In this context, many scientists and teachers are looking for a more efficient path to capability [7].

In order to consider a more efficient learning process of progressing from data to capability, Bloom's taxonomy of learning and knowledge conversion and learning processes are discussed below.

In 'Taxonomy of Educational Objectives' (1956), a seminal work on learning objectives, educational psychologist Benjamin Bloom and his collaborators created Bloom's Taxonomy [25]. The purpose of Bloom's taxonomy was to promote higher-order thinking in education, such as analysing and evaluating concepts, processes, procedures, and principles, rather than just remembering facts. Higher-order thinking was achieved by building up from lower-level cognitive skills [22].

Bloom's taxonomy includes a set of three hierarchical models used to classify educational learning objectives into levels of complexity and specificity namely, cognitive, affective and sensory domains [29]. Six levels, through increasingly more complex and abstract mental levels, within the cognitive domain were identified as depicted in Fig. 2. The six levels, each of which is built on a foundation of the previous level, include remembering (recall previous learned information), understanding (comprehending what facts mean), applying (applying the facts, rules, concepts and ideas), analysing (separating material or concepts into component parts), evaluating (judging the value of information and ideas) and creating (design, combining parts to make a new whole) [22,29]. Design in this instance is an outcome of the evaluation process which comes as a result of analysis. Therefore, evaluation leads to the main objective of the whole process which is to design (or 'create' in Bloom's Revised Taxonomy) [2].

Learning strategies govern the approach for achieving learning objectives which in turn point towards the instructional strategies advising the medium that will actually deliver the instruction [18]. Specific learning objectives can be derived from the taxonomy, although it is most commonly used to assess learning on a variety of cognitive levels [25].

2.3   Knowledge Conversion, Learning Processes and Education

Knowledge and continuous learning are essentials of success in the new economy [34]. The management of knowledge is intrinsically connected to knowledge sharing between individuals and to the collaborative processes involved [17].

Nonaka and Takeuchi defined a model that is based on the fundamental assumption that knowledge is created and expanded through social interaction between implicit—specifically tacit—and explicit knowledge [36]. This interaction is known as knowledge conversion and it is referred to as the SECI model. The process of knowledge conversion advances through four different modes as shown in Fig. 3: socialisation (tacit to tacit), externalisation (tacit to explicit), combination (explicit to explicit) and internalisation (explicit to tacit). Socialisation is the conversion of tacit knowledge among individuals through shared information and experiences by means of observation, imitation and practice. Externalisation is the process whereby tacit knowledge is articulated as explicit knowledge through collaboration with others using conceptualisation and extraction. Explicit knowledge is not only shared via document management systems, e-mails, in meetings, etc., but also through education, learning and training interventions. Combination is the enrichment of the collected information by reconfiguring it or enhancing it by sorting, adding, combining or categorising it so that it is more usable. In order to act on information, individuals should understand and internalise it. This involves the process of creating their own tacit knowledge. The process is closely related to learning-by-doing through studying documents or attending training in order to re-experience to some degree what others have previously learned [36,37].

An individual progresses through five stages in order to acquire new personal knowledge namely, researching, absorbing, doing, interacting and reflecting [31].

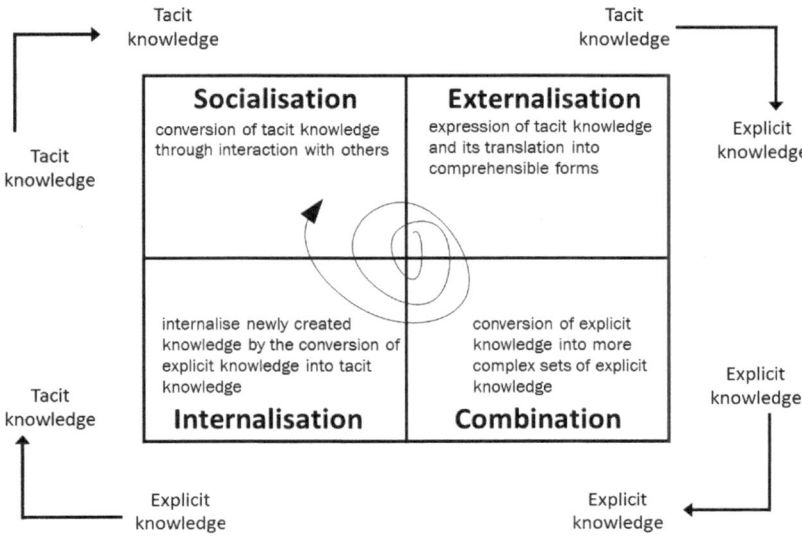

Fig. 3. The knowledge conversion model [37]

During the researching stage, an overview of the topic of study is observed. The absorbing stage follows where an incoherent and disorganised mixture of data and information are formed in the individual's mind while listening, watching, reading and sensing. The doing stage ensues, where different tasks are completed and actions performed in order to organize all pieces of information and connect them with each other with the outcome to form first knowledge. An individual's first knowledge is then enlarged during the interacting stage as own opinions are formed during discussions about the topic of study. The last stage is the reflecting stage during which newly formed knowledge is considered and evaluated in the context of other existing knowledge and personal experience, hence forming an individual's own unique world-view [31].

Practical knowledge and learning strategies may be employed by educational institutions, however very little has been written about it in the educational context or showing direct educational reference [40]. This is unexpected as education is about the creation and application of knowledge; *"the business of education is knowledge"* [40] (p. xiv). Irrespective of this context, the main idea of the knowledge and learning processes is that personal knowledge can only be created by individuals on their own and that they follow particular steps to do so [3]. The background for creating knowledge is information, to create knowledge an individual must observe a sufficient amount of information [30,31].

In the next section we explore the research approach followed to design our knowledge conversion model for education, and how it may inform course design.

3   Design of the Knowledge Conversion Model for Education: Method

Our overall objective for this paper was to design a knowledge conversion model for education supporting programme design. The purpose of such a model is to support academic programme designers to optimise learning by applying knowledge conversion principles and ultimately deliver graduates that can thrive in real-world of work. In order to reach this goal we followed a design-based approach [41]. Design-based research is a *"systematic but flexible methodology aimed to improve educational practices through iterative analysis, design, development, and implementation, based on collaboration among researchers and practitioners in real-world settings, and leading to contextually-sensitive design principles and theories"* [46] (p. 6). Design-based research produces both theories and practical educational interventions as its results [16], and encompasses five basic characteristics [46]:

Pragmatic: Research goals are solving current real-world problems by designing and ratifying interventions as well as extending theories and refining design principles.

Grounded: Design based research is grounded in both theory and the real-world context.

Interactive, iterative and flexible in its research process.

Integrative: Researchers integrate a variety of research methods and approaches from both qualitative and quantitative research paradigms, depending on the needs of the research.

Contextual: Research results are connected with both the design process, by which results are generated, and the setting in which the research is conducted.

With these characteristics guiding our approach, we built upon prior literature about knowledge conversion, learning and education in order to create a knowledge conversion model for education with the aim to solve a real-world problem (pragmatic nature of our research). The knowledge conversion model for education is grounded in educational theory (learning process hierarchy, Bloom's taxonomy of learning) and organisational theory within a real-world context (knowledge conversion model for organisational learning, learning process). Our approach was qualitative, and the context of our research was higher education.

Our study was conducted at a HEI in South Africa that offers a 'Bachelor of Commerce' degree (BCom) in Information Systems. This degree contains a multi-disciplinary subject area, where information, Information Systems, and the integration thereof into the organisation, are studied for the benefit of the entire system (individual, organisation and society). In order to apply the knowledge conversion model designed for education, we used the Information Systems degree and utilised the designed model for the mapping of the entire 3-year undergraduate degree, corroborating the interactive, iterative and flexible nature of our approach.

Next we discuss the knowledge conversion model for education in detail.

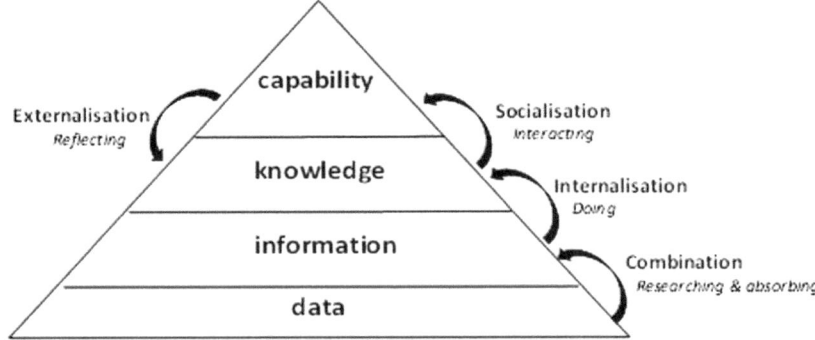

Fig. 4. New knowledge conversion model for education, adapted from [7,37]

4   Exploration of Knowledge Conversion in Education

In order to consider a more efficient learning process of progressing from data to capability, we defined an integrated model utilising knowledge conversion, knowledge exchange and learning processes (Figs. 2 and 3) describing the progression among levels in the learning hierarchy (Fig. 1). The proposed education knowledge conversion model is depicted in Fig. 4. The premise for the design of the proposed education knowledge conversion model is to apply knowledge conversion processes typically found in industry and to consider how it may guide programme and module design in a HEI.

In order to progress from data to capability in the learning hierarchy, we propose the application of particular knowledge conversion processes where, with each knowledge conversion process, particular education programme enablers are associated with. In order to achieve the explicit-to-implicit knowledge and the implicit-to-explicit knowledge transition, we consider the data layer first [6,30].

The attributes of the data layer include facts, events, records, transactions (etc.) without context; thus data has no meaning. It is a description of the world that represents discrete facts about an objective reality and as it can be verified, it can be decisively proven to be accurate or inaccurate. Data as such does not provide meaningful results and is the point of departure towards eventually reaching a meaningful outcome. In the context of a HEI, the data layer refers to the learning of concepts and facts to be committed into memory, as well as quantitative measurements. Some mechanisms utilised in the data layer in an HEI as shown in Table 1, includes on-line message forums, lecture notes and textbooks.

Information attributes point to data with relevance and purpose added as patterns in data reveal relationships. Analysis, categorization and explanation are attributes from a higher education perspective and in this context, refer to understanding and comprehending meaning. Therefore, moving from memory (data) to understanding (information), the process of combination may be applied as it enriches and enhances collected information through sorting and

Table 1. Educ. knowledge conversion model, with enablers of educ. programmes

Learning process step [7]	Level of understanding [23]	Knowledge conversion process [36]	Educational programme enablers (examples)	Literature
Data to information	Researching, absorbing	Combination	E-mail, on-line message forums, gazette, lecture notes, textbook, book marking, learning based on repetition, reading	[30,37]
Information to knowledge	Doing	Internalisation	Lectures, workshops, tutorials, group work, simulations, experiments, virtual reality, e-learning, context-steered learning, blog, 'fishbowls', debate	[7,11,30,37,43]
Knowledge to capability	Interacting	Socialisation	Social activities, industrial training, apprenticeship, hands-on experience, design labs, incubation centres	[4,30,37]
Capability to knowledge	Reflecting	Externalisation	Orals, tests, examination, assignments, peer presentations, tutoring, industry projects, co-operative research, community collaboration, academic spin-offs, mentoring, imitation, observation and practice	[4,37]

categorising it so that it is more usable. The result of combination is about understanding relations. Some educational programme enablers for the combination process from the literature are listed in Table 1 and include lecture notes, textbook, book marking, flash cards, etc.

The knowledge layer deals with the fusion of multiple sources of information over time, in order to create conceptual frameworks. Furthermore, knowledge gives perspective through experiences, values, and insight and contains our beliefs and expectations. From a higher education viewpoint, application enables the use of a concept in a new situation, e.g.: apply what was learned in the classroom into novel situations in the work place. Thus, moving from understanding (information) to application (knowledge), the knowledge conversion process internalisation may be utilised as it is about linking concepts together into a network of ideas, beliefs, memories and forecasts. The outcome of internalisation is about understanding patterns. Some examples in Table 1 of educational programme enablers for internalisation point to simulations, experiments, project-based learning, 'fishbowls', debate, etc.

The fourth layer is the capability layer comprising of the application of knowledge in order to solve problems. Capability talks to a set of principles, providing the ultimate context and frame of reference. From a higher education standpoint, new meaning or structure are built from diverse fundamentals using judgment and evaluation forming a whole. Consequently, moving from application (knowledge) to judgement (capability), the knowledge conversion process socialisation may be utilised where knowledge is conceded through practice, guidance, imitation, and observation. The outcome of socialisation is about understanding principles. Some examples in Table 1 of educational programme enablers for socialisation include consortiums, industrial, apprenticeship, hands-on experience, design labs, etc.

An additional knowledge conversion process, externalisation points to the expression of tacit knowledge and its translation into comprehensible forms. When tacit knowledge is made explicit, knowledge is crystallized, permitting it to be shared with others, and thus forming the basis of new knowledge (capability translated to knowledge). Examples of the reflective nature of externalisation as a knowledge conversion process include mentoring, imitation, observation and practice, as listed in Table 1.

With the pressure on HEIs to ensure that information system graduates are industry-ready, the proposed knowledge conversion model for education may be utilised as a blueprint or guideline to support this requirement. By considering the learning processes and the most efficient path to capability, as well as die particular process of knowledge conversion required to reach capability, the knowledge conversion model for education provides suggestions to instructional designers and educators along each step of knowledge conversion, i.e.: from data to information, from information to knowledge and from knowledge to capability. Therefore, when considering a particular course module in a programme, attention must be given to the basic building blocks (data) that must be placed in context (information) using the different mechanisms listed in Table 1. By combining the information pockets through a project or assignment, knowledge is created where after capability is honed when this knowledge is applied, (e.g. in a case study). This also implies that application may be a challenge if some data, information and prior knowledge are missing. Personal knowledge is shaped by individuals (students) based on a sufficient amount of information provided.

5   Programme Mapping to the Knowledge Conversion Model for Education

In this section we apply the blueprint defined in this section to an Information Systems degree at a HEI.

In order to apply the proposed knowledge conversion model designed for education we looked at the Information Systems degree of a HEI in South Africa. This undergraduate Information Systems programme offers a well-rounded balance of technical and business focused course modules from which students can choose. This particular Information Systems degree is to-date the only Information Systems degree in Africa that is internationally accredited by the Accreditation Board for Engineering and Technology (ABET). In addition, Bloom's taxonomy of learning was utilised to derive specific learning objectives for the modules in the Information Systems programme. The Information Systems programme at undergraduate level is constructed in such a way as to give students exposure to three areas of development:

- Information Systems modules, which include systems analysis and design, programming and database design, are offered at first, second and third year level. Students have a choice of commerce-oriented modules as electives which include business management, accounting, taxation, statistics, internal auditing or marketing management.
- Students are compelled to do an external community project, usually in their second year of study. This project involves working in a team to solve some community problem based on project management principles, i.e.: on-time, with available resources, within a restricted (small) financial budget. The students must report their progress, and their reflections of their experiences, by digital means.
- Critical thinking and problem solving skills are introduced as a separate module in the first year. This module aids the student in different problem solving methods, argumentation, and design processes.

We mapped the entire 3-year degree to the knowledge conversion attributes of our model. The learning process steps for an Information Systems student constitute an iterative process up to where a student can internalise the knowledge obtained throughout his/her years of study. Therefore, every year the student gets exposed to new terminology (data) which he/she needs to make sense of (information) in order to apply it to a case scenario (1st–2nd year) or real-life scenario (3rd year IS project, 2nd year external community project).

5.1   Data to Information

Students are provided with prescribed books and accompanying lecture slides. A combination of tools are used to support students in researching and absorbing the terminology associated with the various modules. The lecturers use the learning management system 'Blackboard' to communicate with the students. Students also have the ability to communicate among themselves or with the lecturer through a discussion board. Quizzes, focused on testing the understanding of discreet elements of a module, are part of the assessment plan. Students must also register themselves for weekly tutorials and practicals where a number of data elements are combined in order to understand the relationships between these elements.

For example, in the systems analysis and design (SAD) module, after having received teaching about the project management aspects of a new information system, students will complete elements of the scope of work in the tutorial sessions and construct a project plan with the 'MS Project' software in their practical session. This allows students to absorb the elements of a scope of work as well as it forces them to research different elements in a project. In the programming module, students are taught the basics of computer programming. It includes the terminology, various programming structures such as loops, and OO 'methods'. In the database module, students learn the introductory concepts associated with databases and are doing weekly practicals to combine different data elements.

5.2 Information to Knowledge

After students have combined the various elements of the particular study unit, students have to internalise their knowledge of the subject area covered. This is accomplished by 'doing'.

In the first year of study, knowledge internalisation is accomplished by using a small case study. In the second year of study, knowledge internalisation is accomplished by doing a larger case study with full project management aspects incorporating multiple relevant elements in context. With regards to programming, students are able after their first year to create a Windows-form-based programme as well as a basic web-based application with HTML, CSS and Javascript. At the end of their second year, absorbing the new terminology learnt, students are able to use the model-view-control (MVC) approach in web development, connect the interface to a database, do object-oriented programming, and can create a complete client-server web-based application.

5.3 Knowledge to Capability

Students have at least two opportunities to socialise their knowledge by interacting with the outside world. In the first instance students, as part of groups containing 5 members, choose an external community project from a pre-defined list of such projects for the year. The list includes projects such as repairing computers at disadvantaged schools, renovation and maintenance work at disadvantaged schools, teaching basic mathematics to pupils at disadvantaged schools, or creating websites for non-profit organisations and disadvantaged schools. Service-learning encourages students by showing them that they can 'make a difference' in society. Jordaan reports that even though the *"students' collective actions are not always successful, they learn from their mistakes by engaging in a continuous sequence of action and reflection"* [27]. Therefore, these types of projects allow students to interact with the world, to apply knowledge learnt in course modules, and to improve general 'life skills'.

In the second instance all Information Systems students need to complete a final year project with a real-world client. The purpose of this project is to deliver an end-to-end working software solution based on their particular client's requirements. The project is project managed by the students themselves, from understanding the problem, designing and developing the system to installation and handover, including training and user manuals. Students combine the skills learnt in the curriculum, which includes their business knowledge from the Commerce modules, with their own unique personal and professional interests to build and implement a computer-based information system in the real-life organisation. Students are assessed throughout the year-long project on various aspects such as project management, logical design, physical design, prototype development, database design, and the complexity of the system. An external examiner from industry examines each of the deliverables of this comprehensive project. However, as the creation of personal knowledge is an individual activity, students are marked (graded) individually as well as per group for their final-year industry project.

5.4   Capability to Knowledge

The externalisation of knowledge occurs in four instances: firstly, reflection from the students on lessons learnt when interacting with a real-life client, what they have learnt from the commercial environment, and how the experience can be improved for the following years' students. Secondly, industry feedback on their experience of working with the students is recorded as industry was now exposed to the capabilities of soon-to-be graduates. Thirdly, the lecturers through the students' interaction with real-life clients, reflect on the business knowledge learnt from different types of industry advice, and finally, through mentorship in the external community projects whereby students identified as 'mentors' share their lessons learnt with the next established community project teams.

6   Conclusion

Employers require students to have both 'soft' skills (such as the ability to work in a team and solve problems) and 'hard' skills that are organisation-specific [26]. Furthermore, students in Information Systems need to stay relevant in a market where technology, methodology (techniques and approaches to develop new systems) and industry trends change quickly [5]. Therefore, students must rather focus on learning processes where 'learning' becomes an act of discovery, rather than focusing on mastering the programme content that might be irrelevant in the near future. Such focus implies understanding and examining a given problem, researching the problem background, analysing possible solutions, developing a proposal and producing a final result. During this process, students develop a deeper understanding of relevant and contextual Information Systems programme contents and skills, as well as the required critical thinking abilities to produce the final result.

The challenges experienced by the students, in addition to the requirements of future employers, make the Information Systems programme complex for both the students, who have a steep learning curve, and the educators, who need to adopt the correct pedagogy to prepare the students for future employment. In order to address this requirement, we have designed a model for knowledge conversion in education where the knowledge conversion and learning processes together with practical mechanisms required to move quickly from data to capability, were defined and addressed.

In order to apply the model for knowledge conversion in education, we have mapped the Information Systems degree from a HEI in South Africa utilising the model and principles as a guide. We assert that the Information Systems programme conformed well with the principles of knowledge conversion, (i.e. data to information to knowledge to capability). We found that the programme was designed to present basic building blocks, create association among the building blocks and then apply the knowledge gained through the process. The capability of the Information Systems graduates is demonstrated through the delivery of a real-world business solution incorporating all required aspects of their commerce modules, critical thinking and problem solving, and Information Systems modules.

By using the model for knowledge conversion for education in HEIs as a blueprint, lecturers and instructional designers can ensure that the design will enable an optimised learning process, delivering graduates who are aligned to the requirements of a competitive industry environment.

References

1. Alavi, M., Leidner, D.E.: Review: knowledge management and knowledge management systems: conceptual foundations and research issues. MIS Q. **25**(1), 107–136 (2001)
2. Anderson, L., Krathwohl, D.: A Taxonomy for Learning, Teaching, and Assessing: A Revision of Bloom's Taxonomy of Educational Objectives. Longman, New York (2001)
3. Andreeva, T., Ikhilchik, I.A.: Applicability of the SECI model of knowledge creation in Russian cultural context: theoretical analysis. Knowl. Process. Manag. **18**(1), 56–66 (2011)
4. Ankrah, S., Al-Tabbaa, O.: Universities' industry collaboration: a systematic review. Scand. J. Manag. **31**, 387–408 (2015)
5. van Belle, J.P., Scholtz, B., Njenga, K., Serenko, A., Palvia, P.: Top IT issues for employers of South African graduates. In: Kabanda, S., et al. (eds.) SACLA 2018. CCIS, vol. 963, pp. 108–123. Springer, Cham (2019)
6. Bhusry, M., Ranjan, J., Nagar, R.: Implementing knowledge management in higher educational institutions in India: a conceptual framework. J. High. Educ. Res. **7**(1), 64–82 (2012)
7. Bleimann, U.: Atlantis university: a new pedagogical approach beyond e-learning. Campus-Wide Inf. Syst. **27**(5), 191–195 (2004)
8. Bruneel, J., d'Este, P., Salter, A.: Investigating the factors that diminish the barriers to university-industry collaboration. Res. Policy **39**, 858–868 (2010)
9. Bruning, R.H.: Cognitive Psychology and Instruction, 3rd edn. Prentice-Hall, Englewood Cliffs (1999)
10. Cascone, L.: Co-operative learning, structured controversy and active learning. Technical report (2017). http://www.gmu.edu/facstaff/part-time/strategy.html
11. Cavusgil, S.T., Calantone, R.J., Zhao, Y.: Tacit knowledge transfer and firm innovation capability. J. Bus. Ind. Mark. **18**(1), 6–21 (2003)
12. Clarke, T., Rollo, C.: Corporate initiatives in knowledge management. Educ. Train. **43**(4/5), 206–214 (2001)
13. Dalkir, K.: Knowledge Management in Theory and Practice. Elsevier Butterworth Heinemann, London (2005)
14. Davenport, T.H., Prusak, L.: Working Knowledge: How Organisations Manage What They Know. Harvard Business School Press, Boston (1998)
15. Driscoll, M.: Psychology of Learning for Instruction. Allyn & Bacon, Boston (2000)
16. Edelson, D.C.: Design research: what we learn when we engage in design. J. Learn. Sci. **11**(1), 105–121 (2002)
17. Edersheim, E.H.: The Definitive Drucker. McGraw-Hill, New York (2007)
18. Ekwensi, F., Moranski, J., Townsend-Sweet, M.: E-learning concepts and techniques. Technnical report, University of Pennsylvania (2006)

19. Fatima, S., Abdullah, S.: Improving teaching methodology in system analysis and design using problem based learning for ABET. J. Mod. Educ. Comput. Sci. **7**, 60–68 (2013)
20. de Azeredo Barros, V.F., Ramos, I., Perez, G.: Information systems and organizational memory: a literature review. J. Inf. Syst. Technol. Manag. **12**(1), 45–64 (2015)
21. Hahn, J., Subramani, M.R.: A framework of knowledge management systems: issues and challenges for theory and practice. In: ICIS 2000 Proceedings of the 21st International Conference on Information Systems (2000)
22. Hakky, R.: Improving basic design courses through competences of tuning MEDA. J. High. Educ. **4**(1), 21–42 (2016)
23. Hey, J.: The data, information, knowledge, wisdom chain: the metaphorical link. UNESCO Interovernmental Oceanographic Commission (2004)
24. Illeris, K.: Towards a contemporary and comprehensive theory of learning. Int. J. Lifelong Educ. **22**(4), 396–406 (2003)
25. Imrie, B.W.: Assessment for learning: quality and taxonomies. Assess. Eval. High. Educ. **20**(2), 175–189 (1995)
26. van Rensburg, J.T.J, Goede, R.: A reflective practice approach for supporting IT skills required by industry through project-based learning. In: Kabanda, S., et al. (eds.) SACLA 2018. CCIS, vol. 963, pp. 253–266. Springer, Cham (2019)
27. Jordaan, M.: Community-based project module: a service-learning module for the faculty of engineering, built environment and information technology at the University of Pretoria. Int. J. Serv. Learn. Eng. (Spec. Ed.), 269–282 (2014)
28. Kolb, D.A.: Experiential Learning: Experience as the Source of Learning and Development. Prentice Hall, Englewood Cliffs (1984)
29. Krathwohl, D.R.: A revision of Bloom's taxonomy: an overview. Theory Pract. **41**(4), 212–218 (2002)
30. Kutay, C., Aurum, A.: Knowledge transformation for education in software engineering. Int. J. Mob. Learn. Organ. **1**(1), 58–80 (2007)
31. Lebedeva, O., Prokofjeva, N.: The use of systems for knowledge search in e-learning. In: Proceedings of the International Association for the Development of the Information Society, pp. 343–348. IADIS Press (2012)
32. Lee, C.C., Yang, J.: Knowledge value chain. J. Manag. Dev. **19**(9), 783–793 (2000)
33. Lindvall, M., Rus, I., Sinha, S.S.: Software systems support for knowledge management. J. Knowl. Manag. **7**(5), 137–150 (2003)
34. Lundvall, B., Johnson, B.: The learning economy. J. Ind. Stud. **1**(2), 23–42 (2006)
35. Moteleb, A.A., Woodman, M.: Notions of knowledge management: a gap analysis. J. Knowl. Manag. **5**(1), 55–62 (2007)
36. Nonaka, I., Takeuchi, H.: The Knowledge Creating Company. Oxford University Press, Oxford (1995)
37. Nonaka, I., Toyama, R., Konno, N.: SECI, BA and leadership: a unified model of dynamic knowledge creation. Long Range Plan. **33**, 5–34 (2000)
38. Polanyi, M.: Tacit knowing: its bearing on some problems of philosophy. Rev. Mod. Phys. **34**(4), 601–606 (1962)
39. Pretorius, H.W., Hattingh, M.J.: Factors influencing poor performance in systems analysis and design: student reflections. In: Proceedings of the SACLA 2017. CCIS, vol. 730, pp. 251–264 (2017)
40. Sallis, E., Jones, G.: Knowledge Management in Education: Enhancing Learning and Education. Routledge, London (2012)
41. Sandoval, W.A., Bell, P.: Design-based research methods for studying learning in context: introduction. Educ. Psychol. **39**(4), 199–201 (2004)

42. Saulnier, B.M.: Towards a 21st century information systems education: high impact practices and essential learning outcomes. Issues Inf. Syst. **17**(1), 168–177 (2016)
43. Schmidt, A.: Knowledge maturing and the continuity of context as a unifying concept for knowledge management and e-learning in learning in process. In: I-KNOW 2005 Proceedings of the Special Track on Interacting Working and Learning (2005)
44. Siemens, S.: Connectivism: a learning theory for the digital age. Int. J. Instr. Technol. Distance Learn. **2**(1), 1–28 (2005)
45. Stephenson, J.: The concept of capability and its importance in higher education. In: Stephenson, J., Yorke, M. (eds.) Capability and Quality in Higher Education. Routledge (2013)
46. Wang, F., Hannafin, M.J.: Design-based research and technology-enhanced learning environments. Educ. Technol. Res. Dev. **53**(4), 5–23 (2005)
47. Williamson, J., Pretorius, E., Jacobs, M.: An investigation into student performance in first year biology at the University of Johannesburg. In: ISTE 2014 Proceedings of the International Conference on Mathematics, Science and Technology Education, p. 181 (2014)
48. Wilson, K., van Alebeek, W.: Analyzing the media narratives in South Africa's #FeesMustFall movement. In: Latiner Raby, R., Valeau, E. (eds.) Handbook of Comparative Studies on Community Colleges and Global Counterparts. SIHE, pp. 1–17. Springer, Cham (2017). https://doi.org/10.1007/978-3-319-38909-7_16-1

Teaching Programming

Contextualisation of Abstract Programming Concepts for First Year IT Students: A Reflective Study

Carin Venter and Tanja Eksteen(✉)

School of Computer Science and Information Systems, North-West University,
Vanderbijlpark, South Africa
{carin.venter,tanja.eksteen}@nwu.ac.za

Abstract. Higher education in South Africa must be transformed. An important dimension that can be addressed in the short term, yet will still have a significant positive impact, is the enrichment of courses with relevant content that resonates with students, i.e. to contextualise the study material. This paper focuses on enrichment of a specific introductory information technology (IT) programming course that is taught to first year students at a South African university. This course is problematic as the students fail to grasp the abstract programming concepts that are crucial for higher-order learning. They can then not apply these concepts practically; this is crucial for them so that they can become good programmers. We applied the soft systems methodology, as a reflective practice, to explore the perspectives of the students, so as to enable incorporation thereof in the teaching material and as such contextualise the material. The outcome of this study is contextualised examples and metaphors relating to the key abstract concepts that will be applied in class.

Keywords: Contextualisation of curricula
Information technology education · Programming skills

1 Introduction

Universities play a crucial role in societies, and even more so in developing countries such as South Africa. Proper education is a fundamental building block to develop countries, so as to expand welfare and foster economic growth. For this, universities must remain relevant. They must respond to the needs of both the local and global societies that they serve; they must also meet requirements of the national and international world of work [17,18].

In this paper we aim to improve the teaching of abstract information technology (IT) programming concepts for first year IT students. Abstract concepts are crucial for higher-order understanding. However, they are difficult to perceive since *"they do not have a bounded, identifiable, and clearly perceivable referent"* [1]. The aim of this study is therefore to enable the students to learn

© Springer Nature Switzerland AG 2019
S. Kabanda et al. (Eds.): SACLA 2018, CCIS 963, pp. 143–157, 2019.
https://doi.org/10.1007/978-3-030-05813-5_10

about abstract programming concepts through the perspective lenses of their respective world views, so as to aid understanding and internalisation of the concepts. A holistic research approach is used to structure the study. It is based on [6] wherein it is suggested that an identified area of concern be investigated using a methodology that embodies a particular philosophical framework, i.e. a linked set of ideas. The Soft systems methodology (SSM) is a methodology that gives epistemological guidance to explore social contexts [3,4]. It provides a learning system that enables problem solvers to explore and understand the world through the perceptions that involved participants' have of their world. So, we applied SSM to guide the reflection process.

The paper is organised as follows: The structure of the study is discussed in Sect. 2. Section 3 gives an overview of the key concepts. Section 4 discusses the empirical study and Sect. 5 gives a short discussion of the research. Section 6 discusses future research. Lastly, a summary is given in Sect. 7.

2   Research Design

This study is structured according to [6], wherein a holistic and reflective research entails three elements: a methodology (M) that embodies a particular linked set of ideas, i.e. a framework (F), that can be applied to investigate a specific instance of an identified area of concern (A). This is referred to as the FMA framework; practical applications and examples are discussed in more detail in [7]. The FMA framework is illustrated in Fig. 1. The application of the FMA framework in this study is discussed next.

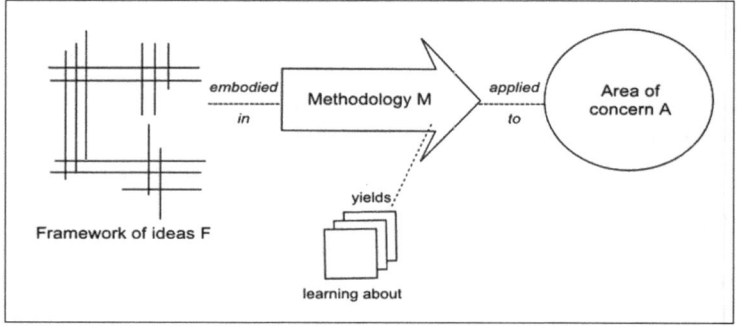

Fig. 1. FMA illustration: elements in research according to [6]

Area of Concern. An area of concern (A) expresses the purpose and motivation of a study. It constitutes a *"real-world situation which seems relevant to research themes which {a researcher} regards as significant"* [6]. The theme of this study relates to teaching of abstract IT concepts to first year IT students;

this is a problematical area as the students find these abstract concepts difficult to grasp. This is discussed further in Subsect. 3.1. The real-world situation of this research theme is as follows: As an example, out of approximately 240 first year students the average marks for specific questions that tested knowledge of abstract programming concepts were 16% and 31% respectively for two consecutive examination opportunities.

Framework of Ideas and Methodology. A framework of ideas (F) and embedded applied methodology (M) outline the research approach of a study. Reflective practice necessitates the inclusion of practices to identify and explore relevant assumptions or questions about the problem being investigated, and the kind of change required to bring about improvement [19]. In this study, the identified area of concern is reflected upon within the holistic framework of systems thinking. It is discussed in Subsect. 3.2. The Soft Systems Methodology (SSM) is a reflective methodology based on systems thinking principles; it enables reflection on a (problematical) status quo so as to define improvement [7]. SSM guides the reflection in this study; it is discussed in Subsect. 3.3.

3   Key Concepts

The key concepts in this study are the contextual teaching of abstract concepts, as well as systems thinking and soft systems methodology. They are discussed in the following sub-sections.

3.1   Contextual Teaching of Abstract Concepts

The concept of 'knowledge' is broad: it refers to knowledge by acquaintance; practical knowledge or skill; and factual or propositional knowledge. These types of knowledge are intricately complex and their relatedness should be appreciated. However, identifying smaller projects and focusing on portions of dimensions that can be implemented incrementally, still contribute to the bigger whole, and add perceptible value in the short-term; it enables a problem solver to overcome enormous complications in a stepwise manner [1]. So, to find a reasonable starting point amidst all the complexity, we decided to focus on impartation of practical knowledge; we focused specifically on teaching of IT programming concepts to first year IT students.

Knowledge is contextual; yet, it is not entirely context bound. Knowledge, when *"correctly seen, is anchored objectively by truth, or facts, that is, by the way of the world is"* [13]. The way that the world is, is, however, perceptively different for different people in different cultures. Concrete concepts, e.g. 'cat' or 'table', are easily and universally understandable and explainable as they can be seen, touched, heard, etc. On the other hand, abstract concepts, e.g. 'love' or 'justice', are more difficult to apprehend, define and explain. They are difficult to grasp as they do not have single, bounded, identifiable referents that are perceivable by the senses [1]. However, abstract concepts are crucial for higher-order cognition.

Teaching of abstract IT programming concepts to the first year IT students is problematic at the South African university where the study was conducted. The students must make sense of concepts such as variables, constants, identifiers, values, syntax, algorithms, etc. They must learn what these are theoretically, and how they are to be applied practically. During the course of a year, it becomes clear that they find it difficult to grasp and apply the concepts. For example, on a yearly basis, an average of 69% of first year IT students are unable to demonstrate theoretical and practical knowledge of these concepts during formal examinations upon completion of the module. Contextual learning is particularly relevant for computer science subjects such as programming. Students must learn to think about computers in the context of solving problems with it, rather than merely using it as utilities. They must learn *"to think about the world in a different way"* [2].

Examples and metaphors should be used in class so as to ground the concepts and engage students. The use of metaphors to teach abstract concepts is applied universally with success [9,14,21,22]. Metaphors, as mental constructions that aid structuring of experiences as well as development of imagination and reasoning, are used by people *"to conceptualise, to represent and to communicate thoughts and actions in their everyday lives"* [14]. However, the metaphors must be relevant and resonate with the students.

3.2   Systems Thinking

The word 'system' is widely used for many different concepts. Ordinarily, it relates to the concept of a system as a mechanism, and describe tangible entities [7]. A 'system' is then a representation of an orderly unit, consisting of components that can be broken down into recognisable individual elements making up the (whole) unit. From this mechanistic systems viewpoint the objectives of a system can be accurately defined; the system can then be constructed to achieve defined objectives; and problematical systems can be systematically analysed, engineered and re-engineered to solve problems [4].

However, from the 1980s onwards, a different view arose where the concept of systems were applied to intervene in, and seek to improve, problematic social situations that involve (unpredictable) human participants, and cannot easily be broken into recognisable parts. From this 'soft systems' viewpoint, a system is concept of coherent whole entities, rather than a description of something in the world [4]. From this perspective, a system is an abstraction which describes the divergent ways in which people conceptually organise their thoughts about the world, rather than what the world consist of [11,16]. A system can now be applied as a conceptual tool to explore and understand social situations as well as social contexts; it facilitates understanding of the status quo [20]. It provides a process of enquiry whereby complex problematical social situations or contexts can be explored; SSM was developed to operationalise these notions of systems thinking [7]. It was therefore applied in this study to explore the contexts and perspectives of the students. SSM is discussed next.

3.3   The Soft Systems Methodology (SSM)

Peter Checkland developed SSM for ill-structured and complex (messy) problem situations where participants generally agree on objectives, but the means to achieve them are still to be selected [7]. SSM gives epistemological guidance to explore appreciative settings in situations that require 'action-to-improve' [3,4]. It models through a learning system that presumes that social reality continuously changes. Never ending purposeful activities of social participants result in ever evolving social developments, and therefore aims to continuously explore models of purposeful activity coherently [6]. It enables problem solvers to understand the world where they aim to intervene through understanding of involved participants' perceptions of their world, i.e. their world views [16].

In the context of SSM, purposeful activity requires that a problem solver engages in a cyclical process where he/she: learns about a problematical real-world situation; selects relevant human activity systems; makes models of them; applies the models to question the real-world situation through comparison; and uses the debate that was initiated by the comparison to define purposeful action to improve the problem situation [7]. It is illustrated in Fig. 2.

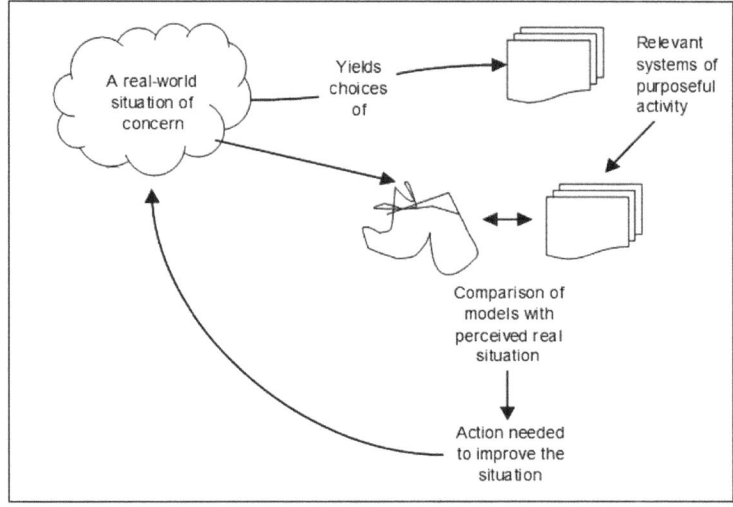

Fig. 2. Basic process of purposeful activity embedded in SSM [7]

A problem solver attempting to intervene in a problematical social context must consider various aspects, e.g. the *"whats and hows of the improvement"* and the people *"through whose eyes 'improvement' is to be judged"* as well as the history of the situation *"of which there will always be more than one account"*; it requires logical analysis of people's perceptions of various purposeful actions (tasks) as well as the various things that people disagree on (issues), and comparing them with perceptions of the portion of the real world that is being examined [7]. The purpose of these comparisons are to initiate and structure debate about change. A detailed and cyclical process of enquiry embedded in SSM is illustrated in Fig. 3 (adapted from [7]).

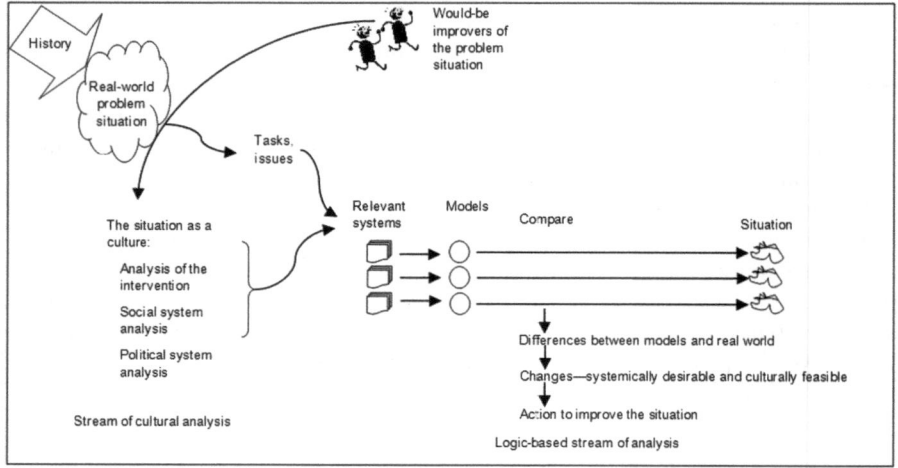

Fig. 3. The SSM process, adapted from [7]

The outcome of the analysis process is presented in the form of a 'rich picture' representing the structure, process and climate of the problem situation or context structure [5]. It allows problem solvers to question real-world situations through comparison, and uses the debate initiated by the comparison, to define purposeful action [7]. So, a rich picture for this study is drawn (Fig. 10); it refers to the perceptive models of the students, as per the analysed interpreted data of Sect. 4.

4   Empirical Study

In this section, we apply SSM to reflect on the IT concepts. These form the foundation of the introductory programming course.

4.1   IT Concepts

The concepts and associated (actual) definitions applied in the study were as follows; the definitions were derived from prescribed text books [10,12,15]:

Sequence Structure: A program structure that contains steps that execute in order. A sequence can have any number of tasks, but there is no chance to branch and/or skip any of the tasks.

Operators: A symbol or characters that represent an action.

Data Type: The characteristic of a value; a variable or constant's data type describes the kinds of values it can hold, and the type of operations that can be performed with it.

Syntax: The formal rules (grammar) of a formal language.

Variable: A named memory location of a specific data type whose contents can vary or differ over time.

Value: The representation of an entity or unit that can be manipulated by a computer program.

Constant: A named memory location of a specific data type whose contents never vary or differ over time.

Algorithm: The steps, and sequence thereof, necessary to solve a problem.

Identifiers: The names of a program's components.

4.2   Participants and Data Gathering

A class exercise were presented to first year students as a game; they played this 'game' in the first introductory class of an academic year. Students were randomly divided into nine groups (they took a number out of a hat upon entering the class). Each of the groups randomly received a concept (name) and its actual definition: see Subsect. 4.1 for details. The groups also received 'game papers' to plan how they wanted to demonstrate or explain the given concept to the class. The only rules were that they were not allowed to use the given definition as-is, and name the concept aloud when demonstrating it to the class; they were reminded of the typical '30 s', 'Pictionary' and 'Charades' type of games. Each group demonstrated or explained a concept, whilst the rest of the class had to guess what the concept was. Thereafter, the groups (that did not see the actual definition of the concept), had to devise a suitable definition of their own, to relate to the concept.

The concept and actual definition represented the relevant systems as per the real world situation. The demonstrations or explanations represented their perceptive models of these concepts. The newly devised definitions represented the different (comparative) models between the real world and the students' perspective models. Their perceptions have to be reconciled with the actual definitions to ensure that they understand and grasp these abstract concepts, for application in programming. This will be done in class during the semester to entrench (anchor) the knowledge so as to enable the students to intuitively apply these abstract concepts. Intuitive application is necessary for higher-order learning; see Fig. 4.

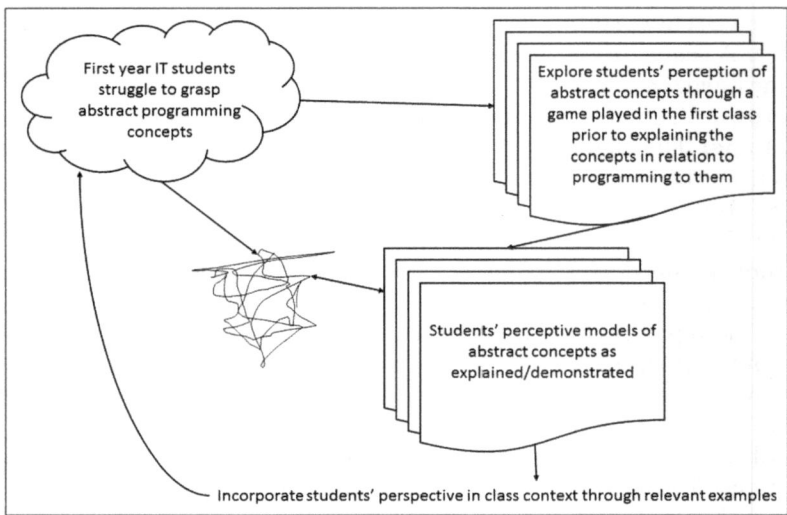

Fig. 4. Planned purposeful activity

4.3   Data Analysis

Data gathered are analysed and presented per concept presented to, and by, the nine groups; this is discussed next. Figures 5, 6, 7, 8 and 9 show the excerpts from the game pages relating to the abstract concepts of the following sub-sub-sections.

Sequence Structure. The concept 'sequence structure' was presented by the first group. They explained it as per the picture below; the example that they used is that of making coffee (Fig. 5). This seem to be a relevant example within the frame of reference of most students. They did not use any words that refer directly to the original definition that was given to them.

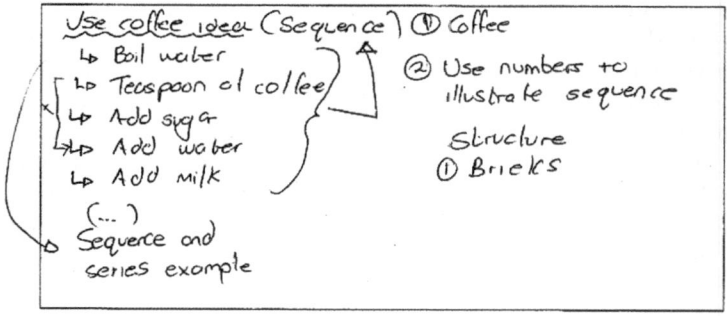

Fig. 5. Excerpt from the game page for 'sequence'

The rest of the class was able to guess the right answer, i.e. that this explanation was that of a sequence structure, within five minutes. The definitions then presented by the rest of the class included reference to 'order' (three of the remaining eight groups); 'steps' (two groups); and organised pattern of tasks or instructions (three groups). The class was thus able to grasp the underlying principles of this concept through this game. The related keywords that the rest of the class then identified to be associated with this concept are all applicable to the formal definition thereof, i.e.: *"A program structure that contains steps that execute in order. A sequence can have any number of tasks, but there is no chance to branch and/or skip any of the tasks"*.

Operator. The concept 'operator' was presented second. The group explained it as something that describes *"a person that drives a car; likewise with an aircraft or a train"* and *"the human intervention that controls the mechanical device"*. They did not use any words that refer directly to the original definition that was given to them. The rest of the class was again able to guess the right answer, i.e. that this explanation was that of an operator, within five minutes. The bulk of the definitions presented by the rest of the class included reference to something that controls the function of something, such as system (six of eight groups). The class was thus able to grasp the underlying principle of this concept through this game. These are applicable to the formal definition thereof, i.e.: *"A symbol or characters that represent an action"*.

Data Type. The concept 'data type' was presented third. This group struggled to visualise the concept and demonstrate/explain it as such. They used examples of data types, e.g. 'integers', 'doubles', 'strings' and referred to *"different kinds of information"*, rather than attempting to explain it through a different or associative example. Still, they did not use any words that refer directly to the original definition that was given to them. The rest of the class took longer to guess the right answer. They also struggled to come up with a definition for the concept on their own. Only two of the eight groups were able to identify the core characteristics of the concept, i.e.: a *"category in which raw information falls"*, and *"data categorised differently by its contents"*; these two groups grasped some of this concept's meaning, i.e.: *"the characteristic of a value; a variable or constant's data type describes the kinds of values it can hold, and the type of operations that can be performed with it"*.

Syntax. The concept 'syntax' was presented fourth. This group struggled to visualise the concept and demonstrate or explain it. They were unable to use words that do not refer directly to the original definition that was given to them. They also struggled to come up with a definition for the concept on their own. The rest of the class were thus unable to devise their own definitions for this concept.

Variable. The concept 'variable' was presented by the fifth group. They explained it as per Fig. 6; the example that this group used relate to the mathematical definition of a variable. They did not use any words that refer directly to the original definition that was given to them. The rest of the class was able to guess the right answer, i.e. that this explanation was that of a variable, within five minutes. The definitions then presented by the rest of the class included reference to something that is 'unknown' (four of the remaining eight groups); something that can be used as a 'placeholder' or 'container' (two groups); and something that is yet to be defined (four groups).

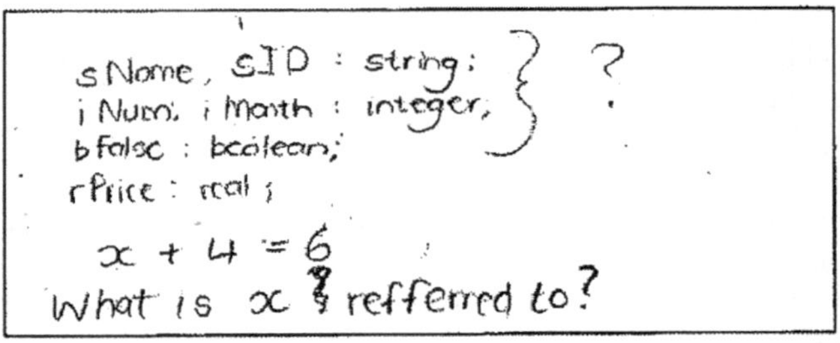

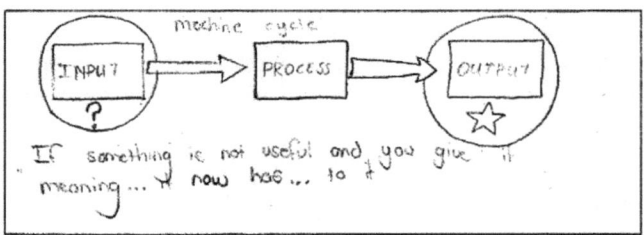

Fig. 6. Excerpt from the game page for 'variable'

The class was thus able to grasp the underlying principles of this concept through this game. The related keywords that the rest of the class identified to be associated with this concept are all applicable to it, i.e.: *"a named memory location of a specific data type whose contents can vary or differ over time"*.

Value. The concept 'value' was presented sixth. The students explained it with the picture shown in Fig. 7; the example that this group used related to a flow diagram where input is processed into valuable output.

Fig. 7. Excerpt from the game page for 'value'

They did not use any words that refer directly to the original definition that was given to them. The rest of the class was able to guess the right answer, i.e. that this explanation was that of values, within five minutes. The bulk of the definitions then presented by the rest of the class included reference to the undertaking whereby something acquires significant meaning or importance (five groups). Some referred to a numerical 'amount' that can be calculated (three of the groups); and one group referred to value as an 'output of an equation'. The class was thus able to grasp the underlying principles of this concept through this game. The related keywords that the class identified to be associated with this concept are applicable to the formal definition thereof, i.e.: *"the representation of an entity/unit that can be manipulated by a computer program"*.

Constant. The concept 'constant' was presented by the seventh group. The students explained it as shown in Fig. 8. They did not use any words that refer directly to the original definition that was given to them.

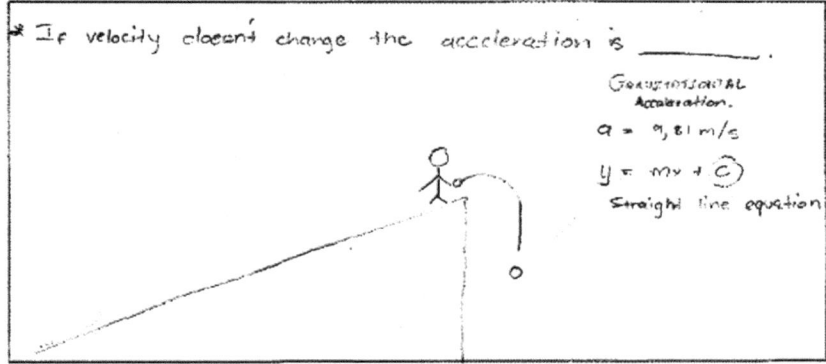

Fig. 8. Excerpt from the game page for 'constant'

The rest of the class was able to guess the right answer, i.e. that this explanation was that of a constant, within five minutes. All the definitions then presented by the rest of the class included reference to something that does not change and/or remain the same. The class was thus able to grasp the underlying principles of this concept through this game. The related keywords that the rest of the class identified to be associated with this concept are all applicable to the formal definition thereof, i.e.: *"a named memory location of a specific data type whose contents never vary or differ over time"*.

Algorithm. The concept 'algorithm' was presented eighth. The students explained it as per Fig. 9; the example that this group used related to instructions for making toast.[1] They did not use any words that refer directly to the original definition that was given to them.

---

[1] For comparison see [8] on algorithms and recipes.

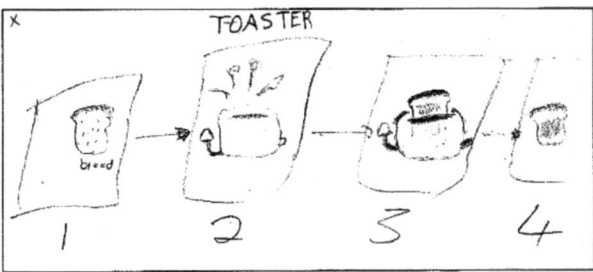

Fig. 9. Excerpts from game page for 'algorithm'

The rest of the class was able to guess the right answer, i.e. that this explanation was that of an algorithm, within five minutes. The definitions then presented by the rest of the class included reference to a set of ordered instructions or rules (five groups); and a problem solving process (three groups). So, the class was able to grasp the underlying principles of this concept through this game. The related keywords that the rest of the class identified to be associated with this concept are all applicable to the formal definition thereof, i.e.: *"the steps, and sequence thereof, necessary to solve a problem"*.

Identifier. The concept 'identifier' was presented last. This group struggled to visualise the concept and demonstrate or explain it as such. They were unable to use words that do not refer directly to the original definition that was given to them. They also struggled to come up with a definition for the concept on their own. The rest of the class were thus unable to devise their own definitions.

5   Discussion

In this study we incorporated the data gathered into a rich picture (Fig. 10). SSM enabled us to reflect on the problem situation and explore relevant assumptions. By exploring the perspectives of the students in the first introductory class, prior to explaining the programming concepts to them, we were able to identify the kind of change required for improvement. We were able to identify relevant examples and metaphors that can now be incorporated in the study material, so as to contextualise the abstract concepts when explaining them to the students in terms of application in programming.

It was interesting that the students applied not only simple, everyday examples in their explanations, but also incorporated examples from mathematics and physics. The students associated the abstract concepts to prior knowledge obtained in school and during formative years. This insight can now assist the lecturer to incorporate these and other similar examples and metaphors in class.

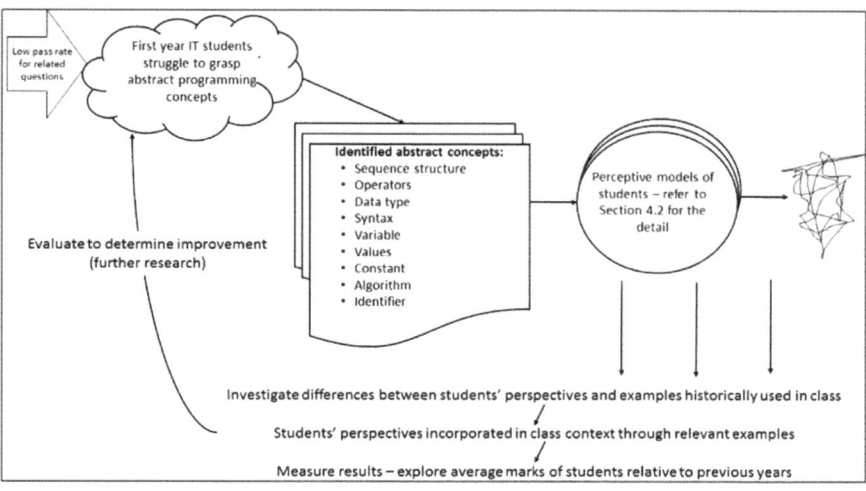

Fig. 10. Research process and outcome

6   Future Research

This research entailed an initial study to identify examples and metaphors to be included in study material, so as to contextualise it. The next step will be to test whether the inclusion thereof yielded positive results. This can only be done after the first examination opportunity upon completion of this course module. Other universities and relevant institutions will also be included in future research, so as to compare and contrast ideas and outcomes.

7   Summary

In this paper we aimed to improve the teaching of abstract IT programming concepts for first year IT students. We applied SSM as a reflective practice to identify relevant contextual examples and metaphors that are representative of the students' perspectives. SSM enables identification of various perspectives in order to understand and reconcile possible differing visions of participants. Contextual learning is important in higher education; students must obtain higher-order knowledge. For this, it is important that they can associate with examples used in class so that they can apply it practically rather than only theoretically. Examples and metaphors were derived from a game that the students played in class. Students were given key concepts and definitions; they were then requested to explain or demonstrate these to class mates (they were reminded of the typical '30 s', 'Pictionary' and 'Charades' type of games). Each group demonstrated or explained a concept, whilst the rest of the class had to guess which concept was illustrated. The other groups had to devise a suitable definition of their own, to relate to the concept, so as to determine whether they really understood the explanation or demonstration. Everyday examples (e.g. making coffee/toast) as well as relevant examples from maths and physics were used by the students. So they associated the concepts with prior knowledge obtained. Therefore, the lecturers are able to incorporate similar examples and metaphors in study material.

References

1. Borghi, A.M., Binkofski, F., Castelfranchi, C., Cimatti, F., Scorolli, C., Tummolini, L.: The challenge of abstract concepts. Psychol. Bull. **143**(3), 263–292 (2017)
2. Caldwell, H., Smith, N.: Teaching computing unplugged in primary schools: exploring primary computing through practical activities away from the computer. Learning Matters Ltd. (2017)
3. Checkland, P.: Autobiographical retrospectives: learning your way to 'action to improve': the development of soft systems thinking and soft systems methodology. Int. J. Gen. Syst. **40**(5), 487–512 (2011)
4. Checkland, P.: Four conditions for serious systems thinking and action. Syst. Res. Behav. Sci. **29**(5), 465–469 (2012)
5. Checkland, P.: Systems Thinking, Systems Practice, 10th edn. Wiley, Hoboken (1981)
6. Checkland, P., Holwell, S.: Information, Systems, and iNformation Systems: Making Sense of the Field. Wiley, Hoboken (1998)
7. Checkland, P., Scholes, J.: Soft Systems Methodology in Action. Wiley, Hoboken (1990)
8. Cleland, C.E.: Recipes, algorithms, and programs. Mind Mach. **11**(2), 219–237 (2001)
9. Condello, A.: Metaphor as analogy: reproduction and production of legal concepts. J. Law Soc. **43**(1), 8–26 (2016)
10. Farrel, J.: Programming Logic and Design, 9th edn. Cengage Learning, Boston (2017)
11. Flood, R.L., Jackson, M.C.: Creative Problem Solving: Total Systems Intervention. Wiley, Hoboken (1991)
12. Forouzan, B.A., Mosharraf, F.: Foundations of Computer Science, 4th edn. Cengage Learning, Boston (2017)
13. Horsthemke, K.: Knowledge, education and the limits of Africanisation. J. Philos. Educ. **38**(4), 571–587 (2004)
14. Kaphesi, E.: Third-year university mathematics education students' metaphorical understanding of mathematics teaching and learning. Afr. J. Res. Math. Sci. Technol. Educ. **18**(3), 276–286 (2014)
15. Lambert, K.A.: Fundamentals of Python: First Programs, 2nd edn. Cengage Learning, Boston (2018)
16. Mingers, J.: Towards an appropriate social theory for applied systems thinking: critical theory and soft systems methodology. J. Appl. Syst. Anal. **7**, 41–50 (1980)
17. Mkhonto, T.J., Muller, A.: Challenges facing higher education curriculum reform, design, and management in the 21st century: an epistemological perspective. J. New Gen. Sci. **7**(1), 109–127 (2009)
18. Mngomezulu, B.R.: What does the Africanisation of a university entail? Lessons from East Africa. AFFRIKA J. Polit. Econ. Soc. **3**(1), 97–113 (2013)

19. Ulrich, W.: Critical Heuristics of Social Planning: A New Approach to Practical Philosophy. Paul Haupt, Görlitz (1983)
20. Vickers, G.: Human systems are different. Bus. Horiz. **27**(5), 83–84 (1984)
21. Wall, T.: Good stories: using metaphors to teach philosophy. Proc. Soc. Behav. Sci. **106**, 1271–1277 (2013)
22. Zhao, J.: Conceptualizing English academic writing via verbal and manual metaphors. Iberica **17**, 119–138 (2009)

Syntactic Generation of Practice Novice Programs in Python

Abejide Ade-Ibijola$^{(\boxtimes)}$

Department of Applied Information Systems, University of Johannesburg,
Johannesburg, South Africa
abejideai@uj.ac.za

Abstract. In the present day, computer programs are written in high level languages and parsed syntactically as part of a compilation process. These parsers are defined with context-free grammars (CFGs), a language recogniser for the respective programming language. Formal grammars in general are used for language *recognition* or *generation*. In this paper we present the automatic generation of procedural programs in Python using a CFG. We have defined CFG rules to model program templates and implemented these rules to produce infinitely many distinct practice programs in Python. Each generated program is designed to test a novice programmer's knowledge of functions, expressions, loops, and/or conditional statements. The CFG rules are highly generic and can be extended to generate programs in other procedural languages. The resulting programs can be used as practice, test or examination problems in introductory programming courses. 500,000 iterations of generated programs can be found at: https://tinyurl.com/pythonprogramgenerator. A survey of 103 students' perception showed that 93.1% strongly agreed that these programs can help them in practice and improve their programming skills.

Keywords: Synthesis of things · Program synthesis
Practice Python programs · Novice programmers
Context-free grammar applications

1 Introduction

Teaching novices how to program takes much time and it requires much patience [19]. Similarly, learning how to program is difficult for novice programmers, with evidences of high drop-out rates in introductory programming courses [8,9,16, 34]. Much research has gone into pedagogy models of teaching this subject and software tools for aiding the learning process. This has given rise to the domain of *novice program comprehension and automatic tutoring* [26,33]—the study of:

1. what misconceptions (or difficulties) novice programmers have [18],
2. what pedagogy models can help them [11], and

© Springer Nature Switzerland AG 2019
S. Kabanda et al. (Eds.): SACLA 2018, CCIS 963, pp. 158–172, 2019.
https://doi.org/10.1007/978-3-030-05813-5_11

3. what technological interventions can be used to support the learning process
of the subject [33].

Novice Misconceptions or Difficulties: Novice programmers often struggle
with comprehending the syntax of programming languages [11], having to
learn a number of different set of skills at the same time [34], the debugging
process [6], lack of practice [25], the complexity of certain topics (such as
arrays, loops, and relational or Boolean algebra for conditional statements)
that are difficult to understand [7,10,36].

Pedagogy Models: Some popular pedagogy models that have been adopted in
teaching programming include: teaching without the vehicle of a language
(e.g. using textual algorithms) [11], adopting the productive failure technique, (i.e. giving students complex problems to solve while hoping they
form their own solutions before giving them direct instructions) [29], and
teaching problem solving before programming [15].

Technological Interventions: Several approaches have been employed to aid
novice program comprehension using technology, such as introducing serious
games [24] with findings revealing that these games add to the fun element
in learning, and students rated the game as an effective way to learn programming [23]. Automatic program summarisation [14], automatic program
narration [3] and program visualisation [32] aids have also been proposed to
aid program comprehension.

One major way to aid novice program comprehension is to get novices to practice
more [12,15,21,28], as emphases has been laid on the lack of practice as one
major reason for high failure rates [25]. This is not only true for programming,
as it has been proven that acquiring long-term knowledge and skill often depend
on the frequency of practice [20].

This paper presents the syntactic generation of programming exercises—that
can be completed with pen and paper—as a practice aid for novice programmers. To achieve this, we have adopted random context-free grammars (CFG) in
the formalisation of programming templates and implemented these formalisms
to produce unique instances of Python programs. These programs cover basic
programming concepts such as assignment statement, function calls, evaluation
of arithmetic expressions and predefined functions, conditional statements and
loops. This process is sketched in Fig. 1.

Fig. 1. Process of Python program generation using CFG rules

In Fig. 1 we take a category of the desired programs (e.g. simple arithmetic programs, programs with loops, programs with if-statements, etc.) and an integer indicating the number of iterations of such programs that is to be generated, and use the predefined CFG rules to generate new and unique instances of the requested program.

We have leveraged on findings that claim that practice can aid novice program comprehension and hence, made the following contributions. We have:

1. designed a random context-free grammar (a set of rules) for the automatic generation of practice programming problems in Python—a programming language widely used in teaching introductory programming,
2. implemented the grammar rules and shown that it generates infinitely many Python programs that can be given to novice programmers as pen-and-paper practice problems, and
3. evaluated the usefulness of the generated programs and shown that novice programmers across two universities find them very helpful.

The remainder of this paper is organised as follows. Section 2 presents the background and related work. Section 3 presents the CFG design for Python programs generation. Section 4 presents the implementation of the CFG rules and iterations of generated programs. Section 5 discusses an evaluation of this idea, while Sect. 6 presents the conclusion and future work.

2   Background and Related Work

In this section we introduce the problem, justify the choice of Python, discuss the motivation and related work.

2.1   Problem Statement

The problem tackled in this paper is summed up in the following questions.

1. Can we aid program comprehension by algorithmically generating more practice programs?
2. How do we design and implement context-free grammars to answer Question 1 of above?
3. What is the perception of novice programmers about automatically generated programs as practice and/or comprehension aids?

These questions are answered in Sects. 3–5 of this paper.

2.2   Motivation

The following are known challenges of teaching and learning introductory programming:

Programming is Difficult: Learning to program is difficult [8,9,34], and more practice can aid this process [12,15,21,28].

High Failure Rates: There are high failure and drop-out rates from introductory programming courses around the world, despite extensive research which attempts to address the issue [9,16].

Wrong Learning Style: Students often find programming difficult when they adopt the wrong style of learning (e.g. memorising programs, practising with past questions, etc.) or have the wrong motivation (e.g. wanting to pass the course and proceed with their mainstream courses)—if its an elective[1] [17].

These challenges have motivated this paper, resulting in a technique for the automatic generation of Python programs that can be used as practice problems by novice programmers.

2.3   Why Python?

In 2016, Python was ranked the second most widely used programming language in teaching introductory programming [30],[2] and recent assessments show that the use of Python has resulted in better successes in teaching programming at first year [35]. This language is used in the university where we have evaluated the results of this paper. All Python programs generated and presented in this paper are of Version 3.x.[3]

2.4   Type and Syntax of Python Practice Programs

This paper focuses on a specific type of programming practice problems, namely: *program tracing*. Program tracing exercises require a novice to determine the values of variables and validity of statements at every program state and, hence, determine the final output (if any) of a program (or report a bug). These types of exercises are well used to test a novice's knowledge of basic concepts such as functions, loops, conditional statements, etc. An example of this type of programming problem shown in Listing 1.1.

Listing 1.1. Sample Program Tracing Exercise 1

```
1 #Determine the output of the following program fragment:
2 x = 5
3 for y in range(1,6):
4         print(x * y)
```

W.r.t. Listing 1.1, the student is given a program fragment to test the knowledge of: assignment of values to variables, range in Python, the use of `for` loops, and print statements. Here, the novice is expected to produce the set of results: 5, 10, 15, 20, 25 on separate lines.

---

[1] Electives are courses not in the mainstream of the offered degree. An example is a student studying towards a Bachelor's degree in Chemistry, who takes an introductory programming course in Python.

[2] Java ranked first.

[3] https://www.python.org/doc/versions/.

Listing 1.2. Sample Program Tracing Exercise 2

```
1  i = -11
2  u4 = 5
3  w = (i - u4)
4  print(w)
```

In Listing 1.2 the task is simpler. A novice is expected to add the values of two variables together i and $u4$, and display the result of the addition. In order to generate this type of a practice problem, we just need to generate a 'random program' that has the structure shown in Syntax 1.

Syntax 1:

$$
\begin{aligned}
&\texttt{initialise identifiers } n \in N \texttt{, assign values } v \in V: \\
&\quad n_1 = v_1 \\
&\quad n_2 = v_2 \\
&\quad \vdots \\
&\quad n_k = v_k, 1 \leq k < |N| \\
&\texttt{set } n_i \in N \longleftarrow \texttt{expr}(n_j \in N | i \neq j) \\
&\texttt{display } n_i
\end{aligned}
$$

The expr function in this syntax is a recursive function that generates simple mathematical expressions as a continuous concatenation of terms. This syntax is generic and can produce the instance shown in Listing 1.3.

Listing 1.3. A Random Instance of Syntax 1.

```
1  x = 4
2  t1 = 20
3  j9 = -19
4  v = ((x + j9)) - ((b - t1))
5  print(v)
```

However, it would be tedious to define many of this type of syntax for the automatic generation of practice Python programs. Hence we have adopted CFGs to formalise this process. With CFGs, non-terminal symbols are created to abstract the repeating components (e.g. identifiers, expressions, conditions, etc.) of templates, thus making it easier to describe the syntax of these programs.

2.5 Target Learning Outcomes

The learning outcomes that we target in this work cover the evaluations of:

1. Built-in functions—mostly mathematical functions (e.g. `floor`, `ceiling`, `abs`, etc.),
2. Expressions (arithmetic, logical and relational),
3. Loops (`for`-loops, and `while`-loops), and
4. Conditional statements, (i.e. `if`, `elif`, `else`).

2.6   Related Work

While there is no work mainly in the automatic generation of practice Python programs, there is related work (using similar techniques) in the areas of:

Synthesis of problems: Generating exercises in algebra for MOOCs [27], generation of problems and solutions for natural deductions and proofs [4], generation of algebra problems to help with mathematics pedagogy [31] using a syntax-directed approach, and grammar-driven generation of regular expression problems and solutions [1].

Synthesis of artefacts: Synthesis of geometry constructions [13] and synthesis of social media profiles using probabilistic context-free grammars (PCFGs) [2].

2.7   Definition of Terms

Here we define some terms used in this paper.

Definition 1 (Symbol, Alphabet, and String [22]). *A symbol is an item or a single token. An alphabet, denoted by Σ is any finite set of symbols. A string is formulated from concatenation of zero or more symbols.*

Definition 2 (Context-free grammar [5]). *A context-free grammar (or CFG) G is a four-tuple: $G = (N, \Sigma, P, S)$ where*

1. *N is a set of nonterminals, also known as 'syntactic variables'. Nonterminal represent phrases/clauses in a sentence. Hence, nonterminals are sometimes referred to as syntactic categories, with every nonterminal defining a sublanguage of the language G.*
2. *Σ is a finite set of terminal symbols, disjoint from N, from which the actual content of a sentence is composed. Σ is referred to as the alphabet of the language defined by the grammar G.*
3. *P is the set of productions, each production consisting of a nonterminal, called the left hand side of the production, a forward arrow, and a sequence of terminal and/or nonterminal symbols, called the right hand side of the production.*
4. *S is the start nonterminal (or start symbol), used to denote the entire sentence. The relation $S \in N$ must always hold.*

More on CFGs can be found in [5,22].

3   Grammar Design for Python Practice Programs

In this section we present the design of a CFG for the automatic generation of Python practice programs. In program design and/or compilation, two classes of languages are often used, namely: regular and context-free languages. Regular languages are used for lexical analysis while context-free languages (CFLs) are used to describe syntax or used for syntax analysis. In this paper, the rules for our templates are mere concatenations of the smaller rules for identifiers, control structures (etc.) of the programming language, hence, it suffices to say that the concatenation of two or more CFLs will always produce a CFL. This is why we have chosen to model these templates using a CFG.

3.1 Building Blocks

We begin the design of our grammar $G = (N, \Sigma, P, S)$ with a building block of production rules $p \in P$ that result in terminal symbols $\alpha \in \Sigma$, such as letters, digits, etc.: see Productions 1–13. Production 1 defines letters that may appear in the formulations of identifier names: this excludes the letters $l, o \in \Sigma_{F_{set}}$. $\Sigma_{F_{set}} = \{l, o\}$ is a forbidden set of alphabets and this constraint is included because of the similarity between $l, 1$ and $o, 0$. In Production 4, we have abstracted a list of parameters to $\hat{p}$, and used this in defining the parameters taken by pre-defined functions in Production 10. Productions 5–9 define operators (arithmetic, logical, and relational). Productions 11–13 are for formatting the final derived string (in this case, a string in this language is a complete Python program).

$$\texttt{<letter>} \longrightarrow l \in \left[\Sigma \cap \Sigma'_{F_{set}} \right] \tag{1}$$

$$\texttt{<digit>} \longrightarrow d \in 0 \mid \ldots \mid 9 \tag{2}$$

$$\texttt{<value>} \longrightarrow v \tag{3}$$

$$\texttt{<parameter\_list>} \longrightarrow \hat{p} \tag{4}$$

$$\texttt{<rel\_op>} \longrightarrow < \mid > \mid <= \mid >= \mid != \mid == \tag{5}$$

$$\texttt{<arth\_op>} \longrightarrow + \mid - \mid * \mid / \mid \% \tag{6}$$

$$\texttt{<logi\_op\_infix>} \longrightarrow and \mid or \mid \wedge \tag{7}$$

$$\texttt{<logi\_op\_prefix>} \longrightarrow not \tag{8}$$

$$\texttt{<logi\_op>} \longrightarrow \texttt{<logi\_op\_infix>} \mid \texttt{<logi\_op\_prefix>} \tag{9}$$

$$\texttt{<pd\_fxns>} \longrightarrow (pow|sqrt|trunc|floor|ceil|\ldots)\texttt{<parameter\_list>} \tag{10}$$

$$\texttt{<nl>} \longrightarrow newline \tag{11}$$

$$\texttt{<tab\_in>} \longrightarrow tab \tag{12}$$

$$\texttt{<spc>} \longrightarrow spc \tag{13}$$

We proceed to define more rules for identifiers, terms, operators, and expressions in Productions 14–18.

$$\texttt{<ident>} \longrightarrow \texttt{<letter>}(\texttt{<letter>}|\texttt{<digit>})^* \tag{14}$$

$$\texttt{<term>} \longrightarrow \texttt{<ident>} \mid \texttt{<value>} \tag{15}$$

$$\texttt{<operator>} \longrightarrow \texttt{<arth\_op>} \mid \texttt{<rel\_op>} \mid \texttt{<logi\_op>} \tag{16}$$

$$\texttt{<expr>} \longrightarrow \texttt{<term>}\texttt{<operator>}\texttt{<term>} \tag{17}$$

$$\texttt{<enclosed\_expr>} \longrightarrow \texttt{<bra\_op>}\texttt{<expr>}\texttt{<bra\_cl>} \tag{18}$$

$$\texttt{<ident\_init>} \longrightarrow \texttt{<ident\_init>}\texttt{<init>} \mid \tag{19}$$

$$\longrightarrow \texttt{<init>} \tag{20}$$

$$\texttt{<init>} \longrightarrow \texttt{<ident>}\texttt{<=>}\texttt{<value>}\texttt{<nl>} \tag{21}$$

At many points in the programs, we desire to display/print outputs in the form of values, expressions or variables. Hence we define a symbol for displaying as follows:

$$\texttt{<display>} \longrightarrow \texttt{<value>} \mid \texttt{<term>} \mid \texttt{<expr>} \tag{22}$$

We proceed to build on this and specify productions for arithmetic, conditional and looping structures.

3.2 Arithmetic Expressions

Simple arithmetic operations are defined recursively in Productions 23–27, allowing occurrences of expressions in enclosed brackets, predefined and functions. This is used in Production 24 for assignment statements.

$$\texttt{<assignments>} \longrightarrow \texttt{<ident><=><sim\_arth\_eval>} \tag{23}$$
$$\texttt{<sim\_arth\_eval>} \longrightarrow \texttt{<sim\_arth\_eval><arth\_op><enclosed\_expr>} \mid \tag{24}$$
$$\longrightarrow \texttt{<sim\_arth\_eval><arth\_op><pd\_fxns>} \mid \tag{25}$$
$$\longrightarrow \texttt{<enclosed\_expr>} \mid \tag{26}$$
$$\longrightarrow \texttt{<pd\_fxns>} \tag{27}$$

3.3 If-Statement Blocks

Here we describe productions for `if` statements.

$$\texttt{<if\_stmt>} \longrightarrow \texttt{<if><chain\_cond><:><nl>} \tag{28}$$
$$\texttt{<elif\_stmt>} \longrightarrow \texttt{<elif><chain\_cond><:><nl>} \tag{29}$$
$$\texttt{<else\_stmt>} \longrightarrow \texttt{<else><:><nl>} \tag{30}$$

The `<chain_cond>` symbol used by the `if` productions is described with Productions 31–37. Production 35 allows the **not** operator to appear in front of some relational conditions in order to negate these statements.

$$\texttt{<chain\_cond>} \longrightarrow \texttt{<chain\_cond><logi\_op\_infix><encl\_cond>} \mid \tag{31}$$
$$\longrightarrow \texttt{<logi\_op\_infix><encl\_cond>} \tag{32}$$
$$\longrightarrow \texttt{<encl\_cond>} \tag{33}$$
$$\texttt{<encl\_cond>} \longrightarrow \texttt{<bra\_op><condition><bra\_cl>} \tag{34}$$
$$\texttt{<condition>} \longrightarrow \texttt{<opt\_not><cond\_expr>} \tag{35}$$
$$\texttt{<cond\_expr>} \longrightarrow \texttt{<ident><rel\_op>(<ident>} \mid \texttt{<value>)} \tag{36}$$
$$\texttt{<opt\_not>} \longrightarrow \texttt{<logi\_op\_prefix>} \mid \lambda \tag{37}$$

3.4 Loops

Here we describe two types of loops, `for`, and `while` loops. The symbol `<initial>` is given as a random number. Since we do not want exercises that will take a lot of time for a novice to complete, it is important to restrict the number of iterations they will have to carry out in the process of tracing the loops.

Hence, Production 40 computes the final values of the `for` loop using random numbers of step length and desired number of executions; these are bounded in the ranges shown in Productions 41–42.

$$\text{<for\_hdr>} \longrightarrow \text{for<spc>in<spc>range<bra\_op><initial>,<final>,}$$
$$\text{(<step> | } \lambda\text{)<bra\_cl><:>} \tag{38}$$
$$\text{<initial>} \longrightarrow \text{<value>} \tag{39}$$
$$\text{<final>} \longrightarrow \text{<step> * <exe\_count> + <initial> } - 1 \tag{40}$$
$$\text{<step>} \longrightarrow 1 \,|\ldots|\, 10 \tag{41}$$
$$\text{<exe\_count>} \longrightarrow 2 \,|\ldots|\, 4 \tag{42}$$
$$\text{<while\_hdr>} \longrightarrow \text{while<bra\_op><condition><bra\_cl><:>} \tag{43}$$

$$\text{<for\_loop>} \longrightarrow \text{<for\_hdr><nl><tab\_in><display>} \tag{44}$$
$$\text{<while\_loop>} \longrightarrow \text{<while\_hdr><nl><tab\_in><display><adj\_cond>} \tag{45}$$

In Productions 44–45, the entire loop structures are defined, allowing for indentations with the `<tab_in>` symbol. `<adj_cond>` is a symbol derived with a function that adjusts the variables within the loop to ensure that the loop is not infinite and that every execution takes it closer to its termination.

3.5   Complete Python Programs

Now we give productions for three types of complete programs. Programs that tests knowledge of: arithmetic operations, conditional statements, and loops. Production 46 is straightforward; it initialises identifiers, does assignments, and displays related contents. Similarly, Production 47 does initialisations and then allows an `if` statement block to appear. Production 48 makes sure that the `else-if` part of the if structure is optional.

$$\text{<prog\_arth\_expr\_eval>} \longrightarrow \text{<ident\_init><assignments><display>} \tag{46}$$

$$\text{<prog\_cond\_expr\_eval>} \longrightarrow \text{<ident\_init><if\_stmt><tab\_in><display> |} \tag{47}$$
$$\longrightarrow \text{<ident\_init><if\_stmt><tab\_in><display>}$$
$$\text{((<elif-stmt><tab\_in><display>) | } \lambda\text{)}$$
$$\text{<else\_stmt><tab\_in><display>} \tag{48}$$

$$\text{<prog\_loop\_expr\_eval>} \longrightarrow \text{<ident\_init><for\_loop> |<while\_loop>} \tag{49}$$

Concluding the rules of G, we define the start symbol $S \in P$ in Productions 50–52.

$$\text{<prog>} \longrightarrow \text{<prog\_arth\_expr\_eval>} \mid \qquad (50)$$

$$\longrightarrow \text{<prog\_cond\_expr\_eval>} \mid \qquad (51)$$

$$\longrightarrow \text{<prog\_loop\_expr\_eval>} \qquad (52)$$

4   Implementation and Results

The grammar rules described in this paper were implemented in a tool called the 'Python Code Generator', using the .Net framework Class Library (FCL). The software produced 1000 iterations of unique programs in 1.04 s, 10,000 iterations in 9.01 s, and 100,000 iterations in 1 min and 30.3 s. We ran the software for one million programs in 4 min and 34 s. 500,000 generated programs can be found at https://tinyurl.com/pythonprogramgenerator. Five iterations of generated programs (for the if statement category) are shown in Listing 1.4.

Listing 1.4. Sample Outputs from Python Code Generator

```
 1 #---------------
 2 # Code Number: 1
 3 p9 = -2
 4 p = 3
 5 h = -17
 6
 7 g = (p - (13%8)) + ((h + p9))
 8
 9 if (h <= -26):
10        print(g)
11 else:
12        print(((p + h)) - (p9 + p))
13
14 #---------------
15 # Code Number: 2
16 k7 = -11
17 z = 4
18 b = 18
19 v = 2
20 t0 = 19
21 z6 = 0
22
23 p = (((z6 + k7)) - (math.ceil(-76.11) - v)) - (t0 + b) + (math.sqrt(16))
24
25 if not (k7 != -3) or (z != 4):
26        print(p)
27 else:
28        print((math.floor(-23.46) + t0) - ((v - b)))
29
30 #---------------
31 # Code Number: 3
32 z4 = 10
33
34 m = (math.trunc(-25.22) - z4)
35
36 if (z4 >= 12):
37        print(m)
38 else:
39        print(((z4 + z4)) + ((z4 - math.trunc(-17.10))))
40
```

```
41 #---------------
42 # Code Number: 4
43 x8 = 6
44 w5 = 12
45
46 a6 = (x8 + w5)
47
48 if not (w5 <= 3):
49            print(a6)
50 else:
51            print((w5 - math.pow(-1,1)) - ((math.sqrt(169) + w5)))
52
53 #---------------
54 # Code Number: 5
55 d1 = 12
56 g = -16
57
58 w3 = ((math.trunc(0.50) + g)) + ((30%5) + d1)
59
60 if not (d1 < 0) or not (g != -9):
61            print(w3)
62 else:
63            print(((math.pow(-1,2) - d1)) + (g - d1))
```

4.1   Solution Generation

For the generated problems to be useful for novice programmers, it is important to also generate solutions that will serve as a benchmark. This is a relatively trivial task. This is because our grammar generates valid Python 3 programs; hence, passing this programs to a Python interpreter give us the output. In Fig. 2 we show how we have generated solutions to every Python file that was generated. Each Python file is fetched in succession, and interpreted until there is no more file left.

4.2   Experimental Proof of Uniqueness

For each category (`<prog_arth_expr_eval>`, `<prog_cond_expr_eval>`, and `<prog_loop_expr_eval>`) we experimented by generating one billion program instances. There were no repeated programs during execution. This can be explained with the large amount of possible permutations of identifiers, initialisations, conditions, and expressions that are derivable from the start symbol. It is possible to conduct a theoretical proof of uniqueness (or a very small number, close to zero, representing the probability of a program recurring) by constructing a parse tree with the production rules, and computing the product of all possible branch of decisions. This is discussed further in the future work section of this paper.

5   Evaluation

In this section we present results from a survey-based evaluation of the students' perception of the generated Python programs and their possible usefulness.

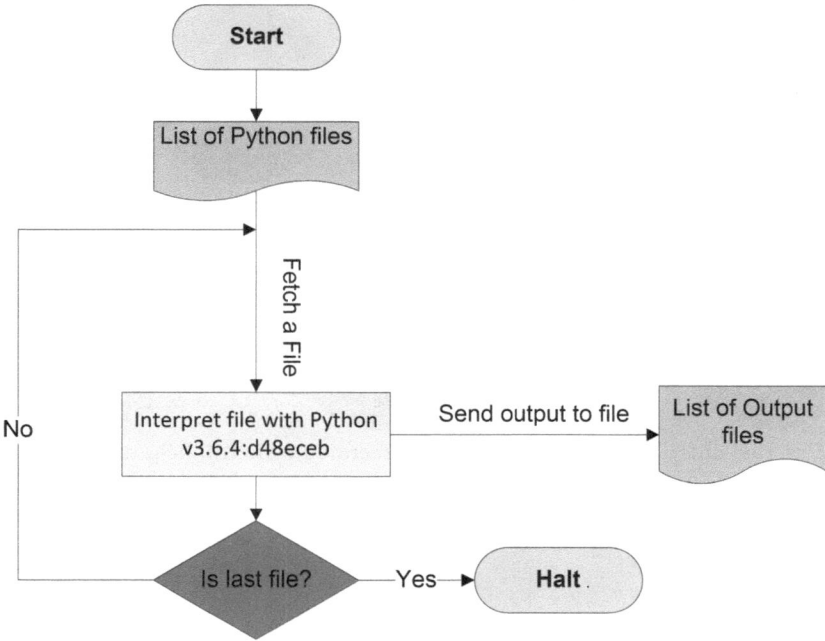

Fig. 2. Process of solution generation

We conducted an online survey at two large universities in South Africa,[4] namely the University of Johannesburg and the University of the Witwatersrand. The respondents were mostly students that were registered for Computer Science or Information Systems degrees.

In total we received 103 responses. 79.6% of the students were in first year, currently taking a Python programming course, and a total of 92.1% are currently doing a programming course across different degrees and levels. Others are Masters and PhD students who admit that they have programmed at some point: see Fig. 3(a). We asked the students if they find programming difficult or too technical, and 73.6% believed it was either too difficult or sometimes too difficult. 26.5% of the students claimed they do not think programming is difficult: see Fig. 3(b)—this difficulty spread agrees with the literatures in program comprehension as discussed in Sect. 2.

An overwhelming 99% agreed that practice can help them in learning programming better: see Fig. 3(c), with 93.1% strongly believing that the generated programs can help them in practice and improve their performance in programming: see Fig. 3(d). An interesting question is if the generated programs for each level are of the same complexity or difficulty. 50.5% of the students strongly thought the difficulty of the programs were the same, despite the difference in

---

[4] https://tinyurl.com/pcg-survey2018.

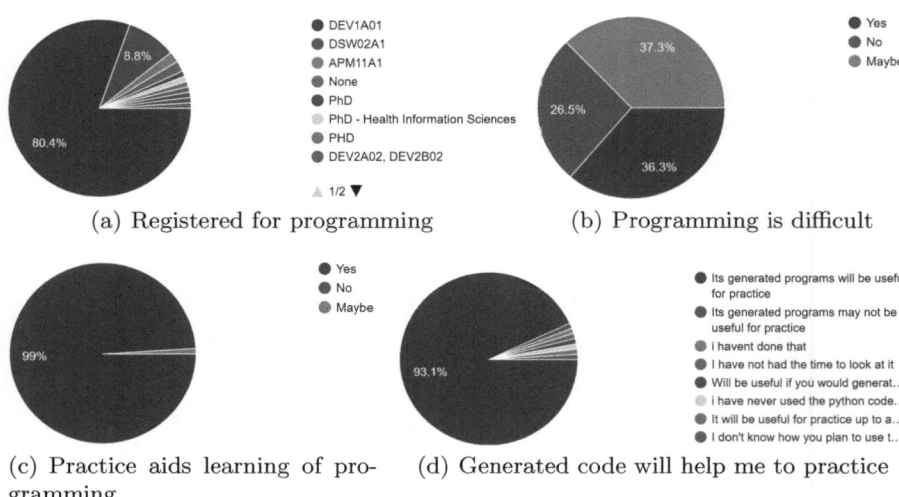

(a) Registered for programming

(b) Programming is difficult

(c) Practice aids learning of programming

(d) Generated code will help me to practice

Fig. 3. Survey: relevance of generated programs

the instances. Total of 79.6% agree to some degree that the programs are of similar difficulty. A total of 90.2% agreed that the programs can be used for tests and examinations. With these feedbacks, we conclude that generating programs for practice, tests, and possibly examinations is worthwhile.

6   Conclusion and Future Work

In this paper we have presented a CFG-based technique for the syntactic generation of practice Python programs and solutions that can be administered to students in pen-and-paper program tracing sessions. We have shown that this technique can generate millions of practice programs in few minutes. Half a million of sample generated programs can be viewed or downloaded from https://tinyurl. com/pythonprogramgenerator. We have also presented an evaluation that shows an overwhelming majority of students agreeing that the generated programs can help them in practising, and can be used in test, and/or examination questions.

From here we will explore the generation of buggy novice programs as debugging is one of the well known activities that improves programming knowledge of novice programmers. We will also make this tool available on a website to the Computer Science Education community. On the formal aspect, we will work on proving (theoretically) that it is possible (or impossible) to have repeated programs after a larger number of iterations.

References

1. Ade-Ibijola, A.: Synthesis of regular expression problems and solutions. Int. J. Comput. Appl. 1–17 (2018) https://doi.org/10.1080/1206212X.2018.1482398
2. Ade-Ibijola, A.: Synthesis of social media profiles using a probabilistic context-free grammar. In: PRASA-RobMech 2017, Proceedings of Pattern Recognition Association of South Africa and Robotics and Mechatronics, pp. 104–109. IEEE (2017)
3. Ade-Ibijola, A., Ewert, S., Sanders, I.: Abstracting and narrating novice programs using regular expressions. In: SAICSIT 2014, Proceedings of Annual Conference of the South African Institute for Computer Scientist and Information Technologists, pp. 19–28. ACM (2014)
4. Ahmed, U.Z., Gulwani, S., Karkare, A.: Automatically generating problems and solutions for natural deduction. In: Proceedings of IJCAI 2013, pp. 1968–1975 (2013)
5. Aho, A.V., Sethi, R., Ullman, J.D.: Compilers: Principles, Techniques, and Tools. Addison-Wesley, Boston (1986)
6. Alqadi, B.S., Maletic, J.I.: An empirical study of debugging patterns among novices programmers. In: Proceedings of the 2017 ACM SIGCSE Technical Symposium on Computer Science Education, pp. 15–20 (2017)
7. Baker, A., Zhang, J., Caldwell, E.R.: Reinforcing array and loop concepts through a game-like module. In: CGAMES 2012, Proceedings of 17th International Conference on Computer Games, pp. 175–179. IEEE (2012)
8. Bergin, S., Mooney, A., Ghent, J., Quille, K.: Using machine learning techniques to predict introductory programming performance. Int. J. Comput. Sci. Softw. Eng. 4(12), 323–328 (2015)
9. Butler, M., Morgan, M.: Learning challenges faced by novice programming students studying high level and low feedback concepts. In: Proceedings of 24th ASCILITE Conference, pp. 2–5 (2007)
10. Dale, N.B.: Most difficult topics in CS1: results of an online survey of educators. ACM SIGCSE Bull. 38(2), 49–53 (2006)
11. Fincher, S.: What are we doing when we teach programming? In: Proceedings of 29th Annual Frontiers in Education Conference, p. 12A4 (1999)
12. Foote, S.: Learning to Program. Addison-Wesley, Boston (2014)
13. Gulwani, S., Korthikanti, V.A., Tiwari, A.: Synthesizing geometry constructions. ACM SIGPLAN Not. 46(6), 50–61 (2011)
14. Haiduc, S., Aponte, J., Marcus, A.: Supporting program comprehension with source code summarization. In: ICSE 2010, Proceedings of 32nd International Conference on Software Engineering, pp. 223–226 (2010)
15. Hill, G.J.: Review of a problems-first approach to first year undergraduate programming. In: Kassel, S., Wu, B. (eds.) Software Engineering Education Going Agile, pp. 73–80. Springer, Cham (2016). https://doi.org/10.1007/978-3-319-29166-6_11
16. Iqbal-Malik, S.: Role of ADRI model in teaching and assessing novice programmers. Technical report, Deakin University (2016)
17. Jenkins, T.: On the difficulty of learning to program. In: Proceedings of 3rd Annual Conference of the LTSN Centre for Information and Computer Sciences, pp. 53–58 (2002)
18. Johnson, W.L.: Understanding and debugging novice programs. Artif. Intell. 42(1), 51–97 (1990)

19. Lahtinen, E., Ala-Mutka, K., Järvinen, H.M.: A study of the difficulties of novice programmers. ACM SIGCSE Bull. **37**(3), 14–18 (2005)
20. Lucariello, J.M., Nastasi, B.K., Anderman, E.M., Dwyer, C., Ormiston, H., Skiba, R.: Science supports education: the behavioral research base for psychology's top 20 principles for enhancing teaching and learning. Mind Brain Educ. **10**(1), 55–67 (2016)
21. Malik, S.I., Coldwell-Neilson, J.: A model for teaching an introductory programming course using ADRI. Educ. Inf. Technol. **22**(3), 1089–1120 (2017)
22. Martin, J.: Introduction to Languages and the Theory of Computation. McGraw-Hill, New York (2003)
23. Mathrani, A., Christian, S., Ponder-Sutton, A.: PlayIT: game based learning approach for teaching programming concepts. Educ. Technol. Soc. **19**(2), 5–17 (2016)
24. Miljanovic, M.A., Bradbury, J.S.: Robot ON!: a serious game for improving programming comprehension. In: GAS 2016, Proceedings of 5th International Workshop on Games and Software Engineeing, pp. 33–36. ACM (2016)
25. Özmen, B., Altun, A.: Undergraduate students' experiences in programming: difficulties and obstacles. Turk. Online J. Qual. Inq. **5**(3), 1–27 (2014)
26. Ramalingam, V., Wiedenbeck, S.: An empirical study of novice program comprehension in the imperative and object-oriented styles. In: Proceedings of 7th Workshop on Empirical Studies of Programmers, pp. 124–139. ACM (1997)
27. Sadigh, D., Seshia, S.A., Gupta, M.: Automating exercise generation: a step towards meeting the MOOC challenge for embedded systems. In: Proceedings of Workshop on Embedded and Cyber-Physical Systems Education, p. 2. ACM (2012)
28. Shargabi, A., Aljunid, S.A., Annamalai, M., Shuhidan, S.M., Zin, A.M.: Tasks that can improve novices' program comprehension. In: Proceedings of IEEE Conference on e-Learning, e-Management and e-Services, pp. 32–37 (2015)
29. Sharples, M., et al.: Innovating Pedagogy 2016. Open University Innovation Report 5 (2016)
30. Siegfried, R.M., Siegfried, J., Alexandro, G.: A longitudinal analysis of the Reid list of first programming languages. Inf. Syst. Educ. J. **14**(6), 47 (2016)
31. Singh, R., Gulwani, S., Rajamani, S.K.: Automatically generating algebra problems. In: AAAI 2012, Proceedings of 26th Conference on AI (2012)
32. Storey, M., Best, C., Michand, J.: SHriMP views: an interactive environment for exploring Java programs. In: Proceedings of 9th International Workshop on Program Comprehension, pp. 111–112. IEEE (2001)
33. Storey, M.A.: Theories, tools and research methods in program comprehension: past, present and future. Softw. Qual. J. **14**(3), 187–208 (2006)
34. Wang, T., Su, X., Ma, P., Wang, Y., Wang, K.: Ability-training-oriented automated assessment in introductory programming course. Comput. Educ. **56**(1), 220–226 (2011)
35. Yadin, A.: Reducing the dropout rate in an introductory programming course. ACM Inroads **2**(4), 71–76 (2011)
36. Zhang, J., Atay, M., Caldwell, E.R., Jones, E.J.: Visualizing loops using a game-like instructional module. In: ICALT 2013, Proceedings of 13th IEEE International Conference on Advanced Learning Technology, pp. 448–450 (2013)

Motivational Value of Code.org's Code Studio Tutorials in an Undergraduate Programming Course

Guillaume Nel[1(✉)] ⓘ and Liezel Nel[2] ⓘ

[1] Department of Information Technology, Central University of Technology,
Free State, Bloemfontein, South Africa
guilnel@cut.ac.za
[2] Department of Computer Science and Informatics, University of the Free State,
Bloemfontein, South Africa
nell@ufs.ac.za

Abstract. As part of an instructional strategy to improve undergraduate software development students' basic understanding of programming constructs, students completed a selection of Code Studio tutorials during the first three weeks of their programming course. Block-based environments, such as the one used by the Code Studio tutorials, typically make it easier for students to learn programming as they can focus on concepts instead of syntax. Students are, however, less likely to regard an instructional strategy as meaningful if it presents no motivational value for them. In this paper, Keller's ARCS Model is used to organize the knowledge gained regarding student motivation and the motivational strategies supported by the Code Studio tutorials. Results obtained from analysis of numeric and narrative data collected through a paper-based self-completion questionnaire confirm the high motivation value of the Code Studio tutorials. The results provide insights regarding students' perceptions of Code Studio tutorials as a motivational instructional strategy in an undergraduate programming course. Since students perceive the Code Studio tutorials to have some educational value, further investigations should be conducted to consider more appropriate and effective ways to integrate Code Studio tutorials with undergraduate programming curricula.

Keywords: Block-based programming · Motivation · ARCS model
Undergraduate students

1 Introduction

The difficulties experienced by undergraduate Computer Science students in introductory programming courses have been documented extensively. Some students, especially those with little or no prior programming experience, struggle to form a sufficient understanding of the process of programming and the working of various control structures [5,25,26]. The amount of theoretical concepts

© Springer Nature Switzerland AG 2019
S. Kabanda et al. (Eds.): SACLA 2018, CCIS 963, pp. 173–188, 2019.
https://doi.org/10.1007/978-3-030-05813-5_12

and techniques students need to master can also lead to a loss of interest in programming [3]. Numerous studies have been conducted to identify instructional strategies that could be used to improve students' understanding of basic programming concepts [7,9,16,24]. The past decade has seen a renewed focus on student engagement as a possible strategy to enhance teaching and learning in higher education [27]. This interest in student engagement is grounded in a sound body of literature that has already established a connection between students' involvement in educationally meaningful activities and student success [2,27]. Barkley described student engagement as both *"a process and a product"* that results from *"the synergistic interaction between motivation and active learning"* [2] (p. 8). It is therefore not enough for students to just be actively involved in meaningful learning activities. They also need to be motivated to engage in such activities. In order to sustain motivation, instructional designs should incorporate strategies to address critical aspects related to attention, relevance, confidence, and satisfaction (ARCS) [11]. Before any learning can occur, however, students' attention must be grabbed. One of the attention-grabbing strategies suggested by Keller is to address students' lack of interest [13]. In order to capture software development students' interest, Kelleher and Pausch suggest a change in the programming environment used by beginners [10]. Various studies have been conducted to explore the potential of block-based programming tools such as 'Alice' [28], 'Scratch' [4,5,21], 'MIT App Inventor' for Android [20] and 'Hour of Code' [6,19] as introductory programming environments. The 'Hour of Code' challenge was launched by Code.org in December 2015 as a one-hour introduction to Computer Science.[1] It was originally designed to show that anybody can learn the basics of programming and to broaden participation in the field of Computer Science. In addition to the 'Hour of Code' event, Code.org has since developed an extended catalog of tutorials and courses that can be accessed via their Code Studio website.[2] The main aim of the Code Studio tutorials is to teach additional Computer Science subjects and programming principles to school pupils up to the age of 18 years.

As part of an instructional strategy to improve undergraduate software development students' basic understanding of programming constructs, students completed a selection of Code Studio tutorials during the first three weeks of their programming course. This paper attempts to answer the following two questions:

1. What is the motivational value of Code Studio tutorials for undergraduate programming students?
2. What are students' perceptions regarding Code Studio tutorials as a motivational instructional strategy in an undergraduate programming course?

A short review of relevant literature is in Sect. 2, followed by a discussion of the research design and method in Sect. 3. Data analysis and results are presented in Sect. 4. The paper concludes with a discussion of our findings in Sect. 5 and recommendations for future work in Sect. 6.

---

[1] https://hourofcode.com/za.
[2] https://code.org.

2   Related Work

2.1   Strategies to Stimulate Motivation in Educational Environments

'Motivation' is often regarded as a vague concept, especially by instructors who want to design learning environments aimed at enhancing students' motivation. In addition to a good understanding of what motivation entails, these instructors also need to consider which *motivational strategies* are best suited for their teaching and learning contexts, and how best to incorporate the chosen strategies as part of their instructional designs. Keller's ARCS model [12] captures four critical aspects (dimensions) that should be addressed in order for students to be motivated to learn: attention, relevance, confidence and satisfaction. He also provides practical strategies that can be used by instructors to achieve each of the four requirements. In using the ARCS model for instructional design [11,13], instructors should first consider strategies to capture students' interest, stimulate inquiry and maintain attention. In order to establish relevance, instructors should set clear goals that are related to the learning material, match students' interests, and provide links to students' prior and future experiences. The suggested confidence strategies should be used to create a learning environment that sets up positive attitudes and boosts students' believes that they can succeed and are in control of their own success. The satisfaction aspect relates students' continued desire to learn to their satisfaction with the process and results of the learning experience [11]. Strategies to promote feelings of satisfaction should describe ways in which intrinsic satisfaction, rewarding outcomes and fair treatment can be promoted. Intrinsic satisfaction is promoted when students feel that *"they have achieved success while studying topics that were personally meaningful to them"* [11] (p. 188). Strategies linked to extrinsic reinforcement (e.g. verbal praise, symbolic rewards and incentives such as marks) can result in rewarding outcomes for students. Instructors should also incorporate strategies to ensure that any rewards given are equitable to the amount of work done by students, and that all students are treated fairly.

2.2   Block-Based Programming Environments as Motivational Tools

In the past decade there has been a steady increase in the use of block-based programming environments to introduce students to programming [29]. These environments aim to make it easier for students to learn programming by focusing on concepts instead of syntax [23]. In this style of programming, blocks (in different shapes and colors) are used to represent the various elements of a programming language (e.g. a control structure, an operator, a variable or a function). Drag-and-drop actions are used to assemble the various blocks (like jigsaw pieces) *"according to a certain planned logic to form a computer program"* [21] (p. 1480). Given the popularity of block-based programming environments, numerous studies have been conducted to explore their use as motivational tools in programming courses of various levels.

Scratch is an open source environment developed by the Lifelong Kindergarten Group at the MIT Media Lab.[3] It facilitates the development of interactive stories, games, and animations that can be shared with others in the online Scratch community. Korkmaz conducted a comparative study to evaluate the effects of Scratch-based game activities on Computer Programming students of an Engineering faculty [14]. The results indicate high levels of motivation but also high levels of negative attitudes towards programming in general. In [5], where Scratch was used in two Computer Science courses for the first three weeks of a 15-week course, the majority of students found the environment to be motivating, funny or easy. A small minority, however, described it as 'difficult' or 'normal'. In [20], where pupils used Scratch for seven weeks, measurements of motivation transition over the 7-week period revealed increased *"intrinsic goal orientation, task value, control of learning beliefs and self-efficacy"* (p. 1042) however no change in extrinsic motivation.

Studies comparing the motivation levels of students using Scratch versus students using traditional text-based programming environments indicated that

- Scratch students were more motivated [5,21];
- Scratch students found the programming environment less boring [21];
- Scratch students were more creative as well as more inclined to create games in their own time [21];
- Scratch students were more motivated to continue with Computer Science studies [4,21];
- The Scratch environment makes it easier for instructors to identify struggling students [5];
- There are no noteworthy differences in retention rates between Scratch and text-programming students [5].

De Kereki urges instructors to consider the impact that an additional learning tool such as Scratch (that is only used for a few weeks at the beginning of a course) will have on students [5]. Students invest time in familiarizing themselves with Scratch, and after a few weeks they have to start anew (without Scratch) in a completely different environment to develop 'real' programs. Such a strategy might have a negative impact on students' motivation towards Scratch and programming in general.

Hour of Code started as a one-hour introduction to Computer Science with the aims to 'demystify code', to show that anybody can learn the basics, and to broaden participation in the field of Computer Science. Although the official 'Hour of Code' event takes place annually in December during 'Computer Science Education Week', all tutorial materials can be accessed throughout the year. The biggest difference between the 'Hour of Code' environment and Scratch is that students cannot create their own programs. In the 'Hour of Code' tutorials, students are confronted with a visualized puzzle-based problem (e.g. a character that needs to move through a maze). Video instructions are used to explain the

---

[3] https://scratch.mit.edu.

aim of the lesson and to introduce new command blocks (representing programming constructs). Students must then move the relevant blocks from a toolbox to a work space and assemble them in the correct order to create an 'algorithm' that will solve the given puzzle. Students can test their 'algorithm at any stage. During testing, students can observe the character's movements as each of the command blocks in their work space are executed. The Code Studio tutorials (an extension of 'Hour of Code') use the same block-based environment as the 'Hour of Code' tutorials. Instructors can use the Code Studio dashboard to build custom courses for their students by selecting tutorials for different subjects and age groups. The tutorials feature popular themes such as 'Star Wars', 'Minecraft', or Disney's 'Frozen' world. An extensive internet search revealed only a small number of studies that investigated motivational aspects of 'Hour of Code' activities. The following two of those studies are of particular relevance:

The study of [19] investigated the learning motivation of high school pupils and first-year university students (non-Computing majors) during 'Hour of Code' activities. The self-reported Situational Motivation Scale (SIMS) [8] was used to measure four motivational components: Intrinsic motivation (doing an activity because it is interesting or enjoyable); Identified regulation (doing an activity because of its perceived importance and value); External regulation (complying with external demands); and Amotivation (the lack of motivation). Both groups showed high levels of intrinsic and identified regulation. The high school pupils found the activities more intrinsically motivated as these activities are probably *"better suited to their lower age level"* [19] (p. 745). Although both groups showed low levels of external regulation and amotivation, the university group showed significantly higher levels of amotivation. Their high levels of amotivation could be attributed to the fact that they were non-computing students who are *"more oriented in their chosen field of studies and may not be interested much in programming"* [19] (p. 745). Overall, Nikou and Economides regard the 'Hour of Code' tutorial as a valuable example of a well-designed educational activity because of its high level of intrinsic motivation [19], but suggest that it should rather be used for students of lower ages.

In [6], 116 undergraduate students studying different majors (including business, accounting, criminal justice, allied health sciences, geography, hospitality tourism management, and psychology) at two universities completed one 'Hour of Code' tutorial. Pre- and post-surveys were used to determine if the tutorial had any effect on the students' attitudes towards programming and if it improved their basic programming skills. The results showed a significant positive impact on the students' attitude but no significant changes in their programming skills. Based on these experiences, Du, Wimmer and Rada recommend that instructors who want to use the 'Hour of Code' tutorials for programming skill development should *"appreciate the learning objectives of the 'Hour of Code' and integrate the tutorials appropriately into their teaching"* [6] (p. 65).

3   Research Design and Method

We followed a mixed methods approach based on the Framework of Integrated Methodologies (FraIM) as suggested by Plowright [22]. The context of this paper was an introductory (first-year) programming course (OPG1) in the Department of Information Technology at a selected South African University of Technology. This is a foundation course aimed at introducing students to basic computer programming principles and constructs through the use of the C# programming language. The main source of data in the study was the population of the 221 students registered for this course. Students were divided into two class groups with two 85-min theoretical sessions (in a traditional lecture hall) and two 85-min practical sessions per week allocated to each group. During the first three weeks of the semester, four practical sessions (two in week 1 and one each in weeks 2 and 3) were set aside for students to work on Code Studio tutorials. The instructor set up a class group for the 'Accelerated Intro to CS Course' on the Code Studio dashboard. This is a 20-h course originally designed for use with pupils between the ages of 10 and 18. It covers core Computer Science and programming concepts and incorporates selected exercises from the Code.org 'CS Fundamentals' syllabus. Each student had to personally register on the Code Studio website and enroll for the custom course set up by the instructor. Although students were encouraged to complete as many of the tutorials as possible during the four dedicated practical sessions, they did not receive any 'rewards' in the form of marks for the completion of these tutorials. Students were also not required to continue working on the tutorials outside of their practical sessions. It should be noted that the majority of the selected Code Studio tutorials were related to programming concepts that were much more advanced than those covered in the first three weeks of the introductory programming course. However, for the remainder of the semester, the instructor intentionally referred back to specific Code Studio examples whenever she discussed new C# programming concepts related to selection, iteration and OO-methods.

In order to collect data on the students' Code Studio experiences, a survey strategy was deemed most appropriate to manage this relatively large data source [22]. As part of this strategy, data was collected by means of 'asking questions' in a paper-based self-completion questionnaire containing both closed and open-ended questions. The questionnaire was distributed at the end of the semester (week 13) for completion during one of the normal lecture sessions. 148 students (the sample) voluntarily completed the questionnaire.

The questionnaire consisted of three sections: Sect. 1 was based on the Reduced Instructional Materials Motivation Survey (RIMMS) [17]. The original Instructional Materials Motivation Survey (IMMS) [11] is a 36-item situational measure of participants' reactions to self-directed instructional materials they have used. After conducting an extensive validation study of the IMMS, Loorbach, Peters, Karreman and Steehouder devised the 12-item RIMMS [17] which they regarded as a more appropriate post-test tool in their instructional setting than the IMMS. The 12 RIMMS items consist of 3 items for each of the four sub-scales of the ARCS model—attention, relevance, confidence, and satisfaction. For the RIMMS, responses are recorded on a 5-point Likert scale with the response scales ranging from 1 (not true) to 5 (very true). Where necessary, the wording of the RIMMS items we adapted to make it more relevant to the context of our study. Care was, however, taken not to change the substance of the items as these relate to specific attributes of the ARCS model [11]. Section 2 of the survey consisted of open-ended questions aimed at soliciting students' views regarding (1) what motivated them to continue with the Code Studio tutorials outside of class; (2) their reasons for abandoning the Code Studio tutorials; and (3) what they regarded as the main educational value of the Code Studio tutorials. The final section of the questionnaire, Sect. 3, was used to collect basic demographic data from the participants. Numerical data collected through the questionnaire was analyzed in 'SPSS 24' while narrative data was analyzed in 'NVivo 11'.

4   Data Analysis and Results

A total of 148 participants completed the survey. There were 105 (70.9%) male participants and 43 (29.1%) female participants. Although students were not required to work on the Code Studio tutorials outside of their scheduled practical sessions, 33 students (22.3%) indicated that they continued to work on the tutorials in their own time.

4.1   Numeric Data: RIMMS

This sub-section describes the analysis and results of the data collected in Sect. 1 of the questionnaire—the RIMMS questions. Reliability estimates were calculated to show the internal reliability of the scales and a correlation analysis was conducted to determine the relationship between the four ARCS categories. The internal consistency estimate for the overall set of 12 items, based on Cronbach's alpha, shows high internal consistency with a satisfactory value of 0.899 for the total scale: see Table 1. The reliability estimates for the attention, relevance and satisfaction scales were satisfactory (>0.6). The low value for the confidence scale (0.591) can be regarded as questionable and might serve as an indication that the three confidence items did not necessarily measure the same underlying concept in the context of this study. It was, however, decided to retain the confidence data for further analysis since the recorded value is very close to 0.6.

The calculated inter-factor Pearson's correlation coefficients indicate a significant positive relationship between all the ARCS dimensions: see Table 2. The highest correlation was between the confidence and satisfaction dimensions ($r = .720$) and the lowest between attention and relevance ($r = .595$). The students' motivation levels were analyzed for each of the four ARCS dimensions as well as for each of the individual items in these dimensions: see Table 3.

In the attention dimension, the total mean score was 3.737, indicating positive motivation levels. Students were positive about how information arrangement (Q1.5; $M = 3.811$) and quality of the tutorial graphics and sounds (Q1.2;

Table 1. RIMMS reliability estimates and descriptive statistics (N = 148)

Scale	Cronbach's alpha	Cronbach's alpha (standard. items)	Mean	SD	# items
Attention	.732	.739	3.7365	0.89785	3
Relevance	.686	.687	3.7703	0.89582	3
Confidence	.591	.592	3.7095	0.82596	3
Satisfaction	.808	.808	3.6757	1.03085	3
Overall	.899	.900	3.6700	0.78927	12

Table 2. RIMMS correlations between ARCS dimensions

Scale	Attention	Relevance	Confidence	Satisfaction
Attention	1	.595**	.621**	.663**
Relevance	.595**	1	.696**	.678**
Confidence	.621**	.696**	1	.720**
Satisfaction	.663**	.678**	.720**	1

**Correlation is significant at the 0.01 level (2-tailed)

M = 3.743) helped to keep their attention. They were, however, less positive about the role that the variety of the tutorials and characters (Q1.9; M = 3.655) played in this regard.

In the relevance dimension, the total mean score was 3.770. Students were most positive about the relation between the tutorials and the concepts they already knew (Q1.1; M = 3.966). The students were, however, less positive about the worthiness (Q1.7; M = 3.676) and usefulness of these tutorials in their programming course (Q1.10; M = 3669).

The total mean score of the confidence dimension was 3.710. By doing the tutorials, students were positive that they could learn the related programming concepts (Q1.3; M = 3.764) and were mostly confident that they would be able to pass a test on it (Q1.8; M = 3.709). They were slightly less positive about how the organization of the tutorials helped them to learn the related programming concepts (Q1.11; M = 3.655).

For the satisfaction dimension, the total mean score was 3.676—the lowest of the four dimensions. Students were most positive about how their enjoyment of the tutorials fueled their interest in programming (Q1.4; M = 3.750). Overall, they enjoyed doing the well-designed tutorials (Q1.6; M = 5.61 and Q1.12; M = 3.716).

4.2 Narrative Data

This sub-section describes the analysis and results of the narrative data collected in Sect. 2 of the questionnaire through mostly open-ended questions. Inductive analysis [18] was used to make sense of the students' responses. This analysis strategy was chosen as it allowed for the emergence of categories from the data itself. For each question the individual responses (or response segments) were

Table 3. RIMMS motivation level per ARCS dimension (N = 148)

Dimension item	Mean	SD
Attention	**3.737**	**.8979**
Q1.2: The quality of the tutorial graphics and sounds helped to hold my attention	3.743	1.2185
Q1.5: The way the information is arranged for each tutorial helped keep my attention	3.811	1.0456
Q1.9: The variety of the tutorials and characters helped keep my attention	3.655	1.0672
Relevance	**3.770**	**.8958**
Q1.1: It is clear to me how the tutorials are related to the programming concepts I already know	3.966	1.1394
Q1.7: The way in which the tutorials were presented convey the impression that the related programming concepts is worth knowing	3.676	1.1618
Q1.10: The programming concepts covered by the tutorials will be useful to me in OPG1	3.669	1.1272
Confidence	**3.710**	**.8260**
Q1.3: As I worked on the tutorials, I was confident that I could learn the programming concepts	3.764	1.0777
Q1.8: After working on the tutorials for a while, I was confident that I would be able to pass a test on it	3.709	1.1737
Q1.11: The good organization of the tutorials helped me be confident that I would learn the related programming concepts	3.655	1.0862
Satisfaction	**3.676**	**1.0309**
Q1.4: I enjoyed the tutorials so much that I would like to know more about programming	3.750	1.2392
Q1.6: I really enjoyed doing the tutorials	3.561	1.2078
Q1.12: It was a pleasure to do such well-designed tutorials	3.716	1.1898

coded based on the main aspect it related to. The resulting initial codes were then compared for duplication and overlapping. Similar codes were grouped together and, where necessary, unrelated codes were re-coded. Refining of the coding system continued until the remaining codes could be grouped into a small set of categories. Responses that were deemed irrelevant to the asked question were omitted from the analysis.

Motivation to Continue. Since participation in and completion of the Code Studio tutorials were not compulsory, students were asked to indicate what motivated them to continue with these tutorials. 83 students (56.1%) responded to this question. Inductive analysis led to the identification of 96 motivational reasons that were grouped into nine categories. Table 4 provides a summary of these motivational categories together with the number of response segments that relates to each category.

Table 4. RIMMS motivational categories for continuation

Category	Count
Learn/improve skills	20
Relate to subject content	19
Fun	16
Engaging	9
Situational interest	9
Challenge	8
Achievement	7
Subjective norm	6
Ease of use	2

The main motivational aspect identified relates to the way in which the Code Studio tutorials helped students to learn or improve various skills such as programming skills and logical thinking skills. Students were also motivated as they could see the relation between the tutorials and the OPG1 subject content: *"This can be useful to me in OPG1"* and *"I learn more skills that I can apply on OPG1"*. The 'fun' aspect also motivated students as they regarded the tutorials as entertaining, enjoyable and *"a game"*. Three students in particular commented on how the tutorials helped *"to make programming fun"*. While some students were motivated by the engagement provided by the tutorials (*"interesting"*, *"keeps me focused"*, *"keeps me motivated"*, *"is addictive"*), others were motivated by the challenge presented by the tutorials (*"increasing level of difficulty"*, *"challenging stages"*, *"I had to think outside the box"*). As students became *"curious"* and *"intrigued"*, the tutorials sparked situational interest as in [15], since they wanted to *"lean more about programming"*. One student, who had no prior programming knowledge, confirmed that the tutorials *"helped to get started with programming"* while another student explained how the tutorials helped to give him a better idea of the skills required to be a successful programmer. Some students were only motivated by achievement. These students said that *"getting a trophy was the best feeling"*. They were driven by the prospect of *"progress to higher levels"* and *"wanted to finish all the tutorials"*. On the other hand there were students who noted that they were driven by subjective norm (i.e. a perceived social pressure [1]) to complete the tutorials. These students regarded their influencers as *"the OPG1 lecturer"*, *"all the famous people who kept on talking about how exiting programming is"* (in the Code Studio introductory video) or even their *"friends"* and *"fellow classmates"*.

Two students remarked that they were motivated by the *"ease of use"* of the Code Studio interface as it was *"very intuitive"*.

Reasons for Stopping. Although the students were scheduled to continue with the Code Studio tutorials until the end of the third week of the semester, 83 students (56.1%) indicated that they stopped doing the tutorials before the time. Inductive analysis of the response segments revealed 83 reasons for stopping. These reasons were grouped into seven categories: see Table 5.

Table 5. RIMMS motivational categories for stopping

Category	Count
Needed time for other subjects	25
Needed time for OPG1	21
Lost interest	12
No challenge	8
Unrelated to subject	7
Too difficult	6
Learned enough	4

As the semester progressed and *"workloads increased"*, most of the students who responded to this question (54.8%) mentioned that the time they were spending on the non-compulsory Code Studio tutorials could be put to better use. They either needed more time to work on their other subjects or they used the scheduled Code Studio sessions to *"catch up on OPG1 practical assignments"*. Students explained that they were *"struggling with the OPG1 work"* or *"falling behind"* and needed to *"do additional C# exercises"* or *"attend extra classes"* in order to improve their OPG1 marks. Some students lost interest in the tutorials since they were either *"no longer motivated to continue"*, or felt that the exercises were becoming *"boring"* as *"some of the things keep repeating"*. While some students stopped doing the tutorials because they were *"becoming too easy"* or *"no longer presented a challenge"*, others stopped because they became *"too difficult"* or *"complicated"* for them. The relations between OPG1 and the Code Studio tutorials were also no longer as obvious for some students. They could either not see how the tutorials helped with programming or saw no improvement in their programming skills and OPG1 performance. A small number of students indicated that they stopped doing the tutorials because they had *"learned enough"*.

Educational Value. In the third open-ended question of Sect. 2, students were asked to give their views on the educational value of the Code Studio tutorials.

Table 6. RIMMS motivational categories for educational value

Category	Count
Related to subject content	65
Improve logical thinking/problem solving skills	39
Easy/fun way to learn	17
Unsure	3

Analysis of the 115 responses (from 77.7% of students) revealed 124 response segments that were ultimately grouped into four categories: see Table 6.

Although some of the students were unsure (3; 2.6%), the majority of the responding students (65; 56.5%) attributed the educational value of the Code Studio tutorials to the relation it had with the OPG1 subject content. Some of these students made specific mention of the role the tutorials played in improving their *"overall understanding of programming"* as well as their understanding of *"selection structures"*, *"repetition structures"* and *"methods"*. 39 of the responding students (33.9%) linked the educational value of these tutorials to their ability to improve *"logical thinking"* and/or *"problem solving skills"*. For others it was just a *"fun"* and *"easy way to learning programming"*.

5   Discussion

The numeric data indicate that students' overall motivation level when doing the Code Studio tutorials was high. There were also strong positive correlations between all four of the ARCS dimensions showing that the motivational elements of each dimensions played an important role in influencing students' overall motivation. High motivation levels were reported for the attention, relevance and confidence dimensions with a slightly lower motivation level for the satisfaction dimension.

From the narrative data it became apparent that the Code Studio tutorials managed to grab the students' *attention* as the entertaining environment captured their interest and added a fun element to programming. It also managed to stimulate inquiry as they were curious and wanted to learn more about programming. The 'addictive' tutorials helped to keep them focused and maintained their attention. The tutorials also produced *relevance* as students could see the relation between the Code Studio tutorials and the programming concepts they were studying in OPG1. The tutorials also matched their personal goals to learn more about programming. In addition, the tutorials also helped students to improve their programming and logical thinking skills. Motive stimulation was provided through the 'social pressure' students experienced from various individuals (either role models or fellow students). Through completion of the Code Studio tutorials, students were able to build *confidence* as the intuitive and easy to use interface increased their believe that they could successfully complete the given tasks. The tutorials also helped students to develop a sense of personal responsibility as they were required to work at their own pace and could measure their own progress. The challenging tasks that gradually increased in level of difficulty also provided students with numerous opportunities to succeed. Finally, the Code Studio tutorials also managed to generate *satisfaction* through the provision of intrinsic satisfaction and extrinsic rewards. Students were able to achieve a desirable level of success while learning more about programming concepts—a topic that was personally meaningful to them. The students wanted to progress to higher levels and finish all the exercises. They were also motivated by the 'trophies' they could earn for correctly completing the tutorials. Since students' solution attempts to each of the Code Studio tutorial exercises were evaluated by the system (and not by a human assessor), the assumption can be made that all attempts were evaluated according to the same standards—i.e.: fair treatment of all students.

Despite the initially high motivation levels reported for the Code Studio tutorials, students' satisfaction levels did not remain high throughout. Due to increasing workloads in OPG1 and their other subjects, students no longer regarded the intrinsic and extrinsic rewards provided by the Code Studio tutorials as equitable to the amount of work they had to put in to complete the tutorials—see [11] for comparison. Some of the students could no longer see the relevance of the tutorials to the OPG1 content. The decline in relevance is not surprising as the more advanced Code Studio tutorials focused on concepts such as repetition structures and OO-methods that would only be covered later in the OPG1 syllabus. Levels of confidence also declined as the tutorial tasks became either too difficult or too easy. Attention levels declined as students became bored with the elements that kept repeating in the tutorials. The drops in confidence and attention could be related to Nikou and Economides' observation that these 'Hour of Code' type tutorials are better suited for students of lower age levels [19]. Given Korkmaz's warning about the possible negative impact that a move between programming environments (e.g. from Scratch to text-based) could have on students' motivation [14], it should be noted, however, that none of the students in this study reported any negative attitudes towards programming in general. One significant difference between the 'Hour of Code'/Code Studio and the Scratch environments is that students do not have to invest a significant amount of time to familiarize themselves with the 'Hour of Code' environment. Students are, therefore, much less likely to experience problems in moving over to a completely different environment (like Microsoft Visual Studio) after first spending a few weeks in the 'Hour of Code' environment. It should also be noted that the students in this study already started working in Microsoft Visual Studio environment in the second week of the semester (after only one week of Code Studio tutorials).

Another aspect of this study, which should not be overlooked, is the fact that students only completed the questionnaire at the end of the semester, 10 weeks after conclusion of the Code Studio activities. At that stage their normal C# lectures and practicals already covered most of the programming constructs that were included in the selected Code Studio tutorials. Students were therefore in a much better position to evaluate the educational value of the Code Studio tutorials with regard to the overall OPG1 course syllabus. They could see the relation of the Code Studio tutorials to the OPG1 course content, the opportunities it provided to students to improve their programming and logical thinking skills, and the way in which the entertaining environment managed to capture their interest.

While the students worked on the Code Studio tutorials, we observed that students tended to follow one of three approaches to solve the puzzle problems. In the first approach, students used a process that included detailed planning and analysis of the whole problem before they started to assemble their command blocks in the work space. The second approach can be linked to 'chunking' where students solved the problem in parts with testing conducted after each iteration. The third approach can be described as trial-and-error. The students who followed this approach would randomly place command blocks in the work space and then make changes based on the test execution results.

6   Conclusions and Future Work

The main aims of this paper were (1) to determine the motivational value of Code.org's Code Studio tutorials for undergraduate programming students, and (2) to gain insights into these students' perceptions of the Code Studio tutorials as a motivational instructional strategy. In this regard, Keller's ARCS Model [11–13] provided a typology to organize the knowledge gained regarding student motivation and the motivational strategies supported by the Code Studio tutorials. Initially, a change in programming environment was identified as a possible attention-grabbing strategy to capture students' interest in programming. Analysis of the numeric data confirmed the high motivational value of the Code Studio tutorials for the targeted group of students. Evidence gathered from the richer narrative data was used to illustrate how integration of the selected Code Studio tutorials served as a motivational instructional strategy. Analysis of the gathered student perceptions also revealed that this particular Code Studio integration attempt was successful in incorporating the following of Keller's suggested motivational strategies [11, 13]:

- Strategies to generate and sustain attention: Capture interest, stimulate inquiry and maintain attention.
- Strategies to establish and support relevance: Relate to goals, match interests and tie to experiences.
- Strategies to build confidence: Explain success expectations, provide success opportunities and develop personal responsibility.
- Strategies to promote feelings of satisfaction: Provide intrinsic reinforcement, provide rewarding outcomes and fair treatment.

It can therefore be concluded that this Code Studio integration attempt was successful in achieving each of Keller's four main requirements for motivation: attention, relevance, confidence, and satisfaction [13]. Given the variety of strategies followed by students in solving the Code Studio exercises, future research could investigate the influence that this type of block-based programming environment could have on students' development processes in a conventional development environment (like MS Visual Studio). The real learning value of the Code Studio tutorials on students' understanding of basic programming constructs such as selection, iteration and methods should also be investigated. Since numerous students pointed out the game-like feel created by the Code Studio environment, the influence of gamification on long-time motivation in Code Studio tutorials could also be investigated.

As noted by Du (et al.), instructors who want to use 'Hour of Code' type tutorials for programming skill development, should *"appreciate the learning objectives of the 'Hour of Code' and integrate the tutorials appropriately into their teaching"* [6] (p. 65). Based on the insights gained from this study, a more detailed investigation could be conducted to consider more appropriate and effective ways to integrate Code Studio tutorials with undergraduate programming curricula.

References

1. Ajzen, I.: The theory of planned behavior. Organ. Behav. Hum. Decis. Process. **50**(2), 17–211 (1991)
2. Barkley, E.F.: Student Engagement Techniques: A Handbook for College Faculty. Jossey-Bass, San Francisco (2010)
3. Bennedsen, J., Caspersen, M.E.: Exposing the programming process. In: Bennedsen, J., Caspersen, M.E., Kölling, M. (eds.) Reflections on the Teaching of Programming: Methods and Implementations. LNCS, vol. 4821, pp. 6–16. Springer, Heidelberg (2008). https://doi.org/10.1007/978-3-540-77934-6_2
4. Coravu, L., Marian, M., Ganea, E.: Scratch and recreational coding for kids. In: 14th RoEduNet International Conference – Networking in Education and Research (RoEduNet NER), pp. 85–89. IEEE (2015)
5. De Kereki, I.F.: Scratch: applications in computer science 1. In: 38th Annual Frontiers in Education Conference Proceedings, pp. 7–11. IEEE (2008)
6. Du, J., Wimmer, H., Rada, R.: 'Hour of Code': can it change students' attitudes toward programming? J. Inf. Technol. Educ. Innov. Pract. **15**, 52–73 (2016)
7. Eranki, K.L.N., Moudgalya, K.M.: Program slicing technique: a novel approach to improve programming skills in novice learners. In: Proceedings of the 17th Annual Conference on Information Technology Education (SIGITE 2016), pp. 160–165. ACM (2016)
8. Guay, F., Vallerand, R.J., Blanchard, C.: On the assessment of situational intrinsic and extrinsic motivation: the situational motivation scale (SIMS). Motiv. Emot. **24**(3), 175–213 (2000)
9. Guzdial, M.: Programming environments for novices. In: Fincher, S., Petre, M. (eds.) Computer Science Education Research, pp. 127–154. Taylor & Francis (2004)
10. Kelleher, C., Pausch, R.: Lowering the barriers to programming: a taxonomy of programming environments and languages for novice programmers. ACM Comput. Surv. **37**(2), 83–137 (2005)
11. Keller, J.M.: Motivational Design for Learning and Performance: The ARCS Model Approach. Springer, Heidelberg (2010). https://doi.org/10.1007/978-1-4419-1250-3

12. Keller, J.M.: Motivational design of instruction. In: Reigeluth, C.M. (ed.) Instructional-Design Theories and Models: An Overview of their Current Status, pp. 383–433. Lawrence Earlbaum Associates (1983)
13. Keller, J.M.: Strategies for stimulating the motivation to learn. Perform. Instr. **26**(8), 1–7 (1987)
14. Korkmaz, O.: The effect of scratch- and lego mindstorms Ev3-based programming activities on academic achievement, problem-solving skills and logical-mathematical thinking skills of students. Malays. Online J. Educ. Sci. **4**(3), 73–88 (2016)
15. Krapp, A., Hidi, S., Renninger, K.A.: Interest, Learning and Development. In: Renninger, A., Hidi, S., Krapp, A. (eds.) The Role of Interest in Learning and Development, pp. 3–25. Lawrence Erlbaum Associates (1992)
16. Lahtinen, E., Ala-Mutka, K., Järvinen, H.: A study of the difficulties of novice programmers. In: Proceedings of the 10th Annual SIGCSE Conference on Innovation and Technology in Computer Science Education (ITiCSE 2005) (2005). ACM SIGCSE Bull. **37**(3), 14–18 (2005)
17. Loorbach, N., Peters, O., Karreman, J., Steehouder, M.: Validation of the instructional materials motivation survey (IMMS) in a self-directed instructional setting aimed at working with technology. Br. J. Educ. Technol. **46**(1), 204–218 (2015)
18. McMillan, J.H., Schumacher, S.: Research in Education: Evidence-Based Inquiry, 6th edn. Pearson Education, London (2006)
19. Nikou, S.A., Economides, A.A.: Measuring student motivation during 'The Hour of Code' activities. In: Proceedings of the 14th International Conference on Advanced Learning Technologies (ICALT), pp. 744–745. IEEE (2014)
20. Nikou, S.A., Economides, A.A.: Transition in student motivation during a Scratch and an App Inventor course. In: Proceedings of the Global Engineering Education Conference (EDUCON), pp. 1042–1045. IEEE (2014)
21. Ouahbi, I., Kaddari, F., Darhmaoui, H., Elachqar, A., Lahmine, S.: Learning basic programming concepts by creating games with scratch programming environment. Procedia Soc. Behav. Sci. **191**, 1479–1482 (2015)
22. Plowright, D.: Using Mixed Methods: Frameworks for an Integrated Methodology. SAGE, Thousand Oaks (2011)
23. Price, T.W., Barnes, T.: Position paper: block-based programming should offer intelligent support for learners. In: Proceedings of the Blocks and Beyond Workshop (B&B), pp. 65–68. IEEE (2017)
24. Sentance, S., Csizmadia, A.: Computing in the curriculum: challenges and strategies from a teacher's perspective. Educ. Inf. Technol. **22**(2), 469–495 (2017)
25. Soloway, E., Bonar, J., Ehrlich, K.: Cognitive strategies and looping constructs: an empirical study. Commun. ACM **26**(11), 853–860 (1983)
26. Spohrer, J.C., Soloway, E.: Putting it all together is hard for novice programmers. In: Proceedings of the IEEE International Conference on Systems, Man, and Cybernetics, pp. 728–735. IEEE (1985)
27. Trowler, V.: Student Engagement Literature Review. Higher Education Academy, York (2010)
28. Wang, T.C., Mei, W.H., Lin, S.L., Chiu, S.K., Lin, J.M.C.: Teaching programming concepts to high school students with Alice. In: Proceedings of the 39th Frontiers in Education Conference (FIE 2009), pp. 955–960. IEEE (2009)
29. Weintrop, D., Wilensky, U.: To block or not to block, that is the question: students' perceptions of blocks-based programming. In: Proceedings of the 14th International Conference on Interaction Design and Children, pp. 199–208. ACM (2015)

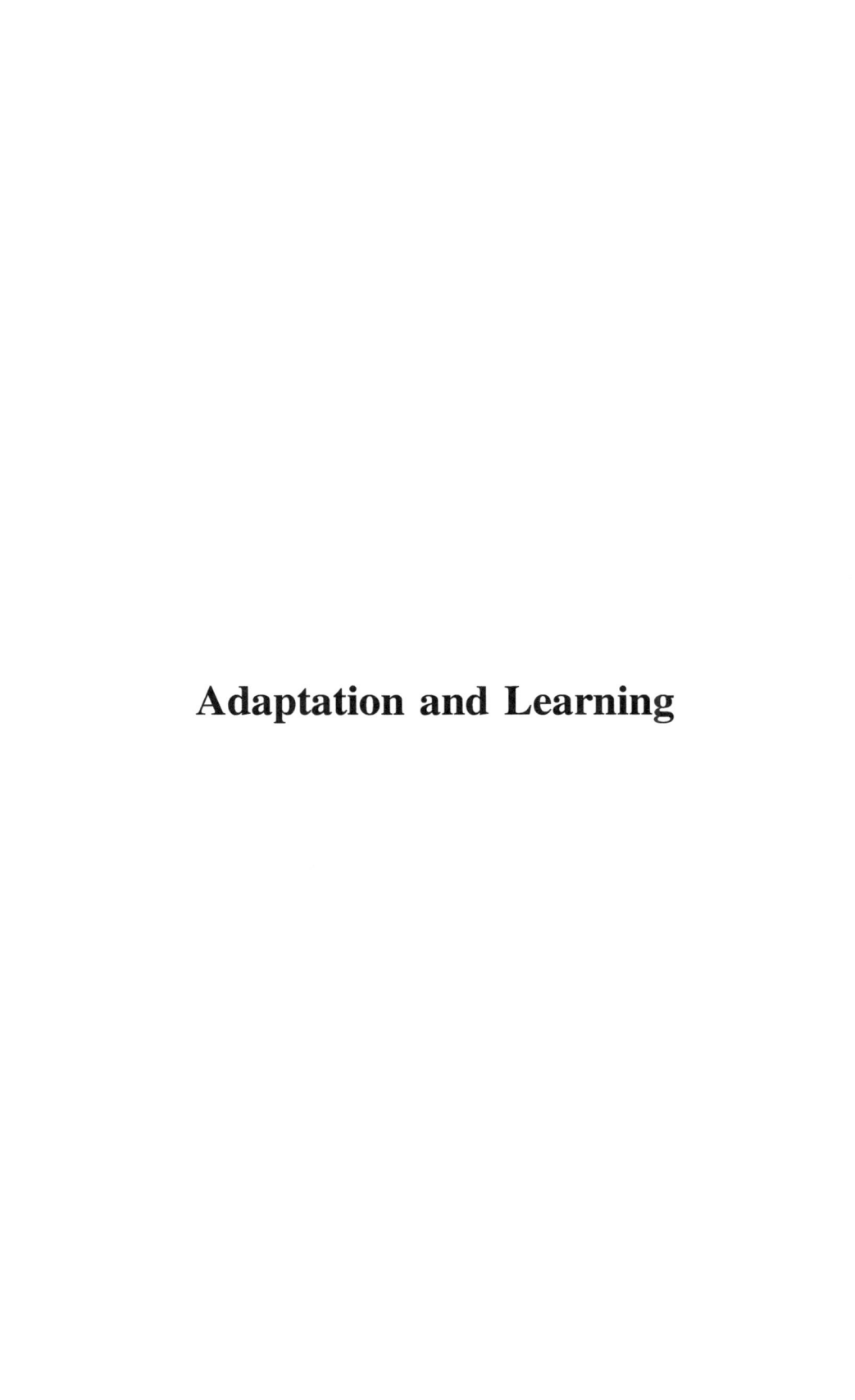

Adaptation and Learning

Towards a Context-Aware Adaptive e-Learning Architecture

George Wamamu Musumba[(✉)] [ID] and Ruth Diko Wario

Department of Computer Science and Informatics, University of the Free State,
Kestell, South Africa
musumbaggw@gmail.com, wariord@ufs.ac.za

Abstract. E-learning is increasingly becoming the preferred delivery mode in learning institutions as it allows any time anywhere learning. However, content delivery, access, distribution and personalization are still a challenge. Moreover, ambiguity of students during decision making for their preferred courses has not been addressed. This paper proposes an adaptive e-learning model, an architecture for the adaptation of learning course materials considering students' profiles and their context information. Integration of fuzziness with processes of customization and selection of adequate material for the user creates a chance to build truly personalized and adaptive systems. This adaptive model is helpful in recommending course materials to students or adapting them depending on their context. It complements instructors' efforts in the delivery of learning materials relevant to their personal profiles. An AeLModel architecture is presented taking a full advantage of ontology, tagging, and users' feedback represented with linguistic descriptors and quantifiers. A prototype was developed and tested using 20 students in a class to assess this model's usability in addition to its adherence to content adaptation, resulting in a 77% of acceptance. It is recommended for this to be used in improving learning processes.

Keywords: e-Learning · Semantic Web · Context-awareness
Context · Adaptation

1 Introduction

The ever-changing state of portable devices in the recent time, coupled with the fact that most of them are pervasively connected to the internet, allows learning to take place anywhere and at any time [32]. This has made it possible for learning management systems (LMS) to provide learning contents to students even outside a school environment. Closely related to this is Ubiquitous Learning, whereby the process of learning can take place virtually everywhere and this can be integrated with people's daily lives [32]. Furthermore, possibility of exploring context awareness in the learning environment and adapting learning to the users' needs and surroundings [5] has increased in the recent times. In mobile learning environment, different context data can be explored.

© Springer Nature Switzerland AG 2019
S. Kabanda et al. (Eds.): SACLA 2018, CCIS 963, pp. 191–206, 2019.
https://doi.org/10.1007/978-3-030-05813-5_13

Portable devices being in use for supporting teaching and learning is no longer new. Mobile learning reality has been made possible by the fact that wireless infrastructure is widely deployed and adoption of handheld computing devices is rapid. Mobile-based learning systems development is discussed in [3,9,27,31]. These systems create practical mobile learning environments that enable students to enjoy the learning mobility with ease. However, when students relocate to areas that are not covered by the local area network, the systems experience challenges, among them the learning functions being disabled leading to inability of tracking the students' learning behaviors, delivery of content, and synchronization of data. Additionally, context-awareness, a concept that is useful in enhancing the learning systems' usability as discussed in [17,30,33,37] is proposed in this work. It is also possible to take the same concept into account in the course caching strategy design for which the main parameters are related context information [8,13].

According to the works in [1], the student context could encompass users' surroundings thus, location information, the learning objective, historical knowledge and preferences. Accordingly, adaptation of content, could personalize the learning object in a bid of meeting this context. As an example, as quoted from [1], "if a learner, driving to school may need information pertaining to the course in which the leaner will have an examination in a few minutes, an application in the learner's mobile phone, using context awareness, can suggest an LO related to the examination. Since the learner is currently driving, the object can be adapted to audible format and transmitted via Bluetooth to the car sound system".

Ontology as a concept of Semantic Web is also proposed in one of the classic works [6] as an idea of machine-process-able information. This form of representation enabled better and more semantic-oriented processing of information, as well as reasoning about it. Its application to e-Learning created opportunities for building systems that were capable of analyzing students' needs and behaviors, and more accurate selection of learning materials. These capabilities notwithstanding, there is a need to deal with missing or inaccurate data [36]. Uncertainty is brought by students when they imprecisely express their needs and opinions. The decisions they make in regard to selection of the most suitable alternatives heavily depend on current circumstances, their understanding of situations, and their needs and requirements—things that are 'equipped' with ambiguity [22].

In this paper, first, we describe an architecture for constructing adaptive human-centric e-Learning systems—systems with capabilities to recognize students's contexts and adapt to students' needs and preferences considering their fuzzy nature in decision making. Such systems combine (1) technologies of the Semantic Web—ontology and forms of its representation, (2) aspects of social software—blogs and tagging, and (3) techniques of Computational Intelligence (CI)—fuzziness and MCDM. Additionally, instructors are also provided with the abilities to enter their suggestions and recommendations and observe students' learning activities and comment on them. Secondly, we propose a model named adaptive e-Learning Model (AeLModel), which depending on the students' context (profile), adapts course materials. In this way, learning is enhanced. The following question is answered: *Putting into consideration the students' context, how could a model for adapting learning materials that is relevant and satisfies the student be developed?* In the process of developing AeLmodel we did not find any other model appropriate for this task. Additionally, existing propositions were not available for either extension or reuse.

Organization of the remainder of this paper is as follows: Sect. 2 discusses related work. Section 3 describes adaptive e-learning concept in some details. Section 4 discusses the technologies and the methodology approach for our study. Section 5 describes the learning model. Sections 6 and 7 present the model's evaluation, results, and concluding remarks.

2   Related Work

Development of e-Learning systems and supporting these technologies represents an ongoing challenge of fundamental interest and practical relevance. Existing approaches in this area are quite diversified enjoying the reliance on various methodologies and effective algorithmic developments. A substantial number of them adhere to the fundamentals of general schemes of web technologies. The domain of e-Learning is expanding quite fast.

In [7,20] it is stated that E-learning allows students to study without the limitations of time and space which is beneficial to some extent. Those studies suggest that ideal systems should classify students and should also provide necessary amount of learning materials that are tailored for the individual student's needs. The 'one size fits all' philosophy results in too much information for users and lacks personalization [4]. However, personalization can bring improvements in Learning Management Systems (LMS). According to [7], LMS in this category do not satisfy the constraints to develop and manage contents to meet the demand of learning institutions. Moreover, most LMS do not provide complete learning solutions [20]. They are unable to provide adequate mechanisms for maintaining consistent instructional presentation or adapting that content to the needs of students. E-learning mode of training is touted as a solution to the above issues. However, student imprecise decision making nature is not managed—hence losing many of them in the process.

According [1], the Semantic Web based on semantic web-rule language (SWRL) rules, providing knowledge representations formats—Resource Description Framework (RDF)[1] and ontology—is already entrenched in e-Learning applications. Features such as formal taxonomies expressed with web ontology languages RDFS and OWL,[2] with rules represented using the web rule language RuleML,[3] have been used in the representation and the dynamic construction of shared and re-usable learning content [14].

---

[1] http://www.w3.org/RDF/.
[2] http://www.w3.org/TR/owl2-overview/.
[3] http://ruleml.org/.

Social networks are among the emerging technologies which can be tapped into when developing education portals. They can provide a platform for exchange of information, and communication between authors, teachers, and educational institutions [21, 39]. These network platforms allow for *"combining educational portals, ontologies, and search agents with functions such as Web mining, and knowledge management to create, discover, analyze, and manage the knowledge of different domains presented in educational material"* [22].

Multiple aspects of e-Learning have been addressed by techniques involving fuzziness. Fuzzy-based methods are used for user profiling, determining students' profiles, evaluating quality of e-Learning systems, as well as enhancing their capabilities. In [19], fuzzy terms were used to describe pedagogical resources as well as users' profiles.

It is apparent that a proper representation of data and adequate processing of information are necessary steps leading towards knowledge-oriented systems. The ability to find and represent different types of relations between pieces of information is a necessary condition for creating semantically conscious applications. This semantic awareness allows for more accurate identification of relevant information. At the same time building any type of system that interacts with a human requires ability to handle imprecision and ambiguity. In this regard we believe that the application of fuzziness and approximate reasoning creates a promising avenue of introducing human aspects to software systems and could lead to the development of more human-conscious-like systems. This aspect is apparently missing in the reviewed works.

3   Concept

Ultimately, our work aims to develop a detailed architecture for development of human-centric adaptive e-learning models. For human-centric aspects to be realized, utilization of fuzziness and approximate reasoning that are able to express and process ambiguity and imprecision—two very characteristic features of human selection and decision-making activities—is needed. We suggest that combining these techniques with RDF and ontology-based representations of knowledge and elements of social networks—blogging and tagging—can lead to a new way of designing e-Learning Systems. Moreover, development of such a system can be a basis upon which to draw conclusions of immediate practical relevance to creation of such applications.

Different from other approaches reported in the literature, this paper considers uncertainty aspects of human nature as imprecision, insufficient available information, and approximate reasoning in order to ensure engaging and comfortable, yet practical and efficient learning environment. Key issues of the proposed architecture include: (1) undisputed ambiguity and imprecision of information provided and used by humans; (2) multiplicity of sources of information influencing the content and (3) the form of course materials that has the following components:

– Personal preferences and feedback, i.e. a student's goals and learning style, as well as the student's involvement in content annotation, tagging, and contributions to blogs;
– Required material, suggestions, and constraints provided by instructors;
– Feedback, content annotations, notes, and evaluations contributed by peer students.

These information sources are often ambiguous. However, they determine relevant components of domain knowledge, greatly influencing the choice of the teaching material considered most appropriate to the student. A variety of ways exist for performing this selection process with varying levels of accuracy and levels of importance assigned to each of these sources. For instance, in courses that are fundamental and need a rigorous approach, the suggestions and constraints imposed on the content by instructors will have higher priority, influence, and precision than preferences provided by the student, as well as the feedback provided by peer students. Construction of course materials becomes flexible with adoption of such approach.

4   Methods and Techniques

4.1   Fuzziness and Semantic Web

Fuzzy theory has proven advantages for dealing with imprecise and uncertain decision situations and models human reasoning in its use of approximate information [34]. Incorporating fuzzy logic in students' decision-making techniques can address the problem on unreliability due to insufficiency in amount of information students have at the point of making decisions. Fuzziness provides a unique approach for dealing with the very human concept of imprecision. Abilities to use such imprecise terms as much, so-so and linguistic quantifiers like more than, most, least, any make fuzzy-based methods most suitable for dealing with human evaluation of different items and their description. Fuzzy set theory implements grouping of data with boundaries that are not distinctly defined. This leads to a critical aspect of fuzziness which is its ability to express levels of membership of terms to specific concepts. Using fuzzy-based mechanisms for processing and reasoning, deduction of new facts and their levels of belonging to specific categories, as well as precision levels of their descriptions is possible.

Software technologies can provide a comprehensive approach to knowledge representation. Ontology is the basic framework usable in representation of concepts, their definitions and instances, in addition to how the concepts are linked and dependent on each other. In some contexts, ontology definition uses the concept of Resource Description Framework (RDF) represented in triple as the foundation of knowledge representation. In this case, the triple is in the form of subject-predicate-object, where: subject identifies the object being described; predicate is the piece of data in the object that a value is given to; and the actual value of the attribute is the object. For instance, the triple 'Anne loves movies' has 'Anne' as its subject, 'loves' as predicate, and 'movies' as object.

The process of tagging is simply labeling or annotation of resources [18] which is performed by users that use tags to easily and freely and without any knowledge of any taxonomies or ontologies annotate resources. These tags are used to represent those strings considered by users, appropriate descriptions of resources. On the other hand, resources could be any items that have been posted and are accessible by users and can lead to an interesting way of describing resources [24, 34]. Those technologies are applied to design and develop elements and features of adaptive e-Learning models.

4.2   Categorization of Students

Another very essential aspect of this work is the identification of categories of students. All students have different learning traits. The differences have been categorized by educators as learning styles, cognitive styles, multiple intelligences or cognitive traits. In creating adaptive learning systems, two approaches have been used: (1) at the outset, cognitive/learning styles are assessed and then the system is presented to match the students' profiles, or (2) having no preset initialization of the system, only allowing adaptations to occur based on the students' use of the system. A test of both approaches is necessary in order understand their advantages and disadvantages.

For the former approach, the exact method for characterizing student profiles is the subject of debates by professionals in education sector. This has been so because some student assessment approaches rely on cognitive style measures arising from psychological theory [29], that is, as discussed in [22], measures of general cognitive tendencies or approaches that endure across numerous types of stimuli. Other assessments modes focus on learning styles, categorizations of students' preferences in educational contexts and finally, some methods employ the measurement of basic cognitive traits (e.g. working memory capacity) as a means to predict what material and style of presentation is desirable for a particular student [12]. From a theoretical standpoint it appears none of these approaches have been unchallenged in regards to their validity and reliability [29].

From the foregoing, the inconclusive nature of research in these areas is vivid. To address this state of affairs, this paper proposes creation of coherence between the initially derived student profiles and the mechanisms for updating their profiles which already exist within a particular adaptive system. A choice of a cognitive style measure that reflects the specific mechanisms in the adaptive system created in this work is taken. This is necessitated as it makes it possible to be modified in a bid to limit the demands of assessment on the student in the initial phase of using the system. Furthermore, for the assessment of the structure of content, the holistic/analytic dimension on the Cognitive Styles Analysis (CSA) [26] is relied upon.

4.3   Representation of Course Material

Students are able to experience new interaction mechanisms with the learning environment with the proliferation of digital technology systems in education. In this regard, of great importance to the teaching process is the effectiveness of digital media. This paper explores how digital representation of material selectively extends but also constrains what a student sees, experiences and has access to, and how it enhances but also shapes instructors' representations and presentations of their knowledge in an e-Learning system. Some of the critical parts of a learning process in whichever level of education are activities such as taking notes, marking important and/or difficult parts of presented materials, and writing feedback comments (i.e. confirmation, corrective, explanatory, diagnostic, and elaborative information). The proposed framework is equipped with a number of techniques and methods, such as content annotation, blogs, and tagging, to allow users to label the teaching material and provide their opinions about its content with particular emphasis put on the use of nonintrusive ways of inputting information, for instance, via voice.

Information provided by users is stored using the knowledge representation schema based on ontology and RDF triples. Algorithms are used to process users' inputs and to annotate course materials with terms and keywords reflecting users' opinions and notes.

4.4   Personalization and Context Dependence

One of the essential challenges of e-Learning systems is to satisfy students' needs and preferences. It is of critical importance to be able to properly elicit and store information about students, their likes and dislikes, and what kind of methods, techniques and media they enjoy during learning activities. The techniques should ensure utilization of two types of information:

- Student's needs, what he/she already knows, his/her goals, things already done, things left to do, timing, ability to learn, ways of learning, most suitable media (slides, notes, short lectures);
- Current context, such as: time of a day, an amount of time a student can spend, place, ability to listen or watch. Special mechanisms and techniques are used to keep track of things that work for the student, i.e. likes, comments, and information about favorite instructors.

All information about an individual student is stored in a specialized ontology. Such ontology is created and maintained for each student. The mechanisms that support storing imprecise (fuzzy-based) information are developed. Students are able to provide their priorities regarding needs and preferences in a suitable form. Special mechanisms for estimating relevance of that information are proposed and validated.

4.5   Instructors' Input Mechanism

The involvement of instructors in the education process is irreplaceable. Therefore, the proposed framework provides a number of ways that an instructor can monitor students' activities and act accordingly. Instructors are able to query the system for items related to available materials and students taking their courses, as well as read comments provided by students and related to the material they prepared. The system also allows instructors to enter answers to students' questions, suggest alternative material to students, and correct them.

4.6   Individual and Collaboration-Based Material Selection

The process of selecting most suitable lecture materials, i.e. choice between multiple versions, multiple sections, multiple media, etc., is the most critical part of any AeLModel-based system. Multiple sources of information about lecture materials have to be evaluated and ranked based on:

- Multiple criteria provided by the student, including student's goals and profile (preferences, likes/dislikes), as well as comments and notes given to similar course materials;
- Instructors' suggestions, recommendations, and constrains, including instructors' notes, observations and expertise, are used as important selection criteria;
- Multiple evaluations of possible material, including the process of collecting students' feedback via social software methods, lead to an extensive annotation of material; also a schema for integrating annotations and extracting most common opinions is required; those opinions play the role of criteria during a selection process.

The proposed selection methods mimic human-amenable aggregation processes from students', other users', and instructors' points of view. The levels of importance are taken into consideration. The methods have to deal with imprecision information (evaluations, criteria, annotation), different priorities, and constraints. This paper examines the following aggregation approaches: fuzzy-based methods; evidence theory; different aggregation techniques including linguistic based aggregation. Overall, the proposed selection mechanisms perform decision-making tasks taking into account:

- What the instructor thinks is important;
- What is important for the student;
- What peers think is important.

5   Description of the Learning System

The architecture of the AeLModel-based system is presented in Fig. 1. In a nutshell, the system knows what the student wants (student's profile) and likes

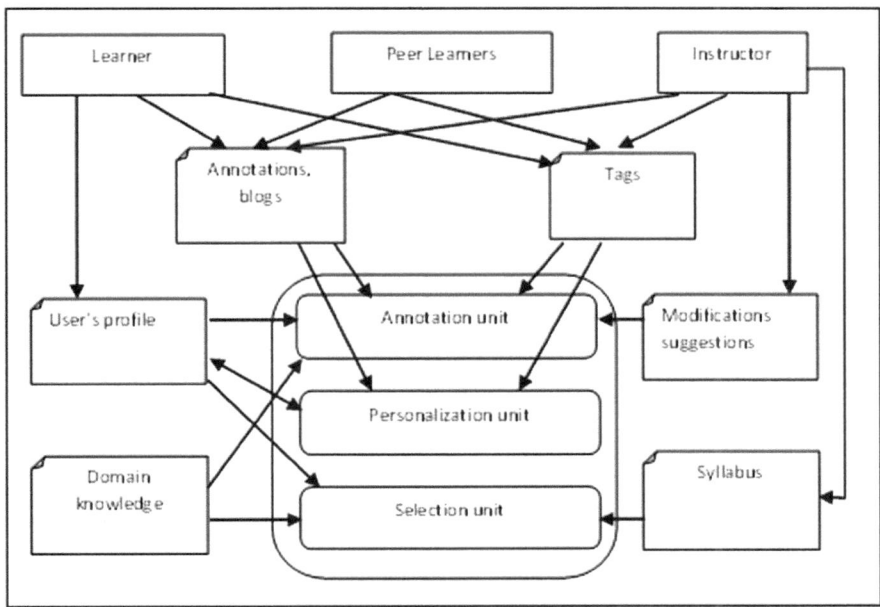

Fig. 1. Architecture of AeLModel-based system

(annotations, blogs, tags), knows what instructors suggest and recommend (modifications, suggestions, annotations, blogs, tags), and knows what peer students say about available material (annotations, blogs, tags). Based on that knowledge and syllabi, the system provides the student with most suitable alternatives regarding sets of education material. The system allows students to make notes and record opinions. At the same time instructors have the ability to monitor the student and provide modifications and additions to the material the student is currently using.

In order to accomplish that, all the tasks performed by the system are divided into three categories:

- Multi-domain annotation of course material stored in a repository combined with techniques and methods of extracting important options based on tag clouds, blogs and students' notes; instructors' suggestions and constrains are also used to annotate available material;
- Personalization that leads to creation and updating of student's profile that contains information about student's preferences, needs, likes or dislikes;
- Prioritization-based multi-criteria selection that performs selection of most suitable material based on student's profile, peer students' opinions, and instructors' inputs.

The annotation activities are presented in Fig. 2. All annotation is performed on course material stored in the repository of the system, and it reflects three

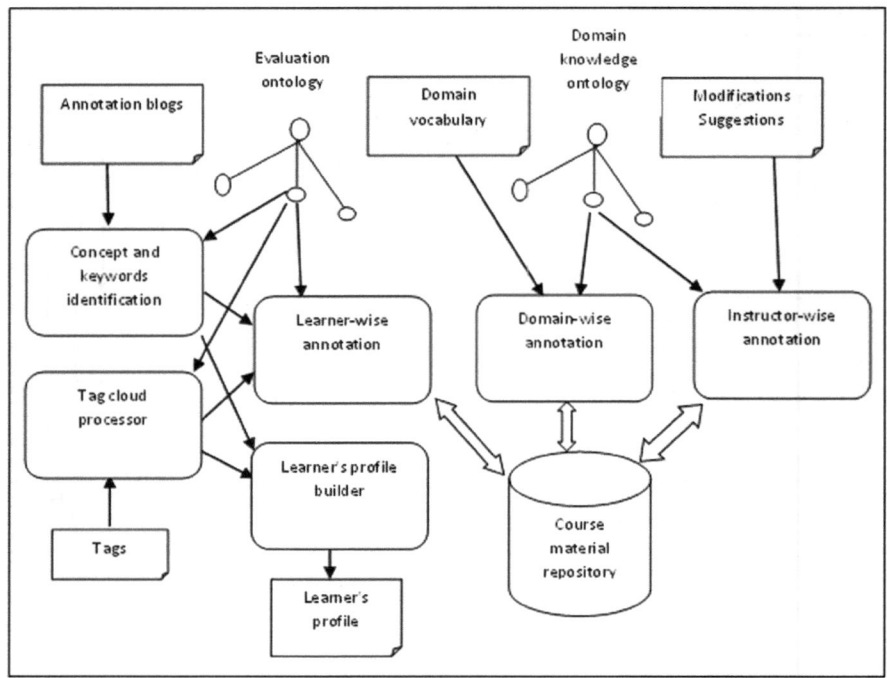

Fig. 2. Annotation activities of AeLModel-based system

domains (dimensions): students', instructors', and knowledge relevant to course topics.

The students-wise annotation is supported by such processes as identification of concept and keywords in annotations and blogs, as well as analysis of tag-clouds. The instructor-wise annotation takes into account all requirements and recommendations provided by instructor. The domain-wise annotation leads to annotation of all repository materials with terms originated from specific knowledge domains.

In the end, all materials are annotated with three types of terms originated from three sources of annotations. The personalization activity is also shown in Fig. 2. It uses results of the same process as annotation: concept and keyword identification and analysis of tag-clouds to extract information that is related to a single student. This information is used for updating of the student's profile. Both annotation and personalization process are continuously performed to keep annotations and profile up-to-date.

The multi-criteria selection mechanisms are presented in Fig. 3. The first step in the process selects a few sets of alternative materials. The selection uses the annotated course material and is based on student's needs and goals and provided syllabi. An important element is extraction of evaluations of those materials done by other students. The last and most important step of selection

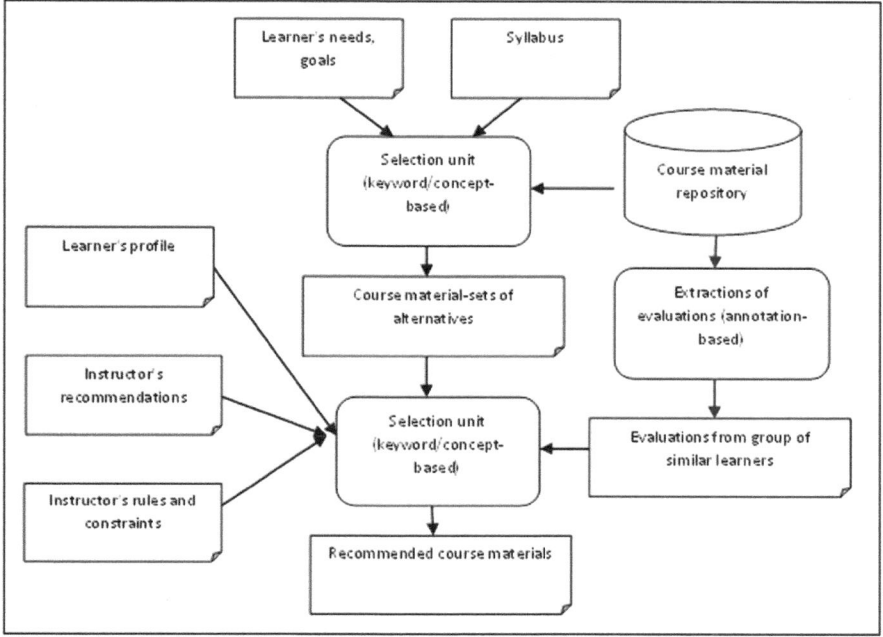

Fig. 3. Selection processes

is identification of the most suitable material. This step relies on a number of different decision-making methods that are able to deal with multiple criteria with multiple levels of priorities [35], imprecise information and human-amenable aggregation of evaluations [23,25]. These processes can use different sources of information, for example RSS-feeds, and different analysis techniques including formal ones, for example FCA [16].

6   Model Evaluation and Results

6.1   AeLModel Evaluation

Model evaluation is a critical component while developing applications. This model is evaluated by analyzing the quality and the fidelity that it provides to fulfill the proposed objective. To accomplish this, a *prototype was developed* and used by undergraduate students taking a course in database systems.[4] An experiment was done with 20 Computer Science undergraduate students, who had experience in e-learning. The experiment was divided into pre-test and post-test. During the pre-test stage, the students were allowed to use the AeLModel application for learning the database systems course. To do this, the application

---

[4] The prototype software is available from the authors upon request.

Table 1. Questionnaire

Q. no.	Statement
1	The course material was appropriately adapted to my profile
2	The course material content was suitable to me
3	The course material was available in the device I was using to access it and was in the right format
4	This model was helpful in my learning and can be useful in online learning (within or outside the premises)
5	This model stirred in me greater interest to learn
6	I could understand easily the content displayed
7	The model can facilitate independent study in disregard to location
8	It was easy to use the model
9	Access of learning material through the model was quick
10	My learning experience was better using the model than other modes I have previously used

was installed to both mobile (Android) and laptops with internet access, and these were given to the students. These devices using web services accessed the course materials stored in a repository. For the post-test, at the end of the semester, participants were asked to fill a questionnaire developed based on the work in [28] in regard to the suitability of the model in answering the research question. Ten statements were worded, and the students rated them using a Likert scale [15]. The scale had five (scoring) choices: 'completely agree' (5), 'agree' (4), 'neutral' (3), 'disagree' (2), and 'completely disagree' (1).

We employed the Cronbach alpha method [10] to test the reliability of the questionnaire administered. This was important as it allowed estimation of the correlation between the responses given by participants. According to [10,11] reliability test results should be more than or equal to 0.7 for them to be acceptable. For our survey the test resulted in 0.8, confirming its reliability. Tables 1 and 2 present the statements in and the results obtained from the survey respectively.

The formulated statements are shown in Table 1. In Table 2 they are represented in the first column, followed by percentages of responses by participants to each item in the following columns, in regard to the Likert scale. For better analysis of the responses, weight average value (WAV) of the items was calculated. The greatest satisfaction to students when they use the model is shown when the WAV value is closer to L(5), while a value closer L(1) indicates the satisfaction level in reverse. For this survey, WAV values were greater than L(3), indicating approval of the model by the students and that they were satisfied in using it.

Results from this survey show that the statement regarding 'presentation' (Q.2) scored lowest. However, its value of 3.32 is above mean and satisfactory

Table 2. Percentage of responses computed from the Questionnaire, with WAV = weight average value = $(5A + 4B + 3C + 2D + 1E)/12$, where A, B, C, D, E are the number of responses in Likert scale L(5)–L(1) with 12 interviewees according to [38]

Response	L(5)	L(4)	L(3)	L(2)	L(1)	WAV
Q.1	26	67	7	0	0	4.17
Q.2	7	54	16	16	7	3.32
Q.3	24	66	7	2	1	4.16
Q.4	59	23	9	1	8	4.26
Q.5	48	48	1	0	1	4.49
Q.6	48	24	24	2	0	4.24
Q.7	44	32	18	6	0	4.09
Q.8	15	65	18	2	0	4.01
Q.9	16	66	17	0	0	4.00
Q.10	40	40	10	3	7	4.09

as it is closer to L(5) than L(1). These results also show the summary of affirmative responses from participants regarding the use of AeLModel. It is shown that there are high incidences of 'agree' and 'completely agree' as responses for statements Q.5 and Q.6 essentially explaining the enhancement of the students' personal interest and understanding by the model. The usability characteristic of the model tested by statements Q.8 and Q.9, was approved by majority of the participants, although it also obtained the highest number of users that were neutral. This could be associated with the fact that a significant number of participants considered that this being just an experiment and the time frame, it would not have been appropriate to evaluate this feature. Notably, adaptation and performance represented by statements Q.1 and Q.9 respectively was good and therefore students who participated in the survey were satisfied with the model. Finally, most participants were satisfied with statement Q.10, stating that the model eased their learning process.

It is noted that our survey employed a relatively small sample and used the Likert scale as a non-parametric scale. Two samples were formed: one with concordant responses ('completely agree' and 'agree') and the other discordant responses ('completely disagree' and 'disagree'). Due to this, the Mann-Whitney-Wilcoxon test [2] was applied to determine the distribution similarity level between the samples using 0.05 as value of significance. Furthermore, the use of R,[5] a statistics software, resulted in the negative. Consequently it is shown that the model of distribution followed by the two sample groups is dissimilar. This means that sample values are independent, effectively showing that inference of any conclusion about one sample that does depend on the results of the other sample.

---

[5] http://www.r-project.org/.

7 Conclusions

One of the strengths of the proposed architecture for development of e-Learning systems is its multidisciplinary nature. This work leads to interesting results in several important areas:

Ontology and RDF triples: those are new and conceptually challenging forms of knowledge representation; activities related to adaptation of these forms to e-Learning systems and their integration with interactive systems should lead to improvements in system's abilities to store, access and analyze information;

Blogs and tagging: incorporation of these activities with e-Learning systems should improve agility of e-Learning systems and their ability to absorb users' feedback, additionally their integration with new forms of knowledge representation should lead to a better analysis of information embedded in blog posts and used tags;

Fuzziness and multi-criteria decision making, as the core technologies of the framework, should play an critical role in the process of creating more human-centric systems; at the same time the framework should provide an evidence of necessity of application of these techniques to development of real-world system able to support users' activities in a personalized way; the combination of fuzziness with the new forms of knowledge representation (ontology and RDF triples) should increase the presence of CI technologies on the Web.

The proposed e-Learning architecture constitutes a very important step towards direct application of fuzziness and new forms of knowledge representation to 'real world' needs of e-Learning systems. The architecture also addresses the challenges imposed by human-centric systems.

References

1. Abech, M., Rigo, S.J., Costa, C.A., Righi, R.R., Barbosa, J.L.V.: A model for learning objects adaptation in light of mobile and context-aware computing. Pers. Ubiquit. Comput. **20**(2), 167–184 (2016)
2. Ahmad, I.A.: A class of Mann-Whitney-Wilcoxon type statistics. Am. Stat. **50**(4), 324–327 (1996)
3. Bae, Y.K., Lim, J.S., Lee, T.W.: Mobile learning system using the ARCS strategies. In: Proceedings of 5th IEEE International Conference on Advanced Learning Technology, ICALT 2005, pp. 600–602 (2005)
4. Bai, S.M., Chen, S.M.: Evaluating students learning achievement using fuzzy membership functions and fuzzy rules. Expert Syst. Appl. **34**(1), 399–410 (2008)
5. Bellavista, P., Corradi, A., Fanelli, M., Foschini, L.: A survey of context data distribution for mobile ubiquitous systems. ACM Comput. Surv. **44**(4), 1–45 (2012)
6. Berners-Lee, T., Hendler, J., Lassila, O.: The Semantic Web. Sci. Am. **284**, 34–43 (2001)
7. Bhaskaran, S., Swaminathan, P.: Intelligent adaptive e-learning model for learning management system. Res. J. Appl. Sci. Eng. Tech. **7**(16), 3298–3303 (2014)

8. Cao, L.Y., Oezsu, M.T.: Evaluation of strong consistency web caching techniques. World Wide Web **5**(2), 95–123 (2002)
9. Chen, Y.S., Kao, T.C., Yu, G.J., Sheu, J.P.: A mobile butterfly-watching learning system for supporting independent learning. In: Proceedings of 2nd IEEE International Workshop on Wireless and Mobile Technologies in Education, pp. 11–18 (2004/2005)
10. Gliem, J., Gliem, R.: Calculating, interpreting, and reporting Cronbach's alpha reliability coefficient for Likert-type scales. In: Proceedings of Midwest Research to Practice Conference in Adult, Continuing and Community Education, pp. 82–88 (2003)
11. Gomez, S., Zervas, P., Sampson, D.G., Fabregat, R.: Supporting context-aware adaptive and personalized Mobile learning delivery: evaluation results from the use of UoLm Player. In: Proceedings of 13th IEEE International Conference on Advanced Learning Technologies, ICALT 2013, pp. 354–358 (2013)
12. Graf, S., Lin, T.: The relationship between learning styles and cognitive traits: getting additional information for improving student modelling. Comput. Hum. Behav. **24**(2), 122–137 (2008)
13. Iyer, R.: Characterization and evaluation of cache hierarchies for web servers. World Wide Web **7**, 259–280 (2004)
14. Jovanovic, J., Gasevic, D., Torniai, C., Bateman, S., Hatala, M.: The social semantic web in intelligent learning environments: state of the art and future challenges. Interact. Learn. Environ. **17**(4), 273–308 (2009)
15. Likert, R.: A Technique for the Measurement of Attitudes, vol. 140. The Science Press (1932)
16. de Maio, C., Fenza, G., Gaeta, M., Loia, V., Orciuoli, F., Senatore, S.: RSS-based e-learning recommendations exploiting fuzzy FCA for knowledge modeling. Appl. Soft Comput. **12**(1), 113–124 (2012)
17. Malek, J., Laroussi, M., Derycke, A.: A multi-layer ubiquitous middleware for bijective adaptation between context and activity in a mobile and collaborative learning. In: Proceedings of International Conference on System and Network Communication, ICSNC 2006, p. 39 (2006)
18. Mathes, A.: Folksonomies: cooperative classification and communication through shared metadata (2004). www.adammathes.com/academic/computermediated-communication/folksonomies.html
19. Mencar, C., Castiello, C., Fanelli, A.M.: Fuzzy user profiling in e-learning contexts. In: Lovrek, I., Howlett, R.J., Jain, L.C. (eds.) KES 2008. LNCS (LNAI), vol. 5178, pp. 230–237. Springer, Heidelberg (2008). https://doi.org/10.1007/978-3-540-85565-1_29
20. Musumba, G.W., Oboko, R.O., Nyongesa, H.O.: Agent based adaptive e-learning model for any learning management system. Int. J. Mach. Learn. Appl. **2**(1.VI) (2013)
21. Raghavan, P.: Social networks: from the web to the identifying some challenging issues and discussing enterprise. IEEE Internet Comput. **6**(1), 91–94 (2002)
22. Reformat, M.Z., Boechler, P.M.: Fuzziness and semantic web technologies in personalized e-learning. In: Proceedings of 8th Conference of the European Society for Fuzzy Logic and Technology, EUSFLAT 2013 (2013)
23. Reformat, M.Z., Golmohammadi, S.K.: Rule- and OWA-based semantic similarity for user profiling. Int. J. Fuzzy Syst. **12**(2), 87–102 (2010)
24. Reformat, M.Z., Yager, R.R.: Tag-based fuzzy sets for criteria evaluation in on-line selection processes. J. Ambient Intell. Hum. Comput. **2**(1), 35–51 (2011)

25. Reformat, M.Z., Yager, R.R., Li, Z., Alajlan, N.: Human-inspired identification of high level concepts using OWA and linguistic quantifiers. Int. J. Comput. Commun. Control **6**(3), 473–502 (2011)
26. Riding, R., Cheema, I.: Cognitive styles: an overview and integration. Educ. Psychol. **11**(3/4), 193–215 (1991)
27. Shih, Y.E.: Language in action: applying mobile classroom in foreign language learning. In: Proceedings of 5th IEEE International Conference on Advanced Learning Technology, ICALT 2005, pp. 548–549 (2005)
28. Ssemugabi, S.: Usability evaluation of a web-based e-learning application: a study of two evaluation methods. Doct. Diss., University of South Africa (2009)
29. Sternberg, R.J., Grigorenko, E.L.: A capsule history of theory and research on styles. In: Sternberg, R.J., Zhang, L.F. (eds.) Perspectives on Thinking, Learning and Cognitive Styles. Lawrence Erlbaum Assoc., Mahwah (2001)
30. Syvanen, A., Beale, R., Sharples, M., Ahonen, M., Lonsdale, P.: Supporting pervasive learning environments: adaptability and context awareness in mobile learning. In: Proceedings of IEEE International Workshop on Wireless and Mobile Technologies in Education, WMTE 2005, p. 3 (2005)
31. Tan, T.H., Liu, T.Y.: The mobile-based interactive learning environment (MOBILE) and a case study for assisting elementary school English learning. In: Proceedings of IEEE International Conference on Advanced Learning Technologies, pp. 530–534 (2004)
32. Wagner, A., Barbosa, J.L.V., Barbosa, D.N.F.: A model for profile management applied to ubiquitous learning environments. Expert Syst. Appl. **41**(4.II), 2023–2034 (2014)
33. Wang, Y.K.: Context awareness and adaptation in mobile learning. In: Proceedings of 2nd IEEE International Workshop on Wireless and Mobile Technologies in Education, pp. 154–158 (2004)
34. Yager, R.R., Reformat, M.Z: Using fuzzy sets to model information provided by social tagging. In: Proceedings of IEEE World Congress on Computational Intelligence (2010)
35. Yager, R.R., Reformat, M.Z., Gumrah, G.: Using a web personal evaluation tool: PET for lexicographic multi-criteria service selection. Knowl.-Based Syst. **24**(7), 929–942 (2011)
36. Zadeh, L.A.: Toward a perception-based theory of probabilistic reasoning with imprecise probabilities. J. Stat. Plan. Inference **105**, 233–264 (2002)
37. Zhao, G., Yang, Z.: Learning resource adaptation and delivery framework for mobile learning. In: Proceedings of 35th Annual Frontiers in Education Conference, FIE 2005, pp. F1H.18–F1H.24 (2005)
38. Zhao, X., Wan, X., Okamoto, T.: Adaptive content delivery in ubiquitous learning environment. In: Proceedings of 6th IEEE International Conference on Wireless, Mobile and Ubiquitous Technologies in Education, pp. 19–26 (2010)
39. Zhong, N., Liu, J., Yao, Y.: In search of the wisdom web. IEEE Comput. **35**(11), 27–31 (2002)

Using Bayesian Networks and Machine Learning to Predict Computer Science Success

Zachary Nudelman$^{(\boxtimes)}$ ⓘ, Deshendran Moodley, and Sonia Berman

Department of Computer Science, University of Cape Town, Cape Town, South Africa
ndlzac001@myuct.ac.za, {deshen,sonia}@cs.uct.ac.za

Abstract. Bayesian Networks and Machine Learning techniques were evaluated and compared for predicting academic performance of Computer Science students at the University of Cape Town. Bayesian Networks performed similarly to other classification models. The causal links inherent in Bayesian Networks allow for understanding of the contributing factors for academic success in this field. The most effective indicators of success in first-year 'core' courses in Computer Science included the student's scores for Mathematics and Physics as well as their aptitude for learning and their work ethos. It was found that unsuccessful students could be identified with ≈91% accuracy. This could help to increase throughput as well as student wellbeing at university.

Keywords: Bayesian Networks · Machine learning
Educational Data Mining · Computer science education

1 Introduction

In the past two decades, the broader field of Educational Data Mining (EDM) has developed into a respected and extensive research field [4]. According to the EDM website,[1] EDM can be defined as *"an emerging discipline, concerned with developing methods for exploring the unique types of data that come from educational settings, and using those methods to better understand students, and the settings which they learn in"*. Using EDM for prediction usually involves developing a model which accepts certain variables (factors affecting the prediction) and outputs an expected result for the predicted variable [3].

EDM, specifically machine learning techniques, can be used to explore factors contributing to the success of high school applicants for the bachelor of computer science curriculum (BSc(CS)) at the University of Cape Town (UCT). While the graduation rate of computer science (CS) majors at the UCT has been reasonably good over the past decade, there is a strong desire to improve throughput and time-to-graduation. Furthermore, in the South African context, UCT needs to consider social redress when admitting applicants. An accurate

---

[1] http://www.educationaldatamining.org.

© Springer Nature Switzerland AG 2019
S. Kabanda et al. (Eds.): SACLA 2018, CCIS 963, pp. 207–222, 2019.
https://doi.org/10.1007/978-3-030-05813-5_14

model to predict student success could allow UCT to continue along its path of social transformation while maintaining and indeed improving levels of success.

Available literature shows that one of the best predictors of academic success at university relates to the marks attained thus far in a student's academic career [17]. However, when using secondary-school marks to predict university performance in South Africa, this may not be the case, because the basic education system in South Africa is worse than *"(almost) all middle-income countries that participate in cross-national assessments of educational achievement"* as well as *"many low-income African countries"* [18]. The South African Department of Basic Education categorises schools into quintiles according to socio-economic status, where Quintile 1 schools have the least resources and Quintile 5 schools the most. Independent or private schools are usually well resourced; the term may also refer to some schools with a non-government syllabus that are poorly resourced (e.g. some missionary schools). For this paper, 90% of the independent schools considered are private and well-resourced.

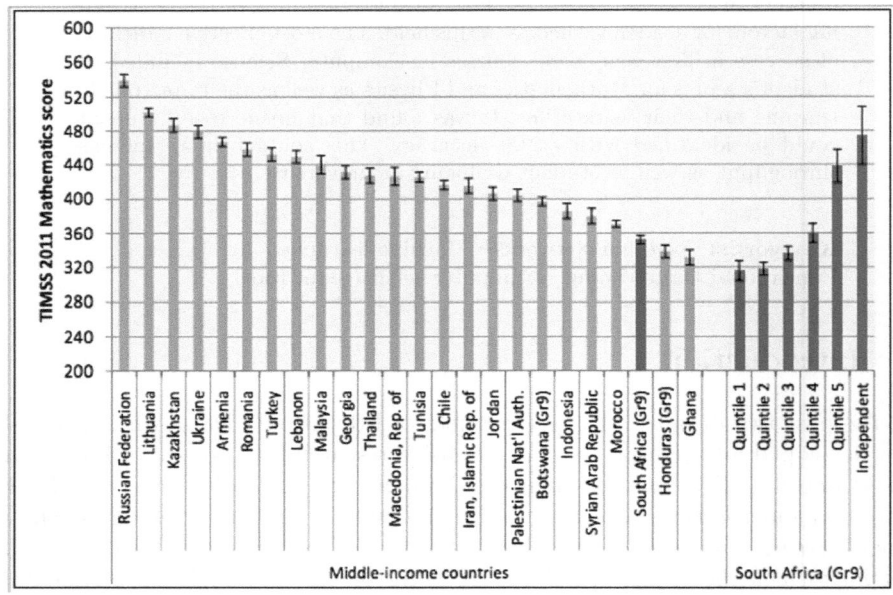

Fig. 1. Average grade-9 test scores for TIMSS middle-income countries, 2011 [18]

Figure 1 shows the disparity in the average mathematics performance of South African school-pupils in different quintiles. A positive correlation exists between quintile and academic performance i.e., in general, the poorer the school, the worse a student's performance in mathematics and science [18]. However, since the quality of education is so varied, a pupil in a lower quintile school may have a greater aptitude for independent learning and/or a better work ethos than a student from a higher quintile school who achieves similar marks.

Another potential factor is the South African province in which a school is located, due to differing standards of education between the provinces in this country. Repeatedly this difference plays a role in the annual *Matric* pass rates, drop-out rates and skills obtained (e.g., literacy) [18].[2] Furthermore, emotional difficulties associated with relocating to a new city may affect academic performance [1]. More than just matric marks, these are potential factors that could also contribute to a more effective prediction model.

This paper aims to explore Bayesian Networks (BN) and Machine Learning (ML) techniques to predict success in the BSc(CS) degree at UCT. Available data included applicants' Matric scores, National Benchmarking Test (NBT) scores, the quintile of their school, and the province in which it is located.

The remainder of this paper is set out as follows: Section 2 reviews related literature on predicting academic performance. Section 3 explains the machine learning methods used in this paper. Section 4 describes how the data was transformed and the model constructed. Section 5 discusses model evaluation and results achieved. Section 6 covers limitations and future work, and Sect. 7 concludes.

2   Related Work

As explained in [16], predicting academic performance of students *"is one of the oldest and most popular applications of DM (Data Mining) in education"* [16]. The most prevalent prediction models include: Decision Trees, Neural Networks, Naïve Bayes, K-Nearest Neighbour, Support Vector Machines, Random Forests and Bayesian Networks [4,17]. Bayesian Networks can handle missing values and have the ability to be queried and give answers that explain their predictions [10]. This allows further enquiry into the causal links between academic success and the predictive variables, i.e., Bayesian Networks are 'white-box' models [20]. This will be crucial for explaining and understanding the predictions of a Bayesian Network model over the typically 'black box' machine learning methods, such as Neural Networks, which do not offer any clear explanations for their predictions. A similar justification is made for using the Decision Tree, Naïve Bayes and Random Forest models as benchmarks for the Bayesian model, i.e., out of the remaining approaches, these model are the easiest to understand [20].

Various papers have compared the predictive performance of these models. The following examples provide a brief overview of the field. Nghe et al. compared the accuracy of Decision Trees and Bayesian Networks in predicting the academic performance of over 21,000 graduate students at two different tertiary institutions [13]. Variables included were grade point average (GPA), prior institution rank, and other factors. They found that Decision Trees were slightly more effective than Bayesian Networks (76.3% vs 71.2% accuracy). Similar results were obtained by [12] for 826 CS students over seven years at the University of the

---

[2] In South Africa, 'Matric' is name of the formal qualification level of pupils who have passed their secondary school (high school) education after school-year 12 before university—somewhat similar to the Austrian 'Matura' or the German 'Abitur'.

Witwatersrand in South Africa [12]. Their Decision Tree model outperformed the Naïve Bayes algorithm with accuracies of 84.5% and 78.9%, respectively. However, those studies investigated different questions: [13] predicted success of students enrolled in post-graduate programmes as well as 3rd-year students' success from their 2nd-year results, whereas [12] predicted 1st-year final grades based on 1st-year 1st-semester results.

According to [14], the Naïve Bayes classifier (76.7%) outperforms Decision Trees (73.9%) and Neural Networks (71.2%) in predicting 1st-years' academic success in Business Informatics [14]. However, their data set had only 257 student records. More recently, Asif et al. produced similar conclusions with their data set of 200 undergraduate students when predicting future performance [2], however with a bigger difference in the accuracy of the compared models, (Naïve Bayes: 83.7%, Decision Tree: 66.0%).

While there are further papers exploring such topics, their results produced are always similarly varied. It thus appears that the accuracy of prediction models is highly dependent on the variables selected, the question addressed, and the context of the investigation. Consequently it seems necessary to investigate specifically Bayesian Network prediction of CS student performance at UCT, and to compare the accuracy with other techniques.

3   Methods

Classification is the assignment of a label or category to a sample of data based on a number of variables [11]. In particular, *supervised* classification allows a model to learn how to classify some attribute of unknown data samples from labeled data samples [14]. The chosen attribute for classification is known as the 'target' variable. There are various methods to address this problem. The four machine learning methods used in this paper are defined and briefly explained below.

3.1   Bayesian Networks

A Bayesian Network is a directed acyclic graph representing a particular domain. Each node of the graph represents a variable from the domain. The nodes are connected by arcs which represent the dependencies between variables. Each arc is assigned a weight using

$$\textbf{Bayes Theorem [11]:}\ P(A|B) = \frac{P(B|A) \cdot P(A)}{P(B)}.$$

Bayesian Networks can be used for a wide range of applications including reasoning, analysis, diagnosis, risk assessment and evaluation [11]. Bayesian Networks are particularly useful for classification tasks as they provide an explanatory model, in contrast to techniques such as neural networks. Constructing a Bayesian Network requires the assumption of the *Markov property* whereby *"there are no direct dependencies in the system being modeled which are not already explicitly shown via arcs"* [11]. It holds for causal and predictive models.

Naïve Bayes. The Naïve Bayes classification technique uses a Bayesian model where the target variable is the parent of all the predictor nodes, i.e., these models assume independence between every predictor variable [11]. Even with these assumptions it is still an accurate and efficient prediction model for many problems [11].

3.2   Decision Trees

A Decision Tree uses the concept of *information entropy* to divide the classification into subproblems which are simpler to solve. Each node's section of the input space is recursively divided into subsections through its descendants. A node with no descendants indicates a prediction made by the model. Thus the higher up in the tree an attribute appears, the more influential it is in dividing the data. When passed a set of input variables, it can produce an expected classification based on the tree that it has learned. There are a variety of algorithms which use training data to construct these trees such as the C4.5 [15]. Tools exist which automatically invoke this algorithm such as WEKA's J48 classification filter [9].

Random Forests. Random Forests construct multiple decision tree classifiers that are trained on different subsets of the data with independent random subsets of the features of the data [6]. Once numerous trees have been constructed, the model classifies a data input by outputting the most popular decision, i.e., the class chosen by the majority of the trees [6]. This method can reduce the 'over-fitting' of data that can occur with Decision Tree classifiers [7].

4   Experimental Design

4.1   Data Pre-Processing and Analysis

The data set used in this paper covered a cohort of 783 students who were admitted into the CS major at UCT between 2007 and 2016. The term 'graduateCS' is used for students qualifying with a BSc(CS); others, who are not 'graduateCS', may graduate with another major instead.

The CS major at UCT is a three-year programme consisting of six 'core' CS courses as well as a mandatory first-year course in mathematics. CS entrant numbers are increasing annually and most courses have consistent pass rates with no clear trends.

UCT offers an option for weak or under-prepared students to complete the same BSc degree over four rather than three years (Extended Degree Program: EDP). CS students are expected to complete Computer Science courses CSC1015F and CSC1016S as well as Mathematics MAM1000W in their first year. EDP students take extended versions of these courses 'stretched' over two years. Consequently, a student who is likely to fail at least one of the three required first year courses should be encouraged to join the EDP. In this context we define 'at-risk' as 'likely to fail CSC1015F, CSC1016S or MAM1000W'. On average 58.83% of all CS entrants who attempt to complete their first-year in one year fail at least one of CSC1016S and MAM1000W.

Only ≈15% of all CS entrants receive financial aid. The majority of these financial aid receivers come from Quintile 4 schools (30%) whereas only 25% come from Quintile 1, 2, 3 schools (cumulatively).

Table 1. Raw data attributes

DATA CONTEXT	ATTRIBUTE (CLASSIFIER)	DATA TYPE
Application	Year	Continuous
Application: *Matric results*	Mathematics	Continuous
	Advanced mathematics	Continuous
	English	Continuous
	Physical sciences	Continuous
Application: *NBT results*	Mathematics	Continuous
	Quantitative literacy (QL)	Continuous
	Academic literacy (AL)	Continuous
Progress	Courses Registered	Continuous
	Courses passed	Continuous
	Cumulative GPA	Continuous
	Financial aid	Binary (y/n)
Throughput	Time to graduate	Nominal
	Dropped out (or excluded)	Nominal
	Course marks for each course	Nominal
Secondary school	Province	Nominal
	Quintile	Nominal

Table 1 lists the data elements in our data set. The South African Master Schools list was also used to retrieve the quintile of the applicants' school. We anonymised all data before continuing to use them with new anonymous identifiers. A preliminary analysis of the data lead to selecting the input variables and to determining the state space of each variable. Firstly, 'AP Maths' was reduced to a categorical variable to indicate if a CS entrant had attempted it, since there are too few data points to make a significant finding with respect to marks achieved for it. Additionally, by means of regression analysis, scores with high correlations (above 65%) were averaged and reduced, since these individually would not provide the model with further information. Secondary school physics and maths had a 69.8% correlation, and NBT maths and school maths had a 66.4% correlation. NBT AL and NBT QL had a 75.3% correlation. Consequently, the following reduced variables were introduced: 'AveSciences' for science, maths and NBT maths, and 'ALQL' for NBT AL and NBT QL.

The distribution of the quintile of the schools the 783 CS entrants had attended was analysed. There were only 9 CS entrants from Quintile 1 schools, 22 from Quintile 2 schools, and 54 from Quintile 3 schools. Consequently, these quintiles were combined under the new variable 'Lower': see Table 2. The quintile of the school attended by 49 CS entrants could not be determined because of insufficient information.

Table 2. Computer science intake per Quintile

	LOWER	QUINT.4	QUINT.5	PRIV.	INT.	NO DATA	TOTAL
# Students	85	61	285	187	116	49	**783**
% of total	10.86%	7.79%	36.40%	23.88%	14.81%	6.26%	100%

The distribution of the quintiles of the school attended across provinces was analysed. The majority of students from low quintile schools attended schools in the Eastern Cape and Limpopo, which are among South Africa's poorest provinces. Most students from independent schools came from Gauteng, which is South Africa's economically most productive province. Consequently, the 'Province' variable was split into the following: 'Eastern Cape and Limpopo'; 'Gauteng'; 'Western Cape'; 'International'; and 'Other'.

4.2   Machine Learning Procedure

Before beginning the machine learning procedure, the data had to be split into training and testing sets to avoid over-fitting. Cross-validation was used to train and test the models during the machine learning process, whereby the last year (2016) was kept aside as a hold-out set for evaluation of the final models. The cohort from each year was used as a fold, e.g., 2007 was used as the test set and all other years (2008–2015) as the training set in the first fold, and so on. Thus, there were nine folds in total, one for each of the years between 2007 and 2015.

Measures of Success. CSC1016S is the second-semester course of our first-year CS degree. It is the first course exclusively required by CS entrants and justifiably so as it introduces a more theoretical foundation of modern day programming with a focus on the Java language. The course introduces concepts such as memory referencing, inheritance, and data type abstractions as well as an introduction to data structures with its module on linked lists. These provide a robust foundation for any construction of CS knowledge and consequently, without it, a CS entrant is unlikely to succeed. Succeeding in the course is defined as achieving over 50%. The probability of CS entrants passing this course was found to be 95.53% and their chance of graduating in CS if this course was passed was 55.8%.

MAM1000W is the first-year mathematics course and is the first-year course for Mathematics majors. It introduces *"fundamental ideas in calculus, linear algebra, and related topics*" [19]. The broad scope of Computer Science requires not only an understanding of these topics, but also fluency with mathematical language and logic. More importantly, MAM1000W requires a far stronger work ethos than what is required at school. Consequently, successfully passing this course allows the CS department to discern whether a student will be able to keep up and succeed in the degree. Succeeding in MAM1000W is defined as achieving over 50% marks for the final course result. The probability of CS entrants passing MAM1000W was found to be 57.39% and their chance of graduating in CS if they passed MAM1000W was 93.64%.

Furthermore, passing all core first year courses (CSC1015F, CSC1016S, and MAM1000W) required for a major in CS on first attempt shows proficient understanding of foundational knowledge for CS as well as an ability to cope with vast jumps in course load and difficulty. Consequently, passing these courses on first attempt provides an even stronger indication of academic success. It was found that the chance of a CS entrant graduating in CS having passed these core first-year courses on first attempt is 97.58%, though their chance of passing them on first attempt is only 41.45%. This consequently shows a student to be 'At-Risk', or not.

After consultation with CS student advisors at UCT, the following target variables for prediction were chosen:

1. Passing CSC1016S, i.e., achieving over 50% on first attempt;
2. Passing MAM1000W, i.e., achieving over 50% on first attempt;
3. At-Risk (*Failing* CSC1015F, CSC1016S or MAM1000W on first attempt);
4. Graduation (eventually, after any amount of time);
5. Graduation (in minimum time as per course-book).

Determining Causal Structure and Parameterization of the Bayesian Network. The network structure was developed over several iterations of development and evaluation with a student advisor.

The variables 'AveSciences', 'AP Maths' and 'ALQL' were included in the structure, since, as explained above, these are often the most powerful predictors of academic success. For reasons explained above, both province and quintile were initially incorporated into the model with links to the Matric score variables. It may seem as though one's school's quintile would be highly correlated with their financial aid state; however, as shown in Sect. 4.1, financial aid is received in fairly equal proportion by CS entrants from all quintiles.

When considering the causal relationships between the variables, it makes little sense to assume that school marks directly affect university results. Rather, there must be some more general (earlier) cause of success for *both* school *and* university. Firstly, a student's success in academic studies is determined by their ability to understand the knowledge that is being provided to them as well as their skills to apply this knowledge. Secondly, the strength of a student's work ethos will affect their academic performance, too. In a Bayesian Network, these variables are known as 'latent' or 'hidden' variables [11]. Similar to any other variable in the network, there are causal links that point to and from these nodes. If a student has a higher aptitude for learning and understanding knowledge, as well as a strong work ethos, one would expect this to affect the school results (the input variables) as well as the University results (the target variables).

In parameterizing a Bayesian Network, the training data are used to determine prior probabilities of each variable; then the conditional and posterior probabilities are calculated [11]. However, by definition, latent variables are unmeasurable. Consequently, the Expectation Maximization (EM) algorithm was used to approximate the most likely values for these variables. The algorithm chooses a value, e, at random to compute the *"probability distribution over the missing values"* and iteratively uses a maximum likelihood to determine a new value e [11]. The algorithm iterates until the maximum likelihood stabilizes.

Upon comparison of results with the Naïve Bayes model, the Bayesian Network was performing suboptimally. Consequently, an iterative process of relaxing the independence assumptions of the Naïve Bayes was undertaken in order to find the best performing structure. This may provide greater insight into which attributes contributed to effective predictions and which introduced noise in the model.

The Bayesian Network was developed using the Norsys *Netica* software package.[3] The software also allows for learning latent variables with an EM learning algorithm.

Discretising Continuous Variables and Selecting Significant Attributes. Discretising variables for machine learning can *"improve the performance of the algorithm and reduce the computation time considerably"* [8]. In order to determine suitable inflection points for each numeric attribute as well as which variables were significant, the J48 Decision Tree algorithm was used on each fold for each model. The resulting trees were then analysed to determine which attributes were to be included in the Decision Tree as well as what values for numeric attributes were to be used. From this, various possible sets of data were produced for each model. After testing each data set, the best performing data set was chosen. The variables and inflection points found were thus shown to be contributive to the target variable according to the machine learning algorithm.

While this procedure was conducted to improve the performance of the predictive models, its outcome is a result itself. These variables and inflection points are significant as they provide an initial understanding of which variables are indeed contributive to the target variables, and consequently, to success in the CS curriculum. This final state space emanating from the data pre-processing, data analysis and initial experiments is shown in Table 3.

---

[3] http://www.norsys.com/download.html.

Table 3. Final state space

ATTRIBUTE	CSC1016S	MAM1000W	AT-RISK	GRADUATION	TIME TO GR.
AveSciences	Low (<68) Mid (68...78) High (>78)	Low (<79) High (≥79)	Low (<79) Mid (79...83) High (>83)	Low (<67) Mid (67...83) High (>83)	Low (<79) Mid (79...83) High (>83)
English	Low (<71) Mid (71...83) High (>83)		Low (<72) High (≥72)	Low (<64) Mid (64...76) High (>76)	Low (<77) High (≥77)
ALQL	Low (<68) High (≥68)			Low (<71) High (≥71)	Low (<71) High (≥71)
Adv. Maths attempted	Yes/no	Yes/no	Yes/no	Yes/no	Yes/no
Financ. Aid	Yes/no			Yes/no	Yes/no
Province	Gauteng Western Pr. ECLP International Other			Gauteng Western Pr. ECLP International Other	Gauteng Western Pr. ECLP International Other
Quintile	Low, Q.4, Q.5, Indep.			Low, Q.4, Q.5, Indep.	Low, Q.4, Q.5, Indep.
Target variable	**Fail** (<50) **Pass** (≥50)	**Fail** (<50) **Pass** (≥50)	**No** (passed all at first time)/**yes**	**Yes/no**	**ThreeYears Over3years NotGradCS**

5   Results and Discussion

5.1   Results

Once the models were constructed and parameterized, each model was tested using the originally withheld testing set. Sensitivity (TPR) and Specificity (TFR) were used to measure the predictive power of each model.

$$\text{Sensitivity} := \frac{TruePredictedPasses}{TruePredictedPasses + FalsePredictedFails}$$

$$\text{Specificity} := \frac{TruePredictedFails}{TruePredictedFails + FalsePredictedPasses}$$

The Matthews Correlation Coefficient (MCC) was also used as a useful measure for model performance on unbalanced data [5]. It measures the correlation between the actual and predicted classifications for all classes. An MCC of 1 indicates a perfect prediction while −1 indicates complete disagreement. A number of experiments were done to predict the five target variables identified earlier, with a focus on predicting At-Risk students. The results are summarized below.

CSC1016S. The Bayesian Network had the highest MCC of 0.38 and the highest TFR of 23%. It also had the joint highest TPR of 98.8%.

MAM1000W. The Bayesian Network and the Naïve Bayes models both scored the highest MCC of 0.43 as well as the highest TPR of 79%. The J48 and Random Forest models attained the best TFR with 70%. The models for this prediction were most effective using only the AveSciences and AP Maths variables as input. This indicates that all other variables did not influence the MAM1000W result.

At-Risk. The variables used for these models were similar to those used for the MAM1000W models, with the addition of Matric English scores. The results for all models for the At-Risk variable are shown in Tables 4, 5, 6 and 7. For this variable, 'Sensitivity' refers to prediction of 'Not At-Risk' students while 'Specificity' refers to prediction of 'At-Risk' students.

Table 4. Performance of the Random Forest for the At-Risk variable

Random Forest	HOLD-OUT SET	AVERAGE	STD.
Specificity	92.42%	90.82%	8.95%
Sensitivity	66.67%	59.70%	13.39%
MCC	61.98%	53.47%	9.30%
F1	84.14%	67.91%	6.71%

Table 5. Performance of the J48 Decision Tree for the At-Risk variable

J48 DT	HOLD-OUT SET	AVERAGE	STD.
Specificity	92.42%	86.92%	13.64%
Sensitivity	66.67%	63.61%	17.58%
MCC	61.98%	53.47%	9.30%
F1	84.14%	67.80%	6.55%

Table 6. Performance of the Naïve Bayes for the At-Risk variable

Naïve Bayes	HOLD-OUT SET	AVERAGE	STD.
Specificity	74.24%	82.40%	18.62%
Sensitivity	70.37%	64.17%	18.71%
MCC	44.54%	49.50%	9.60%
F1	69.72%	65.25%	6.64%

Table 7. Performance of the Bayesian Network for the At-Risk variable

Bayesian Network	HOLD-OUT SET	AVERAGE	STD.
Specificity	92.42%	59.76%	13.77%
Sensitivity	66.67%	90.64%	9.26%
MCC	61.98%	53.34%	8.77%
F1	84.14%	67.91%	6.71%

Table 8. Confusion matrix showing performance of the Naïve Bayes and Bayesian Network models on the 2016 cohort

NAIVE BAYES CLASSIFIED AS			BAYESIAN NETWORK CLASSIFIED AS		
	At-Risk	Not At-Risk		At-Risk	Not At-Risk
At-Risk	49	17	At-Risk	61	5
Not At-Risk	16	38	Not At-Risk	18	36
MCC: 0.445	Specificity: 74%	Sensitivity: 70%	MCC: 0.620	Specificity: 92%	Sensitivity: 67%

Table 9. Quintiles of misclassified At-Risk students compared to quintiles of students from full data set. Note the strong %-discrepancy in the 'independent' category!

	QUNIT.1	QUINT.2	QUINT.3	QUINT.4	QUINT.5	INDEP.	TOTAL
# misclassif. stud.	0	1	5	5	16	20	**47**
% of misclassified	0.0%	2.1%	10.6%	10.6%	34.0%	**42.6%**	100%
% of all students	1.1%	2.8%	6.9%	7.8%	36.4%	**23.9%**	

Table 8 shows the predictive performance of the Naïve Bayes and the Bayesian Network for the 2016 cohort. The Naïve Bayes had the lowest TFR of 74.24% on the 2016 cohort while the Bayesian Network had a TFR of 92.42% and an MCC of 0.62. The J48 and Random Forest models produced results similar to the ones of the Bayesian Network. The final Bayesian Network structure is shown in Fig. 2.

Graduating with CS Major. Similar to the CSC1016S models, each variable was seen as contributing to the predictions. The Bayesian Network had the highest specificity of 61% while the Random Forest performed best at predicting graduating with a sensitivity of 91% and the highest MCC of 0.39.

Time-to-Graduation with CS Major. The Bayesian Network attained the greatest Minimum Time True Positive Rate of 70% as well as the best MCC of 0.24. However, the Naïve Bayes had the best True Positive Rate for not graduating and the Random Forest and J48 were able to predict graduating in more than minimum time with a true positive rate of 9%. None of the models was able to achieve satisfactory results in predicting graduating in more than minimum time.

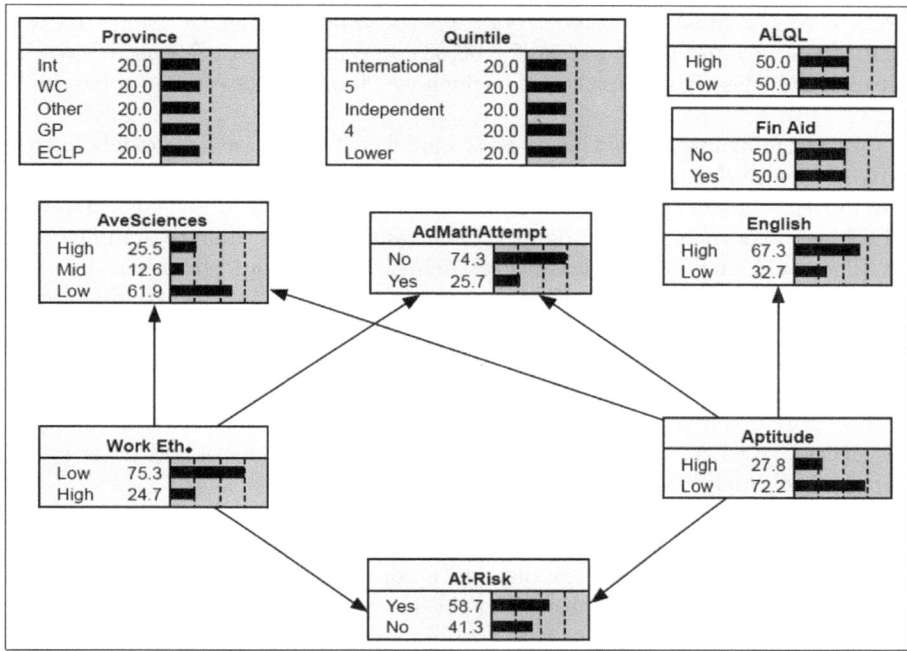

Fig. 2. Bayesian Network for At-Risk students

5.2   Discussion

The *inadequate accuracy for predicting failing* CSC1016S may be a result of the high (86%) CS entrant pass rate of this course—compared to the 61% CS entrant pass rate of MAM1000W. The poor results for Graduating in Minimum Time prediction are less clear; it is possible that there are no signifying features in the given data to indicate how long a CS entrant may take to complete the degree. However, this model performed better than the Graduation model for predicting 'no graduation'. The Bayesian Network achieved 72% accuracy (on average with a standard deviation of 10%) compared to 35% (on average with a standard deviation of 19%) for the Graduation model. Even when using the same data set as the Minimum Time Graduation model (i.e., the same points of inflection and variables included) for the graduation model, the results remained the same. This should be considered in future work.

As far as algorithm performance is concerned, our results were mixed. The Decision Tree and Random Forest models performed similarly to the Bayesian Network for achieving a high specificity (92%) for predicting At-Risk students, while the Naïve Bayes had the highest sensitivity (70%). The findings support the mixed results from the literature which show optimal performance oscillating between the Naïve Bayes, Decision Tree and Random Forest algorithms. In earlier studies, the Naïve Bayes model achieved the highest accuracy of 83.65% [2]

and a lowest accuracy of 76.65% [14]. The best performing Decision Tree was in [12] (84.46%) and the worst in [2] (66.03%). While few studies used Bayesian Network for classification, the one which we found achieved an accuracy of 71.23% [13].

Of particular interest is the At-Risk model. All classification models but the Naïve Bayes performed similarly, with specificities of 92.42%. The prediction errors of this model can be a result of two causes. Firstly, a False Failure Rate (FFR) indicates the model predicted CS entrants At-Risk when they in fact were not. These CS entrants misclassified as being At-Risk would be advised to take the extended courses in vain. However, the second and more pressing source of error is the False Passing Rate (FPR). This figure indicates the number of CS entrants that were classified as Not At-Risk when they in fact were At-Risk, i.e., the model failed to recognise those who are in need of assistance. For the hold-out set, only 5 out of 66 students were misclassified as Not At-Risk. However, it is necessary to try and analyse these misclassified students and determine if there is a prominent reason for their misclassification.

Following such analysis we found that a disproportionate number of CS entrants who were misclassified as not being At-Risk were from independent schools, specifically private schools, (42% compared to 24% for the full data set) as shown in Table 9. Contrary to the initial results found in the Bayesian Network model, attending a private school may be a contributing factor to predicting academic success. Consequently, future research should include this as a variable in prediction models. Furthermore, only 8.33% of misclassified At-Risk students received financial aid compared to 19.8% of students from the full data set. This is another variable that should be explored in subsequent research.

6   Limitations and Future Work

Our data was limited to CS degree applicants over the last ten years. Consequently there were no data for anyone who changed their major to CS or who took CS courses as electives. If larger data sets were used, the models evaluated could have been more accurate or realistic. Additionally, the CS department at UCT has a very limited number of applicants who attend lower quintile schools as well as applicants who are on financial aid. This resulted in the data being biased towards CS entrants in higher quintiles and thus an accurate reflection of success of these categories of CS entrants could not be obtained. Since this study was conducted with UCT students, the situation might perhaps differ at other South African universities.

Bayesian Networks use known data to learn conditional probabilities of the network. Any unknown variable can only be approximated using various algorithmic techniques. Consequently, the variables 'Aptitude' and 'Work Ethos' in the Bayesian Networks may not be realistic or accurate and their addition should be further explored. Future studies into this specific topic should focus on understanding the effect of different partitionings of the state space for different variables to try and attain a more nuanced understanding of the contributing factors of performance. As an example, initial experiments show that using a pass mark of 51% can have a substantial impact on predictive performance.

Finally, while financial aid and quintiles initially seemed to have no effect on the predictive performance of the models, analysis of misclassification of At-Risk students suggested that financial aid and quintile indeed affects the models' results. Hence, further studies should explore the inclusion of these factors (possibly with different partitions) in the experiments.

7   Conclusions

Comparatively, Bayesian networks do not outperform other classifiers, but can attain a similar performance to other classifiers. However, the usefulness of a Bayesian Network does not lie solely in its ability to predict classes. Its visual nature provides insight and greater understanding into the causes of success and the contributing factors to success. Bayesian Networks have a high potential to predict students at risk of not passing their core first-year courses in Computer Science. In particular, failing at least one of the first-year mathematics and computer science courses can be predicted with a 90.64% accuracy (on average). This finding justifies the method of identifying At-Risk-students automatically. Once these students are identified, they can be enrolled in the EDP in order to improve students' academic success and graduation throughput.

The key contributing factors were found to be the marks the students received in secondary school for Mathematics, Science and English, whether or not the student had attempted the AP Maths subject at school, and their aptitude and work ethos. It was initially found that in predicting these At-Risk students, the students' province and quintile did not play a discriminatory role, though deeper analysis suggests that more research will be needed to reach a better conclusion in this matter.

While this paper described the effectiveness of Bayesian Networks to predict and analyse academic success in Computer Science at UCT, further research is required to better 'unpack' these results as well as to improve the predictive performance of the underlying models.

References

1. Andrade, M.S.: International students in English-speaking universities: adjustment factors. J. Res. Int. Educ. **5**(2), 131–154 (2006)
2. Asif, R., Merceron, A., Ali, S.A., Haider, N.G.: Analyzing undergraduate students' performance using educational data mining. Comput. Educ. **113**, 177–194 (2017)
3. Baker, R.S.: Data mining for education. Int. Encycl. Educ. **7**(3), 112–118 (2010)
4. Baker, R.S., Yacef, K.: The state of educational data mining in 2009: a review and future visions. J. Educ. Data Min. **1**(1), 3–17 (2009)
5. Boughorbel, S., Jarray, F., El-Anbari, M.: Optimal classifier for imbalanced data using Matthews Correlation Coefficient metric. PloS One **12**(6), 1–17 (2017)
6. Breiman, L.: Random forests. Mach. Learn. **45**(1), 5–32 (2001)

7. Friedman, J., Hastie, T., Tibshirani, R.: The Elements of Statistical Learning. SSS. Springer, New York (2001). https://doi.org/10.1007/978-0-387-21606-5
8. Gupta, A., Mehrotra, K.G., Mohan, C.: A clustering-based discretization for supervised learning. Stat. Probab. Lett. **80**(9), 816–824 (2010)
9. Hall, M., Eibe, F., Holmes, G., Pfahringer, B., Reutemann, P., Witten, I.H.: The WEKA data mining software: an update. ACM SIGKDD Explor. **11**(1), 10–18 (2009)
10. Heaton, J.: Bayesian networks for predictive modeling. Forecast. Futur. **7**, 6–10 (2013)
11. Korb, K.B., Nicholson, A.E.: Bayesian Artificial Intelligence, 2nd edn. CRC Press, Boca Raton (2010)
12. Mashiloane, L.: Educational data mining (EDM) in a South African University: a longitudinal study of factors that affect the academic performance of computer science 1 students. Doctoral Dissertations, University of the Witwatersrand (2016)
13. Nghe, N.T., Janecek, P., Haddawy, P.: A comparative analysis of techniques for predicting academic performance. In: Proceedings of the 37th Annual IEEE Frontiers in Education Conference, FIE 2007 (2007)
14. Osmanbegović, E., Suljić, M.: Data mining approach for predicting student performance. Econ. Rev. **10**(1), 3–12 (2012)
15. Quinlan, J.R.: C4.5: Programs for Machine Learning. Elsevier, Amsterdam (2014)
16. Romero, C., Ventura, S.: Educational data mining: a review of the state of the art. IEEE Trans. Syst. Man Cybern. Part C (Appl. Rev.) **40**(6), 601–618 (2010)
17. Shahiri, A.M., Husain, W., Abdul, R.: A review on predicting students' performance using data mining techniques. Procedia Comput. Sci. **72**, 414–422 (2015)
18. Spaull, N.: South Africa's education crisis: the quality of education in South Africa 1994–2011. Technical report, Centre for Development and Enterprise, Johannesburg (2013)
19. University of Cape Town: Faculty of Science Handbook (2017). http://www.students.uct.ac.za/usr/apply/handbooks/2017/SCI_2017.pdf
20. Xing, W., Guo, R., Petakovic, E., Goggins, S.: Participation-based student final performance prediction model through interpretable genetic programming: integrating learning analytics, educational data mining and theory. Comput. Hum. Behav. **47**, 168–181 (2015)

AgileTL: A Framework for Enhancing Teaching and Learning Practices Using Software Development Principles

Wai Sze Leung[✉] [ID]

Academy of Computer Science and Software Engineering,
University of Johannesburg, Johannesburg, South Africa
wsleung@uj.ac.za

Abstract. Action research is widely accepted in education circles as an effective practice that brings about change and improvement in the field. Action research is however not as commonly adopted by teachers (or lecturers) in their daily practices due to challenges that include a lack of understanding (in this context, of how to conduct action research), a lack of time, and the daunting prospect of uncertainty in the classroom. These challenges are also faced by software engineers when applied to the domain of software design and development and has been the focus of much research and methodologies aimed at overcoming these challenges. One such approach which has seen high uptake is agile software development which comprises phases that occur in cycles, a concept that is central to the theory of action research. The study, therefore, investigates whether the initial perception of similarities between action research and agile can be leveraged to guide Software Engineering lecturers in enhancing their teaching and learning practices more effectively. The result of this study is a framework that offers lecturers familiar with agile a systematic approach to improving their teaching and learning using familiar software development methods and principles. While this agile-based framework is designed with Information Technology lecturers in mind, it can hopefully be adopted in other disciplines as a framework that uses agile project management principles to overcome some of the identified challenges to carrying out action research in the first place.

Keywords: Agile principles · Action research · Teaching and learning

1 Introduction

Lecturers require better support and guidance when it comes to developing and refining their own pedagogy if we wish to succeed in improving the quality of education at universities.

Presently, specifically in the African context, there is greater emphasis on the academic qualifications of lecturers rather than on their pedagogical knowledge [6]. Primarily, academics are employed not because of their ability to ensure

© Springer Nature Switzerland AG 2019
S. Kabanda et al. (Eds.): SACLA 2018, CCIS 963, pp. 223–233, 2019.
https://doi.org/10.1007/978-3-030-05813-5_15

active student learning, but because they are experts in their disciplines and can thus contribute to the institution's research capacity [1]. The Kenyan Higher Education Regulator's 2014 decision to improve the quality of higher education by enforcing the requirement that all university lecturers hold Ph.D. qualifications by 2018, for example, was accused of being retrogressive, with critics insisting that holding a doctoral qualification does not necessarily equate to research and teaching success [14]. In light of the recent deadline being reached and the Regulator's decision to defer the requirement [18], it may be that some regulatory bodies are arriving at the conclusion that it is unrealistic to assume that academics are equipped with the necessary skills and knowledge for teaching and learning success [1].

In South Africa, both the Department of Higher Education and Training (DHET) and Council on Higher Education (CHE) have acknowledged that successful student learning requires quality teaching that will only be attained if university teachers and academic support professionals are afforded the resources to develop their knowledge and skills in effective pedagogy—one particular principle that is seen to underpin their proposed framework aimed at enhancing academics, is that university teachers should have agency over their own development [1].

In particular, individuals taking responsibility for identifying, reflecting and addressing their own teaching development needs is considered to provide stronger yields than being subjected to external prescription [1].

Action research (AR) is one possible strategy that could be employed by academics to accomplish the aforementioned self-directed teaching development. This form of research is considered to be so beneficial to one's own development of systematic reflection that researchers have argued that it should be introduced to all teachers, either as part of their training [7] or as part of their mandatory duties [13].

This is, however, easier said than done. Research into institutions that have attempted to have their teachers apply AR has shown that chief among other challenges is the barrier due to a lack of understanding of what AR is and how it should be followed [5,13]. For academics who receive limited induction into teaching and are expected to hit the ground running, attempts to encourage them to try out AR may be met with resistance or disaster.

This paper hypothesizes that the principles of Agile software development (Agile) represent an alternative approach that Information Technology (IT) academics (who will likely be familiar with the concept) may follow as an alternative to AR when it comes to applying some systematic approach to introducing changes to the way in which they teach. The aim of the paper is thus to investigate the hypothesis above, and in response, develop a framework that would be suitable for guiding educational action research activities using Agile principles. Specifically, the study will consider the following sub-*questions*:

- To which degree do similarities exist between action research and Agile in terms of their purposes?

- To which degree do similarities exist between action research and Agile in terms of the processes that make up their respective cycles?
- What would an Agile approach to enhancing a teacher's teaching and learning comprise?

To answer the sub-questions mentioned above, the paper is arranged as follows: in the following section, the context of the problem is further unpacked by presenting arguments that motivate why an alternative to action research is being sought. Section 3 will then describe the method undertaken to conduct the study. This is followed by Sects. 4 and 5 which comprise analyses of the two core topics, namely action research and Agile software development. The resultant AgileTL framework is then presented in Sect. 6 before concluding in Sect. 7.

2   Contextualizing the Problem

Traditionally, educational research has been carried out by researchers specializing in educational theory. Such research is designed to develop theories that are universal in nature and to devise generic strategies and principles that would then be put into practice by teachers in the classrooms. Such top-down approaches provide teachers with the foundational knowledge of how to teach in general. However, students are unique and so have characteristics and personalities that differ from one to another. The generic rules thus end up being a source of frustration to teachers as they do not know how exactly to deal with student behaviors or responses that deviate from the 'rule book' [3].

Where the standard, textbook educational theories cannot be applied, the teachers as the persons on the ground must be able to devise their own suitable solution.

As the persons situated in the immediate environment with their students, the teachers have access to the information regarding what makes this particular class unique. In order to teach more effectively, the teachers will need to follow a bottom-up approach in which they learn how to 'read' their students in order to process and correctly identify the problems at hand. Furthermore, they must be able to construct a suitable response that is appropriate for accommodating the present group of students [2,3]. Such an approach is also seen to have the added benefit of liberating the teachers by providing them with a sense of autonomy [2], an element that was earlier identified as one of the underpinning principles as identified by the DHET and CHE.

It should be noted that teachers seeking to follow a bottom-up approach will not be able to do so successfully without the support from their institution. Research has demonstrated that in addition to a lack of training to help teachers better understand a bottom-up approach such as educational action research, other challenges include a lack of support in terms of heavy workloads (hence a lack of time), and a lack of incentive or motivation for teachers to engage in action research [5,13,20].

3   Method

This study aims to test the hypothesis that the similarities between Agile and action research are such that academics, specifically teachers in the IT (and/or related discipline), are able to apply their existing knowledge of Agile principles in their daily teaching and learning practices to improve their pedagogy systematically.

To do this, we will be carrying out a review of the literature on both action research and the Agile software development paradigm. The goal is to identify the overlap between the two in order to develop a framework based on these commonalities. A qualitative content analysis following a deductive approach will thus be carried, starting with an analysis of existing literature on both topics. A deductive approach is applied as the aim is to build on the existing knowledge pertaining to both topics in order to derive the framework for deployment in a 'new setting' [4].

4   Action Research

Action research is regarded as a type of action inquiry, a generic term that describes any process following a four-phase cycle that entails the following [2, 9, 11, 17]:

1. **Plan:** Identify an area for improvement and prepare a plan to practice.
2. **Act:** Implement the planned improvement.
3. **Observe:** Monitor and describe what the effects of the action have been.
4. **Evaluate:** Assess the outcomes of the action, reflecting on the practice and the process, among other elements of the process.

In essence, action inquiry involves taking some action aimed at improving practice, and making inquiries on that action (assessing the effectiveness of that planned improvement) [17], the circumstances, actions, consequences, and resulting relationships of which are subject to scrutiny [10]. It provides a systematic learning process and guides participants into becoming part of a self-critical, collaborative community [10].

Similarly, the methods of Design Research (commonly considered an Information Technology Research Methodology) is seen to involve a similar cyclical approach in which *"knowledge is generated and accumulated through action"*. From this, and several other characteristics, it has been inferred that action research can be considered an approach in design science [8]. Academics in the Information Technology discipline should, therefore, find action research (or similar) concepts to be familiar.

However, as Tripp has remarked, action research is only *"as effective as the people doing it make it"* [17]. Considering that a survey of the staff web pages of Computer Science departments of South African universities revealed the number of academics who received formal training in education to be in the minority, it would be reasonable to assume that IT academics would require some degree of guidance should they wish to engage in action research to inform their teaching practices.

4.1   Educational Action Research

Action research is widely accepted as a prominent method that can be used to support teachers' professionalism as it empowers the teachers to develop their awareness and autonomy in the way they teach and learn [12,13]. It is intended to improve education through change, and learning from those changes' consequences [10].

Essentially, teachers seeking to improve their current practices will attempt to do so by introducing change, observing what the consequences of their change may be, reflecting on those consequences, and coming up with a revised plan moving forward. As is the case with all action inquiry research, these aforementioned phases form part of a single cycle in a self-reflective spiral [10]. The teachers thus become both investigators and participants of their own teaching contexts [2].

4.2   The Action-Reflection Research Cycle

While the aforementioned four phases represent the commonly-accepted action research cycle, several researchers have suggested that the start of an action research project should begin with what some term a 'reconnaissance' period, resulting in the extended Action-Reflection Research Cycle [10,11]. Figure 1 illustrates three such cycles, each of which can be broken down into the following phases [11]:

Reconnaissance:
    Observe: Gather initial data of general interest.
    Reflect: Identify a concern from this initial data which will be the targeted
        problem. Devise a potential solution.
Act: Attempt to solve the identified problem using the potential solution devised
    in the previous phase. Monitor both the solution and how the environment
    responds to the attempted problem.
Evaluate: Evaluate the progress of the solution (based on what has been mon-
    itored in the previous phase).
Modify: Adjust how the solution was implemented (the practice) accordingly.
    This may depend on how successful/unsuccessful the attempted solution has
    been.
Move in New Direction: Consider other aspects of change that should be
    introduced.

For the purpose of our study, we will be comparing the Action-Reflection research cycle specifically with Agile.

5   Agile Software Development

Borne from the desire to address perceived weaknesses present in conventional software engineering, Agile software development is regarded as a 'movement'

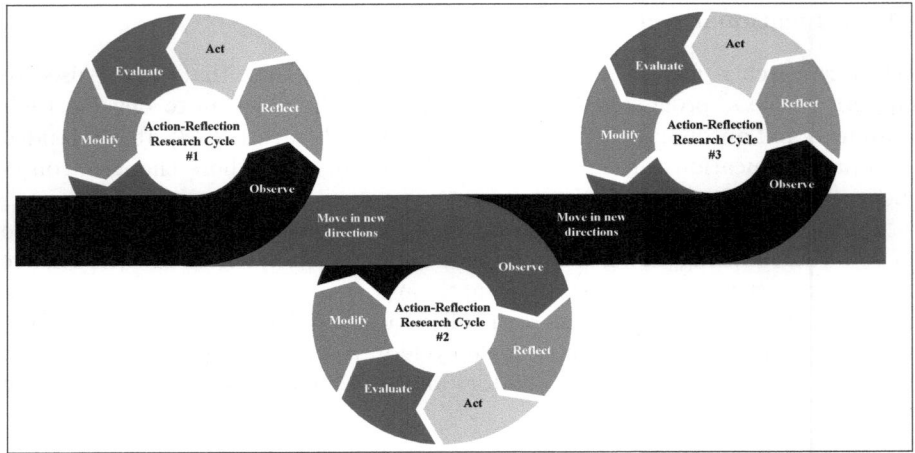

Fig. 1. Action-Reflection Research Cycles based on [19]

that promotes the development of software in a fashion that accommodates for change at a reduced cost. This feature is particularly attractive given the dynamic nature of our modern economy [15], where change is inevitable and traditional software development models such as the Waterfall Model are too rigid to handle customers' requests for change without incurring hefty costs.

Specifically, the group of experts who came together to form what would be called the *Manifesto for Agile Software Development* identified areas which they believed required greater attention to developing software better. These included placing emphasis on individuals and interactions, customer collaboration, and responding to change.[1] Furthermore, the group identified 12 principles which they regarded were essential to achieving agility.

Such principles have proven to be so versatile that it has been adopted in non-IT environments that include marketing and education. For example, the creators of the Agile in Education Compass have made use of Agile's iterative approach to making learning cycles more visible.[2] Similarly, we demonstrate how these principles can apply to guide academics in managing their teaching and learning in Table 1.

The term 'Agile' is an umbrella term which can refer to a number of methods that one can achieve agile (and hence incremental) development with. For the purpose of this study, we restrict ourselves to discussions of two of the more popular agile methods, namely: Scrum and Extreme Programming (XP).

---

[1] http://agilemanifesto.org/principles.html.

[2] http://www.agileineducation.org/.

Table 1. How the 12 agile principles can relate to teaching and learning

Agile principle	Relevance to enhancing teaching & learning
Our highest priority is to satisfy the customer through early and continuous delivery of valuable software	Our students are our customers. It is our highest priority to ensure that they are satisfied by our continuous cycles of improvement to our teaching and learning. This is however not to say that they dictate what is taught in the classroom, but rather should be treated as an important stakeholder in determining how best to present the content
Welcome changing requirements, even late in development. Agile processes harness change for the customer's competitive advantage	Our students are unique. The way they consume the information we present to them can vary from group to group. We should be willing to embrace change and adapt to their needs
Deliver working software frequently, from a couple of weeks to a couple of months, with a preference to the shorter timescale	Deliver results and learning opportunities frequently so that students are able to gauge their progress
Business people and developers must work together daily throughout the project	Our students are our partners in this learning experience. They are learning from us, just as we are learning from them (how to be better at teaching)
Build projects around motivated individuals. Give them the environment and support they need, and trust them to get the job done	Present assessments that engage our students. Ensure that they have the necessary support and knowledge (or means to find it) to complete the assignment
The most efficient and effective method of conveying information to and within a development team is face-to-face conversation	Read the expressions of the students to get a better sense of whether they understand the work that is being presented
Working software is the primary measure of progress	Use a easily quantifiable measurement to assess progress
Agile processes promote sustainable development. The sponsors, developers, and users should be able to maintain a constant pace indefinitely	Provide assessments with enough time between each so that students are able to work on these assignments
Continuous attention to technical excellence and good design enhances agility	Promoting quality will ensure that the students provide consistently excellent work
Simplicity—the art of maximizing the amount of work not done—is essential	The simplest solution is often the most elegant one
The best architectures, requirements, and designs emerge from self-organizing teams	Giving both the lecturer and students autonomy will encourage excellence
At regular intervals, the team reflects on how to become more effective, then tunes and adjusts its behavior accordingly	Ensure that each cycle is not too long. Be sure to have both lecturer and students reflect on their progress on a regular basis

5.1 Scrum

As shown in Fig. 2, the Scrum method shares many similarities with the Action-Reflection Research Cycle. As with action research, Scrum entails phases that require the developers to identify what changes must be made, how to achieve this, carrying out the task, evaluating the result, and as the last phase in that particular run of the cycle, reviewing whether it is satisfactory.

To determine which feature of the overall software project should be worked on next, the developers and customers maintain a backlog, a list of project features that will provide value to the customer. Changes from the customer are introduced via this backlog, with items from the backlog being assigned to a sprint at the beginning of a cycle [15].

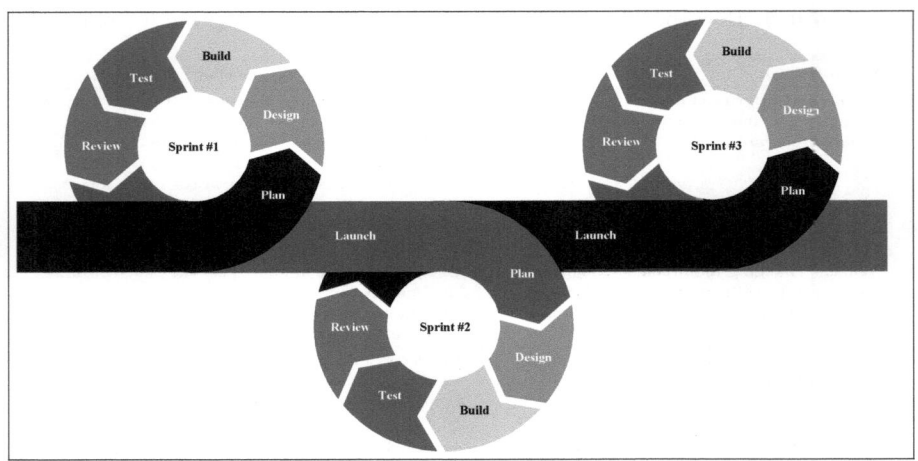

Fig. 2. Agile software development using Scrum [16]

5.2   XP

Similarly to Scrum, the Extreme Programming process is one that can be broken into several smaller activities, namely, planning, designing, coding, and testing [15]. The cycle begins with customers and developers working together to establish what needs to be developed, and what should be developed during the current development cycle.

One key concept of XP that bears mentioning is its promotion of pair programming. This is where XP recommends that programmers work in pairs at one computer at a time, with one creating the code while the other ensures the standard of the code [15]. This is considered to result in the delivery of quality work and could be regarded as a recommended practice when it comes to incorporating mentorship mechanisms for teaching and learning purposes.

6   The AgileTL Framework

Having reviewed aspects of both action research and Agile software development, we now present our proposed AgileTL framework (Table 2) which shows how an academic can follow the phases of a sprint to manage the introduction of some change to their teaching and learning practices in the classroom.

In essence, the idea of adopting AgileTL is for IT academics to take on a more systematic approach to how they introduce changes to their teaching and learning practices. Rather than introduce changes on mere whims, the action research-like approach will help them to reflect and adapt their teaching practices, allowing them to improve, just as action research is intended to.

The following example shows how AgileTL may be applied in the case of an academic dealing with low attendance:

Table 2. AgileTL framework

Action research	Agile	Description/*Agile practices*
Observe	Plan	Gather information to get a view of what is currently happening—as students represent the 'clients', feedback should be obtained from them. Feedback can include their marks (measure of performance) or surveys in which students are asked what could be changed to make the work more understandable. Identify the change that is to be introduced. Come up with the criteria to be used for evaluating whether the change is successful/valid
Reflect	Design	Conduct research to come up with potential solutions of how to introduce the change
Act	Develop	Implement the change according to what was decided in the previous phase. As with Paired Programming, consider pairing up a less experienced teacher with a more senior one to foster mentorships
Evaluate	Test	Evaluate the progress according to the criteria defined during the Planning phase
Modify	Review	Assess whether the change meets the requirements of the goal. If not, restart the current cycle. If requirements are met, move to the next phase
Move in new direction	Launch	Change is verified to work and can be implemented more widely (rest of the class, shared with colleagues). Move onto new cycle to implement next change

Plan: An academic notices that class attendance has been low. In a bid to improve class attendance, they decide to improve this aspect by introducing some change to the way in which they present the class. At present, they observe (from headcount figures) that the attendance averages at 65%.

Design: They decide on introducing roll call as the mechanism.

Develop: Attendance registers are passed out during each lecture, requiring students to sign next to their entry (be it a surname or identifying number).

Test: After two weeks of lectures, the attendance registers are examined, in conjunction with the headcount figures. It is noted that the headcount figures have increased slightly but do not match the number of signatures on the attendance registers.

Review: The change is therefore considered a limited success. The academic must, therefore, consider other possible approaches to tackle the problem more successfully.

When it comes to adapting teaching and learning practices to suit student requirements, AgileTL is similar to the concept of Just-in-Time Teaching (JiTT).[3] However, AgileTL also benefits from the inclusion of the promotion

---

[3] https://jittdl.physics.iupui.edu/jitt.html.

of mentorship when the paired programming paradigm is also adopted. In such a case, a more senior academic serves as an observer to provide feedback to the AgileTL practitioner, an activity that is also recommended in action research.

7   Conclusion

There have been calls for measures to improve the support the development of teaching and learning skills in academics in response to the ever-increasing recognition that academics often lack the necessary training and skills development to deliver quality teaching.

Based on the literature review on action research and Agile software development, we have established that the similarities that exist between the two (in terms of purpose and processes) are significant, suggesting that IT academics, familiar with, and applying agile methods, would likely achieve similar, if not the same outcomes, as if they were to follow action research in attempting to introduce change to the way in which they teach.

From the perspective of the IT lecturer, the proposed AgileTL framework is intended to provide a lightweight approach that encourages them to adopt an action research strategy to their teaching and learning practices by adapting existing knowledge of the Agile paradigm without having to resort to learning about action research from scratch.

This paper is part of a larger research project that aims to investigate how principles in Information Technology can be leveraged to enhance teaching and learning in a broader context. It is envisioned that Agile methods and practices can also be applied outside the IT discipline to assist in promoting environments that not only offer mentoring opportunities in teaching and learning but enable collaboration in this space to benefit the greater community.

Acknowledgments. Thanks for the support received from the *Teaching Advancement at University (TAU) Fellowship Program*, for serving as the driving force behind the formulation of this project.

References

1. Department of Higher Education and Training/Council on Higher Education: A Framework for Enhancing Academics as University Teachers, South Africa (2018)
2. Dikilitaş, K., Griffiths, C.: Developing Language Teacher Autonomy Through Action Research. Palgrave Macmillan, Basingstoke (2017)
3. Efron, S., Efrat, D.R.: Action Research in Education: A Practical Guide. Guildford Press, New York (2013)
4. Elo, S., Kyngäs, H.: The qualitative content analysis process. JAN Res. Methodol. **62**(1), 107–115 (2008)
5. Erba, B.H.: The practice and challenges in conducting action research: the case of Sululta secondary school. Institute of Educational Research (2013)
6. Fredua-Kwarteng, E., Ofosu, S.K.: Improving the quality of university education in Africa (2018). http://www.universityworldnews.com/article.php?story=20180306124842675

7. Hine, G.S.C.: The importance of action research in teacher education programs. Issues Educ. Res. **23**(2), 151–163 (2013)
8. Järvinen, P.: Action research as an approach in design science. Technical report, University of Tampere (2005)
9. Kember, D.: Action Learning and Action Research: Improving the Quality of Teaching & Learning. Kogan Page Ltd., London (2000)
10. Kemmis, S., McTaggart, R.: The Action Research Planner. Deakin University Press, Victoria (1988)
11. McNiff, J., Whitehead, J.: All You Need to Know About Action Research, 2nd edn. Sage, Beverly Hills (2011)
12. Noffke, S.E., Somekh, B.: The SAGE Handbook of Educational Action Research. Sage, Beverly Hills (2009)
13. Norasmah, O., Chia, S.U.: The challenges of action research implementation in Malaysian schools. Pertanika J. Soc. Sci. Hum. **24**(1), 43–52 (2016)
14. Nganga, G.: Over 8,000 non-Ph.D. lecturers face job loss, demotion (2017). http://www.universityworldnews.com/article.php?story=20171107140204898
15. Pressman, R.S., Maxim, B.R.: Software Engineering: A Practitioner's Approach. McGraw-Hill, New York (2015)
16. Srivastava, B.: What is agile methodology? Disadvantage of waterfall model in software development (2017). https://bikeshsrivastava.blogspot.co.za/2017/01/part-43what-is-agile-methodology.html
17. Tripp, D.: Action research: a methodological introduction. Educação e Pesquisa **31**(3), 1–21 (2005)
18. Wanzala, O.: Move on Ph.D.-only lecturers deferred (2018). https://www.nation.co.ke/news/education/Move-on-PhD-only-lecturers-deferred/2643604-4275136-151ejmgz/index.html
19. Yee, J.S.R.: Connecting practice to research (and back to practice): making the leap from design practice to design research. In: Proceedings of International Conference Design Principles and Practices, pp. 1–15 (2017)
20. Zhou, J.: Problems teachers face when doing action research and finding possible solutions. Chin. Educ. Soc. **45**(4), 68–80 (2014)

Teamwork and Projects

The Last Straw: Teaching Project Team Dynamics to Third-Year Students

Sunet Eybers[✉] and Marie J. Hattingh

Department of Informatics, University of Pretoria, Pretoria, South Africa
{sunet.eybers,marie.hattingh}@up.ac.za

Abstract. Educators in Higher Educational Institutions (HEI) are under constant pressure to improve their educational practices such as teaching. Adding to the challenges are the need to expose, and as a result equip students, with practical real life skills such as project management. Lack of behavioural aspects (also referred to as 'soft skills') is often identified as main contributing factor to the failure of projects. Whilst many educational programmes focus on the technical aspects of project management, the behavioural aspects of project management are often neglected. In an attempt to address these challenges, an experiential learning approach (ELA) was adopted to expose students to team dynamics and team roles. The research question was: How effective was the adoption of an experiential learning approach to introduce students to the theoretical constructs of team development and the subsequent roles fulfilled by team members? This question was investigated after allowing students to complete a team-based activity, whereby students had to build a tower using straws, sticky tape and cardboard in an attempt to identify and explain Tuckman's phases as well as Belbin's team roles. The findings of our study, based on survey data completed by students on completion of their activity, indicated the experiential learning approach is successful in teaching students the practical aspects associated with Tuckman's stages of team development as well as Belbin's team roles. The lessons learnt from this experience are given as recommendations to educators to improve the learning experiences associated with ELA in the context of project management.

Keywords: Project management · Behavioural skills
Experiential learning approach (ELA)

1 Introduction

It is well-known that most Information Technology (IT) projects do not meet their objectives [14]. According to [16] as many as nine out of ten transport projects, six out of ten energy projects, seven out of ten dams and five out of ten technology projects fail to deliver on their promises. In 2014 the Journal of African Business devoted an entire special edition to investigate why projects fail in Africa. One of its contributions was a study by Rwelamila and Ssegawa who

© Springer Nature Switzerland AG 2019
S. Kabanda et al. (Eds.): SACLA 2018, CCIS 963, pp. 237–252, 2019.
https://doi.org/10.1007/978-3-030-05813-5_16

investigated the role of project management education as main contributing factor to the failure of project implementation [32] by scrutinizing current project management educational curricula of seven graduate level programmes focusing on Southern Africa Development Community (SADC) countries. They identified (inter alia) the lack of focus on the so-called 'soft-skills' when educating project managers. This view was supported by [9] as one of the fundamental reasons for project failure, namely the inability of project managers to deal with behavioural aspects such as interpersonal communication issues, conflict management and stress management (to name a few) in complex, uncertain and often chaotic environments. A study by Ramazani and Jergeas investigated, from the perspective of current project managers, the areas they have lacked in their project management education [30]. Three main areas were identified, namely: critical thinking skills to deal with complexity; 'soft skills' with a particular focus on leadership and interpersonal skills; and lastly the exposure to real life project management scenarios to provide contextual experience. It therefore comes as no surprise that The Association for Project Management (APM) identifies various domains or knowledge areas in the development of core project management competencies, namely: *technical* ('hard' knowledge and skills focusing on project planning and scheduling, to name a few), *behavioural* ('soft' skills such as interpersonal communication and managing teams), and *contextual competence* (understanding the environment).[1] The discipline of project management therefore should cater for all these aspects in order to produce good project managers. Although many authors acknowledge this [1,9,25,30], the challenge remains in the implementation of educational practices to cater for 'softer' requirements [27]. A similar challenge was recognized at a tertiary education institution in South Africa. This became evident during the third year practical projects of students completing a Bachelor of Commerce (BCom) degree in Information Systems as well as the Bachelor of Information Technology (BIT) degree. There, student groups have to follow the software development lifecycle (SDLC) to develop a fully functional system according to client specifications. Although the teams managed their projects relatively successfully according to Gantt chart project schedules, 'softer' issues, such as interpersonal conflict, almost always prevailed. As a result, the need has been identified to educate students on the softer issues of project management, i.e. behavioural aspects. The obvious starting point for introducing students to behavioural aspects in project management was the focus on team dynamics and as a result team roles. An experimental learning approach was used which sparked the research question for this paper: *How effective was the adoption of an experiential learning approach to introduce students to the theoretical constructs of team development and the subsequent roles fulfilled by team members?* In answering this question the following two sub-questions will be answered, too: after completing the activity,

- can students identify and explain *Tuckman's phases?*
- can students identify and explain *Belbin's team roles?*

---

[1] https://www.apm.org.uk/.

The outline of this paper is as follows: the theoretical constructs students are exposed to are discussed, namely the team development stages of [36,37] as well as the team roles of [3,4] combined with a review of the literature focusing on the topic of project management education (various approaches); a description of our research case and method followed by results from the data gathered; a discussion of the findings; a conclusion section with a summary of our study and possible future research opportunities. Although we acknowledge the fact that the approaches of [3,4,36,37] are well established and relatively old, they remain widely used, relevant and still serve as the main 'building blocks' for understanding teams.

2   Team Dynamics and Team Roles

Team dynamics refer to the effect internal and external influences have on how team members respond [29] (p. 287). How team members respond to influences only becomes evident when there is interaction between team members which has a direct influence on productivity [29]. The type of interaction can furthermore be influenced by the development stage of the team (forming, storming, norming, performance, adjourn) as well the roles played by team members. For example, teams in the storming stage (as opposed to the norming phase) are more likely to experience conflict amongst team members when confronted by negative outside influences like a decision by management to change the scope of a project. Subsequently team members fulfilling the team role of completer or finisher will be devastated to realize that the delivery due date of a project has been moved forward, whilst the implementer will rather focus on re-adjusting milestones and the project schedule to meet the new deadline. On the other hand, research focusing on establishing high performance teams through the influence of different individual team members' cognitive styles [2] provided valuable insights into how project teams should be formed. However, the objective of our exercise was to introduce students on a high level to the various team roles; therefore it seemed applicable and appropriate to include insights from [3,4,36,37] in the project management curriculum (as a starting point).

2.1   Stages of Team Development

Tuckman (et al.) published a model postulating *five stages* of how teams are development [36,37]. These include forming, storming, norming, performing and adjourning:

Forming refers to the initial establishment of a new group, i.e. when team members join;

Storming occurs when team members spontaneously interact with team members to establish individual team roles (normally characterised by some confrontation);

Norming is characterized by cooperation and cohesiveness amongst team members working together to achieve project objectives;

Performing refers to the stage where project groups are optimally working together to meet project objectives. This is the stage project managers aspire to achieve.

Adjourning (and mourning) is the stage where the project is terminated after the project objectives have been achieved. This stage was revised in 1977 by Tuckman and Jensen to cater for the fact that team members might regret their disengagement from the project [37].

The rationale behind the model is that team development can be better understood and managed if project members understand the development stage in which the project team is. Also, the faster the team can advance through all the stages the quicker the stage can perform optimally [29]. Cordoba and Piki postulated that the context in which theoretical constructs are presented are of vital importance to allow students to reflect on their own abilities and skills [9]—in this instance in the context of a simulated project management environment. Although the challenge lies in creating a simulated project management context, various educational efforts attempted and succeeded to achieve this objective. Betts and Healy adopted an experiential learning approach (ELA), using a simple game involving tennis balls, to expose students to the stages of small group development in a classroom [5]. They found that students had a deeper understanding of the various stages at the end of the game. Although the objective of [8] was slightly different—namely to expose students to a real life scenario using an experiential learning approach to teach them project management principles with the main focus on the 'harder' skills—the team dynamics were evaluated at the end of the exercise through a student debriefing opportunity which yielded similar results as the study of [5]. In an interesting application of Tuckman's team development stages, Natvig and Stark used the model as part of a workload management system to perform process analysis with the objective of improving the academic workload management for nurses [23]. The analysis were helpful in understanding and guiding a diverse group of nurses into a highly productive group.

2.2   Team Roles

Belbin (et al.) have done extensive research on the effectiveness of teams [3,4,33]. Accordingly, although there is no specific personality type that makes an ideal team member, the mix of various team members playing different roles is of great importance. As a result, *eight roles* team members can play have been identified. They include:

The Co-ordinator, referring to the team member who provides leadership to the team without being the formally appointed leader. The coordinator typically provides a coordinating role to the team's efforts.

The Shaper drives activities forward due to the dynamic, inspiring role played. This role is often perceived as another type of leadership.

The Innovator provides new ideas but can unfortunately have a personal attachment to these ideas which might not always be practical.

The Resource Investigator is often referred to as the 'link' to people outside the project team who might be of interest to the project. This team role can therefore put the team into contact with useful resources should the need arise. (Unfortunately a team member fulfilling this role is often not interested participating in the team.)

The Evaluator (or Monitor) evaluates various ideas from project team members and propose workable ideas to the rest of the team. This role keeps the project on track without considering the feelings of fellow team members.

The Team Worker is a sensitive team player working hard at keeping fellow team members happy. The personal needs of team members are of utmost importance to the team work.

The Implementer plans and organizes project milestones to produce a schedule. However, should tasks or deliverables change, changes to the schedule or plan is often resisted.

The Completer (or Finisher) is one to whom the delivery of the project according to set deadlines is extremely important. This role entails that the project progress is tracked and that possible risks for the project, that can cause project deliverable delays, are considered.

The ideal team, not necessarily restricted to a project management environment, should consist of diverse team members and have at least one team member fulfilling at least one role. Students should therefore take cognisance of the different roles team members can play on their projects, the subsequent impact thereof as well as potential shortcomings of each role. As a result, project team members can work more effectively together to improve project performance. This is in line with findings of [21] according to which a balanced team composition—i.e. team members fulfilling different roles according Belbin's team roles in collaborative learning groups—yields a higher level of group performance and cognitive complexity. Although the study permitted students to participate in the experiential learning exercise in groups of 5, instead of the ideal team size of 4 according to [33], the objective was to expose students to the different roles within the context of their third year project teams which consisted of 5 members. Later studies made some adjustments to those eight roles and proposed to add a ninth role, namely that of a *Specialist* [33]. The Specialist role was omitted from the original team roles as studies were conducted in a simulated environment without any in-depth knowledge in a particular area. Only when the eight roles were practically tested in a real-life environment the role of a team member with in-depth knowledge in a particular area was identified. During this study students were only exposed to the original eight roles due to the lack of specialist or in-depth knowledge in any participation knowledge area. Although challenging, it is anticipated that the recently proposed 9th role will have to be introduced in subsequent studies. The inclusion of Belbin's team roles in educational curricula are not limited to faculties teaching Information Technology (IT) or related subjects. According to [34], for example, there is a need to expose medical practitioners to what is referred to as 'inter-professional education curricula' in order to understand the various roles when working in project teams as well as to develop teamwork skills. The results of post-study assessments indicated that students experienced an increased level of knowledge about the professional roles of different medical practitioners (such as nurses, doctors and dentists) as well as an improvement in the overall team skills.

3   Experiential Learning

Experiential learning refers to the opportunity offered to students to practically participate in hands-on activities or real-life scenarios with the objective of applying the theoretical constructs they were exposed to [26]. However, it is much more than just the application of theoretical constructs. The experiential learning cycle of [31] allows students not only to participate in the learning activity or real-life scenario, but also to reflect on their experience and to finally apply what they have learned. According to [12] there are *four phases* of experiential learning:

Design, wherein the lecturer contextualises the learning objectives and identifies the activities to be completed by the students.

Conduct: this phase involves the creation of an artefact within specific guidelines.

Evaluation entails the assessment of the task by the lecturer and opportunities for students to review their own experience.

Feedback: continuous information by the lecturer to the students about their progress.

The experiential learning approach is widely used in the teaching of hands-on practical project management skills, all with various levels of success and challenges identified. In [20] one of the many challenges identified was *team composition*, i.e. the selection of specific team members to belong to a team. In real-life scenarios team composition is determined after considering the skills and personality traits of individual team members before members are allocated to groups. However, in the context of the activity, team members could select their own groups. As a result, team dynamics could be perceived as somewhat 'artificial'. Chen and Chuang proposed an experiential learning model for the implementation of experiential learning in a project management course [6]. After the implementation of this module students said that this was an excellent method to bridge the gap between theoretical knowledge and practical constructs. In the study, students were also allowed to interact with industry practitioners which exposed them to real-life scenarios which positively contributed to students' experiential learning experience. Although the value of experiential learning is not to be underestimated and positively correlated with benefits such as increased critical thinking as well as problem solving skills, teamwork and time management skills are often difficult to implement in experiential learning curricula [35]. The main challenge is obtaining the support of institutional members when experiential learning opportunities with external parties are introduced.

Table 1. Rubric for marking the in-class tower artefacts

Assessment criteria	Marks
Stability and Strength: Can the tower stand in an upright position and hold the load of chocolates?	3
Aesthetics: Is it pretty?	3
Teamwork: Did your team work together/conflict experienced/roles by members	3
Debriefing: Lessons learned?	1
Total	10

4   Case Study

As part of the third-year degree programme students were exposed to some of the challenges in a project management environment. As a starting point the focus was on two main theoretical constructs, namely the process of how teams develop according to Tuckman's model, as well as the various roles team members can play according to Belbin. A total of 101 students enrolled during 2017 for their third-year second-semester module, 95% of whom also had to complete their third-year practical projects. Lectures were given once weekly for a duration of 2 h per contact session. The first part of the contact session was for the presentation of theoretical concepts to achieve the following learning objectives:

– Identify and describe the stages of a team's development;
– Name, identify, and explain the different roles of team members according to Belbin;
– Develop ideas for maintaining team performance;
– Identify sources of conflict, and describe the process and possible approaches to conflict resolution.

The second part of the contact session was used to complete a practical in-class activity. The activity focused on the practical exposure to the first two learning objectives of the session, namely the identification and description of the various stages of team development as well as the various team roles according to Belbin. As per the design phase of the experiential learning approach (ELA) [31], the class was given a briefing as to what was expected. The instruction was as follows: teams consisting of 5 members; teams could select their own members; construct a tower by means of ten straws, sticky tape and cardboard. No additional product specifications were stipulated. Teams were given 35 min to complete the activity. A rubric for assessment was provided to evaluate the 'product', i.e. the tower, including criteria such as stability, strength, and aesthetics, as well as teamwork and debriefing. Table 1 shows the according marking scheme.

A prize (chocolates) was offered to the team with the highest marks. An external facilitator was involved in the allocation of the marks to ensure objectivity. For homework the students had to complete an online survey on their experience in class. Additional marks were given to students who completed the survey. A total of 81 students (80%) completed the survey.

5   Method

In order to gain understanding and insight of the team dynamics of the third-year students, we followed the 'interpretive' approach of [11]: it allows for the 'subjective' interpretation of data with the aim of 'understanding' the context in which a survey is done. After the above-mentioned in-class activities, an online survey was conducted with the students. Although no pilot study was conducted, this was the second consecutive year that the same class activity was carried out. The survey questions were formulated such as to support and answer the research questions. The survey consisted of the following questions:

1. Which of the Tuckman stages did you notice in your group? (you may select more than one). Explain your selection.
2. Which stage did your team reach once you have completed the activity? Explain your selection.
3. Now that you are familiar with the different team roles: was it easier to understand the reason why your team members act in a particular way?
4. Which team roles could you identify in your team? (Belbin's team roles)

Thematic content analysis was used to analyse the data. We followed the six steps of [7] to become familiar with the data and to systematically 'code' it into themes and categories as they emerged. Frequency analysis was completed on sections of the data to inform the discussions that follow below.

6   Findings and Discussion

The aim of this paper is to report on the effectiveness of an experiential learning approach to teach third year students team dynamics. On the basis of what has been described above in Sects. 4 and 5, the following sub-sections discuss the data w.r.t. our research (sub-)questions.

6.1   After Completing the Activity, Can Students Identify and Explain Tuckman's Phases?

The thematic analysis of the explanations of the students' choices revealed the extent to which the ELA [31] was successful by highlighting the successes and challenges experienced in the task in identifying Tuckman's phases for team development. Four 'success' and three 'challenge' themes have emerged. Figure 1 illustrates these themes. Each of these themes are discussed in turn.

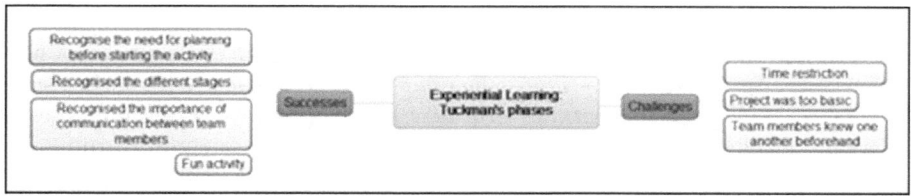

Fig. 1. Themes associated with success and challenges of ELA in learning Tuckman's phases for team development

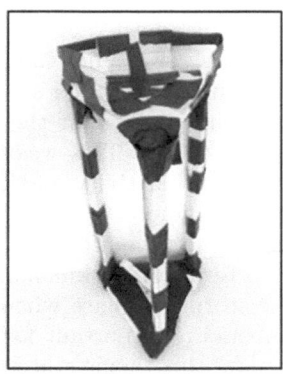

Fig. 2. The winning tower

Successes Associated with ELA in Identifying and Understanding Tuckman's Phases of Team Development. The four 'success' themes associated with the success of the ELA approach in identifying and understanding Tuckman's phases for team development included:

(1) *Recognizing the need for planning before starting the activity.* The planning activity usually occurs in the norming phase according to Tuckman's model. Students indicated that *"it was hard expressing ideas and agreeing on whose ideas to choose because everyone wants to make good impressions"*. Within the ELA, planning is essential in the design phase [6], however through the exercise the students acknowledged the need for planning before starting the activity which is the essence of project management [8].

(2) *Recognizing the different stages.* This is an important theme that emerged as the aim of the ELA was to assist students to recognise Tuckerman's phases within a 'real' project environment. The data indicated that the students reportedly experienced all of Tuckman's stages whilst completing their activity. 73% experienced the forming stage, 54% the storming phase, 70% the norming stage, and 87% the performing stage. It was interesting (though not surprising) that very few teams reached the adjourning or mourning stage (22%). It should be noted that students could select their experienced stages freely in the survey form; hence the numbers will not add up to 100%. In

addition to identifying the different stages, feedback also indicated that students 'moved' between the various stages: *"All four of the first stages were experienced. There were times when our team went back to an earlier stage before being able to continue to a new stage"*. This revisiting of stages in team development might refer to Kolb's theory of experiential learning [18] which states that as a person takes part in completing tasks, the person is influenced by other individuals. People will adjust their thinking after completing the exercise, after observing and reflecting the end result, such that a person will improve the next time when doing the activity [18]. Therefore, as students participate in the new activity of tower-building, they learn through the activity and learn from one another. All students are informed by their own experience; therefore it might require the team to re-adjust their roles and responsibilities. The results mentioned above were further enriched by the students' feedback that indicated that they disengaged from the team after the performance stage (42%). This was supported by the fact that all the teams could complete the activity and deliver a tower as their final products—see Fig. 2 for one example.

(3) *Recognising the importance of communication between team members.* This theme is very important in terms of Tuckman's stages of team development and occurs usually in the storming phase where cooperation and cohesiveness amongst team members are important for the subsequent performing phase. A quote that supports this theme stated: *"No matter the size of the task given—when working in groups with team members communication is important"*. A recent study [24] confirmed that the ELA is an effective way to improve the communication skills amongst students. Further successful examples can also be found in [10, 22].

(4) *Having fun in the activity.* The feedback indicted that the students enjoyed the learning activity and labelled it as a 'fun activity'. Accordingly, Wurdinger and Allison describe the ELA as an approach that is popular with students as it is considered to be more enjoyable and leads to deeper learning when compared to traditional approaches [38]. A reason for this might be the essence of experiential learning as there is a shift in focus from a teacher-centered approach to engaging students to participate in completing activities and to learn from each other [18].

Challenges Associated with ELA in Identifying and Understanding Tuckman's Phases of Team Development. The three themes associated with the challenges of the EPA approach in identifying and understanding Tuckman's phases for team development included:

(1) *Time restriction.* According to [38], time is a factor that inhibits the implementation of ELA. This was also found in our study where the students reported that the time limit on completing the activity has left them unable to experience conflict (conflict resolution had been a theme discussed in the theoretical part of the course) as well as to experience all stages of team development. This is illustrated by the following quotations: *"Because it is*

a project for a very short period of time, we did not experience any type of conflict, as the goal was to finish the project". This was supported by the following quote, which also refers to the specific team development stage that was not experienced due to time restriction: *"As the time span it took to complete the project was very short, it seems that our team skipped the storming stage as we did not have time to fight with one another—completing the project become the most important thing"*. These quotes illustrate that the learning objective set in the 'design phase' [31] were not fully achieved. However, the following quote illustrates that the learning objectives were achieved to some extent as the student was still able to recognise some of Tuckman's stages of team development even though they were not fully experienced: *"It was hard to fully experience all the stages since the activity wasn't too long, but there was definitely presence of certain stages"*.

(2) *Project was too simple.* The feedback from the students indicated that the complexity of the project (building a tower with straws and cardboard) was too low to allow for proper team development: *"We went on with the task to complete it in the time given. The task was too small and basic for any arguments"*. According to [38] the success of the ELA in developing life skills depends on cognitive processes being more complex than mere memorizing. Therefore the relative ease with which our students could build the tower with the given supplies did not require a lot of cognitive processes.

(3) *Some team members knew one another beforehand.* Team diversity—see below—is key to forming an effective team [17]. However, in meeting the research objective of identifying and understanding Tuckman's phases of team development, it was sometimes not possible to experience all the stages as the 'self-selected' team members had worked together before: *"We worked together already, so we did not experience storming"*. For example, the forming and storming stages have been completed during other team activities. The team therefore went straight into the norming and performing stages. The limited duration of the activity could have had an influence on the progression through the stages.

6.2 After Completing the Activity, Can Students Identify and Explain Belbin's Team Roles?

The thematic analysis of the explanations of the students' choices revealed the extent to which the ELA [26] was successful by highlighting the successes and challenges experienced in the task associated with identifying and explaining Belbin's team roles. Three 'success' and three 'challenge' themes have emerged. Figure 3 illustrates these themes, which are discussed in turn.

Successes Associated with the ELA in Identifying and Understanding Belbin's Team Roles. The three 'success' themes associated with the success of the ELA approach in identifying and understanding Belbin's roles included:

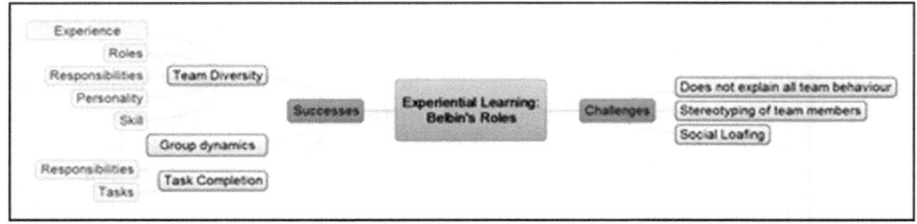

Fig. 3. Themes associated with success and challenges of ELA in learning Belbin's team roles

(1) *Team Diversity.* Team diversity refers to the different or unique characteristics of the individual team members. In [17] this is referred to as 'team membership'. Our data indicated that team members were aware of the individual experience, roles, responsibilities, personalities and skills that team members can contribute in the completion of the task. This is illustrated by the following quote: *"Definitely I realised that each team member has a unique skill that can be used to accomplish a task in a unified manner"*. Students also recognised the strengths and weaknesses as a way to identify or assign roles in a team environment: *"Yes, all persons had their own strengths that they could use to their advantage in the team"*. Team diversity is imperative for an effective team [17]. Students were asked to identify the different team roles played by team members in their teams (whereby team members could fulfil more than one role). This question forced students to reflect on the team activity and to practically apply the concept of the eight team roles on the team members. The most prevalent role was that of 'innovator' (16.2%), followed by 'team worker' (14.6%) and a third position tie for the 'completer' (13.4%) and 'coordinator' roles (13.8%). The high number of 'innovators' was not surprising as the activity required a high level of creativity and improvisation. In addition, the high number of 'team workers' can also be attained to the fact that members had existing relationships prior to the activity.

(2) *Group Dynamics.* Group dynamics is imperative to train students in accountability and responsibility which leads to task completion [17]—see below. The students' awareness of the team diversity (as discussed above) allowed them to understand the group dynamics. Group dynamics in this instance refers to the interpersonal relationships amongst team members: *"It was easier because the group dynamics and the way we completed the tasks showed it"*. The ELA facilitated this experience by allowing students to learn about group dynamics whilst completing their activity. The reflective nature of the survey further gave students an opportunity to evaluate themselves and other team members.

(3) *Task Completion.* Task completion refers to the effective and efficient finalization of a task in accordance with set success or completion criteria. According to [17] the various team roles according to Belbin collectively

contribute to the effective and efficient completion of tasks, in contrast with merely individual efforts. Students acknowledged the contribution of individual roles towards task completion and stated that *"each person acted in accordance to the role in the given task. However the way they acted was in relation to the completion of the overall task. It was vital for them to act in the manner they have acted because everyone saw the task from a different point of view"*.

Challenges Associated with the ELA in Identifying and Understanding Belbin's Team Roles. The 'challenges' themes associated with the success of the ELA approach in identifying and understanding Belbin's team roles included:

(1) *Not all behaviour can be explained.* Due to the awareness created with this ELA activity, students were more conscious of the different team roles (explained above) and illustrated this with the following quote: *"Yes, to a certain degree—but other behaviors from my team members were unexplainable"*. Thus there was an indication that not all team members' behavior could be interpreted according to Belbin's roles. One of the explanations for this might be the time restriction and the simplicity of the project which did not allow for all the different roles to be assumed, or it might be a case of 'social loafing'—see below. Anyway, it was not an objective of our study to look at individual behavior beyond the attributes of Belbin's scheme.

(2) *Stereotyping of team members.* Houghton explained that stereotypes are the grouping of people based on pre-conceived notions of characteristics or behavior of those people [13]. He considered how stereotypes could be managed through an ELA which showed that students can identify stereotypes clearly and can recognize their own stereotypes and stereotyping tendencies in themselves and in other people. Our study confirmed those results where students became aware of the different stereotyping, as indicated by the following quote: *"Only to some degree, since people vary and the Belbin team roles place people into definitive boxes, which may not necessarily be true since people can take on multiple roles or sit on a fence"*.

(3) *Social Loafing.* Social loafing in a team environment refers to some team members not actively participating in the completion of the task. Our data indicated that 'social loafing' was observed by some team members: *"Some members just go with the flow of everyone else; they don't really have their own ideas"*. Social loafing is a common challenge in team work [17]. Laal (et al.) recommended that educators should increase individual accountability as a structural element in collaboration [19] in order to lower the probability of social loafing. These structural elements will typically form part of the design phase in the ELA [31], wherein the lecturer plans the activities.

7   Conclusions and Outlook

This paper investigated the effectiveness of the adoption of an *experiential learning approach* (ELA) to introduce students to the theoretical constructs of *team development* and the subsequent roles fulfilled by team members. This topic is especially important in the context of informatics (IT) in which team work is usually required by the industry [15]. From our observations we can conclude:

- The ELA is an appropriate teaching strategy to teach 'soft-skill' project management concepts where students have to participate practically in completing an activity.
- The majority of our students could successfully identify and understand Tuckman's phases of team development as well as Belbin's team roles and the importance thereof as a result of them experiencing the roles or recognizing roles in fellow team members.
- The ELA was labelled as a 'fun activity' which fosters learning, although from our data it was also evident that there are a few challenges associated with the ELA in the context of team development and role identification.

For these reasons the following recommendations can be made to educators for future implementation:

- Group members should be randomly selected by the lecturer. This will prevent group members from selecting friends or team members from previous team activities which might have an influence on team dynamics; see [28] for comparison.
- The activity task needs to be complex enough to allow students to experience different team roles and to experience the different phases of team development.
- The lecturer needs to increase individual accountability during the design phase in order to decrease the likelihood of social loafing.
- Enough time needs to be given to complete the activity.
- The activity needs to be repeated in order to complete the experiential learning phases.

In the broader context of project management education this paper contributes to the body of knowledge concerning, firstly, how to make project management education more interactive and practical and, secondly, how to teach 'soft skill' theory in a practical manner. The focus on practical skills development is important when considering the requirements for 'real-world-ready' graduates [15].

Future research will focus on increasing the number of activities that can be taught using ELA, as well as increasing the complexity of the type of project in order to allow for a more realistic 'real-life' scenario. The development of a conceptual model or framework based on current literature could provide valuable guidelines on how the ELA can be used to teach team-theoretical topics.

References

1. Ashleigh, M., Ojiako, U., Chipulu, M., Wang, J.K.: Critical learning themes in project management education: implications for blended learning. Int. J. Proj. Manag. **30**(2), 153–161 (2012)
2. Basadur, M., Head, M.: Team performance and satisfaction: a link to cognitive style within a process framework. J. Creative Behav. **35**(4), 227–248 (2001)
3. Belbin, R.M.: Management Teams: Why They Succeed or Fail. Butterworth-Heineman, Oxford (1996)
4. Belbin, R.M.: Team Roles at Work. Butterworth-Heineman, Oxford (1999)
5. Betts, S., Healy, W.: Having a ball catching on to teamwork: an experiential learning approach to teaching the phases of group development. Acad. Educ. Leadersh. J. **19**(2), 1–9 (2015)
6. Chen, K.C.: Building an experiential learning model for a project management course. Am. J. Bus. Educ. **44**(2), 87–92 (2009)
7. Clarke, V., Braun, V.: Teaching thematic analysis: overcoming challenges and developing strategies for effective learning. Psychologist **26**(2), 120–123 (2013)
8. Cook, L.S., Olson, J.R.: The sky's the limit: an activity for teaching project management. J. Manag. Educ. **30**(3), 404–420 (2006)
9. Córdoba, J.R., Piki, A.: Facilitating project management education through groups as systems. Int. J. Proj. Manag. **30**(1), 83–93 (2012)
10. Ellis, R., Watson, C.: Experiential learning: the development of communication skills in a group therapy setting. Nurs. Educ. Today **7**(5), 215–221 (1987)
11. Fitzgerald, B., Howcroft, D.: Competing dichotomies in IS research and possible strategies for resolution. In: Proceedings of International Conference on Information Systems, ICIS 1998, pp. 155–164 (1998)
12. Gentry, J.W.: What is experiential learning. In: Guide to Business Gaming and Experiemtial Learning, Chap. 2, pp. 9–20 (1990)
13. Houghton, S.A.: Managing stereotypes through experiential learning. Intercult. Comm. Stud. **XIX**(1), 182–198 (2010)
14. Hussain, A., Mkpojiogu, E.O.: Requirements: towards an understanding on why software projects fail. In: Proceedings of AIP Conferences Proceedings, vol. 1761, no. 1 (2016)
15. Janse van Rensburg, J.T., Goede, R.: A reflective practice approach for supporting IT skills required by industry through project-based learning. In: Kabanda, S., et al. (eds.) SACLA 2018. CCIS, vol. 963, pp. 253–266. Springer, Heidelberg (2018)
16. Jenner, S.: Why do projects 'fail' and more to the point, what can we do about it? The case for disciplined, 'fast and frugal' decision-making. Management **45**(2), 6–19 (2015)
17. Kayes, A.B., Kayes, D.C., Kolb, D.A.: Experiential learning in teams. Simul. Gaming **36**(3), 330–354 (2005)
18. Kolb, D.A., Boyatzis, R., Mainemelis, C.: Experiential learning theory: previous research and new directions. In: Perspectives on Cognitive Learning and Thinking Styles, pp. 228–247. Erlbaum, Mahwah (2000)
19. Laal, M., Geranpaye, L., Daemi, M.: Individual accountability in collaborative learning. Procedia Soc. Behav. Sci. **93**, 286–289 (2013)
20. Larson, E., Drexler, J.A.: Project management in real time: a service-learning project. J. Manag. Educ. **34**(4), 551–573 (2010)
21. Meslec, N., Curseu, P.L.: Are balanced groups better? Belbin roles in collaborative learning groups. Learn. Individ. Diff. **39**, 81–88 (2015)

22. Namputhiri, M.R.K.: Experiential learning method for enhancing communication skill of tertiary level L2 learners in Thrissur district. Doctoral dissertation, Karunya Institute of Technology and Sciences, India (2013)

23. Natvig, D., Stark, N.: A project team analysis using Tuckman's model of small-group development. J. Nurs. Educ. **55**(12), 675–681 (2016)

24. Nojima, A., Ravia, J., Hongu, N.: Communication skills development through experiential learning in nutritional sciences. FASEB J. **31**(1 suppl.), 975–976 (2017)

25. Ojiako, U., Ashleigh, M., Chipulu, M., Maguire, S.: Learning and teaching challenges in project management. Int. J. Proj. Manag. **29**(3), 268–278 (2011)

26. Ontario Ministry of Education: Community-connected experiential learning: A policy framework for Ontario schools, Kindergarten to Grade 12. Gov. Communic., Canada. http://www.edu.gov.on.ca/eng/general/elemsec/job/passport/CommunityConnected_ExperientialLearningEng.pdf

27. Pieterse, V., van Eekelen, M.: Which are harder? Soft skills or hard skills? In: Gruner, S. (ed.) SACLA 2016. CCIS, vol. 642, pp. 160–167. Springer, Cham (2016). https://doi.org/10.1007/978-3-319-47680-3_15

28. Pieterse, V., Leeu, M., van Eekelen, M.: How personality diversity influences team performance in student software engineering teams. In: Proceedings of IEEE Conference on Information Communications Technology and Society, ICTAS 2018 (2018)

29. du Plessis, Y.: Project Management: A Behavioural Perspective. Pearson, London (2014)

30. Ramazani, J., Jergeas, G.: Project managers and the journey from good to great: the benefits of investment in project management training and education. Int. J. Proj. Manag. **33**(1), 41–52 (2015)

31. Rolfe, G., Freshwater, D., Jasper, M.: Critical Reflection in Nursing and the Helping Professions: A User Guide. Palgrave, Basingstoke (2001)

32. Rwelamila, P.D., Ssegawa, J.K.: The African project failure syndrome: the conundrum of project management knowledge base – the case of SADC. J. Afr. Bus. **15**(3), 211–224 (2014)

33. Smith, G., Yates, P.: Team role theory in higher education: Part 1/3. Belbin Media: Train. J. **March**, 37–40 (2011)

34. Sweet, B.V., et al.: Moving from individual roles to functional teams: a semester-long course in case-based decision making. J. Interprof. Educ. Pract. **7**, 11–16 (2017)

35. Tuberville, K., Danhower, C.: Using experiential learning concepts in new course designs: experiential learning in managing employee wellness and managerial leadership. In: Proceedings of Annual Meeting Southwest Academy of Management, Little Rock, pp. 98–104 (2017)

36. Tuckman, B.W.: Developmental sequence in small groups. Psychol. Bull. **63**(6), 384–399 (1965)

37. Tuckman, B.W., Jensen, M.A.C.: Stages of small group development revisited. Gr. Organ. Stud. **2**(4), 419–427 (1977)

38. Wurdinger, S., Allison, P.: Faculty perceptions and use of experiential learning in higher education. J. e-Learning Knowl. Soc. **13**(1), 15–26 (2017)

A Reflective Practice Approach
for Supporting IT Skills Required by
Industry Through Project-Based Learning

Juanita T. Janse van Rensburg[1]([✉])(iD) and Roelien Goede[2](iD)

[1] School of Computer Science and Information Systems, North-West University,
Vaal Triangle Campus, Vanderbijlpark, South Africa
jt.jansevanrensburg@nwu.ac.za
[2] School of Computer Science and Information Systems, North-West University,
Potchefstroom Campus, Potchefstroom, South Africa
roelien.goede@nwu.ac.za

Abstract. This paper reflects on the concerns that IT graduates lack specific skills required in industry and how project-based learning (PBL) can support these skills. An overview of the instructional design of a course module containing only IT capstone projects received from industry is provided. Feedback regarding the IT skills required of graduates are identified in a pilot study using the industry partners that provided the project scopes. The qualitative data is analysed using open coding. Through reflection on the data analysis, recommendations are made towards supporting required IT skills through PBL in a capstone module in an IT degree.

Keywords: Reflective practice · Project-based learning · IT skills
Capstone projects · Industry requirements

1 Introduction

There is an increasing concern that information technology (IT) graduates lack certain skills expected by industry when they enter the workforce. A large number of reports have appeared in the media as it is an industry issue. An article claimed that 52% of 635 employers (419 of which were specifically responsible for recruiting graduates) indicated that graduates lacked basic attributes such as communication, team work, the ability to cope under pressure and punctuality [12]. 17% of employers stated that none of the recruits were work-ready. Students have also started to notice the gap between theory and practice and are demanding an improved curriculum. In the year 2014, students from as many as 19 countries formed 41 protest groups to object the fact that the curriculum focus in a specific subject is too narrow and the examples are not based on real-world problems [8].

North-West University Ethical Clearance Number: ECONIT-2017-074.

S. Kabanda et al. (Eds.): SACLA 2018, CCIS 963, pp. 253–266, 2019.
https://doi.org/10.1007/978-3-030-05813-5_17

The issue also exists as a gap (already often mentioned in the literature) between IT graduate skills and expectations from industry. These industry-related skills include both soft and hard skills. Soft skills refer to attributes of emotional intelligence, while hard skills refer to the technical skills required to perform specific work-related tasks. Many of these issues suggest that IT graduates need more exposure to project-based assessments, where they can take on different roles in a team environment and exercise different types of skills in the process.

Even in most companies in industry, a project-based learning environment was expected from as early as nearly two decades ago [9]. Especially in IT occupations, job-related tasks are presented in project-based form with employees assigned to specific roles. These roles can include, but are not limited to, the role of a project manager, software developer, database administrator, user-interface specialist, consultant, or administrator who documents the progress of the project. The success of IT projects are frequently measured by the manner in which project management is included, applied and improved upon [10].

Project-based learning (PBL) has also been applied to many different forms of educational instruction. The main idea is that real-world problems are used as part of a student-centered learning process. Furthermore, students take ownership of their learning process if they are intrinsically motivated, and this can be achieved by managing the scope of the project [7]. It can be suggested that a project-based learning exercise that is of personal relevance to students will encourage them to put further effort into the learning process.

At its core, PBL is a reflective practice approach to solving a project-based problem. Reflective practice (RP) is a philosophical term coined by Donald Schön and is described as the process of immediate reflection during the process of fulfilling a task, and also the reflection that takes place after the activity was completed in order to improve a future approach to similar tasks [14].

The remainder of this paper, which continuates our work of [6], is organised as follows. Section 2 provides a short literature review on key concepts of our study. Section 3 provides an overview of the instructional design of a module for IT capstone projects. Section 4 presents the data collection technique and method of data analysis. Section 5 provides recommendations for supporting IT skills required by industry through project-based learning. Conclusion and outlook to future work are given in Sect. 6.

2   Central Concepts (Related Work)

A short section on related work is presented to create a shared understanding on the concepts that inform our study.

Project-Based Learning. Project-based learning (PBL) is the process of 'learning by doing' as well as 'doing with understanding' [2]. Many descriptions of project-based learning revolve around the idea of learning by completing realistic or real-world projects. Six characteristics of PBL are discussed [7]: The first characteristic is referred to as problem-orientated learning, where the project scope encourages the learning activity of the student. Apt project scopes motivate learning amongst students [3]. The second characteristic involves the creation of an artefact by the students. A project scope with specific instructions is provided to the students. During the creation process of the artefact, the students regularly discover gaps in their knowledge. The students then have to do research to solve the problem and take control of their learning process. This is seen as the third characteristic of project-based learning [7]. Project-based learning places the student at the heart of the learning process [5]. Contextualisation of the project where students are exposed to the implementation of the artefact is the fourth characteristic of PBL. The fifth characteristic claims that students are exposed to various types of knowledge representation with respect to resources. They need to develop skills to integrate knowledge from several forms of sources such as text, video and graphs. The last characteristic addresses the reason or motivation for learning of the students. Students are more intrinsically driven and take ownership of their learning experience with project-based learning, more so than in traditional teaching methods [7]. Projects are often the 'flagships' of a syllabus, and students should work collaboratively on real-world activities to solve problems that are important to them [4].

Reflective Practice in Project-Based Learning. Donald Schön argued that design falls within the context of intuitive, artistic processes and that it cannot be boxed within well-formed solutions [14]. Schön maintains that design practice more often deals with disordered and challenging situations. Reflective practice is the dual process of immediate reflection during the situation (reflection-in-action) and reflecting on the situation after it has been resolved in order to better handle future scenarios (reflection-on-action). A characteristic of PBL is that students have to create artefacts and that during the development process, they become aware of gaps in their knowledge [7]. Students then need to research the problem, apply possible solutions by trial and error and, through a reflective approach, find a solution. Reflective practice is an iterative sequence that usually starts with a case study where challenging concerns arise, after which a reflection on possible solutions is conceptualised, leading to a new approach towards solving the problem [11]. Furthermore, the reflective skills of a student is advanced through project-based learning [1].

In this paper, 'reflective practice' not only refers to the iterative process of learning that students go through, but also to the reflective practice approach of the academics to evaluate best practices for reinforcing IT skills through project-based learning.

3   Instructional Design of IT Capstone Projects

As part of the Information Technology degree offered at our university, where this study was conducted, one course module is presented in the last semester of the degree that consists exclusively out of projects (i.e. no tests, assignments, nor written exams). The purpose of this module is to test the combination of knowledge of all previous modules presented at different levels in the degree. An additional outcome of this module is also to immerse students in a project-based environment that would simulate their future working-environment. This module can be seen as the capstone of the IT degree offered.

During the course of this module, students are required to complete 3 projects for marks towards access to the exam project. A fourth project is given as the exam project. As indicated through the use of PBL, students are more intrinsically motivated to take ownership of their learning experience. This idea is further encouraged by the first characteristic given by Helle et al. which indicates that the project scope heartens the participation of the student. As the goal of exit-level students is to obtain employment, it can be reassured that industry-related projects would motivate the learning experience of the student. In the academic year 2017, the four project scopes given to the students were:

Project 1—Internal project scope provided by the university's *robotics* team. The duration of the project was six weeks. Students received a weekly class on topics relating to the robotics project. Students participated in teams of four, divided into groups by the presenter. Project documentation was not expected.

Project 2—Industry project scope provided by 'Company *A*' on *cyber security*. The duration of the project was six weeks. The project was given after project *A*. A guest lecture on cyber security was presented by Company *A* at the beginning of the project. Students participated in teams of two to four students. Students divided themselves into groups. Project documentation was expected, and a detailed rubric was provided.

Project 3—Industry project scope provided by 'Company *B*' on a comprehensive multifaceted project brief relating to bookings and tracking of courier packages. The project was an individual project and was given at the beginning of the semester along with project 1. The duration of the project was 13 weeks and ran concurrently with project 1 and project 2. A guest lecture on the project facets was presented by Company *B* three weeks after the scope was released, so that students could compile a list of questions for the presenter. Students could choose between three problems, i.e., solve the problem of the driver (e.g. via mobile application), solve the problem of the scheduler (e.g. via desktop application), or solve the problem of the customer (e.g. via mobile and/or desktop application). Project documentation was expected, and a detailed rubric was provided.

Project 4—Industry project scope provided by 'Company *C*' on a comprehensive project brief relating to internal event bookings. The project was an individual project and was given after project 3 was completed. The duration of the exam project was five weeks for the 1st examination opportunity. Students who failed the 1st examination opportunity could improve their projects for the 2nd examination opportunity, providing them with an additional two weeks. Students could also elect to miss the 1st opportunity, use seven weeks for the project and present at the 2nd opportunity (with no chance of an

During scheduled class time	PROJECT 1 Team work Robotics	PROJECT 2 Team work Cyber Security	PROJECT 3 Individual work Multifaceted project	EXAM PROJECT Individual work Exam project
Week 1	Commence project 1		Commence project 3 (Company B)	
Week 4			Guest lecture: Company B	
Week 6		Guest lecture: Company A		
Week 7	Submit & Present Project	Commence project 2 (Company A)		
Week 13		Submit & Present Project		
Week 14			Submit & Present Project	Commence exam project (Company C)
Exam Opportunity 1				
Week 19				Submit & Present Project
Exam Opportunity 2				
Week 21				Submit & Present Project

Fig. 1. Schedule of our capstone projects

additional examination opportunity). No guest lecture was provided, and students were encouraged to research the topics related to the project. No project documentation was expected, and a detailed rubric was provided. The company that provided the exam scope also acted as external moderator during the exam presentations.

Figure 1 provides an overview of the schedule followed for the capstone projects. Students had a weekly three hour session during which they had access to the facilitator of the module. Students were encouraged to find the answers on their own as far as possible, but could ask for assistance from the facilitator if proof of unsuccessful research was presented. Students were not forced to attend these sessions, it merely provided a set period for access to the computer laboratories and facilitator. Students could also contact the facilitator during consultation hours or via email correspondence.

4   Industry Perspectives on Lack of Skills of IT Graduates

During unstructured interviews with the partner companies that provided the industry-related project scopes, we engaged in topics related to the perceptions of IT graduates and the expectations of industry. Issues were highlighted that were previously experienced with IT graduates when entering the workforce at Companies A, B, C. As part of our reflective practice approach, in order to improve

Table 1. Pilot study participants, with 'YoE' = Years of Experience, 'Co' = Company

P	Job title	YoE	Co	Location	Project scope
P1	Information Security Consultant (involved in graduate training)	3	A	Johannesburg (RSA)	Project 2: Cyber Security (Web site only)
P2	Consultant (involved in graduate training)	30+	B	Johannesburg (RSA)	Project 3: Multifaceted (Web site, mobile application, and/or desktop application)
P3	Systems developer (involved in graduate training)	10+	C	Meyerton (RSA)	Project 4: Internal event bookings application (mobile application only)

the future iterations of the capstone projects, a pilot study was conducted to identify skills that IT graduates typically lack. Any initial issues identified during this study could possibly be addressed during the 2018 round of student capstone project-based learning experiences with the aim of improving the lack in skills of IT graduates.[1]

Research Method. A pilot study was conducted using a convenience sample of three participants. These participants represented all companies that provided industry project scopes for the capstone projects of 2017. The pilot study was conducted as a first iteration, and baseline, of a reflective practice approach to identifying skills that IT graduates lack. Once initial data has been collected and analysed, a starting point for future research on the same subject can be established. Table 1 contains an overview of participant details.

Data Analysis. Participants were again contacted via email correspondence and asked to provide a written summary of typical skills they found lacking in IT graduates. The email correspondence received was considered as the data collection technique referred to as unstructured written interviews. The data was qualitative in nature. For this reason a data analysis method referred to as open coding was used to find themes in the data. Table 2 provides a summary of the findings from the data analysis.

Additionally, the participating companies also indicated *when* those skills should be addressed or obtained:

Category 1: Skills expected prior to employment (i.e., to be reinforced during undergraduate training *at university*):
  Soft skills: Verbal and written communication, presentation skills, interview skills, research skills, willingness to learn.[2]

---

[1] For comparison see Part III: *Educational Cooperation with the ICT Industry*, pp. 146–205 of SACLA'2017 Revised Selected Papers, CCIS **730**, Springer 2017.
[2] For comparison see [13].

Table 2. Codes assigned to data analysis

Code	Example answers
Communication Skills: Verbal (2 occur.)	*"Lack of clear, concise, communication skills"* (P2). *"Graduates cannot convey their ideas in a clear and concise manner orally, and there is much use of 'uhm', 'ah', and 'like'"* (P2). *"They cannot explain anything on a board"* (P3)
Communication Skills: Written (1 occur.)	*"It is thus very important to us that graduates have the ability to write formal reports in a clear, concise and professional manner"* (P2)
Presentation Skills (2 occur.)	*"These are sometimes found to be lacking, as interns can become very nervous"* (P2). *"I see people are also afraid to write on a white board, everyone thinks presentations are only done in PowerPoint"* (P3)
Critical Thinking, Problem Solving and Attention to Detail (3 occur.)	*"I find the type of conceptual thinking ability, attention to detail and natural curiosity is more of a differentiator"* (P1). *"Graduates should also have a strong aptitude for problem solving, as the environments we work in often require that a non-standard approach be taken"* (P2). *"Most of the graduates with whom I have worked cannot do planning before coding"* (P3)
Professionality, Work Ethics (1 occur.)	*"This point is a non-negotiable one for us. Professionalism and awareness of the environment which you're in is critical in not exposing any information pertaining to our clients"* (P2)[a]
Time Management (2 occur.)	*"One of the big mind shift changes for new members is the reality of challenging deadlines"* (P1). *"It is often required that we familiarise ourselves with various technologies, which we may have not encountered before, in a short space of time"* (P2)
Willingness to Learn (3 occur.)	*"I find the type of conceptual thinking ability, attention to detail and natural curiosity is more of a differentiator"* (P1). *"A graduate's ability to think on their feet and approach problems with an enquiring mindset, where the answer to the problem is not necessarily well-defined, is something which is important to us"* (P2). *"I think one gets too comfortable with only one or two languages; they must see that the same thing can be done with any language"* (P3)
Interview Skills (2 occur.)	*"We often receive CVs and internship applications which appear as if minimal effort has been made to make the application and CV look professional and presentable. Further to this, sending an email with only attachments and no message body can be seen as unprofessional"* (P2). *"They do not have proper interview skills"* (P3)
Research Skills (2 occur.)	*"When one knows one is destined to be a rock'n'roll star, you tend to know your rock n roll heroes really well; I find many developers do not know their industry heroes. One of the core books I recommend every developer owns is Code Complete, which has an in depth discussion of the core practices of professional coding"* (P1). *"It is easy to differentiate a candidate who has a strong interest in information security from someone who has recently been intrigued by something in the news"* (P2)
Programming Languages (1 occur.)	*"Python: for applications that may run on Linux; C#: back-end apps.; HTML, Javascript"* (P3)
GUI Design (1 occur.)	*"C#: front-end apps.; CSS"* (P3)
Data Bases (1 occur.)	*"Entity framework—integration with other databases"* (P3)

(continued)

Table 2. (*continued*)

Code	Example answers
Reusable Code (1 occur.)	"The difference between functional code and production quality code: I have seen project code that works functionally but would not survive any kind of negative or destruct testing. I want people to have a basic grasp of design patterns" (P1)
Architectural Patterns (1 occur.)	"Increasingly people are using MVVM to display tier stuff" (P1)
Code Refactoring (1 occur.)	"I want people to know how and what to refactor" (P1)
Advanced Design Principles (1 occur.)	"I want people to understand SOLID" (P1)
Unit Testing (1 occur.)	"All of the teams I work with use automated unit testing extensively" (P1)
Source Control (1 occur.)	"One of the hardest things for new members to grasp is source control, which becomes much harder to manage in a larger team with shared ownership of code. Merging conflicting code using a merging tool is an essential skill that is expensive to learn while fighting deadlines" (P1)
Internships (1 occur.)	"It is important to do as many internships as possible for a number of reasons. Firstly, it helps to determine the kind of field that you will enjoy working in most. Secondly, it allows you to pick up many of the aforementioned skills with relative ease" (P2)
Certification (1 occur.)	"I want people to know Scrum. The process is not hard to understand, and a formal training course is normally only a day or two, with a certification. I believe a scrum certification can be a career accelerator" (P1)

[a]For comparison see the *Code of Conduct of the ICT Professional* at www.iitpsa.org.za.

Expected technical skills: Understanding of programming languages, understanding of GUI design, understanding of databases.
Category 2: Skills expected prior to (but specifically reinforced during) *internships*, graduate programmes, *employment*:
    Soft skills: Critical thinking, problem solving, attention to detail, professionalism, work ethic, time management.
    Advanced technical skills: Knowledge of reusable code, source control.
Category 3: Skills that would be beneficial prior to (but can be trained during) internships, graduate programmes, employment:
    Advanced technical skills: Knowledge of architectural patterns, knowledge of code refactoring, knowledge of advanced design principles, knowledge of unit testing.

The skills of these categories are further discussed below.

5 Findings and Recommendations

Table 3 provides a summary of the IT skills required by industry and at which point in a student's career these issues should be exercised. Short code keys provided in the table are: 'S' for soft skills, 'T' for technical skills, and 'R' for

Table 3. Reflection on ways to reinforce skills through PBL

Category 1	Reinforcement method	Reflection on inclusion of recommendations in the IT capstone projects at our university
S1: Communication Skills: Verbal	Prompt students to explain their initial project ideas to smaller audiences via a traditional method (e.g. whiteboard)	For all projects, students should explain the initial manner in which they will solve the problem. This will be addressed in a one-on-one setting between facilitator and team. Feedback towards improving verbal communication will be provided
S2: Communication Skills: Written	Prompt students to compile technical project documentation	For each project, students will compile a technical report on the system analysis. Students will be evaluated on relevance of content as well as academic writing standards. Feedback on improving written communication skills will be provided
S3: Presentation Skills	Prompt students to explain their final project to larger audiences via technology-centered methods (e.g. PowerPoint)	Teams or individuals should present their final project outcomes via professional presentation to a panel. The panel could consist of other academics, members from industry and peers. Feedback on presentation skills should be provided
S4: Willingness to Learn	Manage the scope of the project as in [7]. Undergraduate students in their final year will be intrinsically motivated to complete projects that are received from industry (as a reference to what is expected from employment)	Project scopes should not be fictional, but should rather be received from industry. The project scopes should reflect the types of projects companies work on currently. In this manner, students are motivated to learn, as they are exposed to similar projects they will come across during employment
S5: Interview Skills	Additional training in the form of workshops: These can be short presentations offered during class time	A short workshop on interview skills will be presented. A good starting point for structuring the workshop will be to research the STAR method.[a] Furthermore, an informal roleplay activity in which peers evaluate each others' responses to interview questions could pinpoint additional problems that need to be addressed
S6: Research Skills	Technical project documentation: restricting content to recent references on IT (and using the appropriate referencing methods)	In all projects a certain level of research is expected as students need to find methods of addressing the project scopes. A formal research project can also help to train this skill: see T6–T9 below. Students should receive guidance on the structure of a research project in the form of a short workshop

(*continued*)

Table 3. (*continued*)

T1: Programming Languages	Prompt students to complete different projects in different programming languages	Students have completed modules pertaining to different programming languages prior to the capstone projects. To further train different language programming skills, each capstone project will have instructions for a different language the problem needs to be solved in
T2: GUI Design	Provide clear expectations of user interfaces for projects; prompt students to refer to design principles followed in the technical documentation	Students will be made aware of literature on different design principles and prompted to discuss how they implemented these principles in their projects, via the technical report
T3: Data Bases	Prompt students to use a suitable database for each project	Students are required to integrate a database in all capstone projects. Students also receive instruction on database design in additional modules. To further reinforce the skill, a short workshop on database integration and SQL statements will be presented
Category 2	Reinforcement method	Reflection on inclusion of recommendations in the IT capstone projects at our university
S7: Critical thinking, problem solving, attention to detail	Reinforce skills through the planning stages of project development. Students should provide weekly updates on progress and recommendations on how they will address problems. Additionally make students aware of iterative frameworks used for project creation, and prompt them to explain their projects according to the phases of a specific framework (i.e. design science research)	Students will be required to present their capstone projects according to an iterative development framework such as design science research. Students will then be obligated to structure their thought processes in a logical but critical manner, which in turn will train their skills towards reflective practice
S8: Professionalism and work ethic	Additional training in the form of workshops	A short workshop on work ethics and professional conduct will be presented
S9: Time management	Deadline-driven project time-lines: should be feasible, but not overestimated. Create the need for students to work at an acceptable pace at all times	Specific deadlines will be given for each project. These deadlines will be carefully evaluated according to the scope and outcomes of the project. The deadlines will be feasible, but will require students to work continuously
T4: Reusable Code	Additional training in the form of workshops. Guest lectures from industry might be useful	Invite guest speakers

(*continued*)

Table 3. (*continued*)

T5: Source Control	Prompt students to use a version of source control for each project	Source control shall be mandatory for all capstone projects. Students will be asked to use Git for version control[b]
Category 3	Possible recommendations for supporting skill through PBL	Reflection on inclusion of recommendations in the IT capstone projects at our university
T6–T9: Architectural patterns, code refactoring, advanced design principles, unit testing	Difficult to reinforce advanced concepts during a single semester module. Possibly provide a research project to familiarise students with concepts	Students will be required to compile a professional research document with suitable examples on the topics of architectural patterns, code refactoring, advanced design principles and unit testing. In this manner students will become aware of advanced concepts prior to interviews, and reinforce their research skills (S6). This approach will need to be evaluated for effectiveness for future use
Additional learning	Possible recommendations for supporting skill through PBL	Reflection on inclusion of recommendations in the IT capstone projects at our university
R1: Internships	Replace one project with an expected internship at a local company	Facilitator needs to determine whether it will be viable to replace a project with a mandatory internship as part of future employment training. If not, students should be encouraged to attend internships for work exposure and experience. Additionally, students will be motivated to attend 'Hackathons' (short sprints of programming events usually hosted by companies to identify talented individuals). Not only is this a method of exposure for possible employment, but also allows the student to learn about technologies, deadlines and work environments expected in industry
R2: Certification	Suggest additional certifications as part of the B.Sc. degree as a whole	Certifications call for additional funding which does not form part of tuition fees: this will be a problematic issue to implement. In 2018, additional certifications at the students' expense will be suggested. The suggestion will also be discussed with management for including additional IT certifications in the degree as part of tuition fees

[a] https://www.vawizard.org/wiz-pdf/STAR_Method_Interviews.pdf.
[b] https://git-scm.com/.

Table 4. Overview of planned activities

Week	Activity	IT skill addressed via PBL
1	Introduction to module outcomes	Explanation of IT skills required for industry and how these will be addressed during the course of the module
	Workshop on interview skills	S5
	Replace Project 1 with internship at a local company (if feasible)	R1, S8
2	Workshop on professional conduct and work ethics	S8
3	Workshop on research processes	S6
	Commence research project pertaining to architectural patterns, code refactoring, advanced design principles, and unit testing	S2, S4, S6–S9, T6–T9
4	Workshop on reusable code and source control	T4–T5
5	Workshop on database integration and SQL statements	T3
	Students submit research project	S2, S4, S6–S9, T6–T9
	Commence Project 2 (industry scope)	S1–S4, S6–S9, T1–T5
11	Submit and present Project 2; Commence Project 3 (industry scope)	S1–S4, S6–S9, T1–T5
17	Submit and present Project 3; Commence Project 4 (industry scope)	S1–S4, S6–S9, T1–T5
21–22	Submit and present Project 4	S1–S4, S6–S9, T1–T5

recommendations. Furthermore the table provides a reflection on methods of reinforcing the required IT skills through project-based learning in the capstone projects of an IT degree. The last column in the table is a self-reflection on how these recommendation can be addressed in the capstone projects at our university.

6   Conclusion and Future Work

From Table 3 we can now, through reflective practice, suggest a *time line with activities* for supporting IT skills identified in this paper on project-based learning in the IT capstone projects of an IT degree. Table 4 provides a summary towards this initiative. As seen in the table, a clear process for addressing required IT skills is presented through the use of PBL in a capstone module.

Other skills not addressed in Table 4, but that should form part of continuous learning during the course of the semester, are:

1. Project 1 should be a mandatory internship of at least one week that can be completed at any stage during the course of the semester, but needs to be finished before examination as part of the participation mark (R1: S8–S9).
2. Students should be recommended to complete additional internships in their own time to increase learning opportunities (R1).
3. Opportunities should be made available for attending 'Hackathons' hosted by industry (R1).
4. Students should be referred to additional certifications for career acceleration at own cost (R2).

This paper serves as a baseline to an iterative pilot study to determine the effectiveness of the recommendations made, if implemented in the IT capstone projects. On completion of the course module we will reflect on the effects of the changes made to the presentation of the module and suggest improvements. This process shall become a continuous reflective practice exercise, ensuring that best practice is always maintained when facilitating learning through PBL in IT capstone projects.

Many of these IT skills are expected from graduates when entering the workforce. Addressing the support of these IT skills required from industry in the IT capstone projects is a step in the right direction, but may also be too late to viably train the skills before employment. It can be suggested that these skills should be reinforced earlier in an IT degree.

As part of the iterative nature of this study, we will also attempt in future research to improve modules offered in the 'Extended IT Degree'[3] to include skills training through smaller activities of PBL. In this manner the long-term effects of reinforcing required IT skills earlier in an undergraduate degree can be assessed when these students reach their final study-year.

References

1. Ayas, K., Zeniuk, N.: Project-based learning: building communities of reflective practitioners. Manag. Learn. **32**(1), 61–76 (2001)
2. Barron, B.J.S., et al.: Doing with understanding: lessons from research on problem- and project-based learning. J. Learn. Sci. **7**(3/4), 271–311 (1998)
3. Blumenfeld, P.C., Soloway, E., Marx, R.W., Krajcik, J.S., Guzdial, M., Palincsar, A.: Motivating project-based learning: sustaining the doing, supporting the learning. Educ. Psychol. **26**(3/4), 369–398 (1991)

---

[3] Explanation for readers from outside South Africa: in South Africa the 'extended' degree 'stretches' the contents of the regular curriculum into a longer study-duration, for the benefits of weak students who (for various reasons) enter into university rather under-prepared.

4. Boss, S., Krauss, J.: Reinventing Project-based Learning: Your Field Guide to Real-World Projects in the Digital Age. International Society for Technology in Education, Washington, D.C. (2007)
5. Fernandes, S.R.G.: Preparing graduates for professional practice: findings from a case study of project-based learning (PBL). Proc. Soc. Behav. Sci. **139**(1), 219–226 (2014)
6. Goede, R.: A critical systems perspective on project-based learning: guidelines for using industry data for BI student projects. In: Liebenberg, J., Gruner, S. (eds.) SACLA 2017. CCIS, vol. 730, pp. 162–174. Springer, Cham (2017). https://doi.org/10.1007/978-3-319-69670-6_11 .
7. Helle, L., Tynjala, P., Olkinuora, E.: Project-based learning in post-secondary education: theory, practice, and rubber sling shots. High. Educ. **51**, 287–314 (2006)
8. Inman, P.: Economics students call for shakeup of the way their subject is taught. https://www.theguardian.com/education/2014/may/04/economics-students-overhaul-subject-teaching
9. Keegan, A., Turner, J.R.: Quantity versus quality in project-based learning practices. Manag. Learn. **32**, 77–98 (2001)
10. Mitchell, V.L.: Knowledge integration and information technology project performance. MIS Q. **30**(4), 919–939 (2006)
11. Osterman, K.F.: Using constructivism and reflective practice to bridge the theory/practice gap. In: Proceedings of Annual Meeting of the American Educational Research Association, pp. 1–18 (1998)
12. Paton, G.: University leavers lack the essential skills for work, employers warn. http://www.telegraph.co.uk/education/educationnews/10306211/University-leavers-lack-the-essential-skills-for-work-employers-warn.html
13. Pieterse, V., van Eekelen, M.: Which are harder? Soft skills or hard skills? In: Gruner, S. (ed.) SACLA 2016. CCIS, vol. 642, pp. 160–167. Springer, Cham (2016). https://doi.org/10.1007/978-3-319-47680-3_15
14. Schön, D.A.: The Reflective Practitioner. Maurice Temple Smith, Isleworth (1983)

Learning Systems

Enhancing Object-Oriented Programming Pedagogy with an Adaptive Intelligent Tutoring System

Methembe Dlamini⬤ and Wai Sze Leung^(✉)⬤

Academy of Computer Science and Software Engineering,
University of Johannesburg, Johannesburg, South Africa
methembedlamini@yahoo.com, wsleung@uj.ac.za

Abstract. Challenges to teaching programming include a lack of structured teaching methodologies that are tailored for programming subjects while the benefits of providing programming students with individual attention are not easily addressed due to high student-to-teacher ratios. This paper describes how adaptive intelligent tutoring systems may represent a potential solution assisting teachers in delivering individualized attention to their students while also helping them to discover effective ways of teaching a core programming concept such as object-oriented programming. This paper investigates how adaptability in traditional intelligent tutoring systems are achieved, presenting an adaptive pedagogical model that uses machine learning techniques to discover effective teaching strategies suitable for a particular student. The results of a prototype of the proposed model demonstrate the model's ability to classify the student models according to their learning style correctly. The knowledge obtained can be applied by educators to make better-informed choices in the formulation of lesson plans that are more appropriate to their students.

Keywords: Intelligent tutoring systems
Pedagogical decision-making · Adaptability · Artificial intelligence
Machine learning

1 Introduction

Aside from providing students with individualized attention, the deployment of Intelligent Tutoring Systems (ITSs) may also serve as a source of information that helps guide teachers in making better-informed pedagogical decisions.

Much merit exists in introducing programming at lower school levels, as world development is seen to rely on technology [32] and critical thinking skills relevant to surviving the information age are seen to be developed from learning to code [15]. Calls for programming to be taught at early academic stages are increasingly gaining traction [32], however, there are equally voices raising legitimate, realistic concerns: are teachers adequately equipped to *teach* coding [26]?

© Springer Nature Switzerland AG 2019
S. Kabanda et al. (Eds.): SACLA 2018, CCIS 963, pp. 269–284, 2019.
https://doi.org/10.1007/978-3-030-05813-5_18

Unfortunately, the reality is that teachers struggle to come up with effective ways to teach programming [12,15,19,24]. In some cases, teachers are simply not trained to be computer science teachers [26]. This paper, however, focuses on other factors, specifically limited time, limited resources, high student-to-teacher ratios, and student diversity [1,12,19,24], all of which make it difficult for a teacher to devise lessons that cater for particular learning needs [11]. There is thus a need for tools that can assist teachers in monitoring individual students, gathering useful information to improve pedagogical decision-making.

ITSs have been used effectively to offer individual attention to students [8, 21,23,31]. Existing implementations, however, make use of predetermined rules to tailor content, thus lacking the ability to adapt and discover new knowledge about teaching. We propose introducing changes to the traditional ITS model, enabling it to autonomously discover effective teaching strategies and student preferences so that the knowledge generated from such ITSs may be used by human teachers to improve their teaching techniques and make informed lesson planning decisions. This paper presents an Adaptive Pedagogical Model (APM) that is capable of improving teaching strategies by means of machine learning in order to assess the learning preferences for different kinds of students.

The remainder of this paper is organized as follows: Sect. 2 reviews several research areas, specifically on traits that determine academic performance, teaching strategies, intelligent tutoring systems, and machine learning. Section 3 describes the proposed APM, the adaptation approach and its generic adaptation algorithm. Section 2.2 presents the details of the prototype that was implemented to test the APM, leading to an evaluation of the APM in Sect. 5. Finally, the paper concludes in Sect. 6 with a summary of the findings.

2   Related Work

2.1   Need for Adaptive Tutoring

Proponents of student-centered education theory have long highlighted the need for individualized learning mechanisms that allow a student to select their learning path [7,22,34]. The proliferation of eLearning platforms has opened up numerous opportunities to realize student-oriented learning where teachers merely guide and empower their students to take charge of their learning process [22].

The rationale for providing students with individualized learning paths is quite straight-forward: students are diverse—they have different backgrounds, have different learning objectives, and possess different learning styles [3,7].

Given that research has demonstrated a very strong correlation between academic performance and personality traits [9,27] and that students tend to respond better when offered tutorials that are dynamic, intelligent, and catering to their individual attention [1], the aforementioned individualized characteristics are clear indicators that the 'one-size fits all' approach can no longer be considered appropriate. Medical education, for example, believes that students should be allowed to pursue individualized learning while meeting standardized outcomes as this would assist in developing the student's ability to self-regulate their own learning, something considered crucial to staying current in an ever-changing field [22]. Since programming can be closely linked to the rapid pace at which technology evolves, it would stand to reason that cultivating a practice of remaining abreast of developments in the discipline would be quite beneficial.

Personality Models. Over the years, several personality models have been proposed to address the notion that individuals with differing characteristics are seen to learn and digest information differently [9,30]. Because personality traits are used to make pedagogical decisions [16], a system or human tasked with selecting appropriate teaching strategies to deliver content may benefit from having a better understanding of these personality models.

One of the most adopted models is the Five Factor Model of Personality Traits (FFM). The FFM is a framework made up of the dimensions of Agreeableness (likability and friendliness), Conscientiousness (ability to be dependable and always have the zeal to achieve), Emotional Stability, Extraversion (level of socialization with other students and activity), and Openness (imaginativeness, broadmindedness, and artistic sensibility) [29]. For the purpose of this paper, we will be considering the FFM to model our students' behaviors.

Teaching Strategies. Teaching strategies are methods of presenting content to students and are used to personalize learning experiences based on the students's preferred learning style [1]. While students have different learning preferences, it is difficult to discover factors that affect each student's preferred learning style [17]. Among teaching methods, the most common assumption is that students learn better if the instruction is provided in a format that matches the preferences of the student (e.g., for a 'visual learner', the appropriate strategy would be to emphasize on the visual presentation of information) [17].

As with personality models, several theories on learning styles exist, the most common of these following the theory of multiple intelligences [6], and the Visual, Auditory, Read, and Kinesthetic (VARK) Model [17]. These models classify students using different measures and designations, with some classifying the student according to modalities of learning and perceptual styles while others refer to cognitive style, personality type, and aptitudes [5].

Controversy. Although research reveals the existence of learning styles, others argue that this hypothesis has not been adequately and properly tested, citing the lack of sufficient scientific reports to support their rigor [5]. Despite this reservation, researchers argue that there is value in identifying appropriate teaching strategies rather than treating all students the same way [1,6].

As such, it would be beneficial to prepare content in different formats so that they can be presented to accommodate students with their various learning styles. The challenge then lies in ensuring that the most effective teaching strategy can be correctly identified. For ITSs, there will need to be some way in which personality traits can be correctly classified, and an appropriate teaching strategy selected. The next section will look at the components that make up an ITS to establish how the aforementioned tasks can be achieved.

2.2   Intelligent Tutoring Systems

Intelligent Tutoring Systems (ITS) are computerized learning systems that have the ability to personalize the learning experience of students [21]. Figure 1 depicts the traditional ITS model which comprises four components, namely: user interface, pedagogical model, student model, and knowledge base [21]. The arrows in Fig. 1 represent communication flow between the different components. The ITS components work together during the tutoring process as follows:

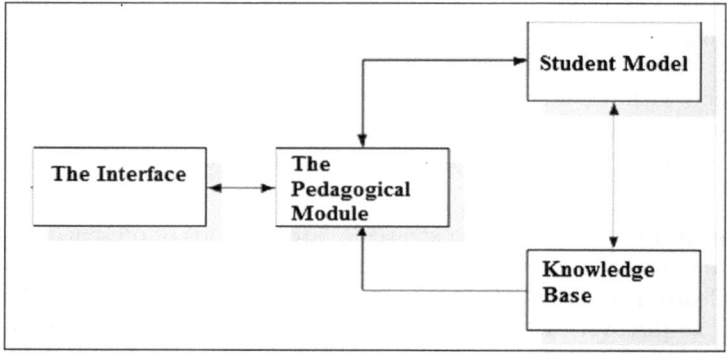

Fig. 1. Components of an ITS according to [10]

1. **User Interface:** The user interface is the main point of communication between the machine and the human user (in this case, the student). Interfaces may vary depending on the ITS implementation although most recent ITSs are conversational in nature and have dialog-based interfaces [25].
2. **Pedagogical Model (PM):** The PM is the reasoning component of the system, forming the decision-making component of the software. It is encoded with a rule interpreter to process and interpret rules [21]. Attempts to improve adaptability within an ITS will require that designers and developers focus on improving the decision-making strategies within this component.
3. **Knowledge Base (KB):** The KB contains the curriculum content and facts necessary for understanding, formulating and for solving problems [21].
4. **Student Model (SM):** The SM represents the student's emerging knowledge and skills. Information such as learning preferences, past learning experiences, and advancement may also be stored to help aid adaptability during the teaching process [21].

ITS implementations vary according to the relative level of intelligence of the components. For example, projects focusing on intelligence in the domain module may generate complex and novel problems while those with an emphasis on teaching strategies may concentrate on intelligence in student models, attempting to identify student characteristics, learning curves, and learning styles among other information.

Adaptability in ITSs generally occurs by tailoring feedback for each individual student to improve their learning experience [14]. This experience can be further enhanced by complementing the personalized feedback with adaptive pedagogical strategies. Such strategies will not only help students but will also ensure that knowledge accumulated by ITSs is accessible to educators.

The ability to achieve autonomy and adaptive pedagogical strategies is often accomplished through the use of Machine Learning (ML) techniques. Given the extensive possibilities and alternatives when it comes to classifying the personalities of students, coupled with identifying an appropriate teaching strategy, it would be challenging, if not possible, to ensure that all outcomes are correctly implemented and catered for. ML thus plays a significant role in the construction of an adaptive ITS that will discover the necessary knowledge that would otherwise take a human a long time to figure out [18]. The following sub-section investigates ways how ML can be applied to achieve adaptive pedagogy in ITSs.

2.3   Machine Learning for Intelligent Tutoring Systems

In essence, ML eliminates the need for explicit domain modeling [2]. Instead, the tasks of engineering the knowledge are automated as ML enables the ITS to learn autonomously from educational datasets. Examples of such systems include AutoTutor and ActiveMath [33].

Although existing ITS implementations have used ML for student modeling, content sequencing, and tailoring feedback [4], little work has been done to use ML to improve pedagogical decision-making. As ITSs operate, they accumulate data about different students and their learning preferences. The data accumulated by the ITS may be used to update the decision-making strategies of the ITS continuously. The ability to continuously train ITSs may be achieved through the use of ML techniques capable of learning over time, these techniques are known as incremental machine learning (IML) [20].

Common IML techniques include Naïve Bayes Classifier (NBC), K-Nearest Neighbor (KNN), and Incremental Support Vector Machines (ISVM). A study comparing these IML techniques for implementation in ITSs revealed that ISVMs perform excellently but at the cost of requiring a large amount of training data. KNN had a tendency to introduce bias which in its selection due to the algorithm's nature of always selecting the most frequent class. Ultimately, NBC was not only generally simpler to implement, but also outperformed its peers. For these reasons, NBC was considered for the implementation of our adaptive ITS.

3   An Adaptive Pedagogical Model for ITSs

This paper proposes an adaptive pedagogical model which uses past tutoring experiences to adjust future pedagogical decision-making strategies. Figure 2 shows the architecture of an ITS that incorporates the proposed model. The proposed model is based on the traditional ITS architecture described in Fig. 1. All basic four components (User interface, Student model, and Knowledge Base are included, however, to make the ITS adaptive some components were added. The proposed model adds a central component to facilitate tutorial dialogs and the expert model for evaluation of student performance during and after tutorial sessions. Feedback from the expert model is used as learning input by the APM. The APM itself is divided into components which are explained in sub-sections that follow below.

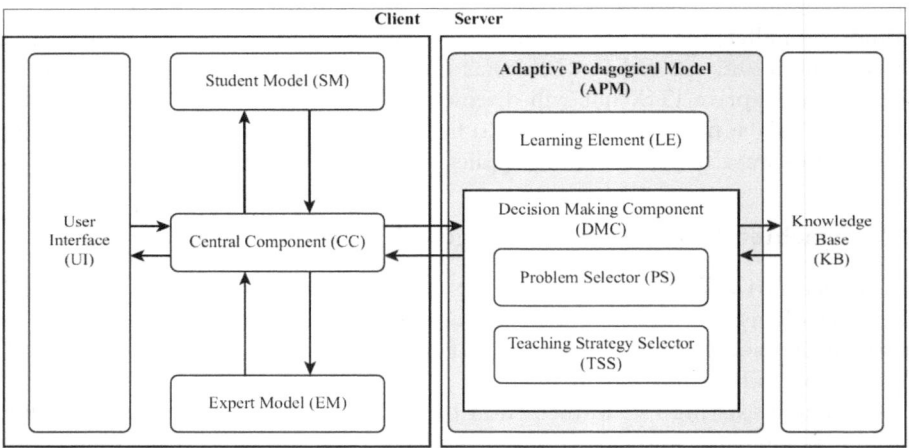

Fig. 2. The adaptive pedagogical model

The APM follows a horizontal approach rather than a longitudinal approach to achieve adaptability. This means that instead of tracking a single student's interaction history, the model records and utilizes the tutorial history of all students using the ITS.

All ITS instances (hosted separately on client devices) interact with a central server. The model uses a machine learning algorithm to parse and discover patterns in the information that is obtained. These observed patterns then become future decision-making policies for the ITS. As the ITS continues to offer tutorial sessions, each upcoming interaction output is then used to update the decision-making policies continuously.

The APM does not act independently but also depends on other ITS components such as the Knowledge Base and Student Model. In Figure 2 the arrows illustrate how information flows from component to computer during tutorial sessions. In the following sub-sections, the components that make up the APM, namely the Problem Selector, Teaching Strategy Selector, and Learning Element, are discussed.

3.1   Problem Selector (PS)

The PS is responsible for deciding on a problem to present to the ITS's student for solving. Ideally, the problem selected is one that is perceived to be neither too challenging to frustrate, nor too simple to bore the student. This decision is based on the Student Model, Problems, and a Selection Policy. Information from the Student Model includes personality traits and information relating to the student's current progress.

As information from tutorial interactions with students continue to flow in, a machine learning algorithm produces a selection policy and continuously improves upon it. The algorithm described below shows the steps and decisions made during the selection of the optimal problem:

Inputs. An array of features extracted from the student model which include:

- Current topic.
- List of questions that the student has already solved successfully.
- Personality dimensions: may assume values 'low'/'medium'/'high'.

Processing. Problem selection involves the following steps:

```
ACCEPT <- list of unsolved problems for the current topic.

FOR EACH problem in problems DO
    Compute pass probability(pPass) of given student model;
    Compute fail probability(pFail) of given student model;
    Calculate the difference between pPass and pFail;
END FOR

RETURN <- Optimal problem (one with the minimum difference
          between the probability of a pass and fail.
```

Output. The optimal problem to be tackled (the problem where the probability of a failure is almost the same as the probability of a pass, hence the problem is deemed as neither too challenging nor too simple).

After problem selection, the next task is to choose the optimal teaching strategy to help the student come to a solution. This process is handled by the Teaching Strategy Selector.

3.2   Teaching Strategy Selector (TSS)

The TSS determines the best teaching strategy for the problem based on the Student Model, selected problem, and selection policy. The goal of the TSS is to identify the appropriate learning style that is proven to be effective in improving the learning gains of the student based on their learning style and the current content that is being delivered. To accomplish this, the TSS makes use of Naïve Bayes to discover patterns in order to predict outcomes of given strategies prior to the delivery of the tutorial.

In this paper we combine the theory of multiple intelligences and VARK to derive teaching strategies. Choosing from these strategies depends on various factors that include the student's cognitive style, personality type, and aptitude. Information on these factors is obtained from the student model for the strategy selector to establish the appropriate strategy.

Inputs. An array of features from the student model include:

- Selected problem (output of the problem selector).
- Personality dimensions: may assume values 'low'/'medium'/'high'.

Processing. Teaching strategy selection involves the following steps:

```
ACCEPT <- list of teaching strategies applicable to the problem(P)
            at hand.
FOR EACH strategy in strategies DO
    Compute pass probability(pPass) of the strategy for P;
    Compute fail probability(pFail) of the strategy for P;
    IF pPass >= pFail THEN
        Calculate difference between pPass and pFail;
        Add strategy to candidate list (item with pass-likelihood);
    ELSE
        Ignore the strategy;
    END IF
END FOR

RETURN <- Optimal teaching strategy (one with the greatest
            difference between pPass and pFail) from candidate list.
```

Output. The optimal teaching strategy for the problem that was selected by the problem selector. Options of the output are either: visual strategy, auditory strategy, kinesthetic strategy, or read and write strategy.

3.3   Learning Element (LE)

The LE basically receives, extract values that are to be used by the Naïve Bayes algorithm during the process of problem and teaching strategy selection described above. Information is received after every tutorial session and the LE extracts the student's personality traits, the student's performance on the problem that was tackled, and the teaching strategy used to deliver content.

To achieve incremental machine learning through Naïve Bayes, the LE updates a frequency table that contains all statistical figures obtained from the LE overtime. During each update values are not converted to probabilities, conversion is done only when a decision has to be made (i.e., during problem and teaching strategy selection). Using such a strategy ensures that the Naïve Bayes always uses updated values as input and thus is adaptive.

In summary, the LE updates values that are used as inputs to the Naïve Bayes algorithms used by the PS and TSS, these updates are done after every tutorial session in order to achieve incremental learning.

4   A Conversational Adaptive Intelligent Tutoring System

To evaluate our proposed adaptive pedagogical model, we developed a prototype mobile conversational intelligent tutoring system (CITS) designed to introduce the programming concept of object-oriented programing (OOP) to Computer Science students.[1]

4.1   Architecture

The ITS is implemented on a client-server architecture. Students are thus able to interact with the system via different client applications that are all connected to a single central server.

The two main functionalities of the server are to store knowledge (curriculum content) and to record previous tutorial experiences which can then be used internally by the ITS to self-improve, and externally by human teachers to derive pertinent student information as observed by the ITS.

4.2   Client Application

The client application serves as the interface between the user (student) and the ITS. The client has an internal database (SQLite) which is used to maintain a Student Model and also store content that is currently being tutored for easy retrieval.

The client application works in tandem with a server maintaining the central database which handles the curriculum information, pedagogical strategies, and previous tutorial data.

Tutorials are presented in dialog format. The ITS initiates a conversation by presenting a problem and engaging the student in a conversation that helps the student to construct a solution. The dialog is also used as a diagnostic tool to measure the student's understanding of a particular concept. The conversation is driven by a six-step cycle which is discussed in the subsection below.

---

[1] The software is available for researchers upon e-mail request: wsleung@uj.ac.za.

As shown in Fig. 3, the main tutorial screen has a dialog section and an input bar. The dialog section displays the chat history as speech bubbles which show messages passed between student and ITS.

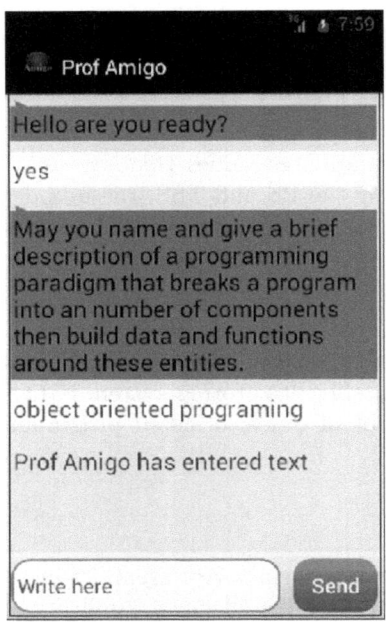

Fig. 3. Screenshot of tutorial conversation between student and ITS client

Since the conversation is in natural language, cosine similarity [28] is used to evaluate the student's inputs. The student's input text is represented as a vector which is compared with all possible responses known by the ITS. The text most similar to the student's input is then considered, ideally if the cosine of two given vectors is close to one then the two texts are considered similar while a value closer to zero denotes different texts.

As an example, the ITS contains a set of expected correct responses and wrong responses for each question. During a conversation, the student's response is compared with all expected responses and the response that is most similar to the student's input is considered. The subsection that follows discusses the speech constructs use to guide the conversation.

The Six-Step Tutorial Cycle. The ITS makes use of six speech constructs adopted from [13] to guide the conversation. The length of the conversation is dependent on the student's performance.

1. The Main Question is output by a Naïve Bayes algorithm and a decision tree. An optimal problem is selected based on previous tutorial experiences.

2. **A Hint** (short question) is presented to highlight a missing concept, given that a student's response is not satisfactory.
3. **A Pump** (question aimed at drawing more information from the student) is presented. For example: *"Do you want to add to your response?"*
4. **Prompts** (leading questions) are presented to the student to help to build an answer.
5. **Assertions** (detailed solutions) are given to the student after all conversation turns have revealed that the student is failing to solve the given problem.
6. **A Summary** (recapitulation of the problem and solution) might be presented by the ITS. In some cases the student provides the summary which is then used to evaluate the student's understanding.

The speech constructs of above form *conversation cycles* whereby each cycle begins with either the ITS's question or a question posed by the student. During the conversation, pumps are presented when there are missing concepts in the student's response. If the student fails to cover all essential concepts, an interior cycle of pumps, hints, prompts, and assertions is formed until the problem is fully solved before a summary is given.

After the ITS has given a summary of the tutorial, the student will be asked if there are any remaining questions about the problem that was just addressed. The cycle then starts again until the problem is solved. In cases where the ITS does not have a solution, an apology is displayed.

The APM uses a student's characteristics to make a prediction of performance to choose the optimal problem and teaching style to suit the characteristic set. These characteristics form part of the student model.

Student Model (SM). Student's characteristics that affect academic performance change as the student learns. In particular, factors that influence change include the frequency of interactions with the ITS, and the mood of the student.

SM variables include personality traits as derived from the FFM. The SM also keeps track of the student's progress, alongside the outcomes of each tutorial. Tracking progress eliminates the possibility of repeating problems. For decision making, the APM depends partly on information obtained from the SM. The SM is dynamically updated, based on feedback from the APM.

4.3 Central Server (CS)

The CS contains the APM and the Knowledge Base (KB). The KB contains the curriculum, teaching strategies, and historical information from previous tutorials. This information is used by the APM to make pedagogical decisions.

In the Knowledge Base, content is organized into topics. Each topic is made up of questions (problems) of varying levels of difficulty. Each question has one or more solutions and is made up of the concepts that the student needs to cover when answering the questions. For each question, there are hints, prompts, pumps, assertions and a summary. After each tutorial session, the student model and results of the interaction are saved in the KB. These values are used to compute frequency tables used by a Naïve Bayes Classifier.

As indicated previously, the information generated by the APM is meant for both internal (the APM itself) and external use. Potentially, teachers seeking to improve their teaching strategies and lesson plans could very well take advantage of the findings established by the APM in their own pedagogical decision-making.

4.4 Pedagogical Analytics for Teachers

Information generated by the ITS during operation may be analyzed by human teachers to improve their pedagogical decision-making. Examples in which the ITS's acquired knowledge can assist are discussed below. Table 1 shows a sample display of information on the percentage of success in using different teaching strategies to teach selected topics. Such information may help human teachers in selecting the most effective teaching strategies to deliver particular content.

Table 1. Sample Data: different teaching strategies to teach different problems

Topic	1st Strat.	2nd Strat.	3rd Strat.
Top. 1	60%	10%	30%
Top. 2	25%	75%	0%
Top. 3	98%	1%	1%
Top. 4	5%	45%	50%

Table 2. Information about students using the ITS

Student	Problems tried per day	Passed	Failed
Stud. 1	20	17	3
Stud. 2	5	0	5
Stud. 3	50	10	40

For example, as shown in Table 1, the first teaching strategy yields better results when used to teach Topic 3, whereas poor performance is obtained when the same strategy is used on Topic 4. Thus, a teacher can easily make an informed choice on which strategy to use when presenting these topics.

Another example of useful information which may be used by human teachers is shown in Table 2: it summarizes the performance of each student using the ITS. This information gives the teacher insights on their students, thus identifying potential at-risk students that require intervention. In our example, the information shows that Student 2 only attempted five problems for the day and failed all attempts. The teacher could seek out the student in question in an attempt to provide them with more personal (and human) attention.

5   Evaluation of the Adaptive Pedagogical Model

The ability to make appropriate pedagogical decisions is at the center of the Adaptive Pedagogical Model. Appropriate in this context is measured by the model's ability to recognize a teaching strategy that yields high academic performance when used to tutor a given problem to a specified student model.

Simulated student models were used during the testing phase where the preferences of each student model group (similar characteristics) were predefined. During simulation, the adaptive pedagogical model's performance is measured by its ability to identify a student model and match it with the appropriate problem and teaching strategy. Analyses from two different perspectives follow.

5.1   Pedagogical Decision-Making Patterns

Instances in which the APM was able to match a student model with the appropriate problem and corresponding teaching strategy are expressed as a percentage of all APM decisions made at selected points in time.

The results reveal inconsistencies in decision-making initially, as shown by the sharp edges at the beginning of the graph in Fig. 4. However, as time progresses, the graph is smoothing. This trend shows that the APM is learning over time and is thus able to make consistent decisions as shown by the gradual smooth increase in elevation after time 56.

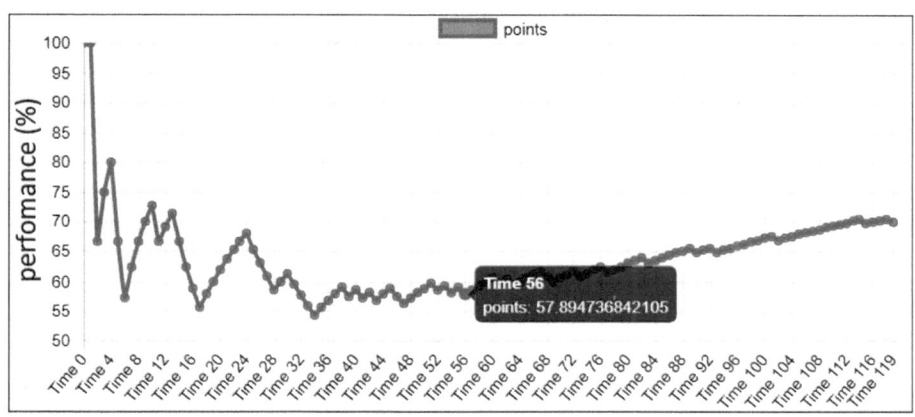

Fig. 4. Representation of past tutorial records based on prediction success statistics

Inconsistency in initial stages may be explained as due to the initial false data that the model was given to start the learning process. When exposed to the actual learning environment the model starts learning and pedagogical decisions made become consistent.

5.2   Teaching Strategy Selection Patterns

Monitoring the decisions made by the APM on choosing a strategy for a given problem for similar student models reveals that the APM is able to identify a strategy that performs well with each distinct group of student model.

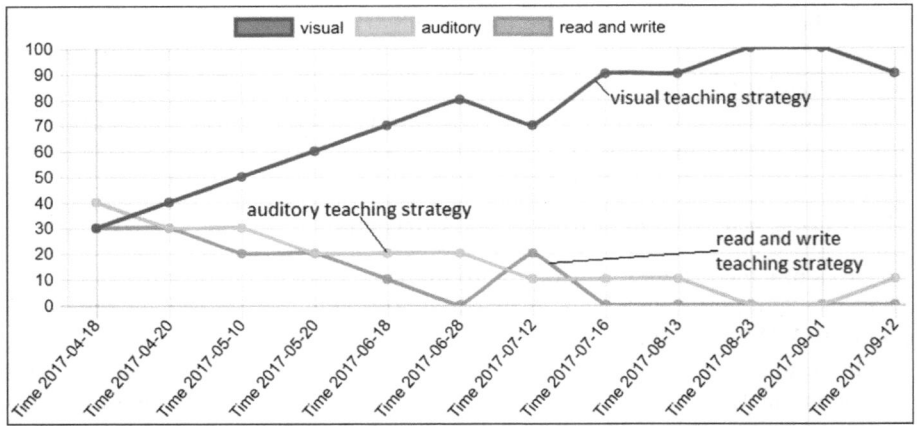

Fig. 5. Graphical representation of teaching strategy selection statistics over time

On identifying an optimal strategy, the APM continues to use the same strategy on students with similar characteristics. This trend can be seen in Fig. 5. As soon as the APM learns the best strategy, the graph of that strategy continues to rise. This rise is due to increases in the selection frequency of that strategy as compared to other strategies.

The two results reveal that patterns are emerging from the pedagogical decision-making data gathered. The results did reveal inconsistencies in decision-making initially. However, as time progressed, the graph smoothed, showing that the APM has managed to learn over time. On the other hand, focusing on the teaching strategy selection choices reveals that the APM can identify a strategy that performs well on a given student model as the APM then continues to use the same strategy on students with similar characteristics.

6   Conclusions

This paper presented the APM which is capable of identifying and adapting its teaching strategies to best suit their student. As proof of concept, an implementation of the APM in the form of a prototype conversation ITS that focused on teaching object-oriented programming principles was deployed for testing. By making use of the Naïve Bayes algorithm, the prototype successfully demonstrated its ability to classify the learning style model of the 'students' it interacted with, coming up with teaching strategies deemed appropriate for the identified learning style.

Such a system can be a useful tool in the programming classroom in the following ways: first, it can serve as a personalized tutoring companion to students, offering them one-on-one revision. Second, through its interactions with students, the ITS can provide human teachers with the necessary information regarding the learning styles of their students, enabling the teachers to make better-informed pedagogical decisions. Lastly, less-experienced programming teachers may also learn from the ITS's successes and failures.

References

1. Baine, D., Mwamwenda, T.: Education in southern Africa: current conditions and future directions. Int. Rev. Educ. **40**(2), 113–134 (1994)
2. Beck, J., Woolf, B.P., Beal, C.R.: ADVISOR: a machine learning architecture for intelligent tutor construction. In: Joint Proceedings of the 17th National Conference on Artificial Intelligence and 12th Conference on Innovative Applications of Artificial Intelligence, pp. 552–557 (2000)
3. Caputi, V., Garrido, A.: Student-oriented planning of e-learning contents for Moodle. J. Netw. Comput. Appl. **53**, 115–127 (2015)
4. Chrysafiadi, K., Virvou, M.: Student modeling approaches: a literature review for the last decade. Expert Syst. Appl. **40**(11), 4715–4729 (2013)
5. Cuevas, J.: Is learning styles-based instruction effective? a comprehensive analysis of recent research on learning styles. Theor. Res. Educ. **13**(3), 308–333 (2015)
6. Davis, K., Christodoulou, J., Seider, S., Gardner, H.: The theory of multiple intelligences. In: Cambridge Handbook of Intelligence, pp. 485–503 (2011)
7. Dorça, F.A., Lima, L.V., Fernandes, M.A., Lopes, C.R.: comparing strategies for modeling students learning styles through reinforcement learning in adaptive and intelligent educational systems: an experimental analysis. Expert Syst. Appl. **40**(6), 2092–2101 (2013)
8. Evens, M.W., et al.: CIRCSIM-Tutor: an intelligent tutoring system using natural language dialogue. In: Proceedings of 12th Midwest AI and Cognition Science Conference, pp. 16–23 (2001)
9. Felder, R.M., Silverman, L.K.: Learning and teaching styles in engineering education. Eng. Educ. **78**(7), 674–681 (1988)
10. Freedman, R.: What is an intelligent tutoring system? Intelligence **11**(3), 15–16 (2000)
11. Ghadirli, H.M., Rastgarpour, M.: A web-based adaptive and intelligent tutor by expert systems. In: Meghanathan, N., Nagamalai, D., Chaki, N. (eds.) Advances in Computing and Information Technology. Advances in Intelligent Systems and Computing, vol. 117, pp. 87–95. Springer, Heidelberg (2013). https://doi.org/10.1007/978-3-642-31552-7_10
12. Gomes, A., Mendes, A.J.: Learning to program – difficulties and solutions. In: ICEE 2007 Proceedings of the International Conference on Engineering Education, pp. 283–287 (2007)
13. Graesser, A.C.: Conversations with autotutor help students learn. Int. J. Artif. Intell. Educ. **26**(1), 124–132 (2016)
14. Gross, S., Mokbel, B., Hammer, B., Pinkwart, N.: Learning feedback in intelligent tutoring systems. Künstliche Intelligenz **29**(4), 413–418 (2015)

15. Kalelioğlu, F., Gülbahar, Y.: The effects of teaching programming via scratch on problem solving skills: a discussion from learners' perspective. Inf. Educ. **13**(1), 33–50 (2014)
16. Kim, J., Lee, A., Ryu, H.: Personality and its effects on learning performance: design guidelines for an adaptive e-learning system based on a user model. Int. J. Ind. Ergonomics **43**(5), 450–461 (2013)
17. Klement, M.: How do my students study? an analysis of students' of educational disciplines favorite learning styles according to VARK classification. Procedia Soc. Behav. Sci. **132**, 384–390 (2014)
18. Knight, W.: AI's language problem (2016). https://tinyurl.com/y7r9haju
19. Koorsse, M., Cilliers, C., Calitz, A.: Programming assistance tools to support the learning of IT programming in South African secondary schools. Comput. Educ. **82**, 162–178 (2015)
20. Kulkarni, P., Ade, R.: Prediction of student's performance based on incremental learning. Int. J. Comput. Appl. **99**(14), 10–16 (2014)
21. Latham, A.M., Crockett, K.A., McLean, D.A., Edmonds, B., O'Shea, K.: Oscar: An intelligent conversational agent tutor to estimate learning styles. In: FUZZ 2010 Proceedings of IEEE International Conference on Fuzzy Systems, pp. 1–8 (2010)
22. Lockspeiser, T.M., Kaul, P.: Using individualized learning plans to facilitate learner-centered teaching. J. Pediatr. Adolesc. Gynecol. **29**(3), 214–217 (2016)
23. Melis, E., Siekmann, J.: ACTIVEMATH: an intelligent tutoring system for mathematics. In: Rutkowski, L., Siekmann, J.H., Tadeusiewicz, R., Zadeh, L.A. (eds.) ICAISC 2004. LNCS (LNAI), vol. 3070, pp. 91–101. Springer, Heidelberg (2004). https://doi.org/10.1007/978-3-540-24844-6_12
24. Milne, I., Rowe, G.: Difficulties in learning and teaching programming – views of students and tutors. Educ. Inf. Technol. **7**(1), 55–66 (2002)
25. Padayachee, I.: Intelligent tutoring systems: architecture and characteristics. In: SACLA 2002 Proceedings of 32nd Annual Conference of the Southern African Computer Lecturers' Association (2002)
26. Partovi, H.: Should Computer Science Be A Mandatory Class In U.S. High Schools? (2017). https://tinyurl.com/yddfe2n7
27. Pashler, H., McDaniel, M., Rohrer, D., Bjork, R.: Learning styles: concepts and evidence. Psychol. Sci. Public Interest **9**(3), 106–119 (2008)
28. Perone, C.S.: Machine Learning: Cosine Similarity for Vector Space Models (Part III). Technical report (2013). http://blog.christianperone.com/2013/09/
29. Poropat, A.E.: A meta-analysis of the five-factor model of personality and academic performance. Psychol. Bull. **135**(2), 322–338 (2009)
30. Saucier, G., Goldberg, L.R.: The language of personality: lexical perspectives on the five-factor model. In: The Five-Factor Model of Personality: Theoretical Perspectives, pp. 21–50 (1996)
31. Schulze, K.G., Shelby, R.N., Treacy, D.J., Wintersgill, M.C., VanLehn, K.: Andes: an active learning, intelligent tutoring system for newtonian physics. Themes Educ. **1**(2), 115–136 (2000)
32. Sterling, L.: An education for the 21st century means teaching coding in schools (2015). https://tinyurl.com/ybuqoh56
33. Susarla, S.C., Adcock, A.B., van Eck, R.N., Moreno, K.N., Graesser, A.: Development and evaluation of a lesson authoring tool for AutoTutor. In: AIED 2003 Supplemental Proceedings, pp. 378–387, Sydney (2003)
34. Wan, S., Niu, Z.: A learner-oriented learning recommendation approach based on mixed concept mapping and immune algorithm. Knowl.-Based Syst. **103**(3), 28–40 (2016)

Interactive Learning of Factual Contents Using a Game-Like Quiz

Abejide Ade-Ibijola[1]([⊠]) and Kehinde Aruleba[2]

[1] Department of Applied Information Systems, University of Johannesburg,
Johannesburg, South Africa
abejideai@uj.ac.za
[2] School of Computer Science and Applied Mathematics,
University of the Witwatersrand, Johannesburg, South Africa
arulebak@gmail.com

Abstract. Computer games are widely recognised for the attention they get from their players. Beyond mere games are 'serious games' created to teach specific subjects or concepts. Arguably, two of the most addictive mechanisms in serious games are: the scoring design, and the game interface. These mechanisms have been proven to increase the interest of players in such games, balancing their learning experience with the fun. Quiz systems, by contrast, are mere educational tools with little or no interesting devices. In this paper we propose a new classification for some mid-point between serious games and quiz systems, suggesting an 'equilibrium' by adding some fun and keeping the educational content of quiz systems. We also describe the development of a new quiz system designed with Abeced. It is designed with game-like interactive feedback mechanisms for testing students on factual contents across different subjects. Abeced, mimicking most serious games, is designed with an interesting interface and a voice feedback to enhance students' learning experience. Students found Abeced very interesting because of its embedded game-like features.

Keywords: Game-like quiz · Serious games · Quiz systems · Abeced

1 Introduction

A game can be described as any form of activity that involves a set of rules or principles where the game players compete for a win using skills and knowledge in attempts to achieve a certain goal [30]. 'Serious' games are purposefully designed to *educate* the player on specific topics during game time [6,25]. These type of games have been reported to be successful in recent years [4], taking advantage of the game 'addiction' (or interest) [35] of students to disseminate educational content. They are used in teaching many topics with increasingly new designs for teaching.

The impact of this category of games cannot be overemphasised. However, creating games for learning is an expensive adventure [18] and, often, players tend

© Springer Nature Switzerland AG 2019
S. Kabanda et al. (Eds.): SACLA 2018, CCIS 963, pp. 285–298, 2019.
https://doi.org/10.1007/978-3-030-05813-5_19

to be carried away with the fun in such games and do not learn as much content as intended by the designers. A quiz system, by contrast, is a tool commonly used in education [31]. It has a different impact on the students. It can be used to measure the students' understanding about what they have learned, and also to measure the standard of what has been learned. A traditional quiz system is regarded as too boring and formal by many students [21]. Quizzes also have a 'fear factor', arousing the feeling of nervousness of writing formal examinations. This makes quizzes not often fun to take [24].

Perhaps it is a good idea to find a point 'between' serious games and quizzes where 'the best of both worlds' can be combined. Let us call this point the 'intersection' of game and quiz. This paper introduces the bridging of serious games with quizzes and also describes the development of a new game-like quiz system called **Abeced** that demonstrates this idea. **Abeced**, unlike a conventional quiz system, is enhanced with three major game-attributes, namely: a scoring design, an interactive graphical user interface (GUI), and voice feedback. The scoring design uses a fuzzy function that determines the percentage of similarity of the player's answer to the system's answer using the Levenshtein distance. Based on the similarity calculated, **Abeced** awards points to the player. The player's reward per answered question is thus not a Boolean score (right/wrong) but a percentage score between 0 and 100.

The following are the contributions of this paper. We

1. propose a new category for classifying game-like quiz systems,
2. suggest that quiz systems can be creatively designed using the proposed category, such as to give quizzes game-like features, and
3. present a new interactive quiz system that aids the learning of factual contents using the our category.

The remainder of this paper is structured as follows. Section 2 describes the background and related work. Section 3 presents the proposed category. Section 4 presents **Abeced** (the first quiz system designed with our category). Section 5 describes the implementation of **Abeced**. Section 6 presents the evaluation of the proposed system. Section 7 presents the conclusion and future work.

2   Background and Related Work

How 'serious' and how 'fun' is it to learn with a conventional learning system? The idea of making learning systems fun is not new [3]; it has given birth to a new research domain called 'serious games' [19,25,28]. Serious games can be virtual environments, simulations, digital games, or mixed reality (amongst others) that allow interactions among players through gameplay, influence, responsive narrative/story, and experience to convey meaning [22].

Recently, interest in serious games has increased. Serious games use the principle of solid game design with aim of entertaining, e.g. to train or educate [32]. In education, the aim of this type of game is in twofold: to be educational and to be entertaining. In this view, serious games are modelled to be appealing and attractive to students (players), with the purpose of meeting certain educational goals. The quality assessment of a serious game must thus take into account the 'educational' and 'fun' categories [4]. Since the aim of having a system that supports entertainment and learning is also the objective of serious games, one could say that serious games present some aspect of 'edutainment'. Micheal and Chen, however, opposed this, and suggested that there is more to serious games than merely edutainment [25]. The distinction made in [25] about the aim of a serious game is that it goes beyond conventional modes of teaching and learning; serious games thus differ from those of older edutainment media. Moreover, whereas edutainment is mostly designed for a specific target audience, i.e. school children, serious games can be played by 'any' audience.

According to most research done in the area of serious games and edutainment, edutainment games constitute a subset of serious games [15,27]. In this paper, the idea of serious games will be used to make quiz systems more 'fun'. A quiz system can be described as a type of mind sport or game wherein the players try to provide the right answer. In some countries such systems are seen as assessment tools for measuring the development of skills, abilities, and knowledge in educational sectors [33]. In this paper we move slightly away from serious games—w.r.t. entertainment—to a 'mid-point' between serious games and quiz systems, aiming at making quiz systems more fun.

A generic decomposition of games into aspects suggests that they have typically: a *story* (or writing), a *virtual world* (wherein the game takes place according to its rules), some *content* (what the game is about), *levels* (of difficulty), *scoring* (who gets what and how), a *system* (the software), and a *user-interface* (what the player sees) [8,16,23]. If quiz systems are to have features from any of the listed aspects, there cannot be a 'story' nor a 'virtual world'. However, a quiz must have content, the system (software), and a game-like user-interface. This paper proposes a new quiz called Abeced with a game-like scoring design and a user-interface and feedback system. Designing a quiz system this way for the purpose of making it more interesting is what we have classified as a new category.

Why is it important to make quiz systems fun? There are several sources that suggest that computer and video game addiction is real [36] and can be channeled into fun learning systems, especially ones based on games [3]. This idea can be extended to quiz systems as shown later in this paper; this will likely increase the interest of students in taking quizzes. There are a number of related papers on serious games and quiz systems. In [9] we can find a support system for learning and teaching medicine. There, a serious game is incorporated into numerous computing devices; the game is used for simulating cases in a hospital in order to assess students' knowledge. The system has gamification features used to motivate its users. Johnson (et al.) did an experiment about students who learn best with the 'Tactical Language and Culture Training System' (TLCTS) [17]. TLCTS is a user-friendly system that helps users to improve their spoken communication skills and aids the learning of foreign culture and language. This system is a type of serious game that brings together interactive lessons and game experience.

Pasin and Giroux designed a new simulation game and described its impact on operations management education [26], whereas Klopfer (et al.) proposed 'Brain Age 2': a handheld console game for teaching arithmetics [20]. Other serious games can be found in [5,29,37,38,40]. There are a number of television shows that are structured in an interactive manner, posting questions to players and giving rewards as well as feedback based on their performance. An example of such a TV shows is 'Who wants to be a Millionaire' [7]. Similarly, a number of electronic quizzes are available online.[1] This paper adopts ideas from *string matching* with the Levenshtein distance [2,14,34,39] and the Fisher-Yates shuffle algorithm [1].

The Levenshtein distance between two strings a, b is given by $L_{a,b}(|a|,|b|)$ where:

$$
L_{a,b}(p,q) = \begin{cases} max(p,q) & if\ min(p,q) = 0 \\ min \begin{cases} L_{a,b}(p-1,q)+1 \\ L_{a,b}(p,q-q)+1 \\ L_{a,b}(p-1,q-1)+1_{(a_p \neq b_p)} \end{cases} & \text{otherwise.} \end{cases}
$$

The indicator function is represented by $L_{(a_p \neq b_q)}$. It is equal to 0 when $a_p = b_q$, and equal to 1 otherwise. Deletion can be done by using the first element (from a to b); insertion is done by using the second, and match or mismatch is done by using the third.

The questions this paper addresses are:

1. *how can we make quiz systems interesting to users (or students) without necessarily turning such systems into serious games?*
2. *how do we classify systems that are neither games nor quiz systems?*

To answer these questions we propose a new game-quiz category that moves a step away from conventional quiz systems and a step closer to serious games, suggesting that there maybe possible gains from optimising the design of quiz systems for fun rather than student assessment.

3   The Game and Quiz System

The main contribution of this paper is the suggestion of a new category (i.e. the intersection of *game* and *quiz*) for the development of quiz systems. The proposed category suggests a 'paradigm shift' from the conventional way of designing quiz systems by adding interesting elements to their designs. By doing so, the systems can 'sit between' conventional quiz systems and serious games as illustrated in Fig. 1: the figure sketches the different categories of learning and game systems w.r.t. the fun and educational content in the design of such systems.

---

[1] http://www.addictinggames.com/.

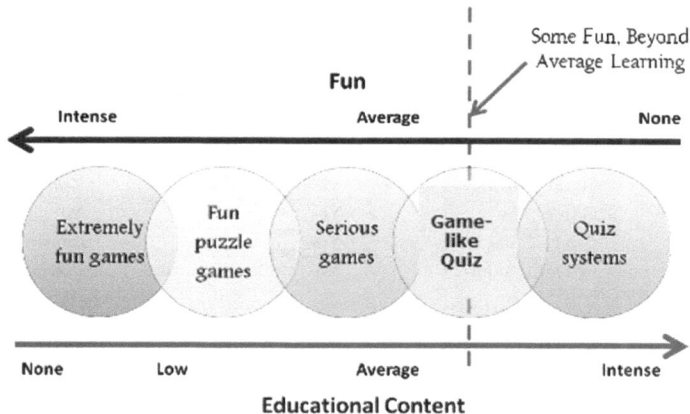

Fig. 1. Fitting game-quiz between serious games and quiz systems

Extremely fun games (leftmost in Fig. 1) have no educational content at all in their design but contain intense fun (or entertainment). An example of such a game is 'FIFA' by 'EA Sports' [10]. Fun puzzle games (such as chess [11]) have low educational content as they teach strategy and rules of play of the real-world game; serious games teach any embedded content and considerably have 'average content' and 'average fun'. Our proposed system is expected to have lesser fun compared to serious games, but should also provide more content, similar to quiz systems. Finally, quiz systems often exclude any fun with intense educational content. We proceed to define more terms for further reference.

In Table 1 we show the following:

- Background Story: a set of occurrences usually leading to the storyline. These stories are often presented to the gamers chronologically or otherwise, partially or in full, as the crucial story unfolds.
- Graphics: the 'look and feel' of the game.
- Gameplay: the activities game developers use to motivate and keep the players engaged to finish each level of the game and the game as a whole.
- Feedback: most games provide players with a good feedback on their results, style of play and actions. These help them to rate their abilities and performance and to think of how they can improve them.
- Learning Content: this is what is learnt by playing the game.

All in all, Table 1 shows what should be left out of (or put in) to the new system designs. It presents the exact definitions and proposals towards the design of our system w.r.t. game and educational features. If too many game features are included, then the system becomes a game; similarly, with too much formality it remains a quiz. As we are aiming for an intersection of game and educational features, we propose that our system should not contain game stories, gameplay, a 'formal' interface, nor Boolean marking. However, it should contain some graphics, many textures or sound, a game scoring engine, some goal

Table 1. Categories of game and quiz systems showing attributes of a game-like quiz

		Video game	Serious game	*Game-quiz*	Quiz
Game features	Background story	Yes	Yes	*No*	No
	Graphics (2D or 3D)	Yes	Yes	*Limited*	No
	Texture & sound feedback	Yes	Yes	*Extreme*	No
	Game scoring	Yes	Yes	*Yes*	No
	Game play	Yes	Yes	*No*	No
	Goal of play	Yes	Yes	*Limited*	No
Educational system features	Learning content	No	Limited	*Extreme*	Extreme
	Formal interface	Yes	No	*No*	Extreme
	Boolean marking	No	No	*NO*	Yes

of play (that reflects some performance metrics and inspires users to improve), and much learning content. The system is aimed at improving the fun in quiz systems; the first system developed as a prototype is described in the following section.

4   Abeced: The First Game-Quiz System

Abeced is a proof of concept to show the practicability of the newly proposed category. As discussed in the previous section, the proposed category excludes some features in games (such as stories and gameplay) and includes some quiz-level of seriousness beyond serious games. The design of Abeced is shown in Fig. 2. Abeced prompts the user for credentials (username and password), verifies the credentials from the database (i.e. user's table) at the back end. The user is then granted access to the quiz system and must select a category of the quiz to be taken; (quizzes are organised in categories in the pool or repository of questions and answers).

The user's chosen category is used in querying the quiz repository, and questions and answers are fetched from the repository based on the category's primary key (that distinguishes each category). The questions and answers are loaded into the quiz engine and are presented to the user one question at a time. The user supplies an answer which is then verified with the fuzzy scoring module. Based on the correctness of the answer the user is given a rich feedback via the system's engine. Next we explain Abeced's components, namely: fuzzy scoring design, content, and feedback design.

Fuzzy Scoring Design: Abeced uses a fuzzy scoring design that does not score a question 'correct' or 'wrong' (Boolean score), but compares the system's answer to the player's answer with the Levenshtein distance algorithms, thereby treating every response as a string response. The fuzzy set for scoring in Abeced is: $F(Score[0, 100]) = \{excellent, verygood, good, passed, failed\}$.

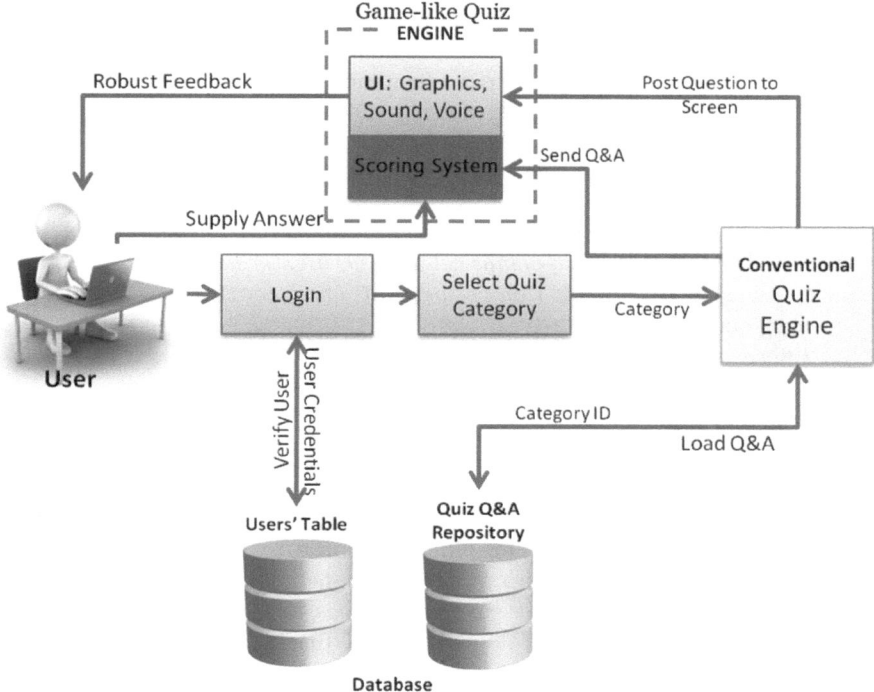

Fig. 2. Flow diagram for Abeced's design

Content Design: Abeced uses a predefined repository of factual contents structured as questions and answers, covering a wide range of subjects such as current affairs, history, art, and science. These Q&As are the challenges posed by the system, displayed to the user at real-time via the game-like interface. The players are prompted to enter the number of questions they want to attempt, and questions are randomly selected from the repository of Q&As using the Fisher-yates shuffle algorithm [13]. For each question displayed in turn, the user is further prompted to supply an answer which is verified against the stored templates.

Table 2. Graphical feedback to players with smileys

Double Thumbs Up	Single Thumbs up	Grin	Surprised	Tongue Out

Feedback Design: The feedback screen for `Abeced` is a quintuple, (I, F_c, R_c, V_c, R_t), where, I is the displayed smiley image; F_c is the font colour of the feedback, R is the inferred recommendation based on user's performance, V_c is the voice feedback, and R_t the user's overall rating. These sets are defined as follows:

1. I = {*"Double thumbs up"*, *"single thumb up"*, *"grin"*, *"surprise"*, *"tongue out"*}
2. F_c = {*"Blue"*, *"Green"*, *"Deep Pink"*, *"Magenta"*, *"Red"*}
3. R = {*"Excellent Performance! You've mastered this subject"*, *"Very Good Performance! You're getting used to this subject"*, *"Good Performance!*
   There are lots of misses though", *"Your performance is just OK! You missed too many facts"*, *"Poor Performance! You should go back and study more"*}
4. V_c = {*"Bravo!"*, *"Good job"*, *"Not so smart huh?"*, *"Mockery Laughter"*}
5. R_t = {*"Legend"*, *"Expert"*, *"Professional"*, *"Wannabe"*, *"Amateur"*}

The image feedback gives a graphical response to the users. As shown in Table 2, the double thumbs up maps to *excellent performance*, single thumb up to *very good*, grin to *good*, surprised to *passed* (the "just-made-it face"), and tongue out to *failed*. Colour-coded feedback (Fc): Depending on the player's performance, `Abeced` is designed to give a customised font-colour feedback. Colours range from Blue to Red and fade out as the user's performance decreases. Recommendation Feedback: `Abeced` also provides textual recommendations to users based on their performance. To excellent players it simply suggests that their performance is perfect; to extremely weak players it suggests that they study more. Voice Feedback: We have used Microsoft's Text-to-Speech library, usable with systems that can connect to the Microsoft Speech Server or API, to synthesise suitable wave sounds for `Abeced`'s main events. The produced wave sounds are played in the background after a user attempts the questions. The sound is either praising or mocking the user.

Fig. 3. `Abeced`'s quiz in progress

Overall User Rating: `Abeced` also rates players' performance on an overall scale. The users get overall feedback in the form of 'titles' based on how well they are playing withih the system. The highest title is 'Legend' (given to users whose overall points are 90% or above) and the lowest is 'Amateur' (for users with points less than 40%).

5   Implementation

We have implemented `Abeced` as a Windows Form Application using the .Net Framework libraries and other utilities (SQLite Databases, Telerik Controls [12]).

Figure 3 shows the `Abeced` game-quiz system at runtime where the user is asked the question *where a university is located*. The user attempted to answer with 'Johannesburg' but misspelled it.

The fuzzy scoring then computed the Levenshtein distance between the model answer and the user's answer, and returns a value. The returned value is used in scoring and providing a robust feedback to the user. In this example, the user scored 75 points (see Fig. 4) and received the feedback of *Very Good!* The correct answer was also displayed. Note that in spite of the wrong spelling the player was not given zero points, whereas in most quiz programs zero points would have been the result.

After the entire quiz, the player is provided with a comprehensive feedback as shown in Fig. 5. It summarises all activities of the player on the system. This includes individual quiz performance as well as all quiz attempts. A recommendation is also provided.

Figure 6 shows how a player can select a quiz category. In this example the player selected the 'general' category with 10 questions and clicked on the 'start' button.

Also note the TV screen and other fancy images displayed in this quiz. This is new in comparison with other quiz systems.

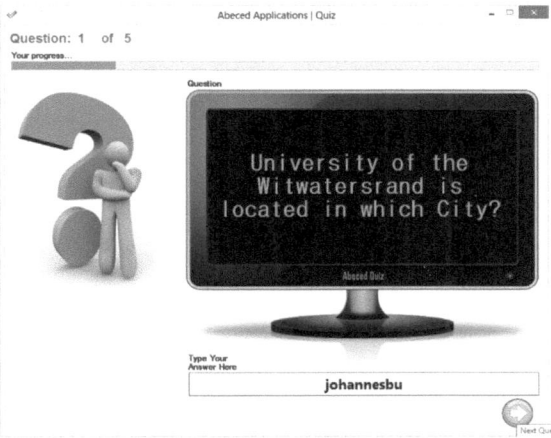

Fig. 4. `Abeced`'s interface showing feedback

6 Evaluation of the Game-Quiz System

Using Abeced as a prototype, we carried out an online survey at University of Johannesburg and the University of the Witwatersrand to determine human

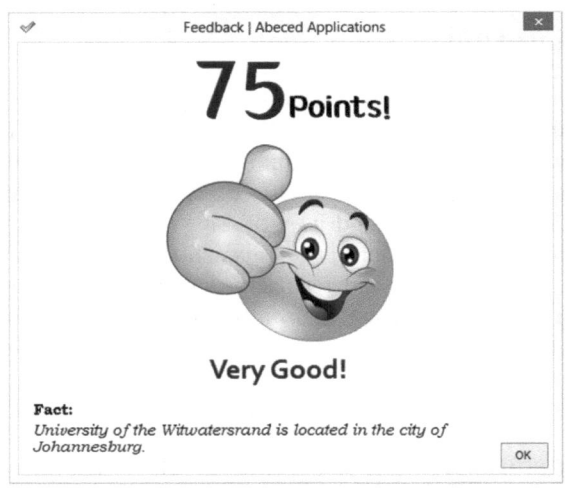

Fig. 5. Abeced showing comprehensive feedback

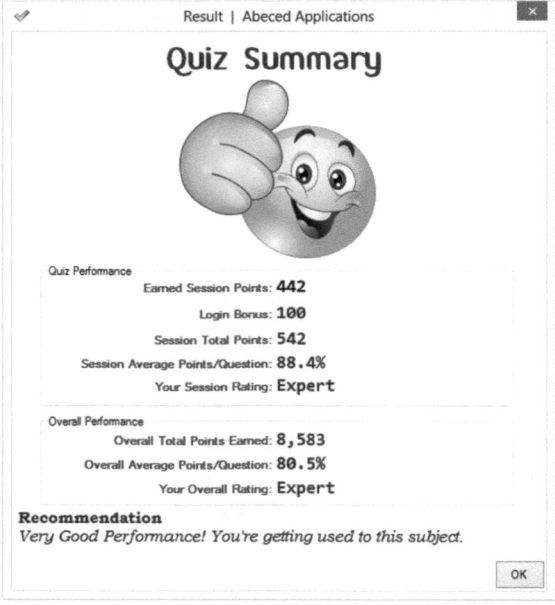

Fig. 6. Abeced game-quiz: category selection

perception about the system. The survey's respondents were mostly undergraduate students. Background information was requested on age range, gender, and degree programme registered for. In this section, we present the responses of these students. We also requested information about the opinion of the players of Abeced w.r.t. use-ability, and impact of the new 'paradigm'. The results of the survey are summarised in Fig. 7.

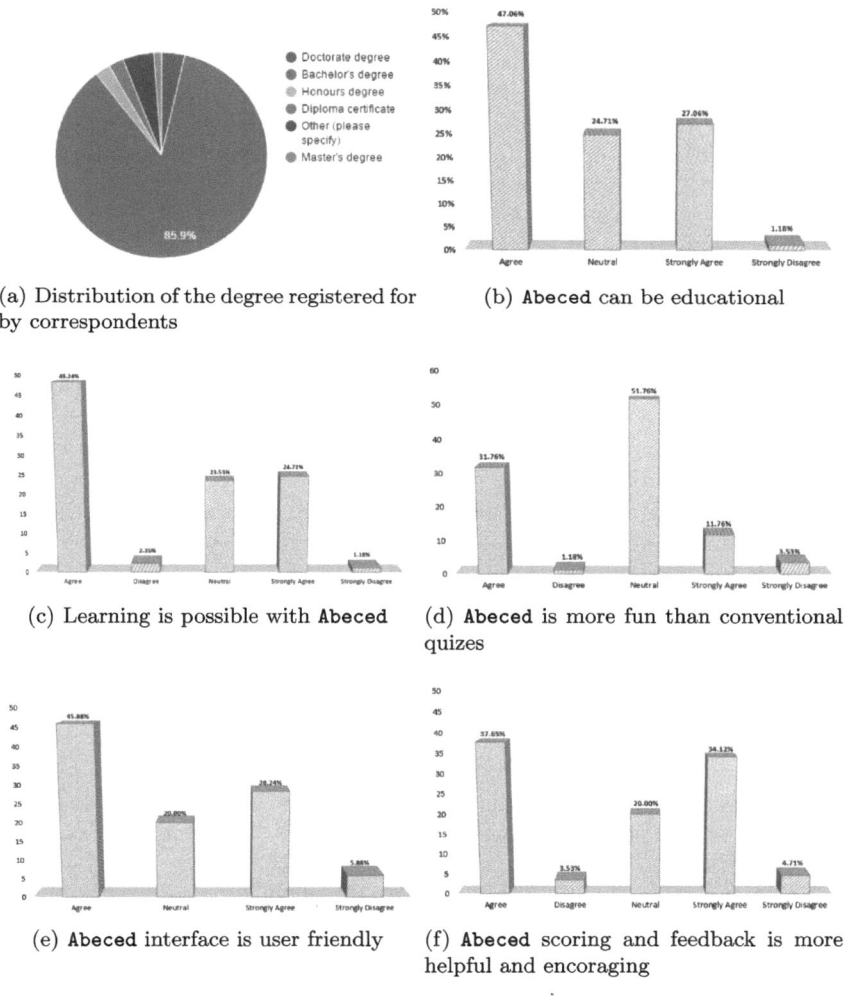

(a) Distribution of the degree registered for by correspondents

(b) Abeced can be educational

(c) Learning is possible with Abeced

(d) Abeced is more fun than conventional quizes

(e) Abeced interface is user friendly

(f) Abeced scoring and feedback is more helpful and encoraging

Fig. 7. Game-quiz system evaluation: survey results

Altogether we had 85 participants. 37.2% of these participants are between 17 and 20 years of age, and 46.5% between the age of 21 and 25. Participants less than 17 years old or older than 25 years were in the minority, in the range of 16.3% of the sample population. With 67.9% male respondents and 32.1% female, we re-confirm that 'gamers' are mostly male—as documented in many other papers. Our respondents are registered for one degree or another at one of the above-stated universities. 86% of our respondents are registered for a bachelor's degree; 4.7% are registered for a postgraduate degree (Masters or PhD's): see Fig. 7(a). Other candidates are registered for diplomas, or other degrees. Many respondents, about 61.6%, agreed clearly that the quiz was fun to fiddle with; 38.4% were 'neutral': see Fig. 7(b). 73.3% claimed that they could learn something from Abeced: see Fig. 7(c). With a comparative bias in mind, about 95.4% agreed (or stayed 'neutral') that Abeced is 'more fun' than a conventional quiz system: see Fig. 7(d). 74.4% agreed that the interface of Abeced is more user-friendly, with even 19.8% staying neutral: see Fig. 7(e). Abeced's scoring/feedback was regarded as 'more helpful' by 72.1% of our respondents, indicating that the scoring of the new system worked well as intended: see Fig. 7(f).

7   Conclusion and Future Work

In this paper we proposed a 'paradigm-shift' from designing conventionally 'boring' quiz systems to highly interactive quiz systems with game-like features. We have also specified precisely how much 'fun' and how much 'content' our game-quiz system includes. Furthermore, we have designed and implemented the first prototype, (Abeced, of this category. Abeced is not merely one test case, but more broadly a 'proof of concept' for the newly proposed game-quiz category. With an online survey of players' experience with Abeced we inferred that learning is possible with Abeced, and also more fun. In future we hope to investigate other applications of the game-quiz with different factual contents.

Acknowledgement. Thanks to Edward J. Nicol Bell who supported the development of Abeced.

References

1. Ade-Ibijola, A.: A simulated enhancement of Fisher-Yates algorithm for shuffling in virtual card games using domain-specific data structures. Int. J. Comput. Appl. **54**(11), 24–28 (2012)
2. Backurs, A., Indyk, P.: Edit distance cannot be computed in strongly subquadratic time (unless SETH is false). In: Proceedings of 47th Annual ACM Symposium on Theory of Computing, pp. 51–58 (2015)
3. Barab, S., Thomas, M., Dodge, T., Carteaux, R., Tuzun, H.: Making learning fun: Quest Atlantis, a game without guns. Education Tech. Research Dev. **53**(1), 86–107 (2005)
4. Bellotti, F., Kapralos, B., Lee, K., Moreno-Ger, P., Berta, R.: Assessment in and of serious games: an overview. In: Proceedings of Advances in Human-Computer Interaction (2013)
5. Bergeron, B.: Developing serious games (2006)

6. Connolly, T.M., Boyle, E.A., MacArthur, E., Hainey, T., Boyle, J.M.: A systematic literature review of empirical evidence on computer games and serious games. Comput. Educ. **59**(2), 661–686 (2012)
7. Deavor, J.P.: Who wants to be a (chemical) millionaire? J. Chem. Educ. **78**(4), 467 (2001)
8. de Leeuw, K.E., Mayer, R.E.: Cognitive consequences of making computer-based learning activities more game-like. Comput. Hum. Behav. **27**(5), 2011–2016 (2011)
9. de Lima, R.M., et al.: A 3D serious game for medical students training in clinical cases. In: Proceedings of IEEE International Conference on Serious Games and Applications for Health, SeGAH 2016, pp. 1–9 (2016)
10. EA Sports: FIFA (2018). https://www.easports.com/fifa
11. Gobet, F., Campitelli, G.: Educational benefits of chess instruction: a critical review. In: Proceedings of Chess and Education: Selected Essays from the Koltanowski Conference, Dallas, pp. 124–143 (2006)
12. Guay-Paz, J.R.: Introducing ASP.NET and Telerik. In: Guay-Paz, J.R. (ed.) Pro Telerik ASP.NET and Silverlight Controls, pp. 1–14. Apress, New York (2010). https://doi.org/10.1007/978-1-4302-2941-4_1
13. Hazra, T.K., Bhattacharyya, S.: Image encryption by blockwise pixel shuffling using modified Fisher Yates shuffle and pseudorandom permutations. In: Proceedings of 7th Annual IEEE Information Technology ,Electronics and Mobile Communication Conference, pp. 1–6 (2016)
14. Heeringa, W.J.: Measuring dialect pronunciation differences using Levenshtein distance. Doctoral dissertation (2004)
15. Jarvin, L.: Edutainment, games, and the future of education in a digital world. New Dir. Child Adolesc. Dev. **147**, 33–40 (2015)
16. Johnson, C.I., Mayer, R.E.: Applying the self-explanation principle to multimedia learning in a computer-based game-like environment. Comput. Hum. Behav. **26**(6), 1246–1252 (2010)
17. Johnson, W.L., Wu, S.: Assessing aptitude for learning with a serious game for foreign language and culture. In: Woolf, B.P., Aïmeur, E., Nkambou, R., Lajoie, S. (eds.) ITS 2008. LNCS, vol. 5091, pp. 520–529. Springer, Heidelberg (2008). https://doi.org/10.1007/978-3-540-69132-7_55
18. Ju, E., Wagner, C.: Personal computer adventure games: their structure, principles, and applicability for training. ACM SIGMIS Database **28**(2), 78–92 (1997)
19. Kim, B., Park, H., Baek, Y.: Not just fun, but serious strategies: using metacognitive strategies in game-based learning. Comput. Educ. **52**(4), 800–810 (2009)
20. Klopfer, E., Osterweil, S., Salen, K.: Moving learning games forward. The Education Arcade (2009)
21. Lightfoot, J.M.: Integrating emerging technologies into traditional classrooms: a pedagogic approach. Int. J. Instr. Media **32**(3), 209 (2005)
22. Marsh, T.: Serious games continuum: between games for purpose and experiential environments for purpose. Entertain. Comput. **2**(2), 61–68 (2011)
23. Mayer, R.E., Johnson, C.I.: Adding instructional features that promote learning in a game-like environment. J. Educ. Comput. Res. **42**(3), 241–265 (2010)
24. McDaniel, M.A., Anderson, J.L., Derbish, M.H., Morrisette, N.: Testing the testing effect in the classroom. Eur. J. Cogn. Psychol. **19**(4/5), 494–513 (2007)
25. Michael, D.R., Chen, S.L.: Serious Games: Games that Educate, Train, and Inform. Muska & Lipman, Cincinnati (2005)
26. Pasin, F., Giroux, H.: The impact of a simulation game on operations management education. Comput. Educ. **57**(1), 1240–1254 (2011)

27. Ratan, R., Ritterfeld, U.: Classifying serious games. In: [28], pp. 10–24 (2009)
28. Ritterfeld, U., Cody, M., Vorderer, P. (eds.): Serious Games: Mechanisms and Effects. Routledge, Abingdon (2009)
29. Rosenfeld, A., Ade-Ibijola, A., Ewert, S.: Regex parser II: teaching regular expression fundamentals via educational gaming. In: Liebenberg, J., Gruner, S. (eds.) SACLA 2017. CCIS, vol. 730, pp. 99–112. Springer, Cham (2017). https://doi.org/10.1007/978-3-319-69670-6_7
30. Rowles, C.: Strategies to promote critical thinking and active learning. In: Teaching in Nursing: A Guide for Faculty, 4th edn. Elsevier (2012)
31. Saga, M., et al.: Development of a multiple user quiz system on a shared display. In: Proceedings of 7th IEEE International Conference on Creating, Connecting and Collaborating Through Computing, C5 2009, pp. 103–110 (2009)
32. Sagae, A., Johnson, W.L., Row, R.: Serious game environments for language and culture education. In: Proceedings of NAACL HLT 2010 Demonstration Session, pp. 29–32. Association for Computational Linguistics (2010)
33. Tinoco, L.C., Fox, E., Ehrich, R., Fuks, H.: QUIZIT: an interactive quiz system for www-based instruction. In: Proceedings of VII Brazilian Symposium of Informatics in Education, pp. 365–378 (1996)
34. van der Loo, M.P.: The stringdist package for approximate string matching. R J. **6**(1), 111–122 (2014)
35. van Rooij, A.J., Schoenmakers, T.M., Vermulst, A.A., van den Eijnden, R.J., van de Mheen, D.: Online video game addiction: identification of addicted adolescent gamers. Addiction **106**(1), 205–212 (2011)
36. Wan, C.S., Chiou, W.B.: Why are adolescents addicted to online gaming? An interview study in Taiwan. CyberPsychol. Behav. **9**(6), 762–766 (2006)
37. Wang, Q., Sourina, O., Nguyen, M.K.: EEG-based 'serious' games design for medical applications. In: Proceedings of IEEE International Conference on Cyberworlds, pp. 270–276 (2010)
38. Westera, W., Nadolski, R., Hummel, H.G., Wopereis, I.G.: Serious games for higher education: a framework for reducing design complexity. J. Comput. Assist. Learn. **24**(5), 420–432 (2008)
39. Yujian, L., Bo, L.: A normalized Levenshtein distance metric. IEEE Trans. Pattern Anal. Mach. Intell. **29**(6), 1091–1095 (2007)
40. Zyda, M.: From visual simulation to virtual reality to games. Computer **38**(9), 25–32 (2005)

Lecturers' Perceptions of Virtual Reality as a Teaching and Learning Platform

Zhane Solomon, Nurudeen Ajayi, Rushil Raghavjee[✉],
and Patrick Ndayizigamiye

Department of Information Systems and Technology,
University of Kwa Zulu Natal, Pietermaritzburg, South Africa
raghavjee@ukzn.ac.za

Abstract. Virtual Reality (VR) is increasingly being acknowledged as a useful platform for education. In South Africa, however, VR is mainly recognized as an entertainment platform. Hence, the potential benefits of VR and its perceived ease of use within the South African higher education setting have not been widely investigated. Therefore, using the Technology Adoption Model (TAM), this paper investigates the perceived usefulness (PU) and ease of use (PEOU) of VR by lecturers. This paper also identifies the perceived challenges to the adoption of VR as a teaching and learning platform from a higher education perspective, and suggests how those challenges may be overcome.

Keywords: Virtual Reality · Higher education · Lecturers

1 Introduction

Education is vital for social, political and economic development of any nation. Therefore, effective teaching is essential and should be based on assisting students to advance from one knowledge level to another [26]. The evolution of technology has created interactive environments for education that now include immersive and interactive three dimensional (3D) learning platforms that are recognized as Virtual Reality [12]. According to [5], Virtual Reality (VR) may be defined as the collection of technological hardware and software that aid in the creation of immersive environments. The VR immersive environment is experienced through devices and components such as computers, head-mounted displays, headphones, and motion sensing gloves [26]. VR is increasingly being recognized as a useful platform for education [36]. VR draws on the strengths of visual representations and provides an alternative method for presenting of course-related content that could enhance teaching and learning. VR caters for students with different learning styles and hence, enhances teaching and learning [30].

South Africa (SA) has recently joined the VR revolution. Therefore, some organizations in SA are competing extensively to be recognized in the VR international market [27]. According to [27], these SA organizations produce VR

S. Kabanda et al. (Eds.): SACLA 2018, CCIS 963, pp. 299–312, 2019.
https://doi.org/10.1007/978-3-030-05813-5_20

devices for use and adoption in fashion and entertainment such as music and gaming. However, VR adoption in SA educational institutions is slow and stagnating according to [28] and research pertaining to the adoption of VR in South African higher institutions is very scarce. This paper attempts, to a limited extent, to address the research gap posed by the scanty literature on VR adoption in South African higher education. It specifically seeks to establish the perceived usefulness and ease of use of VR and the challenges to its adoption from lecturers' perspective.

2   Related Work

The applications of VR in education include, but are not limited to, the use of VR for simulation-based education in the fields of engineering, physical science, and medicine, the use of VR to assist students with disabilities, and the use of VR in gaming [21].

2.1   VR for Simulation-Based Education: Engineering and Physical Science

VR use for simulation-based education in engineering and physical science allows students to utilize equipment and machinery safely for experimental, practical and self-study projects [1,44]. According to [37], Tecnomatix Jack, RAMSIS Automotive, DELMIA Ergonomics Task Definition, SAMMIE, and Santos Human, are some of the VR systems that are used to develop prototypes in the field of engineering. These VR systems assist students in areas such as the automotive industry with the retention of information pertaining to automotive techniques [37]. Similarly, a virtual environment created by the University of Westminster for students of criminal law allowed them to hunt for clues to construct a murder case [19]. In this virtual environment, students can walk around a building and identify the type of crime committed instead of reading witness statements. Students' information retention increased because of the practical exposure in the simulated crime scene [19]. However, another study concluded that not all students are able to retain information obtained from the relevant virtual environment [43].

2.2   VR for Simulation-Based Education: Medicine

VR is utilized in medicine to train students to become nurses, doctors and or surgeons by creating a safe environment where students can practice medical procedures [2]. According to [29], in the VR environment, medical students can safely make errors; they can also gain feedback and standardized experience. A VR system, *Anatomic VisualizeR*, was developed at the University of California for medical students [17]. This VR system contains several 3D anatomic models and allows students to virtually dissect the models. A similar virtual anatomy project, 3D Human Atlas, was developed in Japan to assess students' understanding of the human anatomy [16]. According to [35], VR systems that are based on anatomy allow students to gain experience and feedback. Similarly, VR enhances medical education by standardizing training and providing students with the opportunity to repeat tasks until competency is reached [34].

2.3   VR for Assisting Students with Disabilities

People with disabilities often display limited or no skills necessary for independent living, improving cognition, and practicing social skills [3]. Studies exploring virtual environments as an aid to the acquisition of skills to support people with disabilities have looked at the aspects of grocery shopping, food preparation, orientation, crossing the road, and vocational training [40]. The following paragraphs will focus on the use of VR to assist students who have physical and/or intellectual disabilities.

Physical Disabilities. VR environments developed for people with physical disabilities enable them to develop their navigational skills [9]. For example, a virtual environment that simulates a busy street or shopping center may be used to prepare the physically disabled for a real-life setting. Similarly, physically disabled students can gain knowledge from the virtual environment on how to move around and avoid obstacles in the virtual setting before putting the knowledge into practice in the real world [39]. Food preparation is another aspect looked at to assist with the development of skills. The virtual environment described by [6] was used to teach food preparation to physically disabled students. This environment was based on an actual kitchen setting in which half of the participants were already undergoing a college training course for catering. Students showed significant improvement on the tasks they had learned in the virtual kitchen as compared to the real kitchen environment. However, [41] found no difference in improving learning between virtual and real training environments.

Intellectual Disabilities. Intellectual disabilities consist of learning and cognitive disabilities [40]. The use of VR for autism, a type of learning disability, allows autistic students to be taught road safety [31]. Both [32] and [33] suggest that there is a need to utilise virtual environments for social skills training for autistic students. Students can use the virtual environments to learn rules and basic skills which could be practiced frequently before entering a real-life setting. A VR environment called *The Virtual City* includes a procedure to teach autistic students how to use a pedestrian crossing and how to safely board a bus [11]. An evaluation of the use of VR environments for autistic students specifically showed some transfer of learning from the virtual environment to the real world [40]. VR also assists students with dyslexia, a cognitive disability [23]. Students who are dyslexic have trouble solving problems, writing and communicating [23]. VR aids in the development of virtual environments for dyslexic students, which mainly consist of visual interfaces and related sounds to enable the students to interact with virtual objects [40]. Due to the interaction with virtual objects, dyslexic students have shown improvement in their cognitive abilities [7]. However, [15] found that dyslexic students experience several challenges associated with using the VR environments including information overload if too many objects are shown simultaneously, and imperfect word processing, that is difficultly in recognizing words with similar sounds.

2.4   VR in Educational Games

Generally, VR is used for entertainment purposes such as gaming. However, a study conducted by [20] stipulated that VR in gaming is now being used for educational purposes. A VR game for safety education enhances safe training and education by allowing students to operate hazardous equipment such as a pedestal grinder in the virtual environment. The VR game was adopted to enable students to learn to control and prevent occupational injuries and illnesses caused by improper machine handling [20, 38]. Another game that is used in education is *The Battle of Thermopylae*, which is a virtual gaming environment that aims to portray the historical context and importance of the battle, the warfare strategy of the battle opponents, their cultural differences and the strategic choices they made [10]. *The Siege of Syracuse* is a similar game and is used to educate students about historical events [25]. Similarly, *Heritage Key* is a VR game that also recreates history to educate students about the past, historical monuments, artefacts and archaeological discoveries [8].

Summary of Related Work. As shown in Table 1, most related work focuses on VR adoption for simulation-based education and assisting students with disabilities in various settings. However, none of the reviewed literature specifically investigates the determinants of VR adoption from a South African perspective using a theoretical framework. Thus, this project addresses this gap by investigating factors that may influence the adoption of VR by South African tertiary education using TAM as the theoretical framework.

Table 1. Summary of related work

Literature	Application context	Setting/country
[1, 37, 43, 44]	Simulation-based education: engineering and physical science	Ecuador, Germany, Malaysia, Taiwan, UK
[2, 16, 17, 19, 29, 35]	Simulation-based education: medicine and other disciplines	Japan, Malaysia, Poland, UK, USA
[3, 6, 7, 9, 11, 15, 23, 32, 33, 39, 40]	Assisting students with disabilities (physical and intellectual)	UK, USA
[8, 10, 20, 25, 38]	Educational games	Australia, Greece Japan, UK, USA

3 Theoretical Framework: The Technology Acceptance Model (TAM)

TAM indicates that there are two constructs that influence acceptance and use of a technology [13]. These are Perceived usefulness (PU) and Perceived ease-of-use (PEOU). The former is defined as the extent to which a person believes that a new technology will assist in performing his/her duties better compared to an existing technology. The latter is defined as a person's perception of the required effort to use a new technology. A qualitative study investigated the adoption of a Virtual Reality simulation to train nursing students to use a crash trolley during a medical emergency [14]. Findings revealed that perceived ease of use and usefulness of Virtual Reality are important factors that need to be considered for the adoption of Virtual Reality as a teaching platform. In addition, the study found that perceived innovativeness of Virtual Reality significantly influences the behavioural intention to use the Virtual Reality platform. On the other hand, [18] explored students' acceptance of Virtual Reality in medical education and found that immersion and imagination features embedded within VR applications have an impact on the perceived ease of use and usefulness of VR. Amongst five factors that were investigated in [4]—perceived usefulness, attitude, perceived cost and perceived ease of use—perceived usefulness was the only factor that significantly predicted healthcare professionals' use of Virtual Reality as a therapeutic tool. On the other hand it was found that perceived ease of use did not influence students' intention to use virtual world of Second Life (SL) to learn a chemistry concept [24].

4 Research Method

For this study we used the *exploratory design approach* to investigate lecturers' perceptions about the adoption of VR for teaching and learning. The *purposive sampling technique* was used, too. Data was collected from a sample of 21 lecturers from the discipline of Information Systems and Technology at the University of KwaZulu-Natal (UKZN). A qualitative approach was used to gain an in-depth understanding of the lecturers' perceptions about the adoption of VR as a teaching and learning platform at our university. The aim was to conduct semi-structured interviews with those 21 lecturers. However, data saturation was reached already after 10 lecturers were interviewed. Hence, we collected data from those 10 lecturers. Interviews were conducted in English and voice-recorded with the participants' permission. The recorded interviews were transcribed using Microsoft Word software. The transcribed texts were then analysed with the aid of the 'Nvivo' (version 22) data analysis tool. To this end, each transcribed text was loaded onto Nvivo and then analysed (content analysis) by grouping each participant's responses into three categories also called 'super themes'. These three categories or super themes represented the three constructs on which this project is anchored, that is: perceived usefulness, perceived ease of use and perceived obstacles to the adoption of Virtual Reality for teaching

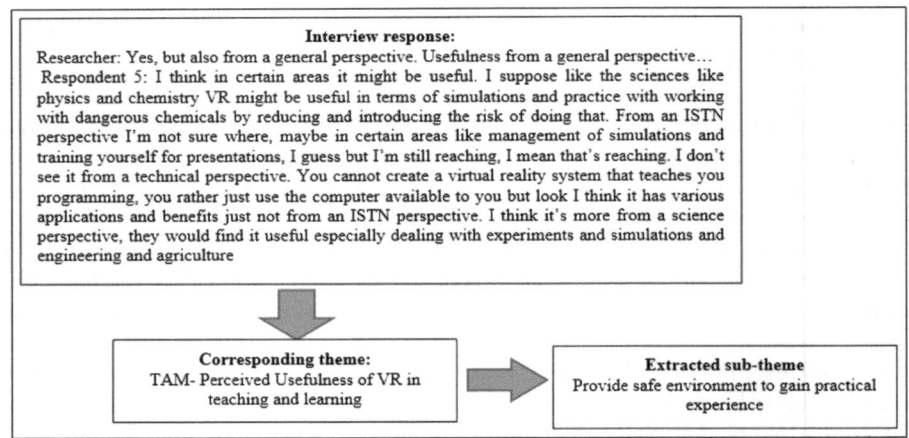

Fig. 1. Data analysis process

and learning. The participants' responses then became the sub-themes and were coded to the corresponding super-themes. The coding process entailed assigning each relevant text to a relevant theme and subsequently linking the theme to the corresponding super-theme. Figure 1 shows the data analysis process using an excerpt of an interviewee's responses.

5   Findings and Discussion

5.1   Demographics of Participants

Table 2 shows that an equal number of lecturers from two campuses (Westville and Pietermaritzburg) of our university were interviewed. Most of the interviewees had the rank of a 'lecturer'.[1] In addition, two professors and two senior lecturers were interviewed. All interviewees were employed in the discipline of Information Systems and Technology in the School of Management, IT and Governance.

5.2   Perceived Usefulness of VR for Teaching and Learning

Specific Disciplines Where VR is Most Appropriate. Most participants stated the disciplines that VR would be most relevant as far as teaching and learning are concerned. These include disciplines whereby safety is of the utmost importance. Participant 5 stated: *"In certain areas it might be useful, like in the sciences, physics and chemistry. VR might be useful in terms of the simulations. It also serves as practice for the students to work with the dangerous chemicals".*

---

[1] Academic ranks in South Africa: 'junior lecturer', 'lecturer', 'senior lecturer', 'associate professor', '(full) professor'.

Table 2. Demographics of respondents

Respondent no.	Designation	Campus
1	Senior lecturer	Pietermaritzburg
2	Lecturer	Pietermaritzburg
3	Professor	Westville
4	Lecturer	Westville
5	Lecturer	Westville
6	Lecturer	Westville
7	Senior lecturer	Westville
8	Lecturer	Pietermaritzburg
9	Lecturer	Pietermaritzburg
10	Professor	Pietermaritzburg

The same participant further elaborated: *"This is because VR reduces the risk of danger in the simulated environment and it teaches students how work with the dangerous chemicals in a real-life situations"*. In the context of medical practice, [2] noted that VR is utilised in medicine to train students to become medical professionals by creating a safe environment where they can practice medical procedures and experience safe exposure to dangerous chemicals. Similarly, [29] stated that in the simulated VR environment, medical students can 'safely' make errors, then gain feedback that can enhance their practice.

Moreover, participant 5 stated that VR simulations can be used to assist biology students to learn about the human anatomy by providing them with an immersive learning environment in which they can experience the course content and gain feedback from their mistakes. Similarly, [35] noted that VR systems based on human anatomy allow students to gain experience and feedback. Some participants felt that VR in the IT discipline could be used to teach abstract concepts such as programming. By contrast, participant 10 did not agree to the adoption of VR in the IT discipline: *"It would not be successful from an IT perspective"*. This participant uses a combination of tutorial and practical sessions to teach course-related content. During the practical sessions, students are required to interact with a computer to complete a task. Hence, the participant believed that VR in the IT discipline would not be useful for modules that are already taught using a computer-based interactive environment.

Some of the participants (3, 4, 5, 7, 8) stated that VR could be used to study law in a courtroom simulation. Likewise, [19] had noted that students' practical exposure to a simulated crime scene or legal environment, such as courtrooms, allow them to retain more information as compared to a non-simulated environment. For example, a simulated environment such as a murder scene allows students to conduct an investigation of the type of murder weapon used, the victim, and other aspects of the crime. This promotes interest for the course and allows students to retain more information for a longer period of time.

By contrast, in a non-simulated environment, students will have to read lengthy witness statements and reports and they will therefore remember information for a short period of time [19].

Benefits of VR for Teaching and Learning. Most participants also stated the advantages of adopting VR for teaching and learning. Participant 1, for example, claimed: *"In the classroom, VR would assist with teaching and learning by creating an active environment to facilitate participation"*. Similarly, [30] had stated that VR promotes active learning and creates an engaging environment to facilitate learning. Some of our participants (2, 3, 4, 5) described the following advantages of adopting VR: *"VR platforms, e.g. second life, eliminate the language barrier and provide flexibility in terms of learning because students can learn at their own pace, hence, promoting effective learning"*. Similarly, [30] noted that VR overcomes language barriers. For example, VR environments with chat rooms and forums provide an equal opportunity for communication between students from different cultural backgrounds. Likewise, [22] had mentioned that VR platforms (such as Second Life and Minecraft) enable students' socialization via the instant messaging feature. Such socialization promotes effective learning as students can communicate with each other to share knowledge of the course work.

Participant 4 stated: *"Utilizing VR in the classroom will cater for different learning styles. Perhaps some student prefer to learn visually; then they can gain more by using VR for learning"*. Similarly, [30] claimed that the visual and interactive strengths of VR makes it suitable for various learning styles. Another participant stated that VR would be useful in modules like history by allowing students to virtually travel to destinations around the world. This assists with creating interest and motivating to learn the course content. Participant 8 further elaborated on the advantage of using VR for promoting motivation with an example: *"A lecturer can try and explain history abstractly, e.g. theoretically explaining the pyramids in Egypt. However, teaching using VR will allow students to formulate an idea on how the pyramids look in terms of the dimensions. Also, by providing the students with an immersive experience they will be more interested in learning about the history of Egypt"*.

Immersive VR environments that are specifically designed to help students to learn and experience course-related material target different learning styles; this cannot be obtained in traditional education, i.e. using blackboard teaching methods [42]. Moreover, immersive VR environments enhance learning retention by promoting interest in the module because students retain more information if they find a module or topic in the course work interesting [42]. Similarly, our participant 1 mentioned that VR depicts a shift from the traditional methods of teaching to the modern methods of teaching. This shift assists lecturers to create dynamic teaching environments to promote students' interest in the course work. Several participants (1, 2, 4, 5, 7, 8) also mentioned VR devices such as VR head-gears and VR platforms such as second life that can create virtual teaching environments to promote students interest in the course work.

5.3 Ease of Use of VR

This theme focused on the participants' reflections on the ease of using and understanding of VR systems in the context of teaching and learning. Most participants briefly explained ways in which the VR systems could be made easy to use and understand. Most participants (1, 2, 3, 4, 5, 8) suggested training as a way of introducing lecturers to VR. Some of the other participants (6, 9, 10) argued that training should continue even when VR is fully implemented. This will enable VR users to keep abreast of new developments and updates within the VR arena. One participant (5) discussed that both lecturers and students will require training to use and understand the VR systems. In addition, participant 3 stated that the UKZN needs to identify educational institutions that have already adopted VR in order to provide a foundation for the adoption of VR from a theoretical perspective. Such a theoretical foundation would enable lecturers to gain insight into changes that need to be made for the successful adoption of VR at UKZN. This would subsequently allow lecturers to understand how to use the VR systems for teaching and learning.

5.4 Challenges to the Adoption of VR and Suggested Solutions

Feasibility. Most participants (2, 3, 5, 9, 10) commented on VR adoption challenges from an infrastructural and financial perspective. They recommended that the UKZN should consider performing a cost-benefit analysis to assess the financial feasibility to adopt VR for teaching and learning. One respondent (2) alluded to the fact that *"VR adoption requires long-term planning; the university is not quite prepared for it right now in terms of the infrastructure required, but perhaps in the future the adoption of VR will be possible"*. Similarly, participant 1 recommended: *"UKZN should take as much time as is needed, no less than two years of time, to decide on the disciplines where VR will be adopted"*.

Most participants suggested a gradual adoption of VR as a solution to the challenge of current feasibility. In addition, other participants (1, 2, 3, 4, 6, 10) advocated having policies for the adoption of VR. These participants expressed that those policies should be optional in order to prevent forcing the adoption of VR to limit instances whereby lecturers would adopt VR just to adhere to the university rules instead of adopting it to its full potential. One participant stated that pilot studies across disciplines should be conducted before deciding on the adoption of VR at UKZN because this would enable the university to gain insights into the capabilities and the potential challenges of adopting VR for teaching and learning.

VR Skills. Some of the participants suggested outsourcing of VR skills to solve the issue of a lack of VR skills among the staff members. By contrast, some of the participants recommended getting VR skills by training existing staff members. Some of the participants explained that the UKZN did not have qualified staff who were familiar with utilizing VR. Training would therefore be fundamental, but it should be complemented by recruiting new staff who have skills in VR.

The recruited staff would be required to help the other staff members by sharing their VR knowledge. This would promote a pool of VR knowledge and skills at the UKZN. In this regard, remarks from the participants include *"do not outsource"* (participants 1, 2), as well as *"yes, UKZN can outsource, although that can be an issue because depending on the external people implies that there is a non-formation of internal skills. UKZN would spend money on outsourcing as opposed to using the existing people at the university"* (participants 7, 8, 9).

Resistance to Change. Resistance to change was a challenge that the participants felt needed to be addressed from an organizational perspective. One participant (2) stated the following: *"The biggest problem is resistance to change. It is really going to take time for the staff to change to newer technologies"*. The transition from old technologies such as projectors and 2D systems to more advanced systems such as 3D interactive and immersive systems like VR can sometimes cause resistance to change because lecturers are accustomed to the old technologies. This is because lecturers have adequate exposure to and experience with using old technologies as compared to their exposure and experience with using VR. The participants focused on 'PowerPoint' as a commonly used technological tool and contrasted it with VR. Most participants perceived 'PowerPoint' as a tool that could be used in conjunction with virtual environments. One participant (1) explained that 'PowerPoint' could be used to teach the theoretical sections of the coursework and it could be used to teach the complex and abstract sections of the coursework. In this way, both 'PowerPoint' and VR could be utilized in conjunction to teach a course. However, some of the participants stated that they would substitute 'PowerPoint' with VR because it would be more beneficial for teaching their modules. In particular, participant 1 stated: *"If VR is used to its full potential, such as creating multiple virtual environments, for example a classroom environment and a business environment, then there is no need for slides"*. The same participant further elaborated: *"This is because theoretical content can be taught in the classroom environment and application will be taught in the business environment, and in this way students will learn better and it will make teaching simpler"*. Some of our participants (2, 3, 4, 5, 10) expressed their concern that the UKZN would need to properly communicate the reasons for adopting VR; failure to do so would result in unwillingness to change. Some participants recommended gradually adopting VR as one of the solutions to the challenge of lack of willingness to change. Generally, people become resistant to change because of a lack of support to facilitate the change. Therefore, to prevent resistance to change, the UKZN needs to implement proper procedures and support facilities to adopt VR for teaching and learning. One participant (2) proposed the following solution: *"An effective change management process, and a clear justification of the need to adopt VR, is required"*. The same participant further elaborated that successful adoption of new technologies such as VR requires acceptance of the technology and that acceptance can only be had once the decision to adopt VR is fully understood by staff members and other relevant stakeholders.

6   Conclusion and Outlook

Several research have highlighted the possibilities and benefits associated with using Virtual Reality within the context of teaching and learning. However, related work reveals that research on the adoption of VR as teaching and learning tool in the South African (or wider African) context is very scarce. This project contributes to the scanty literature on VR adoption Africa as it investigates the perceived ease of use, usefulness of VR and challenges associated with VR as a teaching and learning platform from lecturers' perspectives in South Africa. Current literature highlights the potential use of VR from students' perspective and rarely from lecturers. This paper highlights that VR is particularly useful as it provides a safe learning environment to practice delicate or risky procedures through simulations. Lecturers also believe that VR is useful for teaching abstract concepts in an immersive learning environment. Further benefits include the fact that VR encourages students' participation in the classroom, eliminates language barrier and promotes learning flexibility, cultural diversity and student socialization. In addition, it promotes students' information retention. Lecturers mentioned that due to the evolving nature of technology, there is a need for continuous training (in the pre- and post-adoption phases) to ensure that VR is perceived as easy to use. They further mentioned that there is a need to build knowledge of VR from a theoretical perspective to gain a better understanding on how VR systems could be used for teaching and learning.

In terms of the challenges, lecturers expressed their concerns about the infrastructural and financial capabilities of the UKZN to adopt VR. Thus, they proposed a gradual approach to VR adoption, coupled with pilot studies and flexible policies that encourage voluntary adoption of VR. Some lecturers further advocated for outsourcing VR skills as a way of adopting VR while some were against it. Resistance to change is another identified challenge in the South African context. They indicated that the UKZN should adopt a hybrid approach, combining the use of existing technologies in conjunction with new ones (VR). In addition, the university should engage its academic staff on the need to move to VR systems and create a pathway for the adoption and support for VR for teaching and learning.

This paper suggests a further in-depth study of factors that may influence the adoption of VR in the South African higher education sector. Such a study should adopt more robust theoretical and methodological approach and should endeavor to capture students and lecturers' perceptions on a large scale, that is, from more than one institutions. Particularly, it would be interesting to investigate how perceptions toward VR adoption differ depending on the various types of higher institutions of South Africa (traditional, research-focused or teaching-oriented). Moreover, further studies should be conducted to assess the possibility of adopting VR in South African education in terms of the prevailing infrastructure and financial implications for the South African educational institutions as well as the educational policies put in place by the government that dictate the rules for technology adoption in South African education.

References

1. Abulrub, A.H.G., Attridge, A.N., Williams, M.A.: Virtual reality in engineering education: the future of creative learning. In: 2011 Proceedings of the IEEE Global Engineering Education Conference, EDUCON, pp. 751–757 (2011)
2. Aggarwal, R., et al.: Training and simulation for patient safety. BMJ Qual. Saf. **19**(Suppl. 2), i34–i43 (2010)
3. Ayres, K.M., Mechling, L., Sansosti, F.J.: The use of mobile technologies to assist with life skills/independence of students with moderate/severe intellectual disability and/or autism spectrum disorders: considerations for the future of school psychology. Psychol. Schools **50**(3), 259–271 (2013)
4. Bertrand, M., Bouchard, S.: Applying the technology acceptance model to VR with people who are favorable to its use. J. Cyber Ther. Rehab. **1**(2), 200–210 (2008)
5. Bimber, O., Fröhlich, B., Schmalstieg, D., Encarnacáo, L.M.: The virtual showcase. In: ACM SIGGRAPH 2005 Courses, p. 3 (2005)
6. Brooks, B.M., Rose, F.D., Attree, E.A., et al.: An evaluation of the efficacy of training people with learning disabilities in a virtual environment. Disabil. Rehab. **24**(11/12), 622–626 (2002)
7. Brunswick, N., Martin, G.N., Marzano, L.: Visuospatial superiority in developmental dyslexia: myth or reality? Learn. Individ. Differ. **20**(5), 421–426 (2010)
8. Champion, E.: Heritage role playing-history as an interactive digital game. In: Proceedings of the Design Thinking Research Symposium, Sydney, p. 29 (2003)
9. Chantry, J., Dunford, C.: How do computer assistive technologies enhance participation in childhood occupations for children with multiple and complex disabilities? A review of the current literature. Br. J. Occup. Ther. **73**(8), 351–365 (2010)
10. Christopoulos, D., Mavridis, P., Andreadis, A., Karigiannis, J.N.: Using virtual environments to tell the story: the battle of thermopylae. In: VS-GAMES 2011 Proceedings of the 3rd International Conference on Games and Virtual Worlds for Serious Applications, pp. 84–91 (2011)
11. Chuang, W.: Online virtual training environments with intelligent agents to promote social inclusion. Doctoral Dissertation, Nottingham Trent University (2003)
12. Dalgarno, B., Lee, M.J.: What are the learning affordances of 3D virtual environments? Br. J. Educ. Tech. **41**(1), 10–32 (2010)
13. Davis, F.D.: Perceived usefulness, perceived ease of use, and user acceptance of information technology. MIS Q. **13**(3), 319–340 (1989)
14. Fagan, M., Kilmon, C., Pandey, V.: Exploring the adoption of a virtual reality simulation: the role of perceived ease of use, perceived usefulness and personal innovativeness. Campus-Wide Inf. Syst. **29**(2), 117–127 (2012)
15. Habib, L., et al.: Dyslexic students in higher education and virtual learning environments: an exploratory study. J. Comp.-Assist. Learn. **28**(6), 574–584 (2012)
16. Hamrol, A., Górski, F., Grajewski, D., Zawadzki, P.: Virtual 3D atlas of a human body: development of an educational medical software application. Proc. Comput. Sci. **25**(1), 302–314 (2013)
17. Hoffman, H., Murray, M., Curlee, R., Fritchle, A.: Anatomic visualizeR: teaching and learning anatomy with virtual reality. Inf. Tech. Med. **1**, 205–218 (2001)
18. Huang, H.M., Liaw, S.S., Lai, C.M.: Exploring learner acceptance of the use of virtual reality in medical education: a case study of desktop and projection-based display systems. Interact. Learn. Environ. **24**(1), 3–19 (2016)

19. Hunter, D., Lastowka, G.: Virtual crimes. New York Law School Law Rev. **49**(1), 211–229 (2004)
20. Jin, G., Nakayama, S.: Virtual reality game for safety education. In: 2014 Proceedings of the IEEE International Conference on Audio, Language and Image Processing, ICALIP, pp. 95–100 (2014)
21. Kalay, Y.E.: Virtual learning environments. J. Inf. Tech. Constr. **9**(13), 195–207 (2004)
22. Laister, J., Kober, S.: Social aspects of collaborative learning in virtual learning environments. In: Proceedings of the Networked Learning Conference, Sheffield, pp. 1–7 (2002)
23. Lopresti, F.E., Mihailidis, A., Kirsch, N.: Assistive technology for cognitive rehabilitation: state of the art. Neuropsychol. Rehabil. **14**(1/2), 5–39 (2004)
24. Merchant, Z., Kennicutt, W., Goetz, E.: Predicting undergraduate students' acceptance of 'second life' for teaching chemistry. J. Online Learn. Teach. **11**(2), 233–248 (2015)
25. Mortara, M., Catalano, C.E., Bellotti, F., Fiucci, G., Houry-Panchetti, M., Petridis, P.: Learning cultural heritage by serious games. J. Cult. Heritage **15**(3), 318–325 (2014)
26. Muijs, D., Campbell, J., Kyriakides, L., Robinson, W.: Making the case for differentiated teacher effectiveness: an overview of research in four key areas. School Eff. School Improv. **16**(1), 51–70 (2005)
27. Naidoo, S.: Not just fun and games: virtual reality could revolutionize everything from education to shopping (2017). http://www.seamonster.co.za/not-just-fun-games-virtual-reality-could-revolutionise-everything-from-education-to-shopping/
28. Ng'ambi, D., Gachago, D., Ivala, E., Bozalek, V., Watters, K.: Emerging technologies in South African higher education institutions: towards a teaching and learning practice framework. In: Proceedings of the International Conference on e-Learning, Lisbon, p. 354 (2012)
29. Palter, V.N., Grantcharov, T.P.: Simulation in surgical education. Can. Med. Assoc. J. **182**(11), 1191–1196 (2010)
30. Pantelidis, V.S.: Reasons to use virtual reality in education and training courses, and a model to determine when to use virtual reality. Themes Sci. Tech. Educ. **2**(1/2), 59–70 (2010)
31. Parsons, S., Cobb, S.: State-of-the-art of virtual reality technologies for children on the autism spectrum. Eur. J. Spec. Needs Educ. **26**(3), 355–366 (2011)
32. Parsons, S., Mitchell, P.: The potential of virtual reality in social skills training for people with autistic spectrum disorders. J. Intell. Disabil. Res. **46**(5), 430–443 (2002)
33. Parsons, S., Mitchell, P.: What children with autism understand about thoughts and thought bubbles. Autism **3**(1), 17–38 (1999)
34. Reznek, M.A., Rawn, C.L., Krummel, T.M.: Evaluation of the educational effectiveness of a virtual reality intravenous insertion simulator. Acad. Emerg. Med. **9**(11), 1319–1325 (2002)
35. Rigamonti, D.D., Bryant, H.J., Bustos, O., Moore, L., Hoffman, H.M.: Implementing anatomic visualizer learning modules in anatomy education. In: Proceedings of the 3rd Visible Human Project Conference, Maryland (2000)
36. Rizzo, A.A., et al.: The virtual classroom: a virtual reality environment for the assessment and rehabilitation of attention deficits. CyberPsychol. Behav. **3**(3), 483–499 (2000)

37. Schaub, K.G., et al.: Ergonomic assessment of automotive assembly tasks with digital human modeling and the 'ergonomics assessment worksheet' (EAWS). Int. J. Hum. Factors Model. Simul. **3**(3/4), 398–426 (2012)
38. Smith, M.D.: Virtual reality game. U.S. Patent no. 6,159,100 (2000)
39. Sobota, B., Korecko, S., Pastornicky, P., Jacho, L.: Virtual-reality technologies in the process of handicapped school children education. In: 2016 Proceedings of the IEEE International Conference on Emerging eLearning Technologies and Applications, ICETA, pp. 321–326 (2016)
40. Standen, P.J., Brown, D.J.: Virtual reality in the rehabilitation of people with intellectual disabilities: review. CyberPsychol. Behav. **8**(3), 272–282 (2005)
41. Standen, P.J., Brown, D.J., Cromby, J.J.: The effective use of virtual environments in the education and rehabilitation of students with intellectual disabilities. Br. J. Educ. Tech. **32**(3), 289–299 (2001)
42. Winn, W.: A conceptual basis for educational applications of virtual reality. Technical report TR-93-9, University of Washington (1993)
43. Wu, Y., Chan, T., Jong, B., Lin, T.: A web-based virtual reality physics laboratory. In: Proceedings of the 3rd IEEE International Conference on Advanced Learning Technologies, p. 455 (2003)
44. Zhang, K.E., Liu, S.J.: The application of virtual reality technology in physical education teaching and training. In: 2016 Proceedings of the IEEE International Conference on Service Operations and Logistics and Informatics, SOLI, pp. 245–248 (2016)

Topic Teaching

Generating SQL Queries
from Visual Specifications

George Obaido[2(✉)], Abejide Ade-Ibijola[1], and Hima Vadapalli[2]

[1] Department of Applied Information Systems, University of Johannesburg,
Johannesburg, South Africa
abejideai@uj.ac.za
[2] School of Computer Science and Applied Mathematics,
University of the Witwatersrand, Johannesburg, South Africa
rabeshi.george@gmail.com, hima.vadapalli@wits.ac.za

Abstract. The Structured Query Language (SQL) is the most widely used declarative language for accessing relational databases, and an essential topic in introductory database courses in higher learning institutions. Despite the intuitiveness of SQL, formulating and comprehending written queries can be confusing, especially for undergraduate students. One major reason for this is that the simple syntax of SQL is often misleading and hard to comprehend. A number of tools have been developed to aid the comprehension of queries and to improve the mental models of students concerning the underlying logic of SQL. Some of these tools employed visualisation and animation in their approach to aid the comprehension of SQL. This paper presents an interactive comprehension aid based on visualisation, specifically designed to support the SQL SELECT statement, an area identified in the literature as problematic for students. The visualisation tool uses visual specifications depicting SQL operations to build queries. This is expected to reduce the cognitive load of a student who is learning SQL. We have shown with an online survey that adopting visual specifications in teaching systems assist students in attaining a richer learning experience in introductory database courses.

Keywords: SQL comprehension · Visual specification
Learning via visualisation

1 Introduction

The Structured Query Language (SQL) remains an integral part of the introductory relational database course curriculum in higher institutions of learning, and is considered the most widely used *declarative* and *non-procedural* language for querying relational databases [35]. As a declarative language, many of its statements are 'English-like'. SQL is a non-procedural language because data operations are specified by their intended result rather than their steps towards the result. Since it was adopted by the ANSI and ISO in the late 70's,[1]

---

[1] ANSI: American National Standards Institute, ISO: International Organization for Standardization.

© Springer Nature Switzerland AG 2019
S. Kabanda et al. (Eds.): SACLA 2018, CCIS 963, pp. 315–330, 2019.
https://doi.org/10.1007/978-3-030-05813-5_21

SQL has evolved as a standardised language for most relational database management systems or RDBMSs [24,28]. SQL uses commands to define schema objects (Data Definition Language: DDL) and to manipulate data (Data Manipulation Language: DML) in a RDBMS [15].

Due to the wide-spread application of SQL, being able to formulate queries is an important skill that employers require for graduates in computer science and related disciplines. This skill relates to knowledge of relational databases for the writing of useful and correct queries in SQL [25]. If students' knowledge of the SQL concept is poor, their performance in business sectors would be questionable [5,14]. Despite the triviality of the task of manipulating and retrieving information from relational databases, writing correct queries still remains a well-known problem for many students [15,20,41]. Numerous studies have been conducted with regard to the challenges that students face while learning SQL queries [4,20,25]. Some of the challenges include the burden of having to memorise database schemas, the sometimes misleading declarative nature of SQL (especially when it is learned alongside a procedural or object-oriented programming language), and the naive perception that the semantics of queries would be 'easy' to grasp [10,20]. Other features that students find particularly difficult are the SQL 'join' and 'grouping' functions [24]. Also, writing queries in DML expressions was shown to be difficult for undergraduate students [15]. In order to provide adequate support for these students, we need to build interactive platforms, augmented either with *animation* or *visualisation* aids, to improve the understanding of SQL. In the past decades, a number of tools have been developed to support learning SQL. Some of the existing tools employed interactive visualisations to aid SQL understanding.

In this paper we propose the use of an interactive visualisation technique to aid the understanding of SQL. The visualisation technique ensures the interaction between visual specifications to build queries and will eliminate the need to memorise database schemas, which is a major problem faced by students learning SQL. In our project we have developed an interactive aid which enables visual specifications by 'drag and drop' interactions for generating SQL queries. Although this approach can already be found in programming learning paradigms such as Alice [13], Scratch [39], or StarLogo TNG [43], to the best of our knowledge it has not yet been applied to SQL.

Figure 1 shows the SQL query generation process. In use of the SQL visualiser, images are displayed as visual specifications of a database model. These images can be moved into a query box. When the moved images correspond to a valid `SQL SELECT` statement, a query is generated and shown to the user.

In this paper we make the following contributions:

1. We use predefined images that represent SQL commands to present a user with a 'drag and drop' visualiser.
2. We evaluate the approach using test persons to get feedback on their perceptions of the visualisation.

The remainder of this paper is organised as follows. In Sect. 2 the background related to this paper is discussed. Section 3 presents the methods used. Section 4

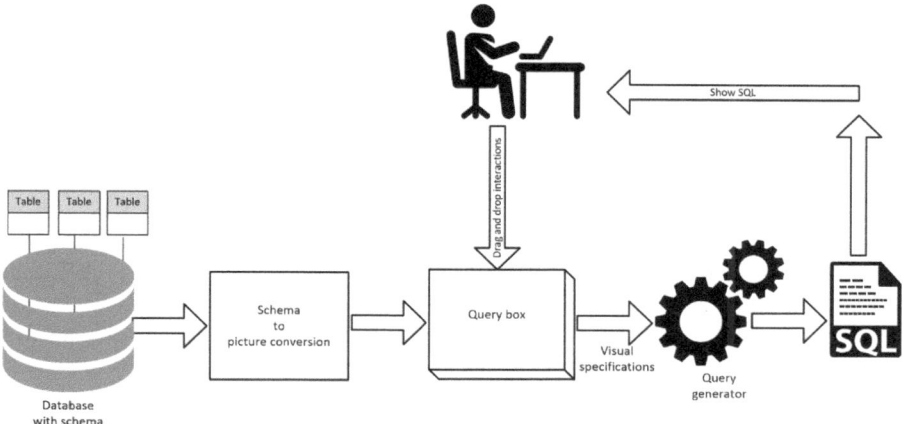

Fig. 1. Framework of the SQL query generation

explains the usage of our new tool. Section 5 presents an empirical evaluation of the SQL visualiser by a group of 121 test participants. Section 6 concludes this paper and hints at future research directions.

2   Related Work

In this section we discuss previous work related to our project. First, the pedagogy models of teaching SQL are identified, followed by the topic of learning through visualisation. Lastly we discuss some of the tools used to aid the understanding of SQL.

2.1   Teaching Patterns for SQL

Different SQL pedagogy models have been proposed over the years. These teaching patterns are either traditional face-to-face instructor-led teaching or teaching through electronic aids. We discuss some of the pedagogy models for teaching SQL. Prior and Lister proposed three-fold objectives for teaching SQL [37]: the first objective aimed to ensure that students developed their query formulation skills, while the second objective described an approach to develop real-world systems using SQL. The third encouraged students to practice and develop their SQL skills using an online method. Renaud and van Biljon proposed another approach which highlighted two pedagogical approaches for teaching SQL [38]: The first method ensured that students used tools for learning SQL, while the second method suggested the use of an instruction-led method of teaching SQL in class before exposing students to tools. Caldeira's approach was similar [9], as it aimed to ensure that students first understood SQL thoroughly by reading and understanding how to write SQL queries before being exposed to electronic aids.

Ahadi (et al.) presented the common semantics that instructors need to consider when teaching students how to write SQL queries [4]. Their paper emphasised the need for a deeper understanding of the common semantics to improve learning outcomes to assist students in the proper writing of SQL queries.

2.2   Learning Through Visualisation

The idea of learning through visualisation is not new. This technique has been extensively used in different application domains to present ideas [17,26]. Ellis and Alan defined 'visualisation' as a systematic way of representing an abstract idea in a way that facilitates human understanding [16]. The respresentation is usually designed in a way that is sometimes 'playful and aesthetically pleasing', so that users can explore how to solve tasks. W.r.t. learning, visualisation can encourage active participation and lead students' critical thought processes [6]. Kellems (et al.) showed that visualisation can even help students with learning disabilities to grasp information more easily [27]. Their study showed that visual aids can also better meet the academic problems of students suffering from Autism Spectrum Disorder (ASD),[2] since they do not require intensive training.

In the area of program comprehension, visualisation has been explored to aid the understanding of programming. Lee (et al.) proposed the use of the drag and drop refactoring visualisation to assist programmers to understand programs written in Java [30]. They showed that their approach was more efficient and less error-prone, and that it could help programmers comprehend programs more easily. Studies conducted in block programming (a technique which represents programs as blocks and uses 'drag and drop' to generate programs) indicated that this type of visualisation increased students' engagement and that it was indeed effective in knowledge transfer [33,40]. A recent study conducted on serious games on the C programming language also applied the drag and drop approach and paved a way for undergraduate students to learn programming [44]. The benefit offered by this visual aid is that it enhances self-pacing, while its entertainment component attracts the attention of students and engages them in the learning process. It is worth noting that most SQL comprehension tools employ visualisation to automatically produce SQL queries and database schemas through either textual or graphical representations [10,19,41].

2.3   SQL Learning Tools

Over the past decades, a number of tools have been developed to aid the understanding of SQL [10,25,34,41]. The majority of these tools are either web-based, desktop or gaming applications, which use visualisation to represent SQL queries. We discuss some of the tools that have been used to aid the comprehension of SQL.

---

[2] A neurological and developmental disorder which results in communication and interaction difficulties.

Table 1. Comparison of other tools versus our approach

Features	eSQL	SAVI	SQlify	sAccess	eledSQL	QueryViz	Our approach
Visualisation of database schema	✗	✓	✓	✗	✗	✓	✓
Visualisation of output data	✓	✓	✓	✓	✓	✗	✗
SQL query generation	✗	✗	✗	✗	✗	✗	✓
Feedback on query semantics	✗	✗	✓	✗	✗	✓	✓
Visual object representation	✗	✗	✗	✗	✗	✗	✓
Ideal for less knowledgeable users (undergraduate students)	✗	✗	✗	✓	✓	✗	✓

One of the earliest SQL learning aids was the eSQL system [25] developed to visualise the SQL SELECT statement (which students usually find confusing). The goal of eSQL is to teach the set-by-step method, where the query selects the output data and behaviour of query operators. The eSQL system displays output data from an SQL query, hence extensive knowledge of SQL is required to use the system.

SQLify [15] was developed as an online interactive, visualisation and assessment tool to aid SQL comprehension. This tool provides comprehensive feedback to students in an automated and interactive fashion. To use the system, a user is required to possess knowledge of SQL in order to test and visualise a database schema.

QueryViz [12] supports users to understand the 'logic' behind the SQL syntax. The advantage of QueryViz is that it allows students to read and understand queries as fast as possible. Also, the tool enables query-reuse and provides a means of visualising schema objects.

The online tool SAVI [10] uses visualisation to teach the semantics of SQL. Hence, SQL knowledge is required to interact with a target database. The goal of SAVI is to overcome difficulties via the way an SQL query interacts with the database.

eledSQL [22] was intended to overcome the problems of teaching SQL education in German secondary schools. This tool ensures that students are able to interact with databases without prior knowledge of SQL.

sAcess [36] is an interactive web-based learning tool which offers a simple, customised interface for learning database manipulation in relational databases. The tool provides a simple interface and eliminates the need for 'mastering' the SQL syntax. As such it is suitable for introductory database education.

While all these tools include visualisation to aid SQL comprehension, none considers our approach of using images to generate SQL queries. Also, most of the tools discussed require knowledge of SQL to 'grasp' the visualisation. Table 1 compares these tools against our approach.

3   Method

In the domain of program comprehension, visualisation tools have been developed to employ the 'drag and drop' approach to aid the understanding of programming. `Scratch` [39], a tool developed to use blocks in order to form a program, minimises the occurrences of syntax errors. Another tool that aids program comprehension is `Alice 2` [11], a 3D animation and interactive system, that uses blocks to build virtual worlds which are primarily designed for novices to learn programming. The intention behind `Droplet` [7] is to facilitate the learning of programs written in JavaScript, and to close the 'learning gap' between using blocks and text for programming. `BlockC` [29] supports students' learning of the C programming language. The tool guides them to focus on the programming 'logic' before they learn the syntax of the language. Together, all these tools focus on using blocks to learn programming without first considering the syntax of the language. This syntax-free approach (SFA) [18] to program comprehension has already been applied by ourselves in the past [1–3]. We have now extended this approach to generate queries using visual specifications without first considering the SQL syntax.

One aspect of queries posing difficulties for students is the `SQL SELECT` construct. This type of query is used to extract data from a relational database [25]. Hence, our main goal is focused on using visual aids to easily generate queries by means of the `SQL SELECT` constructs. This idea can be extended to the system of queries.

It is a common perception that students are better in *recognising* visual constructs rather than in *writing* code for an application. Thus, this paper is motivated by an intention to use visual specifications in order to generate SQL queries. Also, another motive of developing this SQL visualiser is to use it as a teaching and learning aid. Knowing that database schemas pose difficulties for students [15], our intention is to simplify the process of understanding database schemas. We identify three main points to distinguish our visualisation from other approaches.

Intuitive: Our visualisation is intuitive to students who are learning SQL queries for the first time. The visualisation uses images to depict each query statement. It helps students to better understand SQL queries since it allows them to get a 'glimpse' of the corresponding behaviour when an image is selected. Hence, students do not require extensive training to understand how to use the visual aid.

Interactive: The visualisation tool is interactive, which means that students are not required to write any query statement in the application. They can simply click and drag the images across panels. Query statements are then generated immediately.

Helpful: A help facility is provided before the start of the visualiser. A user is provided with an instruction concerning the underlying database schema before the application is used. Also, *hints* are provided in different colours (green or red). These colours indicate whether a query is wrong or correct. In addition, a textual suggestion is offered to ensure that the correct object is selected.

3.1   Design of the SQL Visualiser

The SQL visualiser was implemented as a Windows Form Application and was included as part of the .NET framework for the purpose of creating rich client applications [31]. The visualisation tool consists of some components used for the generation of a query. These components include schema, query box, and query generator.

3.1.1   Schema

The schema shows the logical organisation of the data. In the visualiser, the schema consists of tables and associated fields. An SQL query is based on the underlying schema. If a schema is correct the generated SQL query is correct, and vice-versa. Figure 2 shows an example.

In this schema, each table is shown with its name displayed at the top and its attributes at the bottom. For example:

Lecturer (id, name, phone, email, department)
Courses (id, title, credits, description)
Student (id, name, gender, age, address)

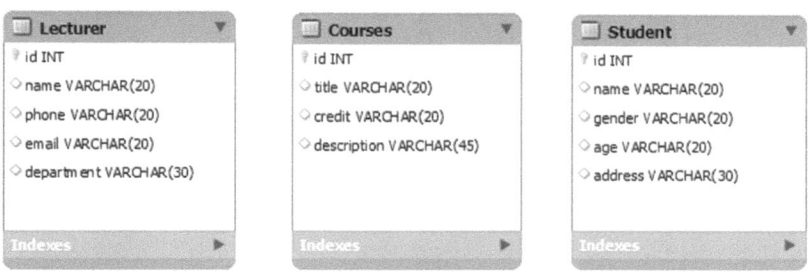

Fig. 2. Logical organisation of the data

Table 2. Operation: symbol and descriptions

Symbol	SQL Block	Description
👆	SELECT	represents the SELECT statement

Each table is linked by a primary key. The unique identifier for the tables is the entity *id*. The visualisation tool relies on the schema to generate the SQL query.

3.1.2   Query Box

The query box is used to specify subsets of the schema that the user is interested in. The query box is the 'building block' for the query generator. In the query box, the schema (represented by images) is extracted into a form used by the query generator to generate the SQL query. Each image is included with a caption for easy identification. Tables 2, 3, 4 and 5 show the pictures and descriptions used to represent a schema.

3.1.3   Query Generator

The query generator transforms the images in the query box and presents a query to the user. As more images are added, the query generator also adds more attributes to the query. The generator phase is very straightforward since the scope is limited (in this paper) to a single relation. The SELECT portion of the query consists of tables and attributes where the FROM clause defines a table and the WHERE clause is defined by a field attribute and its value. We illustrate this with the following Example (Task): *Consider a simple database table with the schema: Student (id, name, age). Now write a simple SQL query to display all information from the student table.*

Figure 3 sketches the process that the query generator uses to present queries. When a user adds the images into box (a), the query generator displays the the corresponding SQL statement in box (b). Additional options are described below.

3.1.4   Additional Options

Operators and Values: In the SQL visualiser we have explored some comparison operators (such as $=$, $<$, $>$). The comparison operators are used in generated queries with values between 0–100 to show an according relationship. For each operator the user can interactively determine which option to select. Moreover,

Table 3. Entity and attributes: 'Lecturer' table

Symbol	SQL Block	Description
	*	denotes 'all' in rows
	id	represents the primary key field
	name	represents the name field
	phone	icon for a phone field
	email	icon for an email field
	Lecturer	icon for a lecturer field

Table 4. Entity and attributes: 'Course' table

Symbol	SQL Block	Description
	*	denotes 'all' in rows
	id	represents a primary key field
	title	represents a title field
	credit	represents a credit field
	description	represents a 'syllabus' (synopsis)
	Courses	represents a course 'module'

Table 5. Entity and attributes: 'Student' table

Symbol	SQL Block	Description
	*	denotes 'all' in rows
	id	represents an identity field
	name	represents a name field
	gender	represents a gender field
	age	represents an age field
	address	represents an address field
	Student	represents a student entity

a user can select the preferred choice of value for use in a query with a 'scroll'-menu provided. Once the 'scroll'-menu is selected, it changes the value in the generated query as desired.

Colours: In the Human-Computer Interaction (HCI) interface design specifications, colours are known to convey information [8]. Within this specification, the association of colours may be used for many purposes if this is implemented conservatively. Colours have salient features, which are useful in human perception [23]. For example, the colour *red* strongly indicates an error, while *green* indicates a normal or acceptable condition. These colours were explored in our visualiser to indicate either an acceptable condition or to respond criticality to a user's error: see Table 6.

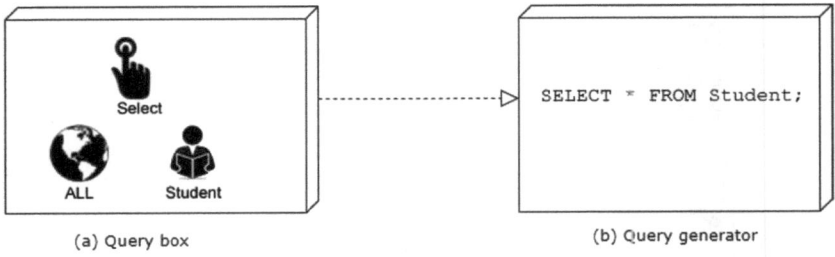

(a) Query box   (b) Query generator

Fig. 3. The process of generating an SQL query

4   Usage of the Tool

Figure 4 shows the feedback screen after adding only the **SELECT** operation into the query box at runtime. The feedback assists the user to specify the required visuals before a query can be generated.

In continuation the example shows that, if the user inserts the correct table and its attributes, a query will be generated. Here the field 'ID' was chosen as the primary key, and the value '50' was selected: see Fig. 5. The help facility, showing advice on how to use the SQL visualiser, is depicted in Fig. 6.

The techniques presented in this paper will find applications in teaching and learning systems. The benefits offered by the visualiser will facilitate human comprehension of SQL queries. This work will particularly aid undergraduate students who are learning SQL queries for the first time.

Another application area of our work can be commercial business systems, where the visualiser may be used to assist non-technical users to comprehend SQL queries. While such users may be aware of databases, their knowledge of SQL queries may be limited. We believe that our technique's clear communication and visualisation features can help industrial users to understand SQL queries better.[3]

Table 6. Colours used to indicate failure or success

Red (indicator of an error)	Green (acceptable condition)
Incorrect query, drag the required field	Fantastic! Your query is correct

---

[3] For comparison see the papers in part 'Academia and Careers' of *this volume* of CCIS.

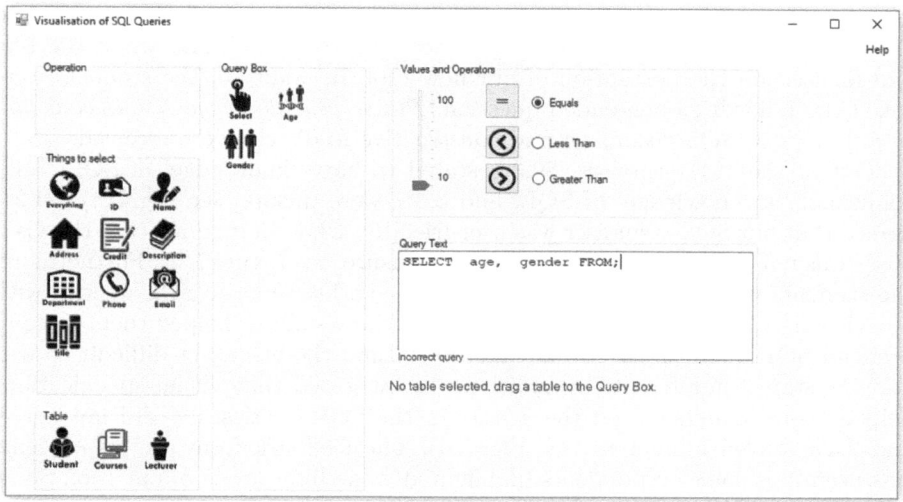

Fig. 4. SQL visualiser: hints provided to the user

5 Evaluation

Our SQL visualiser was evaluated via an online survey by 121 students of the University of the Witwatersrand. The respondents were mostly undergraduate Computer Science students, and majority of them had knowledge of SQL.

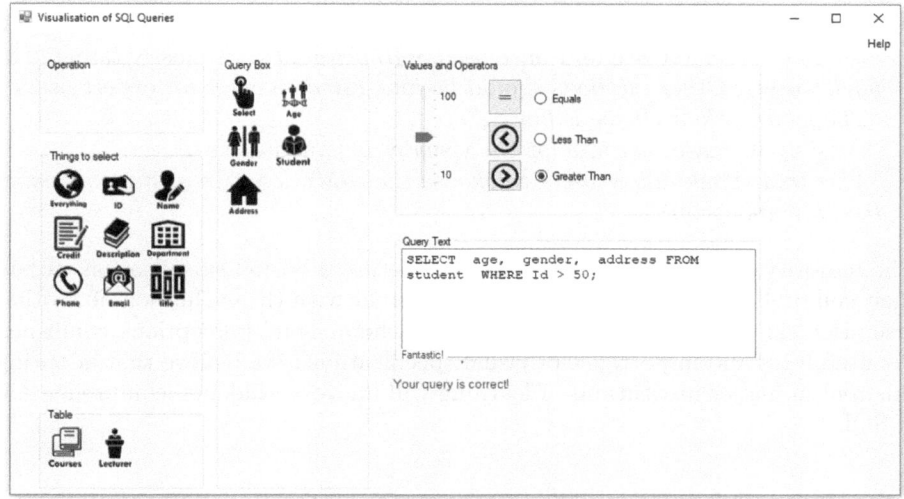

Fig. 5. SQL visualiser: a successfully generated query

The questionnaire was split into two parts: the first required the students to answer general questions about their knowledge of visualisers, while the second focused on the perception of our new tool. In addition, the students were asked the following open-ended question: *Please provide suggestions about how to improve the SQL visualiser*, and constructive feedbacks were received.

Out of the 121 responses, 89.3% stated to have 'knowledge' of SQL; 7.4% confirmed 'no knowledge' of SQL, and 3.3% were unsure: see Fig. 7(a). 94.2% agreed that our SQL visualiser was user-friendly, 4.1% complained that the visualiser was not user-friendly, and 1.7% were unsure: see Figure 7(b). Furthermore, the students were asked if they were able to synthesise basic SQL queries with our visualiser: see Fig. 7(c). 95% agreed that the visualiser helped them to comprehend SQL queries, 4% stated that they found the visualiser difficult to use, and 1% stayed indifferent. In addition, 92.6% stated that visual specifications helped them to understand the syntax of the SQL queries, 5% did not agree, and 2.4% stayed indifferent: see Fig. 7(d). The feedback from the respondents was useful, as some respondents highlighted some limitations of our tool. Some examples of positive comments were:

- *"The visualizer was extremely helpful. I liked the way the pictures assisted in displaying the query. As a learner, I think it will help other students understand SQL queries better and improve our knowledge of the SQL concept".*
- *"Icons were a good idea and helpful. It is not boring".*
- *"Far much better visualiser than l had used so far".*
- *"It seems simple and straight-forward; the user does not have to try hard to understand its functionality and operation".*

Some of the limitations mentioned by the respondents include:

- *"There should be explanations; the use of comments in the query text box would be extremely useful. I have used SQL before; this is mostly targeted at novice users. Other methods should be integrated to cater for expert users".*
- *"The icons' colour choice is boring".*
- *"Possibly increase text size for the visually impaired users".*
- *"This tool should allow users to choose their own icons (e.g. students could be a different icon)".*

The majority of the students commended the use of visual specifications to aid their comprehension. These results are consistent with the evaluation of another visualiser [42] for program comprehension, where users' perceptions confirmed the usefulness and importance of visual specifications. We believe that adopting this tool in higher institutions of learning will improve students' comprehension of SQL.

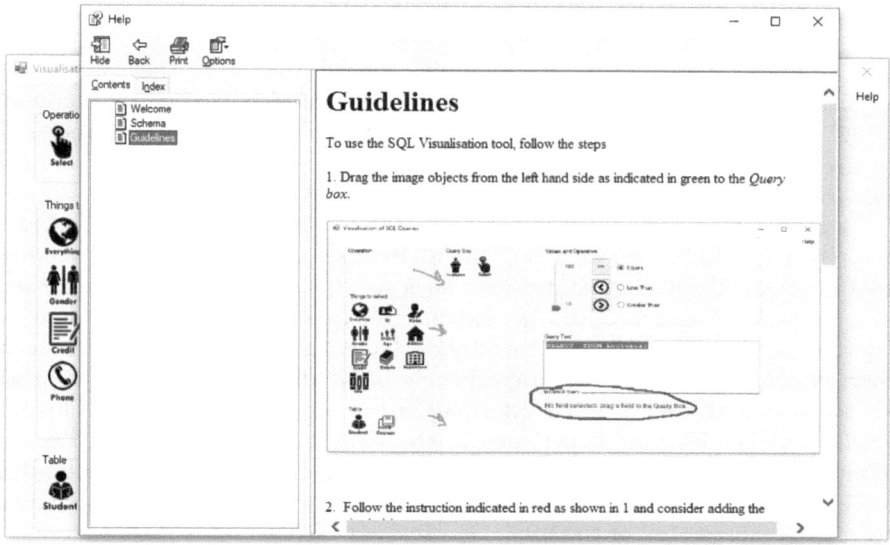

Fig. 6. The help facility gives advice to the user

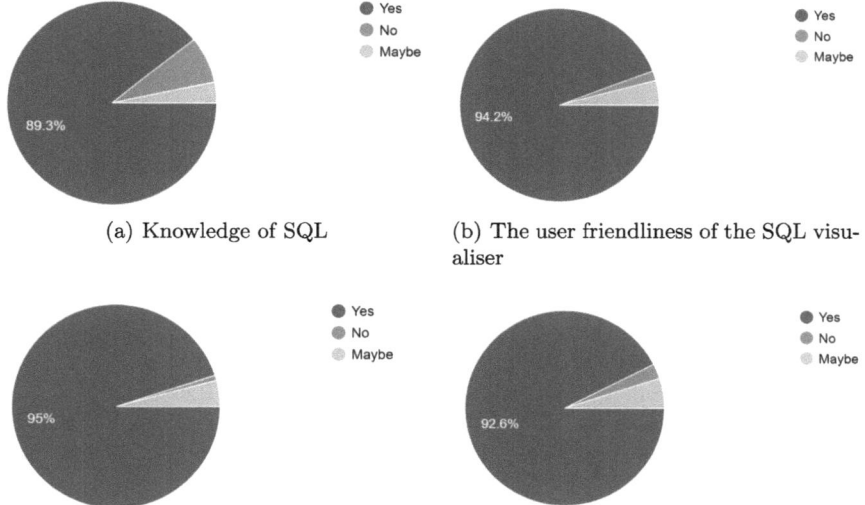

(a) Knowledge of SQL

(b) The user friendliness of the SQL visualiser

(c) Ability to synthesise basic SQL queries using the visualiser

(d) Visual specifications helped comprehend SQL

Fig. 7. Survey results

6   Conclusion and Future Directions

In this paper we presented an interactive visualisation tool that uses visual specifications to build SQL queries from pictures. Our visualisation tool supports the SQL SELECT constructs to improve the students' comprehension process. It is generally agreed that visualisation can encourage active participation and also leads to critical thought processes in students' minds [21, 32].

Currently, we have explored just a few SQL SELECT constructs to aid SQL comprehension. In future, we will create an extended visualiser in an attempt to support other SQL SELECT statements such as JOIN, ORDER BY, GROUP BY and more aggregate functions. Another avenue to explore would be the generation of nested queries. Thus far we have only explored simple (un-nested) SQL query generation. Other areas of exploration could be to allow students to define their own schemas and then use that information to generate SQL queries. This will provide a richer learning experience to the more advanced students. We also anticipate an extended GUI that attempts to use generated queries to manipulate data in a database and then produce a result. This will promote a more extensive and more 'realistic' use of the tool.

Acknowledgements. Thanks to South Africa's Department of Science and Technology (DST) and the Council for Scientific and Industrial Research (CSIR) for the DST-CSIR *inter-bursary support programme* that funds our research (https://www.csir.co.za/dst-csir-inter-bursary-support-programme).

References

1. Ade-Ibijola, A.: Automatic novice program comprehension for semantic bug detection. Doctoral Dissertation (2016)
2. Ade-Ibijola, A.: New Finite Automata Applications in Novice Program Comprehension. Lambert Academic Publishing, Riga (2017)
3. Ade-Ibijola, A., Ewert, S., Sanders, I.: Abstracting and narrating novice programs using regular expressions. In: Proceedings of the Annual Conference of the South African Institute for Computer Scientists and Information Technologists, SAICSIT 2014, pp. 19–28. ACM (2014)
4. Ahadi, A., Behbood, V., Vihavainen, A., Prior, J., Lister, R.: Students' syntactic mistakes in writing seven different types of SQL queries and its application to predicting students' success. In: Proceedings of the 47th ACM Technical Symposium on Computing Science Education, pp. 401–406 (2016)
5. Aken, A., Michalisin, M.D.: The impact of the skills gap on the recruitment of MIS graduates. In: Proceedings of the ACM SIGMIS Conference on Computer Personnel Research, pp. 105–111 (2007)
6. Allenstein, B., Yost, A., Wagner, P., Morrison, J.: A query simulation system to illustrate database query execution. ACM SIGCSE Bull. **40**(1), 493–497 (2008)
7. Bau, D.: Droplet, a blocks-based editor for text code. J. Comput. Sci. Coll. **30**(6), 138–144 (2015)
8. Brown, C.M.: Human-Computer Interface Design Guidelines. Intellect Books, Bristol (1998)

9. Caldeira, C.P.: Teaching SQL: a case study. ACM SIGCSE Bull. **40**, 340 (2008)

10. Cembalo, M., de Santis, A., Ferraro-Petrillo, U.: SAVI: a new system for advanced SQL visualization. In: Proceedings of the Conference on Information Technology Education, pp. 165–170. ACM (2011)

11. Cooper, S., Dann, W., Pausch, R.: Teaching objects-first in introductory computer science. ACM SIGCSE Bull. **35**, 191–195 (2003)

12. Danaparamita, J., Gatterbauer, W.: QueryViz: helping users understand SQL queries and their patterns. In: Proceedings of the 14th International Conference on Extending Database Technology, pp. 558–561. ACM (2011)

13. Dann, W.P., Cooper, S., Pausch, R.: Learning to Program with Alice 2. Prentice Hall, Upper Saddle River (2008)

14. Davis, P.: What computer skills do employees expect from recent college graduates? J. Technol. Horiz. Educ. **25**(2), 74 (1997)

15. Dekeyser, S., de Raadt, M., Lee, T.Y.: Computer assisted assessment of SQL query skills. In: Proceedings 18th Conference on Australian Databases, pp. 53–62. Australian Computer Society, Inc. (2007)

16. Ellis, G., Dix, A.: A taxonomy of clutter reduction for information visualisation. IEEE Trans. Vis. Comput. Graph. **13**(6), 1216–1223 (2007)

17. Ellis, G., Mansmann, F.: Mastering the information age solving problems with visual analytics. In: Proceedings of the Eurographics, vol. 2, p. 5 (2010)

18. Fincher, S.: What are we doing when we teach programming? In: Proceedings of the Frontiers in Education conference, pp. 12A4. IEEE (1999)

19. Folland, K.A.T.: viSQLizer: an interactive visualizer for learning SQL. Master's thesis (2016)

20. Garner, P., Mariani, J.A.: Learning SQL in steps. J. Syst. Cybern. Inf. **13**(4), 19–24 (2015)

21. Gray, C., Malins, J.: Visualizing Research: A Guide to the Research Process in Art and Design. Routledge, Abingdon (2016)

22. Grillenberger, A., Brinda, T.: eledSQL: a new web-based learning environment for teaching databases and SQL at secondary school level. In: Proceedings 7th Workshop on Primary and Secondary Computing Education, pp. 101–104. ACM (2012)

23. Jost, T., Ouerhani, N., von Wartburg, R., Müri, R., Hügli, H.: Assessing the contribution of color in visual attention. Comp. Vis. Image Underst. **100**(1/2), 107–123 (2005)

24. Kawash, J.: Formulating second-order logic conditions in SQL. In: Proceedings of the 15th Annual Conference on Information technology education, pp. 115–120. ACM (2014)

25. Kearns, R., Shead, S., Fekete, A.: A teaching system for SQL. In: Proceedings of the 2nd Australasian Conference on Computer Science Education, pp. 224–231. ACM (1997)

26. Keim, D.A., Mansmann, F., Schneidewind, J., Thomas, J., Ziegler, H.: Visual analytics: scope and challenges. In: Simoff, S.J., Böhlen, M.H., Mazeika, A. (eds.) Visual Data Mining. LNCS, vol. 4404, pp. 76–90. Springer, Heidelberg (2008). https://doi.org/10.1007/978-3-540-71080-6_6

27. Kellems, R.O., Gabrielsen, T.P., Williams, C.: Using visual organizers and technology: supporting executive function, abstract language comprehension, and social learning. In: Cardon, T.A. (ed.) Technology and the Treatment of Children with Autism Spectrum Disorder. ACPS, pp. 75–86. Springer, Cham (2016). https://doi.org/10.1007/978-3-319-20872-5_7

28. Kriegel, A.: Discovering SQL: A Hands-on Guide for Beginners. Wiley, Hoboken (2011)
29. Kyfonidis, C., Moumoutzis, N., Christodoulakis, S.: Block-C: a block-based programming teaching tool to facilitate introductory C programming courses. In: Proceedings of the IEEE Global Engineering Education Conference, pp. 570–579 (2017)
30. Lee, Y.Y., Chen, N., Johnson, R.E.: Drag-and-drop refactoring: intuitive and efficient program transformation. In: Proceedings of the International Conference on Software Engineering, ICSE 2013, pp. 23–32, IEEE (2013)
31. Liberty, J.: Programming C#: building .NET applications with C. O'Reilly, Sebastopol (2005)
32. Lye, S.Y., Koh, J.H.L.: Review on teaching and learning of computational thinking through programming: what is next for K-12? Comput. Hum. Behav. **41**, 51–61 (2014)
33. Malan, D.J., Leitner, H.H.: Scratch for budding computer scientists. ACM SIGCSE Bull. **39**, 223–227 (2007)
34. Mitrovic, A.: An intelligent SQL tutor on the web. Int. J. Artif. Intel. Educ. **13**(2/4), 173–197 (2003)
35. Myalapalli, V.K., Shiva, M.B.: An appraisal to optimize SQL queries. In: Proceedings of the International Conference on Pervasive Computing, pp. 1–6. IEEE (2015)
36. Nagataki, H., Nakano, Y., Nobe, M., Tohyama, T., Kanemune, S.: A visual learning tool for database operation. In: Proceedings of the 8th Workshop in Primary and Secondary Computing Education, pp. 39–40. ACM (2013)
37. Prior, J.C., Lister, R.: The backwash effect on SQL skills grading. ACM SIGCSE Bull. **36**(3), 32–36 (2004)
38. Renaud, K., van Biljon, J.: Teaching SQL—which pedagogical horse for this course? In: Williams, H., MacKinnon, L. (eds.) BNCOD 2004. LNCS, vol. 3112, pp. 244–256. Springer, Heidelberg (2004). https://doi.org/10.1007/978-3-540-27811-5_22
39. Resnick, M., et al.: Scratch: programming for all. Commun. ACM **52**(11), 60–67 (2009)
40. Rizvi, M., Humphries, T., Major, D., Jones, M., Lauzun, H.: A CS0 course using Scratch. J. Comput. Sci. Coll. **26**(3), 19–27 (2011)
41. Sadiq, S., Orlowska, M., Sadiq, W., Lin, J.: SQLator: an online SQL learning workbench. ACM SIGCSE Bull. **36**, 223–227 (2004)
42. Satyanarayan, A., Heer, J.: Lyra: an interactive visualization design environment. Comput. Graph. Forum **33**, 351–360 (2014)
43. Wang, K., McCaffrey, C., Wendel, D., Klopfer, E.: 3D game design with programming blocks in StarLogo TNG. In: Proceedings of the 7th International Conference on Learning Sciences, pp. 1008–1009 (2006)
44. Yassine, A., Chenouni, D., Berrada, M., Tahiri, A.: A serious game for learning C programming language concepts using solo taxonomy. Int. J. Emerg. Technol. Learn. **12**(3), 110–127 (2017)

The Impact of Enterprise Resource Planning Education: A Case Study of the University of Zambia

Mampi Lubasi(✉) and Lisa F. Seymour

Department of Information Systems, University of Cape Town,
Cape Town, South Africa
mampi.lubasi@gmail.com, lisa.seymour@uct.ac.za

Abstract. This paper explores the impact that ERP education has on post graduate students taking an ERP course at the University of Zambia using Sen's capability approach. Through an interpretive case study, capabilities that are enabled by ERP education were identified. We also identified the choices and personal, social and environmental conversion factors that enabled or restricted these capabilities. The choices that impacted the capabilities were that the students were not yet looking for other jobs and they wanted to complete other studies before looking for jobs. Social conversion factors were that the ERP course content does not fit current role, ERP qualification is not valued in the workplace, ERP system is not implemented in the workplace, no role in SAP ERP system in the organisation for IT personnel, hands-on experience from labs, labs lacked an implementation aspect, and a practical local Zambikes case study. Environmental factors were that there are no jobs requiring ERP skills, employers are not aware of ERP graduates in the country and organisations look outside the country For ERP expertise. Universities integrating ERP in their curriculum can benefit from the findings of this paper as it can assist in evaluating the success of ERP education. Employers seeking to hire students with ERP skills can also benefit from this paper as it can assist them in determining how best they can benefit from skills of ERP graduates.

Keywords: ERP education · Capabilities · Sen's capability approach

1 Introduction

Enterprise Resource Planning (ERP) integration in university courses, which we will refer to as *ERP education* has been introduced to help to bridge the gap in ERP competencies required by organisations [12]. One of the hurdles of ERP integration in courses is ensuring that students are not only trained in using the ERP software but in understanding the problems created and solved by the software and the business processes that the software supports [1]. While many universities have invested in ERP education there is scarce evidence of benefits

© Springer Nature Switzerland AG 2019
S. Kabanda et al. (Eds.): SACLA 2018, CCIS 963, pp. 331–344, 2019.
https://doi.org/10.1007/978-3-030-05813-5_22

of ERP education [8] and limited research on the impact or added value of ERP education [2,12]. There has been a call for impact studies to determine whether ERP education has given these graduates an advantage in the workplace or not [2]. There is also a need for empirical evidence on the learning experience of students and their understanding of course content and business processes [4]. Hence the effectiveness of ERP education can be more fully realised by assessing its influence on the students' employment potential, their attributes, skills and knowledge gained and their ability to apply their skills and knowledge in the workplace [15]. In Sub-Saharan Africa, the Enterprise Systems Education for Africa Programme (ESEFA)[1] established in 2013 has partnered with African universities to teach enterprise systems fundamentals using SAP. ESEFA was established to help to meet the demand for skilled ICT personnel by empowering students in African universities with enterprise systems skills. The curriculum which is currently taught is a global curriculum developed by the University of Cape Town and supported by the University Competence Centre (UCC). This curriculum may not be valid in other regions as each region is different, with its own contextual issues. The benefits of ERP education in developed countries may not be the same in Sub-Saharan countries like Zambia hence the need to investigate the capabilities that ERP education enables for students and the contextual issues that impact these capabilities. This paper, with which we continue some of our own previous research in the field of ERP education [10], makes *two new contributions* towards the above-mentioned aim. Firstly, we identify the capabilities enabled by ERP education; secondly, we identify the conversion factors and choices that enable or restrict these capabilities.

2   Theoretical Framework

We use Sen's capability approach as the theoretical framework. Sen's capability approach was pioneered by Amartya Sen, an economist and philosopher and focuses on what people are effectively able to do and to be, that is their capabilities [13]. The conversion of a capability input or resource into a capability is determined by three categories of conversion factors which are personal, social and environmental conversion factors [6]. Personal conversion factors include individual characteristics such as gender, literacy and disabilities. Social conversion factors include norms, policies, rules and regulations and cultural issues such as education structures. Environmental conversion factors include resources and country infrastructure. Sen's capability approach is not an education theory but fits well into education and has been used to assess aspects of education [6]. It was chosen instead of an education theory because of its emphasis on the enhancement of capabilities and opportunities [14]. The approach illuminates the concept that education can have both intrinsic and instrumental value [14]. Education can help individuals to have access to certain opportunities and can help to close income gaps thus expanding people's capabilities [6]. Sen's capability approach can help us to understand the contextual issues that is, personal,

---

[1] http://www.esefa.ac.za/esefa/about/the-programme.

social and environmental conversion factors, and student choices that enable
or restrict capabilities and functionings of ERP education. In Sen's capability
approach, the researcher is responsible for establishing a list of capabilities. We
adopt Gigler's indicators of individual empowerment [5] to identify the list of
capabilities that are enabled by ERP education and the human dimensions that
are impacted. Gigler developed the Alternative Evaluation Framework (AEF)
by operationalizing Sen's capability approach using the sustainable livelihoods
framework. AEF defines a set of impact indicators for evaluating ICT programs.
These indicators were used to evaluate the impact of an online digital library
course on students in South Africa [7]. Table 1 shows the indicators and the
observed outcome indicators proposed by Gigler, and Fig. 1 shows Sen's capability approach. Our paper therefore addresses the following *research questions*:

- *What are the capabilities that are enabled by ERP education?*
- *What are the personal, social and environmental conversion factors and
  choices that enable or restrict these capabilities?*

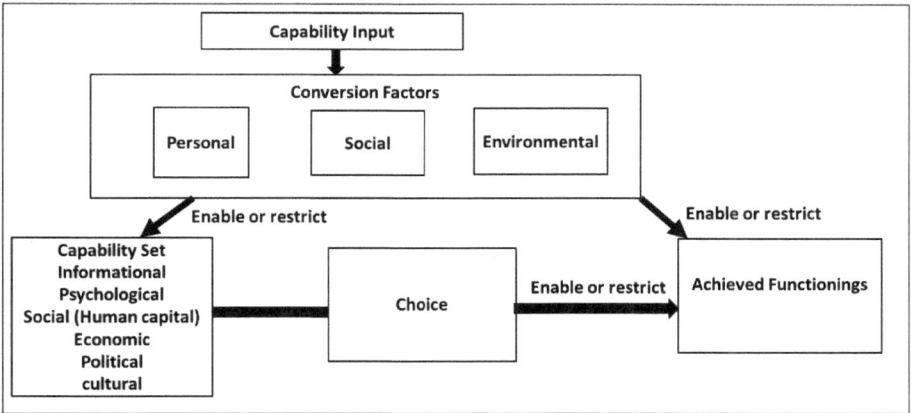

Fig. 1. Sen's capability approach (adapted from [6])

3   Method

The method for this paper is an interpretive case study. An interpretive study
has the potential to produce deep insights in IS research as it seeks to understand a phenomenon of study through the meanings assigned by human actors
[9]. Interpretive case studies can produce generalisations through generation of
theory, development of concepts, drawing specific implications and contributions
of rich insights [17]. The unit of analysis was the ERP course content taught at
the University of Zambia and the unit of observation was postgraduate students

Table 1. Gigler's indicators of individual empowerment [5]

Dimension	Objective	Outcome indicator
Informational	To improve the access to information and informational capabilities	Improved capacity to use different forms of ICTs, enhanced information literacy, enhanced capacity to produce and publish local content, improved ability to communicate with family members and friends abroad
Psychological	To support a process of self reflection (critical conscientization) and problem solving capacity	Strengthened self-esteem, improved ability to analyze own situation and solve problems, strengthened ability to influence strategic life choices, sense of inclusion in the modern world
Social (human capital)	To strengthen people's human capital (skills, knowledge, ability to work and good health)	Enhanced ICT literacy and technology skills (e.g. repair computers), enhanced leadership skills, improved program management skills
Economic	To enhance people's capacity to interact with the market	Improved access to markets enhanced entrepreneurial skills, alternative sources of income, productive assets strengthened, improved employment opportunities, improved income through: (a) lower transaction costs (less time constraints), (b) reduced transport needs, (c) increased timeliness of sales
Political	To improve people's participation in decision-making processes at the community-level and the political system	Improved access to government information and services (e-government), improved awareness about political issues, improved capabilities to interact with local governments
Cultural	To strengthen people's cultural identity	Use of ICTs as a form of cultural expression (e.g. design of computer graphics, websites), increased awareness of own cultural identity

who took the course. Data collection was cross-sectional as the data was collected at one-point in time [3]. Purposive sampling was used in selecting participants for the interviews. Purposeful sampling selects the most productive sample that will aid in answering the research question [11]. Thematic analysis was used to analyse the data using Nvivo software and a deductive approach was used as it is useful for theory testing [16].

4   Case Description

ERP education was introduced at the University of Zambia in October 2014 through the Enterprise Systems Education For Africa (ESEFA) programme. The University of Zambia was one of the first universities in Africa to join the ESEFA programme and the first in Zambia to introduce ERP Education. The ESEFA ERP course content is offered to Computer Science undergraduate students, Computer Science, Engineering and Economics postgraduate students. The course content uses SAP ERP and has a case study component based on a Zambian bamboo bikes producing company (Zambikes), guided workshops (labs) and lectures. The course content was offered as a short course to postgraduate students and ran for about 6 weeks. For undergraduate students, the course content was incorporated into the Database course.

5   Data Analysis and Discussion of Findings

Data was collected from 11 postgraduate students using semi-structured interviews. The availability of the students at the time of the interviews was the most influencing factor when selecting the interviewees. The themes from the analysis and the number of respondents who mentioned each theme are presented in Table 2. Demographics of the postgraduate students interviewed are shown in Table 3.

Table 2. Data analysis themes, with N = number of respondents

Theme	Indicators	N
Capabilities and functionings	Increased marketability	9
	Self-confidence	9
	Gaining ERP knowledge	11
	Improved decision making skills	2
	Ability to run a business	4
	Improved problem solving skills	2
	Increased likelihood of getting a higher salary	4
Choices	Not yet looking for another job	4
	Need to complete other courses	2
Personal conversion factors	Interest in information systems	1
	Background	3
Social conversion factors	Current role different from ERP course	1
	ERP course must be combined with other qualifications	1
	ERP course not appreciated in the workplace	1
	ERP system not implemented in the workplace	4
	No role in SAP ERP system in the organisation	1
	Hands-on experience from labs	4
	Labs lacked implementation aspect	1
	Practical local Zambikes case study	8
Environmental conversion factors	No jobs requiring ERP skills	2
	Employers not aware about ESEFA ERP graduates	1
	Organisations look outside the country for ERP expertise	1

Table 3. Information on participants, with P = number of persons

Profession	Programme of study	P	Code
Accountant	Economics	2	ACC
Teacher	Computer science	2	TCH
IT personnel	Computer science	3	IT
IT manager	Engineering	1	ITM
Administrator	Computer science	1	ADMIN
Unemployed	Computer science	2	UE

5.1   Capabilities and Functionings Enabled

A number of capabilities and functionings were identified as being enabled by ERP education.

Increased Marketability. The majority of the students, 9 out of the 11, felt that the ERP course added value to their qualifications and gave them an advantage thus making them more marketable:

- *"I think it enhances my marketability in the business of accounting and accountancy because I have an advantage"* (ACCI).
- *"I would say I am because I have the skill that if maybe I had to apply for a job someone else who has not done it, I would say I am marketable"* (TCH2).
- *"In terms of getting a better job I think definitely it has increased my market value only that I have not used that to make an application in a different organisation"* (ITM1).

Self-Confidence. The majority of the students, 9 out of 11, felt that the course boosted their confidence in their ability to use ERP systems in the workplace. The accountants who are using ERPs in their current role at work felt that the ERP course had boosted their confidence with the ERP package they use in the workplace:

- *"In my handling of work at the office it has enhanced my confidence, it has improved my confidence with the package we work with"* (ACC1).
- *"It has really given me self-confidence on how to go about certain things and how to just handle a number of transactions which are IT-related"* (ACC2).

Gaining ERP Knowledge. All students noted that they gained knowledge on how ERP systems work and the integration of business processes in an organisation thus strengthening their ability to work on ERP systems. Some students had no knowledge on how ERP systems work but the course gave them an understanding of the different transactions and documents produced during each stage:

- *"The knowledge really increased, because now we are able to break down the activities that go into an organisation"* (ACC1).
- *"It has really strengthened my knowledge and I think even my ability to work because I think like in Sage there are certain functionalities I was not able to explore before, despite me using that program"* (ACC2).
- *"In my case I think I had zero knowledge of ERP technicals behind it, what goes on before you get to the point of creating the delivery note and all these other documents so I think having gone through this I appreciate exactly what goes into all these stages of the business processes"* (UE2).

Improved Decision-Making. Two respondents are now involved in decision making on ERP related issues and other issues in the workplace after taking the course:

- *"I am in the same position but in terms of making decisions for acquiring software for the company I think that has changed very much because of doing the course"* (ITM1).
- *"I was one of the people that was chosen to become a decision maker when they have to do certain things, they will consult you, what do you think we should do"* (ACC1).

Ability to Run a Business. Four respondents felt that the course had also given them knowledge on running a business. The students felt that the course gave them an overview of things that go into running a business. The course has motivated one respondent to start thinking of venturing into customisation of ERP software for small businesses for commercial purposes:

- *"I have been thinking of looking at a venture of customising a certain ERP for commercial basis so I feel empowered in the sense that I can look at a business, look at the business processes that are there and then try and make something that can work for them"* (ACC1).
- *"It gave me a view of what goes on in running sort of companies and also what it would take to start up your own and what would be needed of you in that case"* (UE2).

Improved Problem-Solving. Two respondents noted that the ERP course gave them the ability to solve ERP related problems in the workplace:

- *"Most of the times people call you for troubleshooting, when they have problems they ask you what do you think this would be and that has become common place presently because of the knowledge I have acquired, so, yes, that has really given me that enhanced feeling of being able to handle problems"* (ACC1).

Increased Likelihood of Getting a Higher Salary. Four respondents felt that the course increased their likelihood of getting a higher salary since they had a new skill added. However all 9 respondents that are currently employed have not had any increment in their salary since completing the course as they are still working for the same organisations and have not looked for other jobs outside their organisations:

- *"Most of the multi-nationals operating here I think all rely on ERP systems so I think it would definitely lead to a higher salary"* (UE2).

5.2   Personal Conversion Factors

Two personal conversion factors were identified as having impacted the capabilities and functionings identified.

Interest in Information Systems. Interest in information systems gave one respondent the drive to do the ERP course:

- *"Well, what motivated me is I have interest in Information Systems really because having worked with them at the university and personally having interest in Information Technology gave me a drive to do the course"* (ACC1).

Background. The students' background also had an impact on the capabilities enabled. The two accountants who came from a background where they had experience with other ERP packages before they did the ERP course seemed to have benefited more from the ERP course. One respondent who came from a background where they are involved in sourcing of ERP software in the workplace also seemed to have benefited more:

- *"Yes I did because in our organisation, the accounts department we use Sage ERP for our accounting purposes"* (ACC1).
- *"We use Sage so I had an idea of the ERP system"* (ACC2).
- *"I had theoretical knowledge of course being in the ICT industry but I had not actually worked with one where I would say: 'yes this is a comprehensive ERP system', but in the organisation we are also looking at sourcing an ERP system so that's what made it interesting to participate in the programme and also some background work which we were doing around that"* (ITM1).

5.3   Social Conversion Factors

Several social conversion factors were identified as having enabled or restricted the capabilities and functionings developed.

ERP Course Must Be Combined with Other Qualifications. One respondent recommended that the ERP course be combined with other qualifications in order for it to be beneficial to the employing organisation. Two respondents said they need to complete other professional and academic qualifications they are pursuing in order to reap the benefits of ERP education in the workplace and this had restricted them in some way:

- *"I think you need to have it in conjunction with another course that you become more beneficial to the organisation that employs you"* (ACC1).

ERP Course Does Not Fit Current Role. One respondent noted that the ERP course content does not fit their current role in the workplace hence the course had not benefitted them as they were not using it in their day to day work. Hence in some cases there is a lack of fit:

- *"Right now in my current role I could not say it is beneficial because the actual course and what I am doing are totally different"* (IT2).

ERP Qualification Not Appreciated in Organisation. One respondent noted that the ERP qualification was not appreciated and valued in the organisation where they are employed hence this had restricted the respondent from reaping the benefits of the course in their employing organisation:

- *"If I went into another organisation that appreciated the kind of training I've received in terms of ERPs but otherwise in the current organisation where I am what increases my salary has to do with the other qualifications that I have been pursuing"* (ACC1).

ERP System Not Implemented in the Workplace. Four respondents noted that they are not currently using ERP systems as they are not implemented in the organisations where they currently work. This has prevented them from using the knowledge acquired through the course:

- *"Well, if I was in an organisation where ERP is being used of course that was going to give me competitive advantage"* (ADMIN1).
- *"I am working in an organisation particularly in a department where we are not using an ERP so in terms of an immediate impact of course I am not using that knowledge just now"* (IT1).
- *"Maybe if I was in an organisation that has the system I will be able to practice and be able to use the knowledge"* (TCH2).

No Role in SAP ERP System in the Organisation. One respondent noted that although their organisation uses SAP ERP they do not have a role in the system as IT personnel other than supporting the users of the system. This had therefore restricted the respondent from implementing the knowledge they acquired from the course:

- *"Our organisation does use SAP but then as IT members of staff we do not have a role in the system as yet so we just support other users who use it"* (IT3).

Hands-On Experience Through Labs. Four respondents noted that the labs gave them hands-on experience with SAP ERP systems and helped to develop their confidence in using ERP systems. The students were exposed to transaction processing and document creation at each stage. Some respondents had not been exposed to SAP ERP prior to the course:

- *"It was really nice to have that hands on and it gave you the confidence really because I think if we had just gone through it on the board without having gone to the PC it would not, you know, give you that confidence out there but after the study there was that confidence that remained because we had the hands on experience from the workshops themselves"* (ACC1).
- *"But since it was practical at least I am able to even if I work in an organisation where they use ERP I will be able to use that because the labs gave me hands-on experience with the ERP system"* (ACC2).
- *"It gave us an appreciation of how exactly the systems work because I am sure a number of us had just heard of ERP but that gave us at least the hands-on experience"* (UE2).

Labs Lacked Implementation Aspect. One respondent noted that the labs lacked a practical aspect in that they were not given something to implement but were merely going through what was already implemented. Those from a Computer science background were hoping that the course would involve an aspect of programming:

- *"We lacked a practical aspect, what I mean is we should have been given something to implement ourselves, it i like we were just working on something which is already implemented. We were hoping to be given another part of ESEFA which involves programming which was lacking"* (UE1).

Local Zambikes Case Study. Eight respondents noted that the Zambikes case study made it easier for them to understand the business processes involved in running a business and the role that ERP systems play in the integration of business processes. The case study gave them an idea of what is involved in running a business. The fact that the case study was based on a Zambian company made the case study more relatable to the students:

- *"That was the core of understanding how ERP works"* (ADMIN1).
- *"It was a classic example because it brought the study to life with an organisation that is local and, you know, it made it so real and it was not just theoretical anymore because when you looked at those guys it was practical and then that is an organisation that is operating here in Zambia, in our environment, in our economy"* (ACC1).

- *"I think in our case we had Zambikes as the case study so I think that being a local company I think that was good as well, it made the content a bit more relatable for us because we could see things from the local perspective rather than having a foreign case study"* (UE2).

5.4   Environmental Conversion Factors

Some environmental factors also impacted the capabilities that were enabled by ERP.

No Jobs Requiring ERP Skills. Two respondents noted that there are no jobs requiring ERP skills despite having done the ERP course. They claim that there are no job adverts requiring ERP skills:

- *"I seriously have not seen a lot of job adverts. I have not seen adverts maybe I think when you are already in an organisation and then they want to implement it then you would have that opportunity to, but I have not seen organisations that are going to advertise and say they want someone with this skill"* (TCH2).
- *"I have tried to apply for jobs here and there but it seems even when it comes to the job adverts that are currently in Zambia, it is very rare to find the ERP qualification appearing, which means that most people they still do not know about it"* (UE1).

Employers Not Aware of ESEFA ERP Graduates. One respondent noted that employers are not aware about the ESEFA ERP course and the presence of graduates with ERP skills in the country:

- *"First and foremost employers should understand that the ESEFA graduates are within the country and then two, institutions should be able to sensitise the employers on the kind of graduates they have produced, because to start with, just as you have said, the outsourcing aspect will not stop if employers are not sensitised because most of them seem not to understand that we have this kind of personnel in Zambia"* (UE1).

5.5   Choices

Not yet Looking for Another Job. Four respondents chose not to apply for other jobs and have not used the ERP qualification to look for other jobs:

- *"I am not yet looking for another job I want to finish with my Masters then I can start looking for another job"* (ACC2).
- *"I have not yet ventured into the market as it were"* (ACC1).
- *"In terms of getting a better job I think definitely it has increased my market value, only that I have not used that to make an application in a different organisation"* (ITM1).

Need to Complete Other Studies. Two respondents chose to complete their studies first before looking for other jobs:

- *"I still have to complete my other courses because then with the SAP training itself I am not able to get a job"* (ACC1).
- *"I really like want to concentrate on my masters, finish my Masters then after finishing my masters then I will be able to launch myself again on the market"* (ACC2).

5.6   Resultant Framework

The findings are summarized in the resultant framework in Fig. 2. ERP education is the resource or capability input and how this is converted into capabilities is determined by the context, that is, the personal, social and environmental conversion factors. The capability set shows the capabilities enabled and the dimensions impacted by ERP education as per Gigler's indicators of individual empowerment which are categorized into psychological, social (human capital) and economic dimensions. The conversion factors identified enable or restrict the choices made and the achieved functionings. Choices also enable or restrict the achieved functionings. The psychological and social capability set were identified as capabilities and achieved functionings while the economic capability set were identified as capabilities.

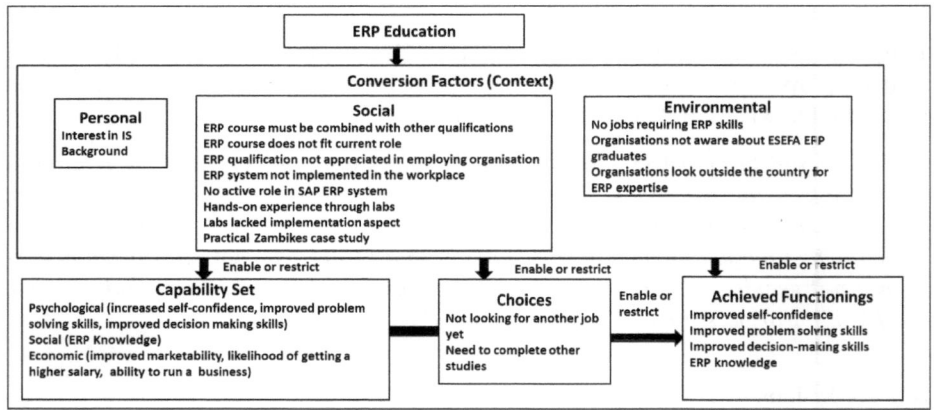

Fig. 2. Resultant framework

6   Conclusion

The aim of this paper was to explore the impact that ERP education has on post-graduate students in Zambia from a capabilities perspective and the contextual issues that impact these capabilities. This was done by means of a case study at the University of Zambia. The study revealed that ERP education enabled seven capabilities for the students: improved marketability, improved self-confidence, enhanced ERP knowledge, improved decision making skills, ability to run a business, improved problem solving skills and increased likelihood of getting a higher salary. ERP education impacts students in the psychological, social (human capital) and economic dimensions. The study also identified choices that enabled or restricted the capabilities and functionings. More significantly, the study also identified how the students' context, that is the personal, social and environmental conversion factors, enabled or restricted capabilities and functionings. These contextual issues show that students in different regions will benefit differently from ERP education and how the education is embedded in coursework has an impact. Hence context has to be considered prior to using global curricula. A limitation of this study was that the majority of the postgraduate students interviewed were from Computer Science. The availability of the students at the time of the interviews was the most influencing factor when selecting the interviewees. Future research is needed to interview more postgraduate students from the other disciplines who took the ERP course to get more diverse perspectives and make the findings of this paper more generalisable. Universities integrating ERP in their curriculum can benefit from the findings of this paper as it can assist in evaluating the success of ERP education. Employers seeking to hire students with ERP skills can also benefit from this paper as it can assist in determining how best they can benefit from skills of ERP graduates.

References

1. Boykin, R.F., Benjamin-Martz, W.: The integration of ERP into a logistics curriculum: applying a systems approach. J. Enterp. Inf. Manag. **17**(1), 45–55 (2004)
2. Bradford, M., Vijayaraman, B.S., Chandra, A.: The status of ERP integration in business school curricula: results of a survey of business schools. Commun. Assoc. Inf. Syst. **12**(1), 26 (2003)
3. Creswell, J.W., Creswell, J.D.: Research Design: Qualitative, Quantitative, and Mixed Methods Approaches. Sage, Thousand Oaks (2017)
4. Fedorowicz, J., Gelinas, U.J., Usoff, C., Hachey, G.: Twelve tips for successfully integrating enterprise systems across the curriculum. J. Inf. Syst. Educ. **15**(3), 235 (2004)
5. Gigler, B.S.: Including the excluded – can ICTs empower poor communities? Towards an alternative evaluation framework based on the capability approach. In: Proceedings 4th International Conference on the Capability Approach, Pavia (2004)
6. Hatakka, M., Andersson, A., Grønlund, Å.: Students' use of one to one laptops: a capability approach analysis. Inf. Technol. People **26**(1), 94–112 (2013)
7. Henke, P., Seymour, L.F., van Belle, J.P.: Impact of an E-learning initiative in the context of ICT4D: a case study of offering an advanced internet course in underprivileged communities. J. Emerg. Trends Educ. Res. Policy Stud. **5**(7), 111 (2014)

8. Hepner, M., Dickson, W.: The value of ERP curriculum integration: perspectives from the research. J. Inf. Syst. Educ. **24**(4), 309 (2013)
9. Klein, H.K., Myers, M.D.: A set of principles for conducting and evaluating interpretive field studies in information systems. MIS Q. **23**(1), 67–93 (1999)
10. Mahanga, K.M., Seymour, L.F.: Enterprise resource planning Teaching Challenges faced by Lecturers in African Higher Education institutions. In: Proceedings SACLA 2016 CCIS 642, pp. 179–186 (2016)
11. Marshall, M.N.: Sampling for qualitative research. Fam. Pract. **13**(6), 522–526 (1996)
12. Ravesteyn, P., Kohler, A.: Industry participation in educating enterprise resource planning. Commun. IIMA **9**(2), 5 (2009)
13. Robeyns, I.: The capability approach: a theoretical survey. J. Hum. Dev. **6**(1), 93–117 (2005)
14. Saito, M.: Amartya Sen's capability approach to education: a critical exploration. J. Philos. Educ. **37**(1), 17–33 (2003)
15. Seethamraju, R.: Enterprise systems (ES) software in business school curriculum: evaluation of design and delivery. J. Inf. Syst. Educ. **18**(1), 69 (2007)
16. Vaismoradi, M., Turunen, H., Bondas, T.: Content analysis and thematic analysis: implications for conducting a qualitative descriptive study. Nurs. Health Sci. **15**(3), 398–405 (2013)
17. Walsham, G.: Interpretive case studies in IS research: nature and method. Eur. J. Inf. Syst. **4**(2), 74–81 (1995)

Qualifications and Skill Levels of Digital Forensics Practitioners in South Africa: An Exploratory Study

Mannis Stenvert[✉] and Irwin Brown

Department of Information Systems, University of Cape Town,
Cape Town, South Africa
mannis.stenvert@alumni.uct.ac.za

Abstract. Digital forensic investigations require competence in skills associated with an investigation which is often measured through qualifications consisting of scholastic education, digital forensic training, digital forensic certification, and digital forensics work-related experience. While prior research has been conducted into the qualifications of digital forensic practitioners within the South African environment, the association between qualifications and measures of skill has not been addressed. This research study utilises a conceptual research framework to test the association between qualifications and the skills levels of digital forensic practitioners in South Africa. The findings show that continuous training and the level of testimony provided by a digital forensics practitioner in a civil or criminal procedure are positively associated with overall skills level. Other factors such as formal education, number of forensics training courses, certification, and work-related experience did not have a direct association with the measured skill. Further research is hence needed to understand the role of these factors in improving skill levels.

Keywords: Digital forensics · Qualifications and skills · South Africa

1 Introduction

In a modern-day crime fighting society, where digital media plays an increasing role as part of evidence, the role of the digital forensic practitioner (DFP) is becoming more relevant. Due to the rapid growth in technology focus has evolved from computer forensics into the digital forensics (DF) domain [30]. DF is defined as the application of predefined scientific procedures and techniques, with the assistance of software, hardware, and other tools, to achieve successful preservation, identification, extraction, and documentation of computerised evidence stored in a magnetically encoded format for the purpose of testimony in a disciplinary forum or a court of law [16,21].

The draft Republic of South Africa Cybercrimes and Cybersecurity Bill stipulates that an affidavit addressing DF can only be completed by an individual

© Springer Nature Switzerland AG 2019
S. Kabanda et al. (Eds.): SACLA 2018, CCIS 963, pp. 345–361, 2019.
https://doi.org/10.1007/978-3-030-05813-5_23

who *"possesses relevant qualifications, expertise and experience which make him or her competent to make the affidavit"* [24] (p. 94). DFPs must thus be qualified with the necessary training and technical knowledge to identify and implement the required methods when handling digital evidence, but the qualification requirements and the way of measure is not defined by the proposed bill. To further complicate this requirement and the assessment thereof, an internationally agreed minimum level of training or certification has not been established for DFPs [9].

The most common method used in measuring national workforce skills, worldwide, is the level of qualification within the applied field of studies [22]. Due to the wide variety of scholastic education, specialised training, professional certification, and work-related experience amongst DFPs, there is a need to better understand the factors that contribute towards the skills levels of DFPs and the measure of the actual levels of their skills [3]. Previous research has looked at the qualification requirements for DFPs internationally [7,25,33] and these guidelines were used as a method in measuring the competencies of DFPs in South Africa (SA) [15]. Research has however not been conducted into the relationship between qualifications and the job-related skills levels of DFPs in SA. The aim of this research is therefore to establish the impact of education, training, certification, and experience on the measured competency levels of DFPs in SA.

The next section reviews literature on the subject matter and develops a conceptual framework for measuring the competency levels of DFPs by means of the skills required in performing a digital forensic investigation (DFI). Thereafter the research design used is outlined followed by the results of data collection and analysis. Finally, the paper is concluded and recommendations for future research are made.

2   Related Work

The following literature review explains the concepts relating to DF, provides an overview of the state of DFPs in SA, and examines standardisation of qualifications within the DF domain. The literature review then addresses the concepts of qualification and skill within the DF domain while outlining DF qualifications and competencies. The focus then shifts to DFP skills levels so as to develop a framework for the purpose of measuring DFP skills.

2.1   Digital Forensics Practice

Forensics incorporates the use of science and/or technology for the purpose of establishing facts and therefore a DFI is the mechanism that uses science and technology to advance and confirm arguments relating to a specific digital incident [4]. A DFI is defined as a specific investigation type pursuing scientific procedures and utilising techniques that will allow the resulting outcome, referred to as digital evidence, to be admissible in corporate disciplinary hearings or a court of law [16]. The objective of a DFP is the answering of questions about past events through the development and application of tests and theories, within science and technology, while examining DFI artefacts which can be evidence admissible in a court of law [4]. Digital forensic practitioners work with law enforcement agencies and private institutions and are trained professionals in the field of data recovery and data analysis of data storages devices, such as computers, cell phones, and other external data storages devices [11].

In SA, research into DF quality assurance within the SA government and private sectors, focussing on full time DFPs supporting criminal investigations and prosecutions has been conducted [13]. The research finds that none of the participants have specialised forensic science training nor DF training that would adequately address quality assurance. These omissions in culmination with excessive caseloads and mediocre supervision would probably account for the inadequate levels of quality assurance practices by DFPs [13].

The state of DFP competence in SA as typified by secondary school education, undergraduate tertiary education, post graduate tertiary education, DF training, competency testing, DF certification, and DF experience has also been examined [15]. The aforementioned research finds that DF in SA is in a poor state as per the crucial elements of DFP qualification, training, competency, and certification. A concern is that DFPs lacking these elements, do not understand the risk of incompetence that comes with inadequate training and education [18]. Digital forensics cases are flawed where DFPs have not continuously updated their skills and knowledge, thus DFPs in SA are becoming outdated and irrelevant [15].

2.2   The Constituents of Qualifications

The combination of *education, training*, and *certification* has been a persistent concern amongst DFPs, and that there is still no standard in the professional certification of DFPs [10,27]. In addressing the Department of Labour of South Africa's Organising Framework for Occupations, as later adopted by the Department of Higher Education and Training [5], Squire states that the performing of a job by an individual incorporates a set or roles or tasks to be performed by that individual [29], and thus the skill level of that job relates to the proficient execution of the deliverables associated with the job. Level of skill can be measured by the extent or standard of formal education, job specific training, relevant work experience and certification [29,32]. Certification is a specifically designed process that assures individual competency and increase the credibility of the certificate holder [25].

Stander and Johnston illustrate the need for formal education in the domain of DF [31], revealing the large financial losses in SA due to the lack of DFPs. They indicate that there was no formal related education available in SA at the time, and that it was required. The SA education element of qualification has thus been absent as recently as ten years ago. Concerning training, in addition to knowledge of tools and techniques, a DFP must be able to explain and defend their reported outcomes to both a layman and an expert in a court or enquiry [8]. Education is aimed at lasting learning with the focus on principles and theories of method, whereas training has the aim of achieving a predefined goal with given tools, hence there is the risk that training becomes tool-centric instead of problem or skill-centric [36]. Training should evolve past apprentice-like showcasing of practices towards scientifically valid principles as entrenched in education [25]. Higher education is desirable when a degree can provide its holder the competence and expertise to testify in a court [8]. Higher education is however not regarded as the most important component of DFP qualifications, as relevant knowledge is substantiated through a professional certification that legitimises training, testing, and work experience, while at the same time assists courts, clients, and employees in assessing the full picture of qualification [8]. Proprietary certification, i.e. certification that focuses on specific vendor products or predefined operating platforms, tends to divide the DF industry as it creates the ill-advised view that DF cannot achieve a generic conceptual approach [27]. The structure and application of a DF process within a case is significantly impacted by individual perspectives and experience [23]. Often these services are performed by a DFP with no education or training, but only experience [25]. The DF process can only be accredited as being forensically sound when the four criteria of meaning, error, transparency, and experience are fulfilled, and of these criteria only experience addresses qualification [23]. Experience is derived from knowledge and skill in the performance of forensic application and is crucial in demonstrating the authenticity of evidence in a court of law [23].

2.3   Skills of Digital Forensic Practitioners

The skills level of a job relates to the proficient execution of the deliverables associated with that job [29]. The skills required by a DFP is encased in a process model for an effective DFI. An acceptable DF process requires that the acquisition of evidence is done in a non-destructive manner, the protecting and conserving of such evidence, the validation of data to initial evidence obtained, and the analysis of such data without changing it [17].

Digital Forensic Process Models. Several Digital Forensic Process Models (DFPM) have been developed over time. All these are overlapping and contain the three phases of acquisition of evidence, examination and analysis of evidence, and reporting of evidence. The Harmonised Digital Forensic Investigation Process Model (HDFIPM) is comprehensive in nature and is constructed out of the benefits of all previous DFPMs [35]. The model is applicable across various DFI scenarios with the aim of expediting investigations through common flow of activities, including pre-incident preparation up to and including evidence dissemination or storage of evidence [12]. Valjarevic and Venter added DF readiness processes to the existing initialisation processes, acquisitive processes, and investigative processes to create the Comprehensive HDFIPM [34]. When a DFI is conducted, a standardised and formalised process is required, for which the HDFIPM forms the basis of ISO 27043 'International Standard Information Technology: Security Techniques: Incident Investigation Principles and Processes' [12].

Skills Measuring of Digital Forensic Practitioners. Education learning theories are important tools in the assembly of a skills matrix. Bloom's Taxonomy of Learning [2] is a central educational framework for the development of learning artefacts and objects [36]. Bloom's Taxonomy has been applied against the tasks and duties performed by DFPs to measure the required core competencies of DFPs [36]. Through this Vendor Neutral Skills Based Framework (VNSBF), skill is expressed through a six-level measurement of expertise to demonstrate the proficiency of process execution by hierarchy progression, where the next level of advancement is only possible by mastering the previous levels of expertise. It is expected that a competency level of six will be difficult to achieve across all phases in the framework, even when the practitioner is remarkably knowledgeable and highly experienced [36].

3   Research Hypotheses and Framework

Skills levels measure the proficient execution of the deliverables associated and connected to an occupation [29] and a better understanding is required of how the factors of demographics, specifically education, training, certification, and experience influence the skills levels of DFPs [3]. Various institutions have different qualification guidelines for DFPs [7,25,33] and research has been conducted in measuring DFP qualifications in SA [15], but the research has not looked at the relationship between qualifications and job-related skills levels of DFPs in SA.

To give credence to the measure of skill by qualification, the skill level of a DFP requires to be measured other than by qualifications, and a set of hypotheses needs to be established and tested to determine if DFP qualifications have an impact on DFP skills levels within the SA context. The skill level of a DFP can be measured by formal education, training, work experience [29], and certification [32], thus these are factors that have an influence on the skill level of a DFP. The poor state of DFPs in SA has been attributed to the low levels of education, training, and certification [15]. The only factor that did not indicate a low level, was experience, where six or more years are regarded as fairly experienced [15]. Taking into consideration previous research [3,15,29,32], the hypotheses to be tested are as per Table 1.

The established variable for each construct in the testing of the hypothesis, as per reviewed literature, is outlined next.

3.1   Education Measures

National Qualification Framework Levels. The formal education level achieved by the DFP is measured by the National Qualification Framework (NQF) level as defined and administrated by the South African Qualification Authority [26], in line with previous research [3,15,29,32].

Course Modules in Digital Forensics. The completion of a module in DF within the formal education domain is measured by the indicated achievement, in line with previous research [15].

Table 1. Research hypotheses H1,..., H9

Area	Hypothesis	
Education	Hypothesis 1	The achieved National Qualification Framework level is positively associated with the skill level of digital forensic practitioners in South Africa
	Hypothesis 2	A module in digital forensics as part of formal education is positively associated with the skill level of digital forensic practitioners in South Africa
Training	Hypothesis 3	The number of relevant digital forensic training courses is positively associated with the skill level of digital forensic level of digital forensic practitiners in South Africa
	Hypothesis 4	Continuous training is positively associated with the skill level of digital forensic practitioners in South Africa
Certification	Hypothesis 5	The number of relevant digital forensic certifications is positively associated with the skill level of digital forensic practitiners in South Africa
	Hypothesis 6	Continuous evaluation is positively associated with the skill level of digital forensic practitioners in South Africa
Experience	Hypothesis 7	The years of digital forensic experience is positively associated with the skill level of digital forensic practitiners in South Africa
	Hypothesis 8	The level of testimony provided is positively associated with the skill level of digital forensic practitiners in South Africa
	Hypothesis 9	The number of court levels where testimony was given is positively associated with the skill level of digital forensic practitioners in South Africa

3.2   Training Measures

Number of Training Courses. The number of vendor specific DF training courses completed is measured by the count of such courses. This is in line with previous research [3, 15].

Continuous Training. The frequency of DF training courses is measured by the regularity of the completion of such courses [15].

3.3   Certification Measures

Number of Certifications. The number of vendor neutral DF training courses completed is measured by the count of such certifications [3, 15].

Continuous Evaluation. The frequency of partaking in DF continuous evaluation is measured by the regularity of the evaluation of such certifications [15].

3.4 Experience Measures

Years of Experience. Experience in number of years in DF is measured by the sum of experience within the DF domain [3, 15, 29, 32].

Levels of Testimony. The highest level of testimony provided as a DFP is measured by the highest level of disciplinary hearing or court representation as derived from the Department of Justice and Constitutional Development [6], in line with [3, 15].

Number of Court Levels. The number of different levels of testimony provided as a DFP is measured by the count of different levels of court representation as derived from the Department of Justice and Constitutional Development [6], in line with [3, 15].

3.5 Conceptual Research Framework

Qualification in the forms of education, training, certification, and experience are hypothesised, as per Table 1, in having a positive impact on the skills levels of DFPs in SA. The conceptual research framework is outlined as per Fig. 1, and demonstrates the expected impact of qualifications on the skills levels of DFPs in SA as determined through the VNSBF on the HDFIPM.

4 Research Method

A positivist deductive quantitative survey was conducted to test the hypotheses in the conceptual framework. The target population is the actual population of DFPs in SA active in the DF domain. Jordaan indicates that the population size of the DFPs in SA is unknown [14], but that estimates put it at no more than 150 practitioners. With an estimated target population of 150 DFPs the required sample size for generalization would be 108 participants, with a confidence level of 95 per cent and margin of error of five per cent [28]. The sample frame for this research makes use of the Association of Certified Fraud Examiners South Africa Chapter (ACFE), with an estimated sample size of 100 practitioners. Probability sampling through simple random sampling was adopted as the sampling technique [28]. All relevant registered members of the ACFE were approached with the random sampling being those that responded to the research intervention. The limitation to this sample frame is the exclusion of DFPs in SA that are not registered with the ACFE. Achieving 108 respondents through the distribution list of the ACFE was not possible, which limits the generalizability of

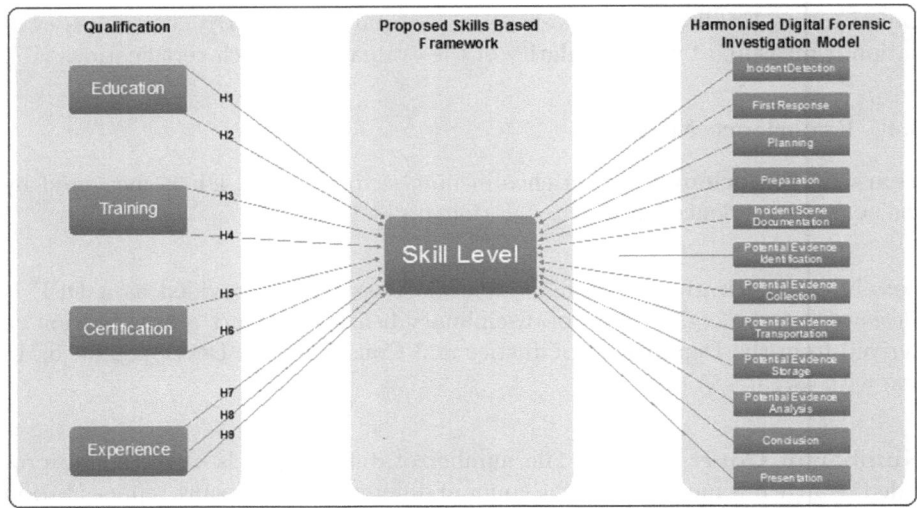

Fig. 1. Conceptual research framework including the hypotheses H1,..., H9

results. The aim was however to achieve a sample population of 100, provided respondents consent and were willing to participate.

The data collection was done through a web questionnaire as a self-completed, internet-based questionnaire [28] utilising the online research instrument *Qualtrics.*[1] The response format of the survey was structured using a combination of the response formats including dichotomous, nominal, ordinal and interval level [1]. All participating DFPs consented to the conducting of the research. Anonymity of the respondents was maintained and data privacy upheld. Participation was voluntary and participants could withdraw at any time.[2]

Descriptive data analysis was deployed for the purpose of demographic layout and measured skills of respondents by means of frequency and descriptive statistical analysis. For the process of reliability of data utilised in the overall skill measure of respondents, the Cronbach's Alpha Test was used in validation. In the process of hypotheses testing, Shapiro-Wilk Normality Test was used for data normality, Kruskal-Wallis H Test and Mann-Whitney U Test used for actual hypotheses testing, and Spearman's Rank-Order Correlation Coefficient for the measure of direction and strength when hypotheses were accepted.

---

[1] www.qualtrics.com.
[2] The research project was approved by our university and complied with the institutionally prescribed codes of ethics.

5   Results and Analysis

5.1   Respondent Profile

The research yielded 54 respondents of whom 26% ($n = 14$) were unusable and 5.5% ($n = 3$) were non-practicing respondents, so omitted from this study. 5.5% ($n = 3$) had incomplete relevant data, so 63% ($n = 34$) complete data forms were left to work with. The sample consists out of 75.68% ($n = 28$) male respondents and 24.32% ($n = 9$) female respondents. The ethnic distribution was 21.62% African ($n = 8$), 24.32% Coloured ($n = 9$), 8.11% ($n = 3$) Indian, and 43.24% ($n = 16$) White. One respondent did not declare ethnicity, and no respondents were measured from the Asian ethnicity group. The age distribution of the respondents was predominantly ($n = 18$, 48.65%) in the bracket of 30 and 39 years, with the bracket of 40 and 49 years the second highest ($n = 16$, 43.24%). Overall 91.89% ($n = 34$) respondents fall within these two brackets. These figures might indicate that the respondents developed into the field of DF instead of entering it as a first choice from high school. Respondents were concentrated in the geographical areas of Gauteng ($n = 21$, 56.76%) and Western Cape ($n = 10$, 27.03%). The two provinces make up 83.78% ($n = 31$) of all respondents with no respondents measured in Limpopo, Mpumalanga, North West, or the Northern Cape. Current sector employment was skewed towards the public sector ($n = 24$, 64.86%) with most respondents active in the domain of public sector law enforcement ($n = 17$, 45.95%).

5.2   Qualification Profile

In analysing the highest level of formal education, 5.41% ($n = 2$) respondents have Masters degrees, 27.03% ($n = 10$) Honours degrees,[3] 64.86% ($n = 24$) a 'National Diploma' or Bachelor degree, and 5.41% ($n = 2$) respondents have a grade 12 highschool education.

With the focus on training, most respondents indicate formal training in DF ($n = 33$, 89.19%) and vendor specific training ($n = 34$, 91.89%). A much lower percentage is however indicated for formal DF certification where 67.57% ($n = 25$) of respondents indicated this. The average number of vendor specific training courses completed by the respective respondents are three, whereas the average number of certifications completed by the respective recipients is one. These figures appear low and might indicate that respondents do not rely on training and certification as a source of development. Continuous training every year is indicated by 43.24% ($n = 16$) of respondents, while 21.62% ($n = 8$) indicate they never partake in continuous training. On the same measure for continuous evaluation, 48.65% ($n = 18$) do so every year while 32.43% ($n = 12$) are never evaluated. These figures are in contrast with the average number of training interventions and certifications, unless these interventions are regularly repeated.

---

[3] In South Africa the 'Honours' degree is an extension of the Bachelor degree which enables a student to commence with Master-studies thereafter. It is thus similar to the final study-year of the (longer) U.S. American Bachelor curriculum.

Table 2. Measured skills levels L1,..., L6; $\checkmark$ = "Skill is required for this level L_i"

Measured skills	L1	L2	L3	L4	L5	L6
Define (Knowledge): Ability to characterise or define the activity	$\checkmark$	$\checkmark$	$\checkmark$	$\checkmark$	$\checkmark$	$\checkmark$
Apply (Comprehension): Ability to apply suitable methods that allow the completion of the activity		$\checkmark$	$\checkmark$	$\checkmark$	$\checkmark$	$\checkmark$
Explain (Application): Ability to employ an activity and explain the concepts and processes involved			$\checkmark$	$\checkmark$	$\checkmark$	$\checkmark$
Evaluate (Analysis): Ability to effectively evaluate and analyse the activity				$\checkmark$	$\checkmark$	$\checkmark$
Critique (Synthesis): Ability to rigorously critique scientific method used in the activity					$\checkmark$	$\checkmark$
Synthesis (Evaluation): Ability to evaluate and fuse information through scientific methods with the aim of producing and authenticated solution to activity						$\checkmark$

In analysing the experience levels of the sample, 64.86% ($n = 24$) of respondents indicated experience levels greater than five years. The largest grouping of respondents ($n = 17$, 45.95%) indicated experience between 5 and 10 years whereas the parameters of 10 to 15 years ($n = 6$, 16.22%) also makes for a notable mention. With the focus on experience obtained through testimony in a disciplinary hearing or a court of law, 54.05% ($n = 20$) of respondents indicate DF testimony. Further analysis of those who have testified indicates that 95% ($n = 19$) has done so up to a High Court level and 60% ($n = 12$) have testified in three or more levels of hearings. A large percentage of respondents had not formally testified and this can be interpreted that those respondents either lacked experience or that they were not active in a sector of DF that require legal testimony.

5.3   Vendor Neutral Skills Based Framework

The measured skills levels of a DFP are as per Table 2. Table 3 provides a consolidation of descriptive statistics. It outlines the results of the method used by the VNSBF in measuring six levels of skill for each of the 12 phases of the HDFIPM and includes the overall skill measured for the HDFIPM. The overall skill level is calculated per individual and rounded down per individual before the calculation of the overall skill mean. This is done in accordance with guidelines [36] where an individual cannot progress to the next skill level unless the previous skill level has been obtained.

The average overall skill measured for the research participants is indicated by the mean value of 3.79 (SD= 1.572), which implies the ability to employ

Table 3. Descriptive statistics w.r.t. vendor neutral skills based framework

	Level by N							Level by N%						Statistics			
	1	2	3	4	5	6	Total	1	2	3	4	5	6	Mean	Median	Mode	Std. Deviation
Overall Skill Measured	4	4	5	7	10	4	34	11.76%	11.76%	14.71%	20.59%	29.41%	11.76%	3.79	4.00	5	1.572
Phase 01: Incident Detection	5	4	8	6	5	6	34	14.71%	11.76%	23.53%	17.65%	14.71%	17.65%	3.59	3.50	3	1.572
Phase 02: First Response	1	3	5	8	5	12	34	2.94%	8.82%	14.71%	23.53%	14.71%	35.29%	4.44	4.50	6	1.481
Phase 03: Planning	1	5	3	7	8	10	34	2.94%	14.71%	8.82%	20.59%	23.53%	29.41%	4.35	5.00	6	1.515
Phase 04: Preparation	4	3	3	9	6	9	34	11.76%	8.82%	8.82%	26.47%	17.65%	26.47%	4.09	4.00	4*	1.676
Phase 05: Incident Scene Documentation	2	4	3	6	5	14	34	5.88%	11.76%	8.82%	17.65%	14.71%	41.18%	4.47	5.00	6	1.656
Phase 06: Potential Evidence Identification	1	6	6	5	8	8	34	2.94%	17.65%	17.65%	14.71%	23.53%	23.53%	4.09	4.00	5*	1.545
Phase 07: Potential Evidence Collection	2	5	2	5	7	13	34	5.88%	14.71%	5.88%	14.71%	20.59%	38.24%	4.44	5.00	6	1.673
Phase 08: Potential Evidence Transportation	1	7	2	3	10	11	34	2.94%	20.59%	5.88%	8.82%	29.41%	32.35%	4.38	5.00	6	1.833
Phase 09: Potential Evidence Storage	2	5	6	3	6	12	34	5.88%	14.71%	17.65%	8.82%	17.65%	35.29%	4.24	5.00	6	1.707
Phase 10: Potential Evidence Analysis	5	3	0	8	10	8	34	14.71%	8.82%	0.00%	23.53%	29.41%	23.53%	4.15	5.00	5	1.726
Phase 11: Potential Evidence Presentation	6	1	4	3	10	10	34	17.65%	2.94%	11.76%	8.82%	29.41%	29.41%	4.18	5.00	5*	1.834
Phase 12: Conclusion	5	2	3	9	12	12	34	14.71%	5.88%	8.82%	8.82%	26.47%	35.29%	4.32	5.00	6	1.821
	35	48	45	66	89	125	408	8.58%	11.76%	11.03%	16.18%	21.81%	30.64%				

an investigation and explain the concepts and processes involved (Level 3). The median value of 4.00, however is reflective of the ability to effectively evaluate and analyse a DFI (Level 4). It is however a concern that 11.76% ($n = 4$) of respondents reported an inability to apply suitable methods that would allow for the successful completion of a DFI (Level 1). At the other extreme 11.76% ($n = 4$) of respondents reported an ability to synthesise (Level 6). The biggest grouping of respondents ($n = 10$, 29.41%) were accounted for in skill Level 5.

5.4 Hypothesis Testing

Hypothesis testing was performed by means of the Kruskal-Wallis H Test, also referred to as the one-way analysis of variance (ANOVA) on ranks, and the Mann-Whitney U Test. The Kruskal-Wallis H Test is a non-parametric technique for verifying whether samples originate from the same distribution, by not assuming normal distribution of the response variables, while focussing on ranked ordinal data [20]. The Mann-Whitney U Test determines the likelihood that variables with an ordinal nature are different within two groups and is used in the circumstances where the research sample is small in size and the data is skewed [28]. The Spearman's Rank-Order Correlation Coefficient was also applied. Spearman's Rank-Order Correlation Coefficient is a nonparametric measure of direction and strength on variables of an ordinal nature, and is therefore used in statistically determining the extent of the positive or negative relationship between the independent and the dependent variables [28].

Hypothesis 1: Education—National Qualification Framework. The results obtained from the applied Kruskal-Wallis H Test ($\chi^2(3) = 0.998$, $p = 0.802$) suggest no statistically significant relationship between the respondents' NQF level and their overall skill measured. This hypothesis is thus *rejected*. The outcome of this hypothesis is inconsistent with research indicating formal education has an impact on the skills levels of DFPs [15, 29, 32], but is in agreement with research to the opposite [3].

Hypothesis 2: Education—Module in Digital Forensics. The results obtained from the applied Mann-Whitney U Test (U = 132.500, p = 0.885) suggest no statistically significant relationship between the respondents' completion of a module in DF as part of formal education and their overall skill measured. This hypothesis is thus *rejected*. The outcome of this hypothesis is inconsistent with research indicating formal education has an impact on the skills levels of DFPs [15, 29, 32], but is in agreement with research to the opposite [3].

Hypothesis 3: Training—Number of Relevant Training Courses. The results obtained from the applied Kruskal-Wallis H Test ($\chi^2(7)$ = 11.274, p = 0.127) suggest no statistically significant relationship between the respondents' number of relevant DF training courses and their overall skill measured. This hypothesis is thus *rejected*. The outcome of this hypothesis is inconsistent with research indicating training has an impact on the skills levels of DFPs [15, 29, 32], but is in agreement with research to the opposite [3].

Hypothesis 4: Training—Continuous Training. The results obtained from the applied Kruskal-Wallis H Test ($\chi^2(4)$ = 11.266, p = 0.024) suggest a statistically significant relationship between the respondents' continuous training and their overall skill measured. The applied Spearman's Rank-Order Correlation Coefficient (rs(32) = 0.498, p = 0.003) suggests a moderate positive correlation of statistical significance between the respondents' continuous training and their overall skill measured. On the basis of the above results, the hypothesis is thus *accepted*. The outcome of this hypothesis is in agreement with research indicating training has an impact on the skills levels of DFPs [15, 29, 32], but is in disagreement with research to the opposite [3].

Hypothesis 5: Certification—Number of Relevant Certifications. The results obtained from the applied Kruskal-Wallis H Test ($\chi^2(4)$ = 7.237, p = 0.124) suggest no statistically significant relationship between the respondents' number of relevant DF certifications and their overall skill measured. This hypothesis is thus *rejected*. The outcome of this hypothesis is inconsistent with research indicating certification has an impact on the skills levels of DFPs [3, 15, 29, 32].

Hypothesis 6: Certification—Continuous Evaluation. The results obtained from the applied Kruskal-Wallis H Test ($\chi^2(4)$ = 7.376, p = 0.117) suggest no statistically significant relationship between the respondents' continuous evaluation and their overall skill measured. This hypothesis is thus *rejected*. The outcome of this hypothesis is inconsistent with research indicating certification has an impact on the skills levels of DFPs [3, 15, 29, 32].

Hypothesis 7: Experience—Years of Digital Forensic Experience. The results obtained from the applied Kruskal-Wallis H Test ($\chi^2(4) = 7.826$, $p = 0.098$) suggest no statistically significant relationship between the respondents' years of DF experience and their overall skill measured. This hypothesis is thus *rejected*. The outcome of this hypothesis is inconsistent with research indicating experience has an impact on the skills levels of DFPs [15,29,32], but is in agreement with research to the opposite [3].

Hypothesis 8: Experience—Level of Testimony Provided. The results obtained from the applied Kruskal-Wallis H Test ($\chi^2(5) = 12.418$, $p = 0.029$) suggest a statistically significant relationship between the respondents' level of testimony provided and their overall skill measured. The applied Spearman's Rank-Order Correlation Coefficient ($rs(32) = 0.498$, $p = 0.003$) suggests a moderate positive correlation of statistically significance between the respondents' level of testimony provided and their overall skill measured. On the basis of the above results, the hypothesis is thus accepted. The outcome of this hypothesis is in agreement with research indicating experience has an impact on the skills levels of DFPs [15,29,32], but is in disagreement with research to the opposite [3]. It has to be noted that said research [3] measured a relationship between the number of court appearances and measured skills levels.

Hypothesis 9: Experience—Number of Levels Testified. The results obtained from the applied Kruskal-Wallis H Test ($\chi^2(6) = 10.945$, $p = 0.090$) suggest no statistically significant relationship between the respondents' number of court levels where testimony was given and their overall skill measured. This hypothesis is thus rejected. The outcome of this hypothesis is inconsistent with research indicating experience has an impact on the skills levels of DFPs [15,29,32], but is in agreement with research to the opposite [3]. It has to be noted that said research [3] measured a relationship between the number of court appearances and measured skills levels.

6 Discussion and Implications

In the skills level measuring, the average DFP in SA demonstrates a skill level between Explain (Application) and Evaluate (Analysis). This translates as the ability to conduct a DFI and the proficiency to explain the concepts and processes involved (Level 3) while almost achieving the ability to effectively evaluate and analyse a DFI (Level 4). The extremities have to be noted, as nearly 12% of DFPs in SA are not able to conduct a DFI (Level 1) while 12% are able to do so at the level of Synthesis (Level 6).

This study finds that qualifications, as measured through education, training, certification, and experience cannot be statistically confirmed as having an association with the skills levels of a DFP in SA on all tested hypotheses in this study.

Qualifications through continuous training and the level of civil or criminal testimony provided are statistically accepted as having a positive association with the skills levels of DFPs in SA. Qualifications through formal education, formal education DF modules, number of DF training courses or certifications, continuous evaluations, years of DF work-related experience, and number of court levels where testimony has been provided do not have an association with the skills levels of DFPs in SA. The outcomes of this study contribute towards research on DF skills [3,15,29,32] and warrant further research in exploring the exact relationship between education, training, certification, experience, and skill. It may be that the relationships are indirect, for example, education sets the foundation to enable professionals to acquire skills over a period of time, hence there may not be a discernible direct relationship. Experience may also act as a moderating influence on the relationship between qualifications such as education, training and certification, and skill levels.

7   Conclusions and Outlook

A conceptual research framework, derived from previously published literature was utilised in testing nine hypotheses to determine if qualifications have a positive association with the skills levels of DFPs in SA. This research finds that only continuous training and the level of testimony provided in civil or criminal procedures has an impact on the skills levels of the respondents. Literature likewise indicates a disconnect between the impact of qualifications on skills, as studies find for both relationships and non-relationships between qualifications and skills. The outcome of this study further adds to this uncertainty and the challenge in the proposed legal requirements of *"relevant qualifications, expertise and experience"* [24](p. 94). With a larger sample size, however, hypotheses may have been supported.

As the total population of DFPs in SA is not known and even the ACFE has no exact figures on the number of registered DFPs, the number of respondents used in the hypotheses testing (34) limits generalisation. A further limitation is the listing of training and certification courses in the survey. These lists cannot be considered as complete and the additional listing of courses by respondents was only counted as a value of one to the sum of listed courses selected by the participants. A further complication is the non-standardisation of courses. An expert panel review and supply of relevant courses will be more appropriate in this environment.

The method used in determining the skills levels of respondents is not a validated method. The method was however used due to its direct design towards DFPs. In addition, skills were measured by self-assessment. The DF domain in SA is still in its infancy, and although strides are continuously made in the technical scientific aspects of DF, ongoing research is required in the human development part.

Future research is required into the development of an attainable relevant DF qualification program that is vendor neutral and will meet legal requirements for the purpose of testimony in a court of law. Strengthening DF in SA further will be research into the establishment of a regulatory authority for DFPs in SA. This will contribute towards the advancement and standardisation of DF in SA.[4]

References

1. Bhattacherjee, A.: Social Science Research: Principles, Methods, and Practices, 2nd edn. University of South Florida Press, Gainesville (2012)
2. Bloom, B.S., Engelhart, M.D., Furst, E.J., Hill, W.H., Krathwohl, D.R.: Taxonomy of Educational Objectives: The Classification of Educational Goals. David McKay Company, Philadelphia (1956)
3. Carlton, G., Worthley, R.: Identifying a computer forensics expert: a study to measure the characteristics of forensic computer examiners. J. Dig. Forensic Secur. Law **5**(1), 5–19 (2010)
4. Carrier, B.D., Spafford, E.H.: An event-based digital forensic investigation framework. In: Proceedings of Digital Forensic Research Workshop, pp. 11–13 (2004)
5. Department of Higher Education and Training: Organising Framework for Occupations (OFO), Guideline No. 2013, p. 33, South Africa (2013)
6. Department Justice and Constitutional Development: Courts in South Africa. Governm. Communic. http://www.justice.gov.za/about/sa-courts.html
7. European Network of Forensic Science Institutes: Guidelines for Best Practice in the Forensic Examination of Digital Technology. In: Best Practice Guide 6(FIT-2005-001), p. 30 (2009)
8. Foit, D., Vukalović, J., Hausknecht, K.: Competencies and Skills needed for Digital Forensic Trainer. In: MIPRO 2015 Proceedings of 38th IEEE International Convention on Information and Communication Technology, Electronics and Microelectronics, pp. 1376–1381 (2015)
9. Grobler, M.: Digital forensic standards: international progress. In: SAISMC 2010 Proceedings of South African Information Security Multi-Conference, pp. 216–271 (2010)
10. Harichandran, V.S., Breitinger, F., Baggili, I., Marrington, A.: A cyber forensics needs analysis survey: revisiting the domain's needs a decade later. Comp. Secur. **57**, 1–13 (2016)
11. INFOSEC: Computer Forensics Investigator. https://www.infosecinstitute.com/career-profiles/computer-forensics-investigator
12. IOS: Information Technology – Security Techniques – Investigation Principles and Processes. Standard ISO/IEC 27043:2015 (2015)
13. Jordaan, J.: A Sample of Digital Forensic Quality Assurance in the South African Criminal Justice System. In: ISSA 2012 Proceedings International Information Security for South Africa Conference (2012)
14. Jordaan, J.: An Examination of Validation Practices in relation to the Forensic Acquisition of Digital Evidence in South Africa. M.-Diss., Rhodes Univ. (2014)
15. Jordaan, J., Bradshaw, K.: The current state of digital forensic practitioners in South Africa. In: ISSA 2015 Proceedings of International Information Security for South Africa Conference (2015)

---

[4] Such advancement might even be expected to motivate *educational innovation* in tertiary-academic digital forensics courses: see for example [19].

16. Köhn, M.D., Eloff, M.M., Eloff, J.H.P.: Integrated digital forensic process model. Comp. Secur. **38**, 103–115 (2013)
17. Kruse, W.G., Heiser, J.G.: Computer Forensics: Incident Response Essentials. Addison-Wesley, Boston (2001)
18. Laykin, E.: Investigative Computer Forensics: The Practical Guide for Lawyers, Accountants, Investigators, and Business Executives. Wiley, Hoboken (2013)
19. Leung, W.S.: Cheap latex, high-end thrills: a fantasy exercise in search and seizure. In: Liebenberg, J., Gruner, S. (eds.) SACLA 2017. CCIS, vol. 730, pp. 265–277. Springer, Cham (2017). https://doi.org/10.1007/978-3-319-69670-6_19
20. Liu, H.: Comparing Welch's ANOVA, a Kruskal-Wallis Test and Traditional ANOVA in case of Heterogeneity of Variance. M.-Diss., Virginia Commonwealth Univ. (2015)
21. Lunn, D.A.: Computer Forensics – An Overview. Technical report, SANS Inst., (2000)
22. Manca, F.: Why Do We Need to Measure Skills Better? Better Indicators for Better Policies! Technical report (2013). https://oecdskillsandwork.wordpress.com/2015/12/04/why-do-we-need-to-measure-skills-better-better-indicators-for-better-policies/
23. McKemmish, R.: When is digital evidence forensically sound? In: Ray, I., Shenoi, S. (eds.) DigitalForensics 2008. ITIFIP, vol. 285, pp. 3–15. Springer, Boston, MA (2008). https://doi.org/10.1007/978-0-387-84927-0_1
24. Minister of Justice and Correctional Services: Republic of South Africa Cybercrimes and Cybersecurity Bill (2017)
25. National Research Council: Strengthening Forensic Science in the United States: A Path Forward. National Academies Press (2009)
26. Republic of South Africa: National Qualifications Framework Act 67 of 2008. Government Gazette 32233(25) (2009)
27. Rogers, M.K., Seigfried, K.: The future of computer forensics: a needs analysis survey. Comp. Secur. **23**(1), 12–16 (2004)
28. Saunders, M.N.K., Lewis, P., Thornhill, A.: Research Methods for Business Students, 7th edn. Pearson, London (2015)
29. Squire, D.: Understanding the Organising Framework for Occupations. Technical report (2012). https://www.skillsportal.co.za/content/understanding-organising-framework-occupations
30. Srinivasan, S.: Digital forensics curriculum in security education. J. Inf. Technol. Educ. **12**, 147–157 (2013)
31. Stander, A., Johnston, K.: The need for and contents of a course in forensic information systems and computer science at the University of Cape Town. Informing Sci.: Int. J. Emerg. Transdiscipl. **4**(1), 63–72 (2007)
32. Taylor, C., Endicott-Popovsky, B., Phillips, A.: Forensics education: assessment and measures of excellence. In: SADFE 2007 Proceedings of 2nd International Workshop on Systematic Approaches to Digital Forensic Engineering, pp. 155–165 (2007)
33. United Nations Office on Drugs and Crime: Staff Skill Requirements and Equipment Recommendations for Forensic Science Laboratories (No. ST/NAR/2/REV.1), p. 138, UNO (2011)
34. Valjarevic, A., Venter, H.S.: A comprehensive and harmonized digital forensic investigation process model. J. Forensic Sci. **60**(6), 1467–1483 (2015)

35. Valjarevic, A., Venter, H.S.: Harmonised digital forensic investigation process model. In: ISSA 2012 Proceedings International Information Security for South Africa Conference (2012)
36. Valli, C.: Establishing a vendor neutral skills based framework for digital forensics curriculum development and competence assessment. In: Proceedings of Australian Digital Forensics Conference (2006)

Balancing Theory and Practice in an Introductory Operating Systems Course

Bennett Kankuzi(✉)

Department of Computer Science, North-West University, Mmabatho, South Africa
bennett.kankuzi@nwu.ac.za

Abstract. Operating systems is one core course of many computing curricula. However, many students find the course difficult and boring as they cannot practically relate to the inner workings of an operating system. This paper presents an approach which was used in delivering an undergraduate second year introductory operating systems course with the aim of balancing theory and practice in order to keep students motivated in the course. The students, however, did not have sufficient programming background to undertake kernel-level programming projects. The approach, therefore, involved complementing theory lessons with a series of practical tasks spread throughout the whole period of delivery of the course. An evaluation of the course showed that the performance of students taught using this approach was significantly higher than those taught theoretical operating system concepts only. Through a survey, students also expressed strong satisfaction that the approach contributed to a positive learning environment as the students also specifically found the course relevant and well balanced in theory and practice.

Keywords: Teaching operating systems · Student motivation

1 Introduction

Operating systems is one core course of many computer science, information systems and computer engineering curricula [5, 24]. It is a core course because many of the fundamental concepts learnt in an operating system course have wider applicability in other computing areas such as concurrent programming, algorithm design and implementation, modern device development, virtual environments, system security and network management [5]. Many students, however, find the course difficult [16]. This has been attributed to several reasons. Most operating system concepts are abstract and thus not easily understood [16]. For example, the abstract concept of a process is difficult to understand [16]. It is therefore difficult for many students to create correct mental models of operating system concepts [16]. Students also lack the pre-requisite knowledge expected of most operating system textbooks like advanced programming skills and as a result, they cannot easily work with low-level code such as the operating system kernel [16]. This leads to situations where a course is delivered

© Springer Nature Switzerland AG 2019
S. Kabanda et al. (Eds.): SACLA 2018, CCIS 963, pp. 362–375, 2019.
https://doi.org/10.1007/978-3-030-05813-5_24

based on theory only. However, there is need for balancing theory and practicals so that students see practical relevance of material being learned in class [16]. In general, it is also imperative that computing students are exposed to a wide range of applications and case studies that connect theory and skills learned in academia to real-world occurrences to appreciate their relevance and utility [24]. Nevertheless, achieving such a balance is often a challenge [16].

There are several approaches to teaching an operating systems course. A pure theoretical approach involves teaching fundamental concepts of operating systems by just following a prescribed textbook without any practical work [16]. However, many students never fully understand the relevance or meaning of the concepts and theory without having practical application [16]. Another approach is to give students several unrelated programming projects through which students at the end get to understand more of the functionality of an operating system by themselves [16]. The programming projects could be about concepts related to operating systems without actually involving programming an operating system such as implementing a solution to a critical section problem [1]. Another approach is to use simulations where a functionality of a real operating system can be simulated [16,20]. Instructional operating systems also simulate the functionality of real operating systems and students can be given programming assignments to modify or extend the simulated operating system [1]. Another approach is to give students modify or develop the kernel of real-world operating system [16,20]. This can be quite challenging for many students as source code for real-world operating systems is huge and hence difficult to comprehend [1]. Others have also proposed a 'middle-ground' teaching approach whereby the various approaches are combined without labouring students with details such as full operating system implementation [19]. For example, lectures on theoretical concepts are supplemented with practical programming projects and simulations in [23].

Prior knowledge is one factor that affects student's learning in science [12]. An instructional strategy should therefore take into consideration the learner's existing knowledge and skills [13]. It would therefore not be appropriate to introduce an operating system course by giving programming projects that will involve modifying the kernel source code of an operating system to students who do not have sufficient background in programming. However, a pure theoretical approach is also not appropriate for computing students [24]. In this paper, we present an approach which we used in an attempt to balance theory and practice in an introductory operating systems class which did not have enough programming background but, on the other hand, we wanted to have a course that balances theory with practice which could in turn keep students motivated in the course. Studies have shown that motivated students perform better academically [26]. We also present a detailed evaluation of our approach through various course evaluation metrics.

The rest of the paper is organized as follows: in Sect. 2, an overview of related work is presented. Our teaching approach is presented in Sect. 3 while its evaluation is presented in Sect. 4. Concluding remarks are in Sect. 5.

2   Related Work

There are several approaches to teaching an operating systems course such as presenting only theoretical concepts without any practical work, use of programming projects, use of simulations, and use of real-world operating systems.

Crossword puzzles and games have been used in [14] to teach operating system concepts, particularly, process management using a process state transition game. A virtual platform in which kernel-level projects using the Linux operating system can be developed and debugged by students has also been used in [20]. The rationale for this approach was to enable a large class of students to have hands-on kernel-level project experience with a real operating system, which can be difficult to achieve with a large class [20]. A virtual platform allows many students to share the same physical machine hence cuts on expense and administrative difficulties of providing a dedicated physical machine for each student [20].

A web-based interactive software tool in which students could by themselves have a simulation of memory management techniques particularly page replacement algorithms was developed in [8]. An interactive website that simulates the Ubuntu operating system inside a web browser was also developed in [9]. Using the website, students could explore both the graphical user interface (GUI) and the command line of an Ubuntu operating system environment. Additionally, students could self-test their acquired knowledge through an automated examination [9]. A Java-based, simulated operating system to teach operating system concepts through animations and to actively experiment with the algorithms, data structures and services of an operating system, was also developed in [16].

Operating system concepts have also been introduced through a series of Android kernel programming projects in which students had to modify the kernel code [2]. The projects were to introduce operating system concepts such as system calls, process management, virtual memory and file systems through modifying Android kernel code. The use of a mobile operating system to teach an operating system course was a departure from the use of desktop and server operating systems to introduce operating system concepts. A student evaluation of the course indicated that students preferred the use of a mobile operating system over the use of traditional desktop and server operating systems to learn operating system concepts [2].

Programming assignments have also been used to teach an operating systems course [10]. The programming assignments included user-level projects as well as basic kernel-level projects [10]. An evaluation of the approach showed that the programming assignments enhanced learning experience in the course and students had better grades [10].

Instructional operating systems such as Nachos [4], ICS-OS [11], GeekOS [15] and Qutenix [22] have also been used to teach operating system concepts. Instructional operating systems are smaller operating systems specifically designed to serve as a platform for instruction, rather than as fully-functional operating systems [1]. With instructional operating systems, students may be provided with a very minimal skeleton of the operating system and they extend the functionality of the operating system [1]. Students may also be tasked to modify existing code [1]. Instructional operating systems have smaller source code bases compared to mainstream operating systems, making them ideal for instruction as it is easier to comprehend and modify [11]. However, most instructional operating systems are not formally evaluated on their effectiveness [1].

Most of approaches that involve programming projects involve using derivatives of the Unix/Linux operating system. However, it is also possible to use the Microsoft Windows operating system [21]. However, unlike stable Unix-based curricula, a Windows-based operating system curriculum has to take into account of the continuous changes in versions of Microsoft Windows operating systems [21]. Accessing Windows source code is also a challenge as it is a proprietary operating system [21]. Moreover, even though Windows source code has been made available to academic institutions, managing complexity of the source code is a huge challenge [21].

Others also use a mixed approach to teaching an operating systems course. For example, a theoretical approach coupled with programming projects and simulations has been used in [23]. An informal evaluation of the approach showed that students enjoyed using simulations and student performance in exams also improved [23].

Many of the approaches that involve programming projects also require some considerable level of competency in programming and as such, may not be applicable to students without enough programming background. In our case, the students did not have sufficient programming background to do kernel-level programming projects. As such, we had to come up with an approach that takes this fact into consideration when trying to balance theory with practice. Many of the approaches, stated above, also lack formal evaluation on their effectiveness. In our case, we have also provided a formal evaluation of our approach.

3   Our Approach

The main objective of the course at our institution is to introduce students to fundamentals of operating systems. The course, in the 2017 class, had seventy-three registered students. The course was delivered through a series of eleven lectures and six practical assignments spread across a period of eleven weeks with one lecture per week.

Each lecture was allocated one hour and thirty minutes. Lecture topics delivered are given in Table 1. The course content is mainly taken from a prescribed textbook [25]. The lectures comprised a series of fundamentals of operating systems. Lecture 1 and lecture 2 involved introducing an operating system as an important piece of software on a computer system; functions of an operating system; and types of operating systems. Lecture 3 involved introducing the concept of system calls in relation to modes of operation of a CPU and how that affects the way application programs access privileged services from the operating system. Lecture 4 introduced various architectures of operating systems. Lectures 5, 6 and 7 introduced various concepts in how the operating system manages processes. This included topics such as the notion of a process; process states; process scheduling algorithms; threads; interprocess communication; and process synchronization. Lecture 8 and lecture 9 introduced various memory allocation techniques used by the operating system to manage memory on a computer system. Lecture 10 involved introducing how the operating system through the I/O subsystem manages I/O hardware. Lecture 11 introduced the concept of a file and related concepts such as file systems and directories as provided by the operating system. The lecture also introduced different security mechanisms provided by the operating system.

Table 1. Lectures delivered during the course

Lectures 1–2	General introduction to operating systems
Lecture 3	System calls
Lecture 4	Operating system structure
Lectures 5–7	Process management
Lectures 8–9	Memory management
Lecture 10	I/O device management
Lecture 11	File management and system security

Table 2. Practical tasks assigned during the course

Task 1	Downloading and installing any Linux distribution side by side with any Windows operating system
Task 2	Downloading and installing the latest NetBeans IDE and the latest Java Development Kit (java compiler) on a Linux platform
Task 3	Downloading and installing LibreOffice in MS Windows OS and Linux OS
Task 4	Introduction to the Linux command line
Task 5	Introduction to Shell Scripting in Linux
Task 6	Part 1: Introduction to Operating System Virtualization;
	Part 2: Introduction to Programming for the Android Operating System

The students were also given six practical assignments spread throughout the course delivery period. The tasks given are presented in Table 2. The practical tasks were done during their free time or during an allocated weekly two-hour practical period. Students could do the tasks on their own computers or institutional undergraduate laboratory computers, where possible. Each student was asked to write documentation in LaTeX about the steps they took to accomplish the task (including screenshots) and if possible, state the challenges they encountered. Documentation had to be submitted as a portable document format (pdf) document through the university's online learning portal for marking. In marking the tasks, students also had to demonstrate, individually, to the instructor the practical work they had done.

In Task 1, students had to install a Linux distribution of their choice side by side with a Microsoft Windows operating system. The objective of Task 1 was to demonstrate several concepts including disk partitioning, modification of the boot process and the fact that many operating systems can be installed side by side on a single machine. The objective of Task 2 was to demonstrate how to install application programs in other operating systems other than Microsoft Windows. Students had to follow installation instructions from the software owners which included working with the Linux command line and modifying configuration files. The objective of Task 3 was to demonstrate that a cross-platform application program running on different operating systems might not have the same code base as it has to make different system calls corresponding to the hosting operating system. Task 4 included executing process management commands on the Linux command line. With the commands, students could visualize processes through process trees, create and kill processes, check memory and hard disk usage, among other things. Students also had to learn to navigate the Linux directory structure using the command line. Security concepts were also explored through setting file permissions through the command line. Task 5 included students writing simple shell programs. The aim of this task was to provide a glimpse to the tools and skills needed to understand, modify, compile, install, and debug the Linux kernel. The first part of Task 6 involved students installing a Linux virtual machine inside a Microsoft Windows machine. The aim of this task was to demonstrate modern trends in operating systems, such as virtualization, which are making it possible to have services like cloud computing. The second part of Task 6 involved writing an Android application and deploying it on an Android mobile phone. The aim was to indirectly introduce students to the architecture of a mobile operating system.

4   Evaluation of Our Approach

4.1   Method

The pedagogical approach was primarily evaluated by comparing the performance of students, based on the final grades obtained with respect to the first opportunity examinations in the 2016 class and the 2017 class. Students whose final grade after writing first opportunity examinations is less than 50% are deemed to have failed and are therefore given a second opportunity examination. In this paper, we compare performance of students, based on the final grades obtained with respect to the first opportunity examinations.

In the 2016 class, students were taught by another lecturer and were taught operating systems concepts without any practicals. In the 2017 class, students were taught using the approach presented in this paper. The final grades of students in the two classes, with respect to the first opportunity final examinations, were compared. The 2016 class had sixty-seven students who wrote the first opportunity examination while the 2017 class had seventy students who wrote the first opportunity examination. However, ten students in the 2016 class also failed the second opportunity examination and thus failed the course and therefore retook the course in 2017. Performance comparison for the ten students who retook the course was therefore done separately from the rest of the students.

A course final grade for each student in the 2016 class was derived by taking 50% from first opportunity final written examination score and 50% from written tests score. On the other hand, a course final grade for each student in the 2017 class was derived by taking 50% from first opportunity final written examination score, 25% written tests score and 25% from practical submissions score. All the six practical submissions were used in calculating the practical submissions score. A student is deemed to have passed the course if they get a final grade of 50% or above.

Student evaluation of the course by the 2017 class was also considered. Student evaluation is used to gauge the perception of students of their learning environment with respect to the course. Student evaluation of the course by the 2017 class was independently done by the department of the university concerned with the development of teaching and learning at the institution. The department administers questionnaires to students at the end of each course to gather student feedback on a course. Questionnaires are completed anonymously so that students should be able to express their experiences freely. The questionnaire has twenty-five statements with five categories, namely preparation, presentation, instructor friendliness, assessment and subject content. The students mark their experiences against a particular statement on a rating of a scale of 1 to 4 with 1 for 'Strongly disagree', 2 for 'Disagree', 3 for 'Agree' and 4 for 'Strongly Agree'. For purposes of this paper, we also specifically looked at three questions that focused on student's perception of subject content, i.e. how relevant students found the concepts and theories taught in the course; how students found theory being taught in the course to be related to practice; and how students found what was taught in class to be in tandem with relevant recent developments in the subject. Thirty-one out of the seventy-three registered students completed and submitted the questionnaires.

4.2 Results

The minimum mark in the 2016 class for the ten students who retook the module in 2017 was 31% and maximum mark was 47%. The average grade of the ten students in the 2016 class was 41% with a standard deviation of 4 % points. The minimum mark for the ten students in the 2017 class was 35% and maximum mark was 68%. The average grade of the ten students in 2017 was 53% with a standard deviation of 11% points. A box-plot illustration of the final grades of the ten students in the two classes is given in Fig. 1.

Using Q-Q plots and histograms, the final grades of the ten students were found to be not normally distributed. A non-parametric test, Wilcoxon Signed Ranks Test, was therefore used to test if the difference in the average grades for the year 2016 and year 2017 for the ten students was statistically significant.

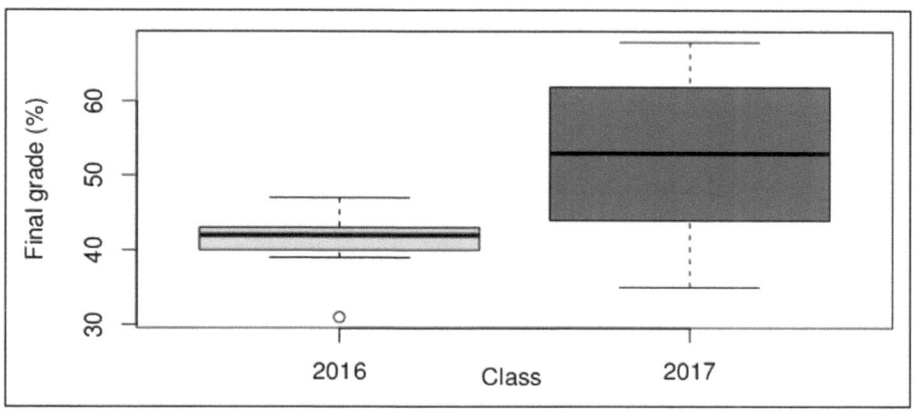

Fig. 1. Box-plot illustration of final grades of the ten students who failed the course in 2016 and retook it in the 2017 class

At significance level of .05, the Wilcoxon Signed Ranks Test indicated that the average grade (53%) for the ten students in the 2017 class was significantly higher than the average grade (41%) for the ten students in the 2016 class; $Z = 6.5, p = .03$.

The minimum mark for the remaining fifty-seven students in the 2016 class was 25% and maximum mark was 86%. A follow-up of student records show that the student who scored a minimum mark of 25% also failed the second opportunity examination but did not retake the course in 2017. The average grade of the remaining fifty-seven students in the 2016 class was 53% with a standard deviation of 9% points. The minimum mark for the remaining sixty students in the 2017 class was 29% and maximum mark was 89%. The average grade of the remaining sixty students in the 2017 class was 61% with a standard deviation of 12% points. A box-plot illustration of the final grades of the remaining students in the two classes is given in Fig. 2.

Using Q-Q plots and histograms, the final grades of the remaining fifty-seven students in the 2016 class and the final grades of remaining sixty students in the 2017 class were found to be normally distributed. A parametric test, Welch Two Sample t-test, was therefore used to test if the difference in the average grades for the year 2016 and year 2017 for the these remaining students was statistically significant. At significance level of .05, the Welch Two Sample t-test indicated that the average grade (61%) for the remaining sixty students in the 2017 class was significantly higher than the average grade (53%) for the remaining sixty-seven students in the 2016 class; $t(112.21) = -4.0865, p = .00008$.

A summary of the 2017 class general perception of the learning environment under each evaluation category is given Fig. 3. The average evaluation score for the preparation category was 3.49 out of 4.0 while the average evaluation score for presentation was 3.47 out of 4.0. Instructor friendliness had an average evaluation score of 3.82 out of 4.0. On the other hand, the average evaluation

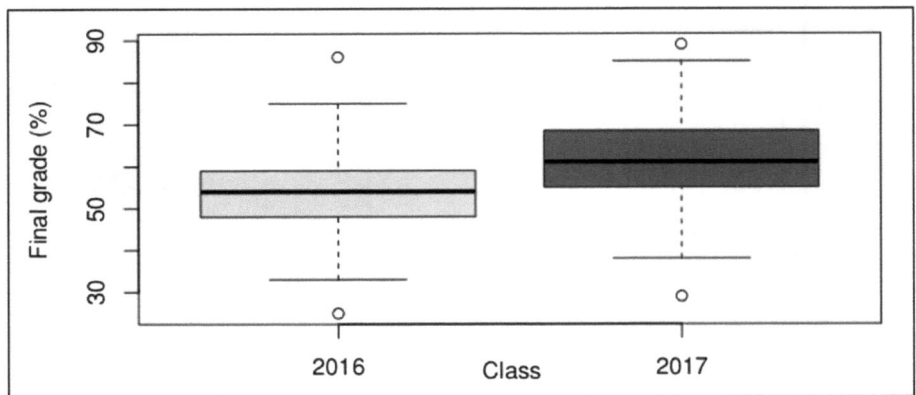

Fig. 2. Box-plot illustration of final grades of the rest of the fifty-seven students in the 2016 class and rest of the sixty students in the 2017 class

score for the assessment category was 3.41 out of 4.0 while average evaluation score for subject content was 3.44 out of 4.0.

A summary of the results of student evaluation, specifically, with respect to the three questions pertaining to perception of subject content are presented in Fig. 4. For example, none (0%) of the respondents strongly disagreed that they found the concepts and theories taught in the course to be irrelevant while 3% of respondents disagreed that they found the concepts and theories taught in the course to be relevant. On the other hand, 40% of respondents agreed that they found the concepts and theories taught in the course to be relevant while 57% of respondents strongly agreed that they found concepts and theories taught in the course to be relevant.

4.3   Discussion

The results indicate that performance of students in the 2017 class was significantly higher than in the 2016 class. This is true for students who retook the course in 2017 as well as for non-repeating students. However, it is important to note that there are several factors that could influence academic performance in a class as presented in a model in [26] and illustrated in Fig. 5. In the model, student performance is directly influenced by two factors, namely, the aptitude of a student and the amount of effort a student puts in a course [26]. The effort put by a student in a course is in turn influenced by the student's grade history, motivation, extra-curricular activities, work responsibilities and family responsibilities [26]. Motivation is influenced by the student's self-expectations and their perception of the learning environment [26]. The learning environment is affected by several factors such as appropriate use of class time, a caring instructor, good instructional materials and teaching methodology, which in turn increase student's level of expectancy and thus increasing motivation [26]. A positive learning environment as perceived by a student, leads to greater student motivation

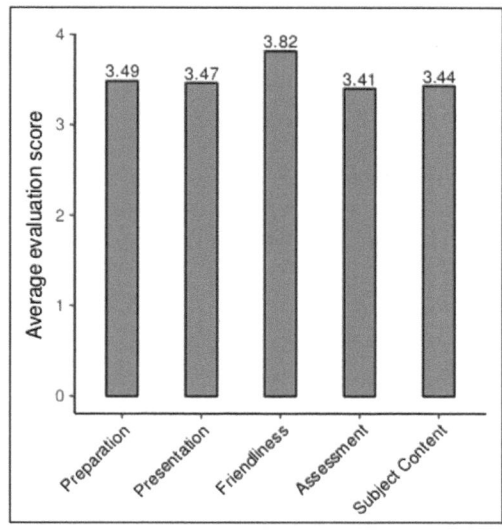

Fig. 3. Average evaluation scores in each evaluation category in the 2017 class

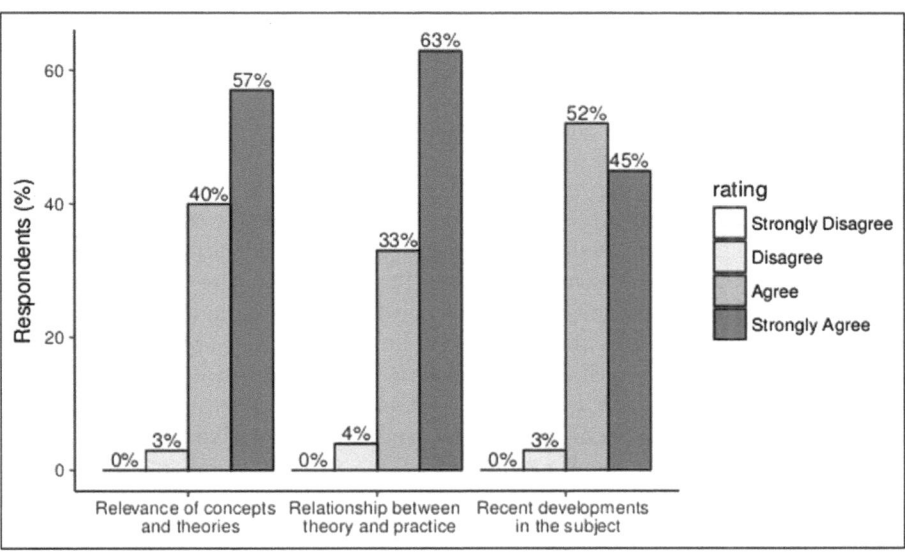

Fig. 4. The 2017 class evaluation of the learning environment with respect to subject content

which in turn leads to greater effort and correspondingly higher academic performance [26]. Motivation was also found to be a major factor in influencing effort as compared to grade history, work, extra-curricular activities and family responsibilities [26]. This implies that, student's expectations and learning environment, which are factors which influence motivation have a major influence on student performance. It is therefore also important to gauge whether our teaching approach contributed to improving student's expectations and their perception of the learning environment, which in turn, might explain the significantly higher performance of the 2017 class.

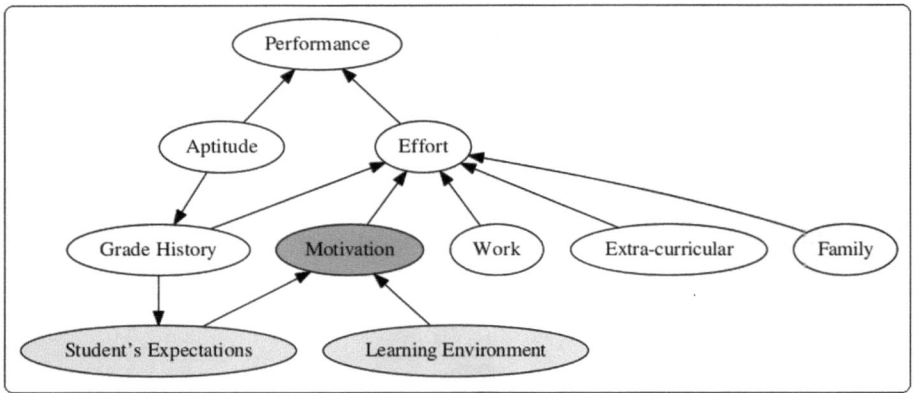

Fig. 5. Model of factors that affect student performance, adapted from [26]

The student's perception of their learning environment was very positive as illustrated in Fig. 3. In all evaluation categories, the average score was more than 3 out 4.0. In other words, students generally agreed that the learning environment was good in all categories. We also specifically note, as in Fig. 4, that the students rated highly the subject content, i.e. relevance of concepts and theories, relationship between theory and practice and connection to recent developments in the subject. This indicates that the teaching approach contributed to a positive learning environment for the students. A positive learning environment leads to greater student motivation which in turn leads to greater effort and correspondingly higher academic performance [17,26]. Other studies have also shown that more motivated students perform better in class [6,7]. Research has also shown that students are also motivated with classes in which they are exposed to practical work as it provides an opportunity to practice their creativity [6]. We can therefore conclude that our teaching approach contributed to the significantly higher performance of the class.

As posited in [26], there are several factors that can affect academic performance of students. We, therefore, investigated further our conclusion that our teaching approach contributed to the significantly higher performance of the class. We did this by interviewing some students, who retook the course in 2017. We managed to interview only three of the ten students who retook the course in 2017 as others had graduated and left the institution. The students were interviewed separately and each was shown their 2016 final grade in the course as well as their 2017 final grade. Each student was then asked to explain factors that influenced them to perform better after retaking the course in the 2017 class. All the students explained that they hard to work harder in order not to retake the course again and also specifically indicated that the teaching approach motivated them to have a positive outlook of the course. This finding further confirmed our conclusion that our teaching approach contributed to the significantly higher performance of the class. This finding agrees with the model in [26] that student's expectations and a positive learning environment can influence student motivation. The conclusion, that our teaching approach contributed to the significantly higher performance of the class, also agrees with the findings in [10,23], namely that adding a practical component to an operating systems course enhances student learning experience and consequently leads to better academic performance in the course.

We, however, take note of several possible limitations to our evaluation approach. First, we have mainly centred our conclusion on motivation as a predictor of academic performance. However, other studies have also confirmed that the motivation is a valid predictor of academic performance [3]. Second, it could be possible that the questions in the 2017 examination were easier than the 2016 examination. However, both examinations were based on the same syllabus and questions in both examinations were set at the same recommended level of the revised Bloom's Taxonomy [18]. For a second year class, level 2 of the revised Bloom's taxonomy was used. At level 2 of the revised Bloom's Taxonomy, students were tested of their understanding of operating system concepts by interpreting, summarising, paraphrasing, classifying, inferring, comparing and explaining of concepts. Third, not all seventy-three students in the 2017 class participated in the course evaluation survey as it was administered at the very end of the semester. However, we believe that the thirty-one students who participated, are a representative sample of the whole class.

In general, some of the practical exercises used in our approach do not seem to directly deepen theoretical concepts like scheduling and memory management. However, the primary emphasis of the approach was to motivate students with tasks that they could immediately relate to and find practical relevance. We, however, recommend correcting this shortfall by complementing our approach with relevant simulations.

5   Conclusion

This paper presented an approach which was used to teach an introductory operating systems course with the aim of balancing theory with practice in order to captivate student engagement and interest in a course which otherwise is considered boring and abstract to students. The approach had to take into consideration the fact that the students did not have sufficient programming background to undertake kernel-level programming projects. Traditional lectures were complemented with a series of hands-on practical tasks.

An evaluation of the course showed that the performance of students taught using this approach was significantly higher than those taught theoretical operating system concepts only. Through a survey, students also expressed strong satisfaction that the approach contributed to a positive learning environment as the students also found the course relevant and well balanced in theory and practice. We, therefore, recommend our approach to other instructors, particularly, in situations where students do not have sufficient programming background to undertake kernel-level programming projects but they still want to balance theory and practice in the delivery of the course. Moreover, the practical skills students may gain using our approach may also prepare them for industry jobs such as system administration as well as self-employment.

As part of future work, the same approach will be used in the next class and an evaluation will be conducted accordingly.

References

1. Anderson, C.L., Nguyen, M.: A survey of contemporary instructional operating systems for use in undergraduate courses. J. Comput. Sci. Coll. **21**(1), 183–190 (2005)
2. Andrus, J., Nieh, J.: Teaching operating systems using Android. In: Proceedings 43rd ACM Technical Symposium on Computer Science Education, pp. 613–618 (2012)
3. Campbell, M.M.: Motivational systems theory and the academic performance of college students. J. Coll. Teach. Learn. **4**(7), 11–24 (2007)
4. Christopher, W.A., Procter, S.J., Anderson, T.E.: The Nachos instructional operating system. In: Proceedings USENIX Winter Conference, pp. 481–488 (1993)
5. Cross, J., Denning, P.: Computing curriculum 2001. The Joint Curriculum Task Force IEEE-CS/ACM Report (2001)
6. Devadoss, S., Foltz, J.: Evaluation of factors influencing student class attendance and performance. Am. J. Agric. Econ. **78**(3), 499–507 (1996)
7. Durden, G.C., Ellis, L.V.: The effects of attendance on student learning in principles of economics. Am. Econ. Rev. **85**(2), 343–346 (1995)
8. Garmpis, A.: Design and development of a web-based interactive software tool for teaching operating systems. J. Inf. Techn. Educ. Res. **10**, 1–17 (2011)
9. Garmpis, A., Gouvatsos, N.: Innovative teaching methods in operating systems: the Linux case. In: Proceedings Conference on Innovative Approches in Education: Design and Network, pp. 155–163 (2012)
10. Giraddi, S., Kalwad, P., Kanakareddi, S.: Teaching operating systems – programming assignments approach. J. Eng. Educ. Transform. **31**(3), 68–73 (2018)
11. Hermocilla, J.A.C.: ICS-OS: a kernel programming approach to teaching operating system concepts. Philippine Inf. Techn. J. **2**(2), 25–30 (2009)
12. Hewson, M.G., Hewson, P.W.: Effect of instruction using students' prior knowledge and conceptual change strategies on science learning. J. Res. Sci. Teach. **20**(8), 731–743 (1983)
13. Hewson, P.W.: A case study of conceptual change in special relativity: the influence of prior knowledge in learning. Europ. J. Sci. Educ. **4**(1), 61–78 (1982)

14. Hill, J., Ray, C.K., Blair, J.R., Carver, C.A.: Puzzles and games: addressing different learning styles in teaching operating systems concepts. In: ACM SIGCSE Bulletin, vol. 35, pp. 182–186 (2003)
15. Hovemeyer, D., Hollingsworth, J.K., Bhattacharjee, B.: Running on the bare metal with GeekOS. In: ACM SIGCSE Bulletin, vol. 36, pp. 315–319 (2004)
16. Jones, D., Newman, A.: RCOS.java: a simulated operating system with animations. In: Proceeding Computer Based Learning in School Conference paper #28 (2001)
17. Karemera, D., Reuben, L.J., Sillah, M.R.: The effects of academic environment and background characteristics on student satisfaction and performance: the case of South Carolina State University's school of business. Coll. Stud. J. **37**(2), 298–308 (2003)
18. Krathwohl, D.R.: A revision of bloom's taxonomy: an overview. Theor. Pract. **41**(4), 212–218 (2002)
19. Machanick, P.: Teaching operating systems: just enough abstraction. In: Proceedings SACLA 2016, CCIS 642, pp. 104–111 (2016)
20. Nieh, J., Vaill, C.: Experiences teaching operating systems using virtual platforms and Linux. In: ACM SIGCSE Bulletin, vol. 37, pp. 520–524 (2005)
21. Polze, A., Probert, D.: Teaching operating systems: the windows case. In: ACM SIGCSE Bulletin, vol. 38, pp. 298–302 (2006)
22. Qu, B., Wu, Z.: Design and implementation of tiny educational OS. In: Qian, Z., Cao, L., Su, W., Wang, T., Yang, H. (eds.) Recent Advances in Computer Science and Information Engineering. Lecture Notes in Electrical Engineering, vol. 126. Springer, Heidelberg (2012)
23. Robbins, S.: A three pronged approach to teaching undergraduate operating systems. ACM SIGOPS Oper. Syst. Rev. **42**(6), 93–100 (2008)
24. Shackelford, R., et al.: Computing curricula 2005: the overview report. ACM SIGCSE Bull. **38**, 456–457 (2006)
25. Silberschatz, A., Galvin, P.B., Gagne, G.: Operating System Concepts Essentials. Wiley, Hoboken (2014)
26. Wooten, T.C.: Factors influencing student learning in introductory accounting classes: a comparison of traditional and nontraditional students. Issues Account. Educ. **13**(2), 357–373 (1998)

APPENDIX: Summaries of Affiliated Workshops

Workshop of the South African Computing Accreditation Board (SACAB)

Summary

Curriculum accreditation has become important nowadays since more and more institutional 'players' —including private and/or commercial ones— are offering tertiary education of varying (often unknown) quality.

In this context the South African Computing Accreditation Board (SACAB) workshop was organised under the umbrella of the SACLA'2018 conference in Gordon's Bay (Western Cape) by *Sue Petratos* (Director of the School of ICT at the Nelson Mandela University),[1] and *André Calitz* (Chairman of SACAB and the SACLA organisation). The purpose of this workshop was to discuss Document #6 in the series of six documents that make up the SACAB Degree and Diploma Accreditation Document Set.[2] These six documents are:

1. SACAB General information (Doc. #1);
2. SACAB Administrative Guidelines (Doc. #2);
3. SACAB Application Guidelines (Doc. #3);
4. SACAB Guidelines for Submissions (Doc. #4);
5. SACAB Submission Forms (Doc. #5);
6. SACAB Diploma Programme Criteria for Comprehensive Universities and Universities of Technology (Doc. #6).

The workshop was attended by 17 representatives of Comprehensive Universities and Universities of Technology in South Africa, with the *objectives* to:

- Discuss the role of the old *TECLA* (Technikon Computer Lecturers Association) in curriculum development;
- Confirm the specialisation fields offered in diploma programmes (for example: software development, business applications, communication networks, and the like);
- Establish a SACAB Diploma Advisory Board;
- Expand the SACAB assessment panel to include the new SACAB Diploma Advisory Board to set proposed curricula for diploma programmes;
- Provide administrative guidelines for diploma programmes;
- Propose evaluation criteria for diploma programmes (Diploma Standards Document #6).

---

[1] E-mail: sue.petratos@mandela.ac.za.

[2] Explanation for readers from outside of South Africa: In the South African context a 'diploma' certifies a 2-year vocational qualification below the level of a B.Sc. degree. It must not be confused with —for example— the German diploma which is Master-equivalent.

© Springer Nature Switzerland AG 2019
S. Kabanda et al. (Eds.): SACLA 2018, CCIS 963, pp. 379–380, 2019.
https://doi.org/10.1007/978-3-030-05813-5

The workshop firstly focused on the processes and criteria for the accreditation of Computer Science, Information Systems and Information Technology degree programmes offered by universities in South Africa. Delegates attending the workshop agreed that there is currently a lack of guidelines for the accreditation of diploma programmes in South Africa and also no collaboration between academic institutions regarding standards for diploma programmes. Attendees also agreed that there is a need for such an accreditation body and that they would want to establish criteria to obtain accreditation. The support of the Institute for IT Professionals in South Africa (IITPSA) —also a sponsor of the recent SACLA conferences (2016–2018)— is appreciated on this journey.

The main objective is to find a way forward for the content development for Document #6 of the SACAB. The SACAB composition and representatives were further explained and it was decided that the Comprehensive Universities and Universities of Technology must have a stronger presence in order to drive the accreditation of diploma curricula.

Deciding on the way forward it was clear that Universities of Technology need to form a sub-task team to work on the vocational diploma- and career-focussed tertiary qualifications. It was also clear that there is no need to create criteria from scratch but rather to use the existing structures (e.g. the ACM/IEEE IT 2017 curriculum recommendations) and work the diplomas into this framework by just creating different levels of requirements for diplomas within the specified criteria.

Also the role of the old *TECLA* organisation was discussed which had become inactive for a number of years. It was decided that all universities should support and participate more actively in the *SACLA* organisation, which is now a revived and functioning body for all computer lecturers in South Africa. An annual workshop for diploma programmes was proposed were diploma programmes' curriculum criteria and standards could be discussed every year.

Last but not least it was decided to use the next *SAICSIT* (South African Institute of Computer Scientists and Information Technologists) conference as a 'platform' for the next SACAB planning session for Universities of Technology and Comprehensive Universities, for the sake of even better discussions and better representation of those types of institutions. For the proposed SACAB meeting in September 2018 in Port Elizabeth (RSA), delegates were requested to send the following information to Sue Petratos:

- Which diploma programmes does your institution offer;
- Name of a contact person for curriculum discussions at your institution;
- Name of a delegate to attend the next SAICSIT'2018 conference with the aim of being actively involved in the accreditation of diplomas in the near future.

A task team and committee will then be formed at SAICSIT'2018.

Sue Petratos
André Calitz

Workshop on the IT Dividing Line Between Schools and Universities: Who Should Teach What

Summary

This panel discussion workshop, which took place on 20 June at SACLA'2018 in Gordons Bay (South Africa), was to explore the interface between high school teaching and university teaching in IT-related topics. The perception exists that there is a large degree of overlap in some areas between introductory courses at universities with the school syllabus, while a gap exists in other aspects of the syllabi.

The panel discussion was moderated by *Linda Marshall* from the Computer Science department at the University of Pretoria, supported by *Lisa Seymour* from the Information Systems department at the University of Cape Town, (both RSA).

The panelists comprised of members representing the high school examination bodies and universities. The high school examination bodies had representation from *Ighsaan Francis* from the government's Department of Basic Education (DBE), supported by two IT Specialists, namely *Ian Carstens* and *Shamiel Dramat*. Moreover, *Delia Kench* and *Jakkaphan Tangkuampien* represented the Independent Examinations Board (IEB) high school body. Computer Science and Information Systems higher education were represented by *Aslam Safla* and *Pitso Tsibolane* from the respective academic departments at the University of Cape Town. Last but not least there were also some academic guest-hearers, lecturers and professors from the audience of the SACLA'2018 conference under the umbrella of which this panel discussion workshop has taken place.

To provide a baseline from which a discussion could take place, each panelist provided a short presentation on the computing syllabus they represented. The following main points came from these presentations and the discussions which followed.

- The numbers of learners taking Information Technology (IT) as a subject is low. About 1.4% of all learners writing the DBE CAPS examinations have IT as a subject. The percentage for IEB is 6.6%. From the discussion, it became clear that these numbers could be attributed to:
  - a high dropout from IT in school grades 10 and 11. Many learners find the subject challenging and time consuming. At many universities, IT is not a requirement to study a computing related degree programme and therefore is dropped for subjects which provide a broader entrance possibility to university degree programmes.

© Springer Nature Switzerland AG 2019
S. Kabanda et al. (Eds.): SACLA 2018, CCIS 963, pp. 381–382, 2019.
https://doi.org/10.1007/978-3-030-05813-5

- IT is not offered in many schools, probably as a result of not enough qualified teachers and access to infrastructure. In both cases, the financial implications are the main contributing factor. An IT teacher is able to earn more in the corporate environment. Providing IT infrastructure to schools is costly.

The low take-up of IT is a concern as this impacts on the ability of South Africa as a country to meet its computing demand.

- The two high school IT examination bodies differ in their focus in terms of the application of the curriculum content. The overall content, however aligns well. Both bodies require theoretical IT-related topics and a practical component which includes programming and basic database manipulation. The programming language used in this practical component differs with the DBE preferring Delphi and the IEB Java. This in itself should not be a concern, however the way in which the foundational content of the languages are taught is. It is possible, by using an IDE, that a learner writes very little code themselves and therefore misses out on the fundamental building blocks required in programming and algorithm development.
- IT or computer literacy is not foundational and introducing learners to computing in earlier grades may help reduce the perception that IT is not only for a specific grouping.

In summary, potential *solutions to the main points identified are required*. These may include:

- Providing school level IT on devices that most learners have, such as mobile devices.
- Limiting the content of the presentation of the syllabus, making it less overwhelming to the general school going learner.
- Change the name to better reflect the content being presented.
- Etc...

The panel discussion workshop by no means identified all the problems; neither did it provide implementable solutions. It was however a first and very important step in a long process required to make IT more accessible to high school learners and university students in South Africa.

Hopefully this will be only the first of many forthcoming discussions to take place between the basic education and higher education in order to further the IT 'footprint' within South Africa and abroad.

Linda Marshall

Author Index